CONFLICTS ABOUT CLASS

Debating Inequality in Late Industrialism

a selection of readings
edited by
David J. Lee and Bryan S. Turner

Longman
London and New York

Longman Group Limited,
Edinburgh Gate,
Harlow, Essex CM20 2JE, England
and Associated Companies throughout the world.

Published in the United States of America
by Longman Publishing, New York

© Longman Group Limited 1996

First published 1996

ISBN 0 582 275679 PPR

British Library Cataloguing-in-Publication Data

A catalogue record for this book is
available from the British Library

Library of Congress Cataloging-in-Publication Data

Conflicts about class: debating inequality in late industrialism:
  a selection of readings/edited by David J. Lee and Bryan S. Turner.
     p.   cm.
  Includes bibliographical references and index.
  ISBN 0–582–27567–9
  1. Social classes—Research. I. Lee, David J., 1938– .
II. Turner, Bryan S.
HT608.C66   1996
305.5—dc20
                                                        95–42106
                                                           CIP

Set by 5 in 10/11 Pt Palatino

Produced through Longman Malaysia, PA

In Memoriam

Joan B. Freeman, M. Ed

of Newman College, Birmingham
1932–1995

who was 'Arntee Jone' to David, Adrienne, Rebecca and Suzanna
for longer than they want to remember
and whose kind of class analysis will always have a future
even though she'd never heard of Bryan and the others.

· · · · ·

But come with old Khayyam and leave the Wise
To talk. One thing is certain: that life flies . . .

Contents

Preface

The origins of this book lie in an exchange of published writings between the two editors, as a result of which we realised that we disagreed about practically everything. (We have written separate conclusions as a tangible expression of these disagreements.) It must seem to outsiders that such an admission might be made by sociologists as a whole – a 'contention' of sociologists would be a fitting collective noun. Quarrelsome behaviour is particularly evident in the area of sociological work known as class analysis. We have, however, agreed amicably to edit this book in the belief that sharp disagreement can be intellectually productive. We are reminded that it was, for example, Marx's total disagreement with Proudhon, Mill and Say that produced contemporary class theory in the first place.

Familiarity with class analysis itself will show why disagreement is fundamental to this topic. Moreover, many sociologists have spent their lives studying class and take unkindly to the conviction of some colleagues that they have been wasting their time. Nor does it help to note that colleagues in several cognate disciplines like history have of late decided to jettison the term class altogether.

Our justification for compiling this book is that the latest turn in the debate about class epitomises current controversies about the future nature and direction of sociological enquiry itself. We would like to think that in the end both sociology and class analysis will emerge leaner but fitter from the critiques and research collected together here. Furthermore, while we are literally poles apart in our attitude to the idea of intellectual progress in the social sciences, there is an implicit agreement in the chapters to this collection that, regardless of the idiom of class analysis, there remain important issues about inequality and justice in contemporary societies which deserve a wider audience than the readership of sociological journals.

We have certainly managed to agree too that the real heroes of this book are certain members of the Essex University Computing Service in particular Brett Giddings and Glyn Daniels. Only through their patience and skill were we able to overcome the diverse electronic terrors which comprise the hyper reality of international academic collaboration nowadays: scrambled email; unintelligible binhex, crashing Windows, imported boot sector viruses and corrupted discs. With their help the individual texts eventually appeared as old-fashioned manuscript and we were reminded of Steve Bell's celebrated question: 'Can there be text without paper?'

We are grateful, too, to the Fuller Bequest Research Fund of the University of Essex Sociology Department for generous assistance toward the costs of preparing this collection for publication.

We are equally grateful to those who encouraged us at bad moments or provided invaluable contacts, help and advice: in particular, in strict alphabetical order, Rosemary Crompton, Jay Gershuny, John Goldthorpe, Bob Holton, George Kolankiewicz, David Lockwood, Ray Pahl, Jan Pakulski, David Rose, John Scott, Malcolm Waters, and John Westergaard. We are also extremely grateful to all of the authors for the general alacrity with which they agreed to have their work used and revised or even wrote entirely fresh contributions. Their willingness to respond in record time to our interventions and arm-twisting is gratefully acknowledged. Monika Loving, Maureen Rhodes and Diane Streeting took over at the computer when we flagged. Sue Aylott never minded loaning the use of her printer. Adrienne Lee provided not only encouragement but endless real-life examples of class relationships in British Primary Education. Lastly we owe an enormous debt to our editor at Longman for her patience and her willingness to promote sociological debate.

David Lee,
Colchester, England

Bryan Turner,
Geelong, Victoria, Australia

June, 1995

Acknowledgements

We are obliged to the following for permission to reprint material in revised and/or edited form: Blackwell Publications Limited; Routledge Limited; British Sociological Association Publications Limited; Annual Review Publications Ltd, Santa Monica, USA; the Editors of *Annual Review of Sociology*, *British Journal of Urban and Regional Research*, *International Sociology* and *Sociology*.

The research reported in Chapter 17 was undertaken as part of the Economic and Social Research Council's East–West Programme. Grant no. Y 309 25 3025, 'Emerging Forms of Political Representation and Participation in Eastern Europe' awarded to Geoffrey Evans, Stephen Whitefield, Anthony Heath and Clive Payne.

Introduction: Myths of classlessness and the 'death' of class analysis

David Lee and Bryan Turner

As the world knows, in early January, 1995 a violent earthquake occurred around the Japanese port of Kobe. A few days later, a British newspaper, the *Guardian*, published a special report on the disaster under a clumsy headline: 'Japan's poor bear brunt of quake that ended middle class myth'. Two arresting photographs appeared alongside it. One, taken in the city centre, showed pulverised apartment blocks and cold homeless victims. The other showed an affluent suburb where the spacious houses had mostly survived intact and 'the rich merely had to lower their standard of living a notch or two'. The disaster it seemed had hit most severely those whose income and life style was least fitted to cope and revealed in the process the stark inequalities which exist in Japanese society. To those familiar with sociological studies of divisions in the Japanese labour market and with the best available survey evidence from Japan on the pattern of socio-economic inequalities, the report's conclusions come as no surprise. Yet the overwhelming majority of the country's citizens (on some reckonings 90 per cent) regularly describe themselves as 'middle class' (*Guardian*, 26 January 1995; cf. Ishida 1993).

Sociological surveys have found a readiness to identify with the middle class in other industrial countries – the United States and Australia, for example – though much depends on the way the question is put in the first place. In Europe, where after all the political and social rhetoric of class originated, willingness to see society in terms of 'us' and 'them' is reportedly greater – especially in Britain (Marshall *et al.* 1988:143–7). Even here though, a fair degree of ambiguity about class exists in people's minds and their perceptions of class shift according to the political climate and the method of enquiry (Marshall 1983). Public ambivalence and confusion surrounding the term is mirrored in the world of scholarship. Several writers now recommend the word 'class' be jettisoned simply on the grounds that the multitude of possible political and philosophical meanings of 'class' make it useless for detached analysis (e.g. Calvert 1982, Hindess 1987).

1

Thus, it is not really surprising that in sociology too so-called 'class analysis' should periodically come into serious question. 'Class analysis' is itself a diffuse term. It means in practice little more than any sociological research which tries to identify and explain class divisions and/or to gauge their effects empirically. It has been dominated by three influential traditions of sociological theory: Marxism, neo-Weberianism and to a much lesser extent functionalism. By using these alternative theoretical perspectives as the basis for empirical research into social stratification, however, it comprised, until recently at least, one of the most confident specialisms in mainstream sociology. Class was described by a leading American theorist and methodologist, albeit with a degree of tongue in cheek hyperbole, as sociology's 'only independent variable' (Stinchcombe cited in Wright, 1979:3) and a future chairman of the British Economic and Social Research Council could write (of large scale survey research on 'social stratification'): 'This is not an area in which sociology needs to be defensive or apologetic' (Newby 1982:2).

In the eyes of a surprisingly diverse group of critics, however, the validity of this entire spectrum of work is now in question. In part this reflects simply the seemingly endemic disorderliness in sociology itself. It has always been split between those of its practitioners who seek to develop sociological knowledge through rigorously conducted empirical research and wish to claim the discipline as a social *science*; and on the other, those who argue that its subject matter, human society, inevitably means that sociology must remain a reflexive discipline whose assertions and 'findings' – including those about the class-divided nature of society – are not incremental but essentially contested.

Certainly, the social and political context of class theory and analysis has always been particularly important for understanding its analytical preoccupations and – as some now see it – its failures and weaknesses. Although early on in the Industrial Revolution 'class' was used relatively uncontroversially by liberal political economists and conservative social commentators, all that rapidly changed with the appropriation of the term by Marx. In his hands, class became a key concept of revolutionary politics. Class struggles, he claimed, are the motor of history and the vehicle by which society could be changed. So as the notoriety and power of Marxism spread, these older discourses of 'class' were displaced, first by its significance in the economic and political struggle between capital and labour, and then in the bitter global rivalry between liberal capitalism and communism which culminated in the Cold War.

This social and political context to class analysis has now suddenly and profoundly altered. The collapse of communism in the USSR and Eastern Europe, exposing a history of authoritarian rule, environmental destruction and abuse of human rights, has rendered the once strident frameworks of Western Marxism intellectually problematic and even emotionally unsustainable for many erstwhile supporters.

In the West, political programmes of economic deregulation seemed to sweep all before them during the 1980s, challenging socialistic accounts of the inevitably exploitative and class-ridden character of capitalism. Deregulation exposed the established industrial societies to global recession and the restructuring of multinational investment. An assortment of liberal journalists and liberal thinkers, however, have asserted that capitalism is now the only triumphant world economic system in existence and that the end of history has arrived (e.g. Fukayama 1992). Thus although the supposed 'classlessness' of society still retains considerable ideological significance, the issue which dominated sociological class analysis for years – the relative validity of competing liberal and Marxist accounts of inequality under capitalist industrialism – has suddenly lost its force. Are not the very words 'class' and 'capitalism' in any case simply nineteenth-century concepts creaking under the strain of late twentieth-century developments? What, if anything, is there left for class analysis to do?

It is with the debate on this last question that we have been primarily concerned in compiling this collection. For many sociologists, whether they actually do class analysis themselves or not, the answer to it remains: 'plenty' – notwithstanding the changes just described. Many of them have always sought to wean class analysis away from the constraints of ideologically inspired debate and to treat it as an area of empirical, non-dogmatic even scientific enquiry into the nature and causes of contemporary inequality. Characteristically inspired by the stratification theory of Max Weber, the practitioners of this form of class research have claimed to have long since demonstrated the limitations of both Marxist and liberal scenarios for the development of class structure. As John Goldthorpe, one of the most eminent proponents of this view, and his colleagues at Nuffield College, Oxford, argue in this book, capitalist societies may not have been sundered by revolutionary upheaval but they are demonstrably not classless either. Understanding the persistence and stability of class inequality thus continues to give a clear agenda for sociologists to work at, even in the 'post-Marxist' times we live in (see Chapters 7, and 14 to 16). But as will soon become apparent, this version of class analysis too is under attack.

We are, however, already plunging into the debate about class itself. Before doing so properly, we think it helpful to distinguish two kinds of critique of class analysis which are not always clearly separated by the participants. The first, which we have not attempted to cover systematically, we will call 'myths of classlessness': substantive assertions about the actual distribution of class power and privilege in modern industrial nations. The second, which we consider much more pivotal, is the rumoured 'death of class' itself: that is, the theoretical and methodological issue of whether class is simply a metaphor for socio-political aspirations or really works as a concept and a tool for sociological research.

Myths of classlessness

Claims as to the 'withering away' of class have played an important role in liberal defences of free-market or 'capitalist' democracy from its critics. But to study the controversy surrounding the issue of classlessness is to uncover the ambivalence within Marxist political theory too about the issue. What is arguably the oldest 'myth' of classlessness originated in Germany at the end of the nineteenth century when Eduard Bernstein attempted to persuade the Marxist Social Democratic Party to adjust its strategy to the actual conditions, as he saw them, of the time (Bernstein 1899). Bernstein made claims about improvements (or 'embourgeiosement') in the economic situation of the masses which have become standard to 'revisionism' and reformism within and without socialist labour movements (cf. for example Crosland 1956). Bernstein rejected the Marxist argument that polarisation and pauperisation were taking place, recognised a significant improvement in the wages of the working class (largely, he thought, because of the technological advances wrought by capitalism), noted a significant increase in the size of the middle class, rejected the argument of increasing economic crisis and suggested that capitalism could be reformed through parliamentary politics rather than by its revolutionary overthrow. Technical change, the growth of the middle class, the growth of income, mobility and political and social differentiation – these themes were picked up by many non-Marxist writers too during the first half of the twentieth century (a useful overview is Goldthorpe *et al.* 1987:Introduction). These sort of arguments seemed especially plausible to scholars in the United States where, compared with Europe, working-class living standards were high, political rhetorics of socialism and class conflict much weaker, and the analysis of ethnic and communal differences more salient than social class.

It was also from the United States that a second highly influential myth of classlessness originated and took hold: the thesis of the separation of ownership and control. The pioneering empirical work of Berle and Means (1932) on US manufacturing companies purportedly demonstrated that the development of joint stockholding and the growth of large industrial corporations had marginalised the significance of the old-style capitalist. Control of business was passing to professional managements who increasingly were recruited 'meritocratically' (i.e. according to certificated technical competence), so their authority did not essentially rest on legal ownership of the company. Here too both Marx himself and his followers in the early twentieth century, despite working from a European context and having very different political objectives, had already suggested that ownership interest was being displaced by managers and effective control by finance capital (Hilferding, 1910; Lenin, 1916). By accepting this change, with its implications of managerial revolution, they saddled themselves and later generations of Marxists with having to explain how the capitalist class nevertheless remains both cohesive and *capitalist*. By contrast, liberal theorists ever since have found it easy to argue that because capital holding now substantially derived from the savings, insurances and pensions of ordinary workers, capital *ownership* has become largely democratised and the capitalist class is no more (for a recent example see Saunders 1990a:91).

The implication of these two influential myths is that neither of Marx's celebrated phases of class formation, and the 'predictions' he had made about them, could any longer be sustained: class had ceased to exist both 'in itself' as an objective social cleavage defined by relations of ownership and non-ownership of the means of production and 'for itself', as emergent groupings of economic interest with potential for oppositional 'class consciousness'. As early as 1959 sociologists were being urged to forget about class (Nisbet 1959). During the years of the Cold War such arguments were incorporated, mainly by US sociologists, into a detailed theory of the 'withering away' of class with the clear political implication that capitalism was in no danger of revolutionary upheaval and that it was communism that was likely to change (Kerr *et al.* 1969).

Classlessness, citizenship and post-modern capitalism

As we shall see below, the theory of the withering away of class was never without strong critics, and was profoundly shaken by the unexpected renaissance of Marxist thought and politics in Western societies during the late 1960s. Within the past two decades or so, however, the rise of the neo-liberal New Right in Western politics has overlapped with a wider intellectual shift involving renewed claims that by the late twentieth century, capitalism had so fundamentally changed as simply to render the terms of class analysis redundant. As this collection shows (see the chapters by Holton, Pakulski, Waters and Turner) these arguments have had a particular appeal not only in the USA but in Australia, a country which Crook and his colleagues have portrayed as epitomising the changes in question (Crook *et al.* 1992).

No less than four 'new' myths of classlessness have been involved here: in rough order of emergence, those of citizenship, post-industrialism, post-Fordism and post-modernism.

Citizenship

The study of democracy and citizenship has in fact long been a necessary adjunct to the study of class inequality. One of the peculiar features of capitalist society has been the combination of systemic and profound social inequalities (namely the existence of social classes) and a parallel set of institutions relating to democratic participation and citizenship (namely the welfare state). It was T. H. Marshall (1981) who referred to welfare-capitalism as 'the hyphenated society' to suggest that welfare and the market were essential if ultimately irreconcilable ingredients of modern capitalism. His analysis established a tradition in post-Second World War sociology that theoretical class analysis must address fundamental questions relating to democratic processes and citizenship as a form of political membership. And in so far as 'citizenship' (and welfare) reduced the salience of class divisions, it always provided the potential for a myth of classlessness.

A more usual liberal argument these days, however, is that the incompatibility between citizenship and inequality is more apparent than real and that there is a parallel between market-based inequality and the freedoms of the political market place (Holton and Turner 1989). That is, economic markets provide the best institutional context for the realisation of equality of opportunity, but equality of opportunity is perfectly compatible with inequality of outcome (Turner 1986). The parliamentary system also functions as a type of political market place within which political parties compete for power and influence with similarly unequal political outcomes. Within this liberal framework, freedom of choice as a consumer in the economic arena is a necessary component or support for political individualism within the democratic arena, and their co-existence makes radical class interpretations of inequality redundant.

Post-industrialism

The notion of post-industrialism absorbed something of earlier liberal theories of the meritocratic logic of twentieth-century industrialism. In a post-industrial society theoretical knowledge as such, rather than private capital formation, forms the axial principle of society and is the primary source of social innovation and policy development. The idea is particularly associated with the writings of Daniel Bell (1973; 1976) who attempted to describe how this change in the organisation of capitalist society was associated with developments in the economy: the decline of manufacturing as the principal form of economic activity, the growth of the service industry and a corresponding decline in the agricultural sector. This axial principle of knowledge gave supremacy to professional and technical occupations which, Bell argued, constituted a New Class. It also gave fresh significance to the role of university intellectuals as the producers of new knowledge. The theory of post-industrial society has given rise to a variety of debates in class analysis with respect to the importance of the new middle class, the role of technicians, the deskilling of the labour force, the creation of a new working class and the productive significance of the intellectual worker.

Post-Fordism

The thesis of 'post-Fordism' was developed just a few years later (Piore and Sabel 1984; cf., however, Wood (ed.) 1989). Post-Fordism, it is argued represents a very different form of capitalism characterising the world economic system of today which increasingly is highly globalised and also deregulated. The new forms of 'disorganised' capitalism do not operate on the basis of full mass employment. Rather there is a high degree of what is called 'flexible specialisation' in the use of labour and post-Fordist production systems are highly automated in order to introduce some degree of flexibility into dedicated machinery. Post-Fordism also relies on numerical flexibility, that is, the labour market itself is highly deregulated, depending heavily on semi-skilled labour bought on a non-contractual basis. In a post-Fordist environment it is also the case that there is a considerable flood of women into employment. For example in the United Kingdom women constituted almost 44 per cent of the labour force in the 1990s. As women have entered the labour force so they have abandoned many of their traditional social roles, particularly within the domestic arena. The emancipation of women in many social contexts is now also associated with increasing divorce rates and marital breakdown. With the erosion of the nuclear family, there has also been a feminisation of poverty since most single-parent households are in fact led by women.

In post-Fordist society the functional relationship between the economy and the household has supposedly been broken and many right-wing critics of contemporary society have blamed the welfare society of the post-war period for the unintended consequence of driving men from the household. Nathan Glazer (1988) and Daniel Moynihan (1973 and 1989) have been particularly concerned with the problem of black poverty, particularly with the growth of the socially isolated and fragmented black, single-parent households, where women are wholly dependent upon welfare payments for their survival. Certainly in North America, post-Fordism has disrupted class communities which might form the basis of opposition to the social system. European writers too have embraced the implications of post-Fordism by arguing that these structural changes spelt the end of the working class as an organised, fully employed, coherent social group. For example, in his famous commentary on these developments the former Marxist André Gorz pronounced a farewell to the working class (Gorz 1982; see also Harvey 1989).

Post-modernism

With the growth of post-modern theory, the last of the four developments we are considering, it is clear that much of what had gone before, Bell's work in particular, anticipated theoretical developments in the analysis of post-modern culture. For example Bell's emphasis on theoretical knowledge and the role of computerised information in many respects anticipated the account of the post-modern condition presented by writers like J.-F. Lyotard (1984) and furthermore Bell's focus on the importance of hedonism within a consumer society also laid some of the foundations for later analyses of the aestheticisation of everyday life in terms of new cultural practices. Although post-modernism as a theory and post-modernity as a condition of society are surrounded by a large measure of theoretical uncertainty and conceptual confusion (Turner 1990) it may be defined as involving in social and economic terms a society in which social classes are no longer important because the social structure is extraordinarily complex and chronically fragmented along a variety of dimensions including gender, age, ethnicity and culture. It is also a society in which the main locus of social division has shifted from the sphere of social production to that of consumption and culture. Post-modernity thus involves the growing importance of the culture industry such as tourism, the aestheticisation of everyday life through new patterns of consumerism, the construction of social identity by individual choice rather than by traditional location, the pluralisation of personal identity and the life course, and the disappearance of the structured life span or life project. In economic terms post-modernity means a post-Fordist economy with highly specialised production systems involving multi-skilled workers, a globalisation of markets which are also segmented, and a dependence upon new management techniques to bring about more precise levels of industrial control. Finally, in political terms, there are new ideologies of self-reliance and competitiveness.

Commentators have noted that many of these so-called post-modernist themes contain echoes of the political analysis of the New Right, and this is particularly evident in a reassessment of the significance of the 'citizenship' issue. Among recent influential critiques of class analysis, Clark and Lipset are somewhat unusual in that their case still rests on arguments about the growth of welfare – as well as on familiar liberal claims for working-class emancipation through affluence and education (see Chapter 2 below and also Clark, Lipset and Rempel 1993). The paradox to which post-modernist analyses point, however, is that the processes which have to some extent undermined the reproduction of social classes in the late twentieth century are also the conditions which have largely undermined the forms of social citizenship recognised within the Marshallian framework. The latter emerged under conditions of Keynesian economic and political policies: a consensus about the importance of full employment, a commitment to a democratic revolution in the education sphere, the maintenance of the household and a general commitment to social security. It is becoming more usual to argue instead that the supports of 'welfare' citizenship, such as the conventional family and the nation state, appear to be disappearing (Roche 1992). Welfare regimes lack the capacity adequately to respond to current patterns of internal migration, labour market flexibility or the globalisation of various key legal and political authorities. Thus Beck (1992, 1994), working in the German context and Anthony Giddens in Britain (Giddens 1990) argue that conventional notions of class, citizenship and capitalism appear to be dated, if not obsolete. We need an entirely new vocabulary to describe the fragmented structures, individualistic processes and deregulated social and natural environment of late twentieth-century society.

All these new myths of classlessness, however, and their implications for the conceptual structure of sociology, command little support among many of the academics who have been associated with empirical class analysis. They complain of the tendency of the relevant authors to treat speculative assertions about the direction in which all societies are supposedly heading as if they were securely established fact. They point out that claims of post-Fordism, post-industrialism and the shift from production to 'consumption cleavages' have generated a great deal of critical research and discussion in rebuttal. A vital part of the defence of traditional forms of class analysis as the chapters by Hout *et al.*, Westergaard and Goldthorpe and Marshall illustrate well, has been that liberal and post-modernist myths of classlessness persistently ignore the findings of rigorously conducted research, research which has increasingly employed very sophisticated techniques of data gathering and analysis and which are already sufficient to show the survival of class divisions within the new world order. On this view then, the existence of class divisions and their profound effects on peoples' lives is an objective finding which sociology can claim to have established. But this brings us to the conceptual issues surrounding the sociology of class.

The death of class metaphors? (i) 'Strong' class theories

The reaction we have just described was in part triggered by a perhaps understandable feeling that critics of class analysis were motivated by a political desire to gloss over extensive but inconvenient research evidence of the persistence, indeed widening of economic inequality. Confronted by this accusation, however, the critics have responded by denying or drawing back from any suggestion of a lessening of inequality and have insisted that their principal concern is the varying and inconsistent or elusive ways in which the defenders of class analysis use the term class as an explanatory tool.

A crude division can be made between 'strong' and 'weak' usage of class in sociology. Strong class theories, of which Marxism is by far the major example, can be said to adopt a holistic approach: that is, class is or was in some sense a causal factor in historical change and the overall organisation of society and its institutions. It impinges on the lives of individuals even though they themselves may be unaware that their own actions contribute to its continuance. Weak class explanations, by contrast, reject the suggestion that class may be 'more than the sum of its parts' or that classes are independent entities in any sense. Their approach to class is what Myles and Turegun (below) call 'positional'. Classes are in the first place simply empirically identifiable groupings of individuals who have certain analytically significant situations (such as their possession of property or highly paid skills) in common. Weberian sociologies of class have been the foremost representatives of this form of explanation. They reflect Max Weber's commitment to interpretative methods in sociology and his view that any link between class membership and other aspects of meaningful or communal action must be regarded not as necessary but contingent. This involves much less ambitious claims for class as an explanatory concept, especially in respect of the problem of 'class formation', the intentional process by which the members of classes act together in various ways (for example by supporting a particular political party) and in doing so form what Weber called a *social class*.

Now, this broad division in class explanations, it might be argued is a chronic instance of the pervasive 'explanatory failures' of sociological theory as a whole (cf. Holmwood and Stewart 1983). Explanatory failure arises out of the co-existence of two incompatible ways of accounting for social phenomena embodied in the terms 'structure' and 'action'. Putting the matter somewhat crudely, structural approaches have attributed causal priority to the persistent, *supra*-individual and typically universal features of social life, such as economic or communal organisation – and, of course class. Action approaches, on the other hand, often denying the existence of causal 'structures' altogether, have depicted wider social processes as the product, not the source, of the intentions and strivings of individuals. Arguably neither approach in the end carries conviction because the one approach tends to collapse into the other, or to lead its followers eventually into an agnosticism about the possibility of any sort of explanation, in the conventional sense, at all. This it might be argued is the problem with the major theories used in class analysis: 'strong' approaches fall back on 'weak' ones and vice versa.

Furthermore, as Holton argues in Chapter 1, the term 'class' itself is all too often an imprecise metaphor for the moral and political aspirations which give rise to failed explanation in the first place. As Holton himself makes clear, however, his main target in this respect is Marxism whose 'strong' approach to class explanation shows a number of well rehearsed difficulties, not least over the non-occurrence of the expected proletarian revolution. Marx's much quoted treatment of the proletariat as a class 'in itself' (by virtue of its structural location in capitalist production) which becomes a class 'for itself' (by pursuing its supposedly objective class interests) conceals a real gap in his thought. What is the precise causal linkage between the broader changes in society and the consciousness and actions of individuals? Marx's own writings contain contradictory answers. Mostly, as Lockwood argues in a celebrated essay (Lockwood 1981), Marx glossed over the problem with assumptions mirroring nineteenth-century utilitarianism: proletarian revolutionary action is guided by the rational pursuit of objectively identifiable (class) interest (e.g. in overthrowing exploitation). At other times, however, he embraces a mind-as-blank-paper behaviourism which depicts people as puppets or what Marx himself calls bearers (*träger*) of the structures they inhabit. Arguably, these contradictory theories of action account for the subsequent division of Marx's followers into 'humanist' and 'structuralist'.

When strong explanations fail a characteristic response is to protect the original theory by *ad hoc* resort to contingent historical and dispositional factors which diverted action from its 'true' course. The absence of revolution might, for example, be explained by schisms in the labour movement due to nationalistic fervour, say, prior to the First World War, or by the power of the post-war 'bourgeois' state or the mass media – with the implication that eventually these veils over capitalist exploitation must fall. The issue of citizenship provides another example. Many radical critics have dismissed citizenship as merely a ruling-class strategy (Mann 1987), an ideological mask covering the 'real' structural inequalities of the mode of production. Such arguments fail, however, to take into account different forms of citizenship and different historical patterns of development in welfare states. The tradition of citizenship in North American democracy and in the French revolution, for example, assumed a more active and radical form than the passive type of citizenship which has been characteristic of Great Britain (Turner 1990; on the different worlds of welfare capitalism see Esping-Andersen 1990).

True, with the renewal of Marxist thought and politics during the late 1960s and early 1970s, Marx's *Weltanshauung* was radically reinterpreted so as to address these cruder explanatory failures and more effectively to account for contemporary events and institutions. Arguably, however, theorising and substantive research pulled in opposite directions. The tendency in Marxist theoretical writing, sometimes implicit at others explicit, was to abandon class altogether as an explanatory concept. As Becker points out in an important review, the assumption of a necessary link between class interest and political action came to be seen as 'reductionist', that is it presupposed a much too rigidly deterministic causal linkage between the economic organisation of society and politics, ideology and culture (Becker 1989). However, such theoretical manoeuvres intentionally or unintentionally give the impression of a shift in Marxism closer to those 'weak' theories (like Weber's) which regard consciousness of class and class interest as contingent on historical circumstances and intentional action.

The valuable stimulus given by post-1960s Marxism to substantive research, on the other hand, strengthened rather than weakened the use of class explanations. Liberal myths of classlessness were vigorously attacked. Marxist scholars began, for example, to re-examine the empirical structure of wealth, ownership and company control. Class explanations using Marxist concepts were extended into the analysis of a wider range of sociological topics than ever before: notably in cultural studies, and in the sociology of education, urbanism and criminology. There was also greater engagement of sociological debates on class with historical studies of working-class formation as carried out by the post-war generation of Marxist historians such as E. P. Thompson and Eric Hobsbawm.

Another important intellectual development of this period was the so-called deskilling debate. Harry Braverman, a Marxist from outside academia, challenged conventional claims that the proletariat of traditional Marxism was being displaced as machinery eliminated many former manual jobs. Braverman claimed that mechanisation in the office, as in the workplace generally, entails a deskilling of skilled labour – and hence that many so-called white-collar (middle-class) jobs, including even management itself, were actually being 'proletarianised' (Braverman 1974). This thesis struck a resonant chord in the era of spreading electronic technology and Braverman's attempt to reassert Marx's thesis of progressive proletarianisation redirected the attention of serious class research to the complexities of the 'labour process', that is to the shifting technical and social organisation of individual industries and workplaces behind gross changes in the size of different occupational groups.

By the early 1980s, however, with the absorption of many erstwhile student radicals into academic life, a substantial interpenetration had developed between Marxist and non-Marxist class research. For example, the vast number of detailed studies of historical and contemporary labour processes which followed the publication of Braverman's polemic soon showed up the simplistic character of his ideas (e.g. Wood 1982) – so much so that in due course it became difficult to say what was distinctly 'Marxist' about this new branch of class analysis.

But perhaps the most striking example of the routinisation of the Marxist renaissance is to be found in the work of the American Marxist, Erik Olin Wright (see especially Wright 1978, 1985). Wright's approach is distinguished not just for the originality with which it addressed some acknowledged difficulties in the Marxist account of late twentieth-century industrialism but also for its willingness to regard Marxist theory as a set of scientific hypotheses which could and, indeed, should be tested by advanced empirical methods. There are innumerable summaries and critiques of Wright's work and the so-called 'no-bullshit' or positivist school of academic Marxism with which he was associated. They include an important volume on the 'debate about class' edited by Wright himself (Wright (ed.) 1989b). What matters here is that within a relatively short space of time Wright had published several methodologically sophisticated attempts to develop the broad contours of Marx's class theory into a precise analytical framework for operationalising standard Marxist class categories (capitalists, the proletariat, the petit bourgeoisie) and demonstrating to an audience of 'mainstream' sociologists their salience in US society. At the same time, through his notion of contradictory class locations, he attempted to address those developments in twentieth-century capitalism that had raised especial difficulty for Marxist explanation: such as, the relative decline of heavy manual work and the rise of the 'white-collar' middle class. He also initiated an ambitious programme of comparative survey research, with the aim of validating his schema of class measurement using large-scale data sets, gathered from several industrial nations. Argument continues as to how far the results provide support for his original framework but Wright began radically to revise it anyway, using neo-Marxist reformulations of the concept of exploitation using rational choice and game theory (Wright 1985).

Undoubtedly, the sophistication of Wright's work was a serious challenge to established liberal theories of classlessness in the United States. Significantly, however, as both Holton, and Myles and Turegun point out in their respective chapters, by embracing notions like class *location* and explanatory strategies from 'bourgeois' traditions of positivism, Wright lessed the distinctiveness and historical focus of 'strong' Marxist theory and neo-Weberians could acknowledge convergences with their own work (e.g. Marshall *et al*. 1988, Chapter 2). Nevertheless, even as late as 1989 he was making a case for the distinctiveness of 'strong' Marxist class explanations as opposed to empiricist class analysis maintaining that:

> the explanatory force of the abstract macro level Marxist concept of class would be greatly compromised if it was unconnected to corresponding micro-level concepts, concepts that are closely tied to the lives and conditions of individuals. . . . If Marxist class analysis is to be theoretically powerful and politically useful, then it seems necessary to continue the attempt at forging concepts at the concrete micro-level. (Wright, 1989b:314)

Although, unlike Goldthorpe, he has intervened relatively little in the post-communist conceptual debates represented here, Wright, like other radical critics of capitalism, would no doubt still maintain that the collapse of communism has no implications whatsoever for the intellectual and theoretical distinctiveness of Marxist sociology. It is notable that in this volume, however, that Hout, who has been a colleague of Wright's, and Westergaard, a British sociologist who has always defended the empirical viability of Marxism, are prepared to define class in a very catholic fashion in their chapters, so as to unite the supporters of all variants of class analysis in its defence.

The death of class metaphors? (ii) Weak class explanations

It is at this point that we must consider the crucial role which the authority of Max Weber's theoretical ideas about social inequality has played for (non-Marxist) supporters and critics of class analysis alike. In the last fifty years, major phases in the debate have been associated with careful reinterpretation of Weber's incomplete and ultimately somewhat elliptic writings.

When the texts first became widely available (albeit incompletely) in English, Weber (along with his contemporary Emile Durkheim) was typically represented to students as a critic of the Marxism of turn-of-the-century German politics, who attempted to separate (and 'salvage') from Marxism's purely political programme those theories which remained of scientific interest (see for example Weber 1948: editorial introduction). In the course of their attempt to demonstrate the withering away of class, liberal writers of the 1950s and 1960s made particular use of two key Weberian ideas, *Schichtung* and *Stand*, normally conveyed in English, perhaps not very helpfully, by the words 'stratification' and 'status'. Stratification, for Weber, denoted in the first place the subdivision of individuals and/or households into unequally and hierarchically ordered groupings. So 'class', broadened out from its association with property to include other forms of economic interest including 'ownership' of occupational skills, was simply one form of stratification. Equally important, however, was *status* stratification, which included divisions based on religious or legal rights but also distributional inequalities of esteem, consumption and 'life style'.

Weber's writings enabled more sophisticated liberal sociologists in the USA and elsewhere to accept that some class inequalities, in Weber's sense, would continue to exist, as a result of the operation of the labour market. But many nevertheless proposed that as class recedes in significance 'stratification' becomes centred around divisions of status in the sense of consumption and life style. Status inequality in this sense, however, really implied a metaphor of gradations between points on a continuum, rather than dichotomous fractures (Ossowski 1963). Several scales of occupational 'status' were devised and in the USA became the principal device through which to measure 'social background' and its effect on life courses, and in particular the social mobility of individuals between positions of different prestige or socio-economic status (cf. Glass (ed.) 1954; Blau and Duncan 1967). Functionalist theorists had meanwhile devised a sociological version of the human capital theories of Chicago neo-classical economics. The residual class inequalities which exist in market societies, they argued, reflect not so much property divisions as the functional importance of a social role and the amount of training and talent required for its adequate performance (Davis and Moore 1945; cf. Karabel and Halsey 1977:Introduction). Arguably, post-modernist claims about what Waters (Chapter 5, this volume) calls the 'succession of stratification' systems have roots in these older liberal functionalist appropriations of Weberian thought.

It was also to Weber's work, however, that a group of mostly British sociologists appealed in an attempt to challenge the general factual and theoretical adequacy of these liberal functionalist myths of classlessness (for a review see Gallie 1990; and for a US example Collins 1971, 1975). As Westergaard points out in Chapter 11, the study of social class has been fundamental to the development of contemporary British sociology. Arguably, this is closely related to the distinctive history of industrial capitalism in the United Kingdom and the relatively stark nature of class differences in its social and cultural history. Much of the radical historiography of Britain has also been dominated by class studies although this tradition too is now under challenge (Cannadine 1992; Joyce 1995).

In the work of David Lockwood and John Goldthorpe, its leading representatives, British neo-Weberian class analysis rejected (as did Weber) the historicism of Marxist/materialist theories of the relation between class 'in itself' and class 'for itself'. Nevertheless, it was argued, Weber treated conflict as endemic to social order and considered all forms of stratification as 'phenomena of the distribution of power'. Class stratification rather than status stratification is characteristic of market capitalism since, as Weber himself put it in a celebrated phrase, in such a social order 'market situation' acts as the '*causal* component' (our emphasis) of individual 'life chances' (Weber 1967:928) and classes are, therefore, in the first instance identifiable statistical aggregations of causal components deriving from individual market situations. Goldthorpe in particular rejected the 'status continuum' approach dominating American stratification research and devised his own class classification which draws on Lockwood's celebrated distinction between the 'market' and 'work' situation of occupations (Lockwood 1958; Marshall 1990; Goldthorpe, this volume, page 206). The result has been a systematic and increasingly comparative research programme, using, like Wright, large data sets to locate the precise extent to which, in societies like Britain, the USA, France or Germany, objectively measured class explains social grouping (or class 'formation') and can predict social mobility, education, political attitudes and so on.

As Part Two reveals, however, in the last few years the neo-Weberian 'research programme' rationale for class analysis used by Goldthorpe and others has not escaped searching criticism. The following is an attempt to give a balanced assessment of the issues in dispute.

One undoubtedly is that anti-scientism is currently very influential, especially in British sociology. Much of its influence can be traced back to the attack of late 1960s radicals on positivist philosophy and on the scientific aspirations of mainstream sociology. Marxist and feminist radicals of the time, for example, dismissed the idea of social *science* as mere 'bourgeois' or 'malestream' ideology and sought to revive philosophical disputes going back to the nineteenth century or earlier as to the nature of our knowledge of society. In doing so they contributed substantially to an emergent crisis of method within the discipline, associated with renewed interest in language and the anti-positivist writings of post-Wittgensteinian philosophers (for a review see Giddens 1976). This has resulted in widespread preference for conducting research using 'humanistic' and 'qualitative' research methods and a willingness to disparage the validity of large-scale surveys. Leading names have embraced 'self-reflexivity' as a necessary and inevitable methodological strategy in

15

all areas of sociological work (e.g. Giddens 1976, Bourdieu 1993). 'Self-reflexivity' rules out in principle the possibility of showing that class is an objective (that is, observer-free) feature of modern societies. To stalwarts of class analysis, however, this relativism of method appears self-contradictory, suspiciously like 'word-spinning' and an excuse for sociologists to avoid having to study statistics and read tables.

Anti-scientism within the sociological community itself, ironically enough, prepared the ground for the political challenge to the idea of social *science* which soon followed from the right rather than the left. With the rise of so-called New Right ideas, mainstream class analysis found itself included in the general attack on subversives who, allegedly, masked an anti-capitalist agenda behind a facade of disinterested professionalism and scholarly expertise. New Right critics of sociology, some of whom held senior posts in the subject, sought to expose the discipline's obsession with inequality, which, it was said, obscured the more positive aspects of a market-driven industrial society and misrepresented and exaggerated the actual level of deprivation within it (Berger 1987, Marsland 1987). In Britain, even the statistical methods used to generate the 'findings' of class research, were attacked as constructs of an unexamined left-wing consensus in sociology as a whole (e.g. Saunders 1989, 1995).

These issues of philosophy and politics provide a context to the debate, however, rather than its core. Many of the most outspoken critics of class analysis in the English language literature have themselves contributed to the sociology of class in the past and say they broadly accept the methods and findings which show continuing strong associations between life-chances and occupational and socio-economic inequality. What they question is the habit of describing these findings as being about 'class'. Given that there are many sources of inequality in modern societies – gender, racial and age discrimination – what justifies the privileging of class in particular as an explanatory term?

A special instance of this is the critique raised against conventional class analysis by feminist sociologists. As Crompton argues in a review of the controversy below (Chapter 9) the analysis of what she calls employment-based 'class' relationships, far from being the key to understanding the structure of households, is itself only explainable by reference to the unequal household division of labour between men and women (see also Davidoff and Hall 1987). Similar arguments might be advanced in relation, say, to the history of 'racial' and ethnic divisions. As Anthias points out in an influential review of the latter issue:

what appears in the guise of 'race and class' is a number of heterogenous questions concerning processes of class formation, race formation, racism, exclusion, and economic and social position and disadvantage. Such questions cannot be collapsed together under the links between race and class for they involve looking at wide social processes. . . . The terms of the 'race and class' debate itself usually imply an answer which posits some sort of effectivity or determination of one by the other, or total autonomy, denying any relation. Both these positions appear as more or less inevitable outcomes of the ways in which the question is posed. (Anthias 1991:20)

She argues further that asking simply about the linkage of 'class' versus 'race'

conflates different levels of analysis, the conceptual and empirical. This conflation results from the assumption that the possibility of analytically separating these categories finds expression in their concrete manifestation as given groups. (Anthias, 1991:ibid.)

What explanatory mileage, then, does the term 'class', once stripped of its Marxist associations, contain? Clearly, much depends on whether resort to the Weberian explanatory framework avoids falling into the trap of 'explanatory failure'. We noted Holmwood and Stewart's (1983) complaint that, having generally failed to show the link between abstract class concepts and concrete events, social theorists had the habit of appealing to the uniqueness of the circumstances to protect the theory from rejection. But whereas this criticism seemed principally aimed at Marxism and historical class analysis, the polemic by Pahl which we reprint here as Chapter 6 directed a somewhat blunter version of the explanatory failure argument at *all* class analysis, regardless of pedigree. True, as he was to explain later, his words were intended for a non-sociological audience concerned with urban affairs. His main target was the simplistic way in which urban analysts had linked the existence of urban problems (deprivation, pollution, planning blight and so on) to the rise of protest movements. In doing so they invoked what Pahl calls the 'false mantra', by which consciousness and action are linked to a determining structure. But the implications for mainstream class analysis were soon recognised. It is possible, moreover, to find passages in neo-Weberian writings which seem to bear out Pahl's argument (see for example Marshall *et al.* 1988:6 and Crompton's assessment 1993:60). In Chapter 7, however, Marshall and Goldthorpe reject the idea that their work necessarily makes such assumptions.

It can in fact be argued that Weberian class explanation is more vulnerable to the opposite criticism, namely, that its very reluctance to conceptualise classes as having independent causal force in themselves results in the smuggling of a series of inadequate metaphors of 'structure' ('stratification', 'closure', 'mobility') by the back door in lieu of a theory explaining the coherence of class positions (Lee 1994). Much debate, for example, surrounds the issue of what constitutes the boundaries of classes themselves and what provides the common element of the occupations which positional class schema include within class categories – other than the imposed decision of the investigator to adopt this particular grouping. This has in fact been hotly debated ever since, in researching social mobility in Britain,

Goldthorpe and his colleagues sought to separate the measurement of class from the measurement of status stratification (see Marshall 1992). Goldthorpe's analysis of the putative 'service class' also turns upon specifying a common characteristic which marks out this particular class position from those around it (Goldthorpe 1982; cf. Savage *et al*. 1992). Scott (Chapter 10) seeks to resolve the boundary issue partly by regarding it as a problem of the construction of class measures; and partly by invoking Weber's notion of social class formation. But as the chapter by Lydia Morris demonstrates, current suggestions of an emergent underclass have presented a comparable problem which cannot be solved so easily, since it involves a more subtle understanding of labour market processes (surely a Weberian aim?) than can be got either from formal measurement or the notion of 'class formation' alone.

A related debate surrounds the concept of 'closure' used by some Weberian sociologists of class as well as by Weber himself. Weber was concerned to understand how monopolies were created in the control and the management of scarce resources, whether these resources were spiritual or material. By the notion of social closure, he indicated those complex processes by which social groups seek to increase and to control their rewards by limiting access to scarce resources and opportunities to a small group of eligibles. This monopolisation of resources against competitors necessarily divides the world into insiders and outsiders.

Is this Weberian idea of closure, however, consistent with the idea of class as an aggregate of individual positions? Critics could argue that it implies a set of enduring interests and relations that orchestrates the consciousness and actions of its individual members across space and across generations. Weber's recent followers arguably inherit the problem. An approach to class differences as a form of social closure has been developed by several neo-Weberian scholars such as Collins in the USA and Parkin in Britain (Collins 1971, Parkin 1971, 1979). Both open up the whole question of how individual differences in 'human capital' or 'market situation' are connected to the emergence of knowledge stratification. Educational credentialism, they argue, is an essential aspect of in-group and out-group processes for the management, control and monopolisation of scarce knowledge resources. The creation of professional monopolies, typically reinforced by state licensure, is simply one illustration of a more general structure of occupational exclusion. In his discussion of the concept of property as social closure, for example, Parkin draws upon the work of Pierre Bourdieu to make a comparison between cultural capital and economic capital. Bourdieu has made great use of the idea of cultural capital both in his study of the educational system and the exclusionary force of educational attainment (Bourdieu 1984, Bourdieu and Passeron 1970). Here, too, however, the concepts of cultural capital and credentialism imply a 'strong' understanding of class even though they also do not fit easily into the Marxist language of economic ownership and modes of production either.

Because of such difficulties there have also been numerous attempts to create a synthesis between strong and weak class concepts, of which Giddens's (1973) attempt to devise a theory of 'class structuration' could be considered an early example. Mann's monumental examination of the sources of social power seeks to understand how economically structured class is related to Weberian questions about variations in consciousness (Mann 1973) and coercion, state formation and military mobilisation (Mann 1986a and 1986b). Turner's discussion of status (Turner 1988) seeks to incorporate economic class analysis with an approach to status as cultural exclusion and the notion of citizenship as political involvement. Most striking of all, however, is that Crompton's magisterial review of class and stratification research (Crompton 1993:40–41 and 202) has come down in favour of such a way of resolving the issue. In support she notes how the Marxist social historian E. P. Thompson urges us to regard class as 'something which in fact happens' (ibid.:37; cf. Thompson 1968:9). Unfortunately, too, social history now has its own debate about class in which Thompson's approach has been severely censured. Thus just as neo-Marxist and neo-Weberian empirical work on class had by the early 1980s tended to merge, so various kinds of fusion and *confusion* took place on a conceptual level too.

There is no doubt, then, that all forms of class analysis have become very vulnerable to critique at a number of levels: theoretical, philosophical and above all, in the political climate of academia in the 1980s and 1990s, ideological. At the heart of this critique, a kind of Weberian fundamentalism is evident which seems to be seeking to rescue the writings of the master from the structural apostasy of existing class analysis in any form. Neo-liberal sociologists in particular have been able to make an impact because the tradition of political theory on which they draw, stemming from the work of writers like Popper and Hayek, is heavily committed, like Weber himself, to individualist methodology. But neo-liberalism overlaps with the postmodern philosophical critique of 'grand narratives' (Lyotard 1984) which sees Weber as a forerunner of its enthusiasm for irony and relativism. Thus, a fundamental re-reading of Weber is again at the heart of change – as action theorist, individualist, philosopher, and early post-modernist. But is it this time to preside over the death of class analysis *per se* – or not?

Conflicts over class: the organisation of the volume

This has been the major consideration in shaping the selections in the volume. In Parts One and Two we have reprinted the principal contributions in two influential and parallel exchanges about class analysis, the first among sociologists from the USA and Australia which chiefly featured in the journal *International Sociology*, the second a debate in British sociology which followed the publication of the polemic by Pahl discussed above. These two sections feature many of the themes and authors we have been discussing here. Part Three contains some recent research papers, mostly specially written for this collection, which, in addressing some of the empirical themes which have arisen during the debate, raise important matters of class explanation and imagery. Each part is preceded by a short overview which introduces the individual contributions.

The volume as a whole reflects our belief that sociological research on contemporary society will emerge strengthened by these critical debates about class analysis. Whether or not 'class analysis' itself should survive is, however, a matter on which, as we explain in our separate conclusions, we ourselves differ completely and must thus ultimately leave to the reader's judgement.

Part One

Class in a Post-Communist World

Class metaphors and triumphant individualism

Over this opening selection of papers looms the theme of the triumph of individualism in late twentieth-century society and its implications for the analytical viability of the sociology of class. All of the authors were either born in or work in non-European societies, specifically the USA or Australia, where class traditions are, at best, weak and where the market economy and individualistic values (the 'American Dream', the 'Lucky Country') are deeply entrenched in the political and social culture. From this vantage it has been perhaps easier than in Europe to claim that the type of society which Toennies called *Gesellschaft*, based on the predominance of impersonal, heterogenous and largely contractual relationships between autonomous and legally 'free' individuals, provides the *general* paradigm for what is now virtually a world social order. Moreover, for political liberals in both the New and the Old world, *Gesellschaft* is the model of order which people in uncoerced situations will 'naturally choose'.

On the other hand, as Holton argues in his highly influential paper, the 'idiom' of class in European social theory emerged out of nineteenth-century pessimism about the stability and desirability of *Gesellschaft*. It and the socialist political rhetoric with which it was associated embodied a nostalgia for *Gemeinschaft* (community), and for traditional forms which the individualistic order had destroyed. In its specific form of communism (not, admittedly, to be confused with Marxism as a whole) political class struggle became an attempt to redirect history and define circumstances in which community may again triumph over atomism. Has the recent collapse of that experiment provided final vindication of both liberal political theory and of individualistic theories of *Gesellschaft* in sociology?

The core of Holton's case is what he calls the difficulty of distinguishing between the value concerns underlying class theory and the efforts of sociological class analysis to develop scientific procedures for measuring and analysing class. He accepts, however, that it will not be possible to drop class analysis altogether because economic inequality will continue to be part of the distribution of power in late twentieth-century *Gesellschaft*. But the conceptualisation of class itself will become progressively 'weaker' in the sense used in the Introduction.

The difficulty of making any clear separation between the representation of the actual nature of contemporary social conditions and the choice of a conceptual and evaluative framework within which to do so is well illustrated in the critique of class analysis by Clark and Lipset on one hand and the response to them by Hout, Brooks and Manza, on the other. Careful scrutiny of these chapters will show that the formal definition of class by both sets of authors is remarkably close. Both are prepared to see it in very broad terms as structured inequality between individuals arising out of ownership of property or out of market advantage. Their usage is very different, however. Clark and Lipset introduce a separate notion of 'hierarchy' and are clearly concerned with how far perceptions of class and hierarchy influence behaviour in what they call 'situses' (or institutional segments) of society, in particular work, politics and the family. They make, in fact, an astonishing range of substantive claims some of which are addressed by the chapters in Part Three (see e.g. Goldthorpe on politics) but the major theme to emerge is the fragmentation of stratification taking place within each of these situses as a result of the advance of individualistic values and the death of the old solidarities which fostered class identity and struggle.

Hout and his colleagues are on the other hand keen to direct our attention back to the central issue, the empirical persistence of class as a major organising principle of economic inequality in contemporary US and other highly industrialised societies. Their paper not only provides a useful overview of some of the principal studies and sources on this topic of the last few years but also cites fresh findings of their own.

The last two chapters in Part One are both by authors from the University of Tasmania who have already written about the post-modernisation of society (Crook *et al.* 1992) and whose papers were printed in *International Sociology* in the wake of the Clark/Hout exchange. The first author, Pakulski, accuses the disputants of talking past each other. Clark and Lipset are talking about the fragmentation of stratification, whereas Hout and his colleagues are talking about the persistence of economic inequality which, Pakulski thinks, is not at issue. Conceptually too Hout *et al.* retain some elements of a Marxist theory of class as objective material interest which Pakulski sees as unsustainable in the wake of the individualising changes which have occurred. In the interest of clarification he proposes a useful fourfold typology of class conceptions which would distinguish descriptive from explanatory usages and the objective aspect of class from the subjective. Water's starting point is also the link between the conceptualisation of class and the issue of whether or not class exists. His is an ambitious attempt to demonstrate not just the fragmentation of stratification but the succession of different systems of stratification over time. He argues that this makes it possible to not only to retain the Marxist concept of class (as a description of a now superceded set of conditions) but also to comprehend Marxist society itself as a superceded order of stratification. The work of both of these authors usefully contains overviews of the substantive changes which they and others believe characterise post-modernity and which might be regarded as the ultimate point which individualisation and *Gesellschaft* can reach. The celebration of this state of affairs might in turn be regarded as the late twentieth-century form taken by political liberalism.

CHAPTER 1

Has class analysis a future? Max Weber and the challenge of liberalism to Gemeinschaftlich accounts of class[1]

Robert Holton

Class has often been presumed dead (Nisbet 1959), or less and less able 'to do useful work for sociology' (Pahl below, p. 113). Many of the bolder propositions of class theory have proved false or inadequate, not least Marx and Engels's celebrated expectation of proletarian revolution in the advanced capitalist world. Meanwhile the idea of a unitary general theory of inequality linked to class has given way to an increasing emphasis on the multiple intersections between class, gender, race and ethnicity. Yet for all this the language of class continues to be widely used in popular culture and political debate (see, for example, Crompton 1993:9). The discourses of class also continue to haunt social theory and social research.

The meaning of class terminology appears to vary considerably between the domain of popular culture (where it is often synonymous with status), and that of social theory (where it is usually treated as a *sui generis* component of social inequality linked to the structure of economic power). But there is little unanimity of definition or conceptualisation in intellectual circles either. Meanwhile, political actors invoke class as a means of dramatising their claims to be organic leaders of mass opinion. In this situation the persistence of the language of class may simply signify intellectual confusion, and the conflation of analysis with rhetoric, or perhaps conceptual piety to an enduring piece of intellectual artifice.

A more likely interpretation of the persistence of class, however, is its powerful and multi-dimensional metaphoricality. Metaphors are figures of speech 'in which a name or descriptive term is transferred to some object to which it is not properly applicable' (*Oxford English Dictionary*). For Ossowski (1963) metaphors function to combine intuitive understanding with routine application in a way that evades comprehensive and systematic definition. Class, he argued, is one such metaphor, able to draw on a wide range of possible meanings or allusions. These include the methodological practice of categorising, the labelling of cohesive social groups possessing a quality distinct from other social groups, and the use of spatial allusions to suggest distance between social groupings, as well as more rhetorical political allusions to the existence of organic agents of conflict and social change in society and world history. Class is simultaneously an objective feature of the world – 'something which in fact happens' (Thompson 1968:i) – and a subjective idea. Its metaphorical flexibility is also reflected in the proliferation of dichotomic, gradational and functional class schema.

There are a number of further ways in which we can unravel the metaphoricality of class. One of these involves the serviceability of class concepts in both *Gemeinschaft*-based and *Gesellschaft*-based accounts of society. In other words, class is equally used to discuss community formation, as it is to refer to the distribution of individuals within roles available within structures of economic production and exchange. Developing this point it is possible to identify three typical idioms of class analysis on the *Gemeinschaft–Gesellschaft* spectrum. Speaking metaphorically, it is possible to specify a strong class idiom at the *Gemeinschaft* end of the spectrum, a weak class idiom at the *Gesellschaft* end, and certain intermediate positions.

The strong class idiom operates both as a structural account of relationships of power, inequality and exploitation, and simultaneously an account of consciousness, group formation, and social movements as emancipatory social change. As in most conventional accounts of class, these relations derive in a fundamental sense from economic relations of production and exchange instituted in property rights. However, in the strong class idiom these relations are not only contained within the economy, but suffuse politics, culture, and so on. The strong class idiom presents a unitary account of society, whereby the theory of class is coterminous with the theory of society. Its most influential formulation is to be found in Marx's and Engels's emphasis on class as the motive force of history.

To describe the strong class idiom in terms of *Gemeinschaft* relations is more a metaphorical than a literal procedure. This is because the literal sociological usage of *Gemeinschaft* is generally related to pre-modern particularistic accounts of community tied together by blood, kinship, and locality; whereas the classic Marxist account of class under capitalism takes as its starting point the cash nexus of the *Gesellschaft*, or society of 'free' individuals. Yet the strong class idiom is precisely an attempt to define the circumstances under which community may again triumph over individual atomisation. In this sense, it is legitimate to describe the strong class idiom, metaphorically, as a *Gemeinschaftlich* view of class.

The 'weak' class idiom, by contrast, treats class as one of several patterns of power and inequality, which may exist in any given society. This idiom not only rejects a unitary account of class in society, but also argues against any necessary connection between class positions and the development of group formation, class communities, social change, and the course of world history. A typical formulation of this approach is to be found in Weber's tripartite account of the distribution of power in terms of class, status, and party. Here, class is again derived from economic relations, but the centre point of the approach concerns the character of class positions occupied by individuals. Social class formation is a contingent possibility, but there is room here for some sense of exploitation.

Weber's approach is typical of what might be called the radical liberal perspective on class. This accepts the *Gesellschaftlich* account of modern society as a given and seeks out dimensions of market-place exchange where power inequalities affect the life chances of individuals. There is an underlying commitment here to *Gesellschaft* relations as the foundation for equality of opportunity, but also space for justifications of class inequalities of condition, especially where these result from differences in marketable skill and human capital endowment. The metaphorical flexibility of class permits its continued usage in this very different context, though its provenance is restricted to the analysis of economic inequality and its contingent social consequences.

Between the strong and weak class idioms there has grown up a range of intermediate positions. These have generally arisen as a result of perceived weaknesses in the strong class idiom as originally formulated in the nineteenth century. Class continues to be seen as a major dimension to social inequality, and as having a connection with group formation, conflict, exploitation, and change. On the other hand, the strong claim for class as a unitary account of inequality, and as the motive force for history, is no longer advanced with confidence. Far more typically, class is projected as a manifestation of economic conflict within the work-place, which generally fails to achieve radical political expression. This goes further than the weak idiom in its continuing emphasis on conflict and collectivist organisation, as well as in the elusive search for a more robust understanding of class politics. This search has, however, led some to abandon key elements of the older *Gemeinschaftlich* position, such as the labour theory of value, while still maintaining a critique of capitalism and liberalism as inegalitarian and exploitative.

The main aim of this chapter is to evaluate this relationship between *Gemeinschaft* and *Gesellschaft* elements in class theory in the light of Weber's earlier statement of the 'weak' *Gesellschaft* idiom. Although there are relatively few enthusiasts any longer for the strong class idiom, it remains clear that there has been some regrouping around a 'transitional' position on the *Gemeinschaft–Gesellschaft* spectrum. The argument of this chapter is, first, that the case for any kind of *Gemeinschaft* component of class theory is getting progressively weaker. Much of the debate between neo-Marxists and radical liberals is now taking place on the terrain of the *Gesellschaft* idiom. This is particularly evident in the deployment of rational choice and game theory assumptions within Marxist and radical discourse. A further feature of my argument is that *Gesellschaft* theories of class offer limited but significant justifications for retaining class analysis. The analysis of contemporary social structures, and relations between markets, households, organised interests, and the state, cannot dispense with class analysis altogether. Weber's radical liberal legacy has been of some use in encouraging social theorists in this direction, although Weber himself failed to follow through a thoroughgoing radical liberal account of market relations, linking production and distribution to consumption.

Class and the problem of Gemeinschaft in Western social thought

It is important to re-emphasise that class has always been far more than a sociological concept debated among intellectuals. The language of class, and the social movements activated in the name of class, were a fundamental emergent feature of European capitalist industrialisation (Briggs 1976, Williams 1976). In the process, the linguistic meaning of 'class' was massively extended and transformed. What began as a generic classificatory device became both a political and industrial rallying cry and a major discourse within social analysis. In both cases, issues of inequality and exploitation were linked with social conflict and the problem of how to overcome emergent social cleavages.

Until then, inequalities between social groups had generally been understood in terms of a complex status hierarchy of ranks, orders, and degrees. The new terminology of class now shifted attention to the 'economic' basis of social divisions and conflicts, and their expression in political action and cultural identity. This shift still left room for disagreement over precise specification of the nature of the economic processes involved. Of particular interest is the debate over the relative importance of inequalities of exchange relations in the distribution of income (as in Ricardianism), compared with the Marxist emphasis on inequalities in the social relations of production. None the less, the fundamental *formal* principle at stake in class theory was, and continues to be, the structural location of the causes of social inequality, exploitation, conflict, and change within socio-economic relations. However much such relations may influence or depend on political and cultural institutions, class theory is grounded in economic relations.

Having said this we immediately encounter a paradox, namely the perpetuation of evaluative, status-ridden, cultural values in popular, and much academic, language usage concerning class. It is not of course surprising to find that social classifications are value relevant. What is striking is the difficulty of making a sharp distinction between the ostensibly scientific, formal analytical procedures of class theory, on the one hand, and the value-concerns underlying class theory, on the other. [. . .]

Marxist political economy is certainly not value-free. Marx's value theory, with its attempt to locate a universal equivalent with which

29

to measure value, is constituted precisely to assert the need for a type of community to meet the social problems engendered by the alienation, atomisation, and fetishism of commodities under capitalism. Whereas the sphere of exchange appears constituted by individual atoms subject to a self-regulating allocation process beyond human intervention, Marx sees in the sphere of production an essentially co-operative enterprise – albeit currently under highly exploitative conditions. The potential for social improvement comes not by emphasising the market-place choices of the individual consumer, rich in needs, but through the creation of a community of free producers, individually autonomous, but collectively bound through an objective *Gemeinschaftlich* labour theory of value.

Marxist value theory, with its origins in medieval Christian theology and peasant communism, represents an attempt to replace the *Gesellschaftlich* categories of market exchange – price, wages, profits, and so on – each accruing to self-interested individuals, with an alternative account of social life grounded in co-operation among producers. For Marx, we need categories like value and surplus-value in order to demonstrate that the market is embedded within more fundamental social relations. Under some conditions the more fundamental relations of production may engender exploitation, but under others they may lay the basis for the transcendence of exploitation itself. This is not, however, a merely technical or scientific argument. For the categories of value and surplus-value contain a strong normative component. They assert the dignity of labour – to be more precise, productive labour – the parasitical character of non-productive occupations geared merely to the realms of market profitability, the exploitative character of private property rights which provide selective control over the necessities of life, the pathological nature of market-oriented consumption, and the need for an organic consensus about principles of just distribution.

All this assumes that there ought to be a communitarian basis upon which the different wants of individuals could be measured and made commensurable with one another. There is no suggestion that wants may be incommensurable, for to raise this spectre would undermine the search for an objective basis to value, and an objective grounding of the route to a reassertion of community over the 'fetishism of commodities' and reversal of the alienation of the producer. In all these respects Marx has a fundamental moral antipathy to *Gesellschaftlich* relations of individual exchange, where value is linked subjectively to the wants of individuals. He cannot accept that the conception of individuality involved could be anything other than an abstraction from social relations. Here Marx leaves no space for the possibility that liberalism could come up with a theory of socialised individuals, consistent with the existence of a social order. This position has been extremely influential, bequeathing to modern social theory the highly problematic axiom that market exchange cannot legitimise itself and has therefore to rely on sources of legitimacy that lie outside capitalist social relations (see, for example, Habermas 1976).

The value-relevant character of the labour theory of value is not in itself an argument against its sociological usefulness. There is, however, a second major problem with the theory: namely, its dubious status as a technical argument. Marx's argument, we may recall, is that wherever we find private property rights in the means of production and conditions of wage-labour, there is necessarily exploitation of labour through the extraction of surplus-value by capital. In other words, labour does not receive the full value it has added to potential commodities during the production process. Part of the value created is siphoned off as surplus-value. Without this, further capital accumulation would not be possible.

A major logical difficulty with this argument, as John Roemer (1982a) has pointed out, is that it can be made to apply to any resource utilised in economic activity. Any commodity is in fact capable of producing more value than it embodies through the value added during the production process. If we choose corn as a universal equivalent or measure of value, we can calculate the embodied corn values of commodities. From this we can prove that the economy can produce a surplus only if corn is exploited – that is, that the corn value of a unit of corn is less than one.

One consequence of this argument is that there is nothing unique about the status of labour as a universal equivalent. Marx's labour theory of value is therefore flawed. The significance of the theory concerns its value-relevance in that we are generally more interested in people and human labour than corn. The *Gemeinschaftlich* moral resonance of the theory arises from the belief that people should not be 'exploited', while there is widespread indifference to the exploitation of things. If we want to reconstruct a theory of exploitation according to Roemer, we must look elsewhere. His own strategy is to mobilize game-theoretic and rational choice assumptions of an inherently *Gesellschaftlich* character. Exploitation is said to exist where an individual or set of individuals could gain more if they withdrew from the current relations of production, compared with staying in. Here exploitation is linked not to the normative assumptions of a community of free producers but rather within the optimizing strategies of utility maximising individuals. The search is on for a version of *Gesellschaft* which optimises returns to individuals. [. . .]

Marx's comments on the eventual 'withering away' of the state as socialism moved towards communism are again redolent of the anarchistic peasant *Gemeinschaft*. In Marx's view, post-capitalist free producers will require the state, as a body differentiated from the *Gemeinschaft*, only if it is necessary to preserve their existence. Once this condition lapses with the productive upgrading of the post-revolutionary system, the need for a separate state will disappear. Once again we see a *Gemeinschaft* critique of excessive differentiation at work, though not of course a return to 'primitive' communism.

Within these *Gemeinschaftlich* parameters – with their minimal need for special differentiated bodies geared to the co-ordination of exchange, integration of the social fabric, state administration, and so on – the proletariat represents for Marx the emergent social force with the requisite community-like characteristics. It has been massed together in factories, and homogenised in condition by the imperatives of capital accumulation, most notably the rising organic composition of capital. This homogenisation, and the consequent polarisation of the class structure, encourages a collective interest in the abolition of private property rights in the means of production. Given the evaluative yardstick of the moral economy of free producers, social differentiation between owners and non-owners of capital, and the consequent hierarchical division of labour, is untenable since it breaks the *Gemeinschaft* aspirations and links between producers. Because capital requires wage-labour to function, contemporary proletarians cannot be emancipated as a class without destroying private property rights over the means of production. The revolutionary political mobilisation of proletarian community is, however, synonymous with the conditions necessary to prepare a *Gemeinschaft* of humanity. Within the 1848 revolutions and the Paris Commune of 1871, Marx believed he detected the first stirrings of the imminent transition to socialism. [. . .]

The language of class in the century since Marx has witnessed an increasingly dualistic development. On the one hand, status concerns have persisted in class categories, reflecting a continuation of the evaluative vocabulary of moral distinction. On the other hand, theorists have searched for a more sociologically grounded vocabulary linked with observable structural features of economic life, and with social movements. 'Class' has become a 'shorthand' concept we cannot seem to do without when discussing socio-economic groups, political action and cultural behaviour, and yet the ambiguities in its meaning and intellectual function seem to be proliferating in an ever more confusing way than before.

The ubiquitous term 'middle class', which has emerged to prominence in class discourse since Marx's time, is a particularly graphic example of the conflation of status elements with the socio-economic characterisation of structural locations within the division of labour. The middle class is often coupled with notions of 'upper class' and 'working class' in a three-class schema. Yet the nature and the boundaries of the middle class in this framework are never very clear. Is it meant to reflect a distinction between landowners (upper class), capital owners (middle class) and wage and salary recipients (working class)? Or is it that capital owners are the upper class, salaried workers such as professionals/managers and service providers the middle class, and wage-workers the working class? It is very difficult to sort out these issues since the terminology itself is capable of interpretation both as a gradational status hierarchy (such as upper middle class, lower middle class, and so on) and as a structural account of qualitatively different socio-economic positions, albeit using terminology drawn from popular culture. [. . .]

While there is a good reason to believe that popular conceptions of class, and many class labels, include a strong element of evaluative status considerations, this does not rule out arguments in favour of structural accounts of class. Such accounts are justified to the extent that the set of positions available for individuals to enter arises independently of human volition. Within the strong class idiom, with all of its *Gemeinschaftlich* connotations, it is, however, very hard to aggregate the multiplicity of class positions into categories, without having recourse to evaluative cultural criteria. These criteria, as we have seen, embrace moral issues such as 'productiveness' as opposed to 'unproductiveness', or capacity to generate organic community as against simple collectivities of individuals. Considerations of what community should be like structure the ostensibly scientific discourse of what it is like. In the process, strong class theorists have now found themselves on the defensive as the *Gemeinschaftlich* preoccupations of nineteenth-century moral critics of market capitalism seem increasingly outmoded in late twentieth-century conditions of advanced *Gesellschaftlich* social relations.

The erosion of the strong class idiom

The erosion of the strong class idiom in recent social analysis can be seen in three key areas. The first involves the increasing rejection of *Gemeinschaftlich* theories of class, in which classes are portrayed as having organic interests, expressed in specific 'class' agencies or institutions. The problem has been put very clearly by Hirst (1977). His claim is that classes as such do not act, and that politics is not conducted, in terms of the direct contact between classes. Instead, we find agencies such as political parties, campaign organisations, trade-union and employee organisations, riotous mobs, and so on, which are at best 'representative' of classes, though only indirectly. To say that particular organisations 'stand for certain economic classes is either simply to accept the claims of a party, organisation or apparatus to represent a certain class, or to argue that the party's programme and actions somehow correspond with the "interests" of that class' (Hirst 1977:130).

To accept the former means accepting organisational rhetoric very naively at face value. To accept the notion of class 'interests' formed on the economic plane and then projected into politics assumes an organic homogeneity of interests, and that interests are somehow constituted independently of 'politics'. This last option represents a kind of unacceptable economism. Hirst's conclusion is that 'there is no necessary correspondence between the forces that appear in the political (and what they "represent") and economic classes. . . . Classes do not have "interests", apparent independently of definite parties, ideologies etc., and against which those parties, ideologies etc. can be measured' (ibid.: 130–1). [. . .]

This challenge to organicist theories of class and of the organic connection between economic class and political action is very striking because it is advanced as an argument within Marxism, and yet it is critical of the overwhelming idiom of Marxist class analysis. For our present purposes it represents an attempt to avoid the assumption that classes are communities in a socio-political sense, while retaining a continuing sense of economic inequality and political conflict under capitalism. Elsewhere there are of course a range of arguments to the effect that economic inequalities at the point of production tend to generate sectional and instrumental conflict rather than outright political mobilisation and radicalisation (Goldthorpe *et al.* 1969, Mann 1973). Such criticisms have either led to a reconceptualisation of class around non-organic *Gesellschaftlich* relations (Roemer 1982b, Wright 1985) or a historicisation of class analysis around the few contingent moments when economic class has seemed to correspond with social class (Thompson 1968).

A second related development, however, concerns the growing historical scepticism concerning 'ouvrierist' or rank-and-filist accounts of working-class social history. Although the study of rank-and-file community-level movements played an important role in correcting an earlier institutional bias in labour history (see especially Holton 1976), an over-preoccupation with this issue to the exclusion of sectionalism, instrumentalism, and non-economic social cleavages has created an over-romanticised distortion of working-class history. At its worst this genre has perpetuated the search for empirical instances of *Gemeinschaftlich* class relations, without testing for their typicality (see especially the work of the History Workshop movement in Britain). There are comparatively few studies like John Foster's magisterial *Class Struggle and the Industrial Revolution* designed to test the strength and limitation of class formation under different structural conditions (Foster 1974). There are also comparatively few studies of the 'unmaking' of class communities on a par with Gareth Stedman Jones's seminal essay on working-class politics and culture in late nineteenth-century London (Stedman Jones 1974).

A third manifestation of the erosion of the strong class idiom is the declining support for the labour theory of value and the insistence on distinctions between productive and unproductive labour. The challenge here, as we have already seen, has been couched in terms of the overly moralistic and at times metaphysical character of the categories involved. This has been clearest in the self-styled 'no bullshit' theory of Marxism, which leaves aside Hegelianism, the labour theory of value, and organicist constructions of class in favour of models of rational choice and the critique of institutional frameworks which distort the achievement of individual interest.

Such changes in the intellectual climate can of course be connected with structural and cultural changes in modern Western societies. First, there is the decline of heavy industry and associated transport occupations, characteristically organised through occupational communities (for example, miners, shipyard workers and dockers). The decline of occupational community is clearly linked with an erosion of *Gemeinschaftlich* views of class. This has been further accelerated with the shift to more organisationally diffuse forms of service work. In parallel with these changes is the diffusion of private home ownership, car ownership, and the general expansion of household privatism. Home ownership, alongside economic restructuring, has dissolved many of the older working-class communities.

Second, there is the erosion of class voting, and in certain Western societies a decline in trade-union and left-wing political party membership (such as US trade unions, British trade unions, and parties of the left). New social movements such as feminism, the peace movement, and the ecology movement are neither work-centred (in the conventional sense of paid work outside the household) nor class-specific (Feher and Heller 1984, Gorz 1982). The feminist theorization of gender relations, personality development, and sexual politics within the household has been particularly corrosive of the largely male-centred work-place-oriented 'class' *Gemeinschaft*. Feminist theory has not only rejected the idea that women get their economic 'class' from their husbands/fathers (Allen 1982), but has in some cases gone further to reformulate class as an exploitative relation between men and women (Walby 1986, Delphy and Leonard 1986).

Such changes have also encouraged a more differentiated conception of propertised classes. There never was an entirely unitary ruling class with an organic solidarity (Abercrombie, Hill and Turner 1980) but the continuing differentiation of propertised and credentialled social positions since the mid-nineteenth century has reduced the likelihood of this even further. The strong class idiom, with its increasingly polarised view of relations between the organic class communities of labour and capital has now been sharply revised. One prominent area of revision is to be found in New Class theory (Gouldner 1979) or service class theory (Renner 1953, Dahrendorf 1969). While earlier attempts to differentiate the capitalist class from a managerial class proved inconclusive, there is now a far greater weight of support for the need to differentiate between property-based and knowledge- or credential-based class positions or class strategies. This debate has been encouraged in part by the realisation that economic inequality and social stratification have also been evident in socialist as well as capitalist societies. If class is to be deployed as a means of understanding group formation under conditions of economic inequality, then it becomes necessary to develop a class analysis of socialism alongside that of capitalism (Djilas 1966).

It is evidently worth pursuing the possibility of a more generic theory of class, linked not merely to private property ownership, but also to the characteristics that make for inequality in socialist societies. This search led Dahrendorf to develop the neo-Weberian criterion of authority-relations as a generic basis for class divisions, whether under capitalism or socialism (Dahrendorf 1959). However, this advance was achieved by abandoning a concern for organic class community formation, in favour of the pursuit of class analysis within any 'imperatively co-ordinated organization'.

Communitarianism also disappears from Erik Wright's second class model. This went beyond Wright's first class model, based as it was on the fusion of property and authority relations. In the second model Wright sought to define class in different social systems by individual control over types of assets (private property under capitalism, organisation under socialism) (Wright 1985).

The erosion of the strong class idiom has not led in any simple way to the decline of class theory itself. In spite of the exuberant claims of the New Right to be setting the terms of the intellectual and political agenda, there remain some striking attempts to reformulate an 'intermediate' or 'strong-as-possible' class theory short of objectionable elements and more appropriate to late twentieth-century conditions. And yet the challenge of the rejuvenated liberal social philosophies of some sections of the New Right is not so easy to evade in an era when 'the working population has developed institutions which reflect . . . individualism, egoism and economic calculation' (Marshall et al. 1985:271).

This revival was, for one thing, completely unexpected by class analysts. Many still regard liberalism as a bizarre and outmoded atavism, which aims to restore a mythical world of sovereign individuals that never existed even in the time of John Locke. This blanket rejection is, however, misconceived. In particular, it fails to comprehend the popular appeal of Gesellschaftlich ideologies designed to recognise individual autonomy and the differentiation of the private household from strong cultural and political controls. Popular culture simply does not experience the expanded public functions of the modern state as an unambiguous good, or as a timely rescue from the atomisation of Gesellschaft. The alleged atomisation of the Gesellschaft is experienced by many as a kind of 'freedom' – notably freedom to determine one's own values and objectives.

There may often be illusions here as to the capacity of households to be free-standing without the underlying public support of citizenship rights. At the same time the issue of atomisation may usefully be re-cast, as in much post-modern theory, as cultural pluralisation. This it seems to me offers a clearer sociological grounding of what is typically mis-labelled atomisation, insofar as it highlights the existence of multiple life-worlds. But what of inequality within this framework? Does it necessarily disappear from view in favour of liberal triumphalism, or can it retain some analytical cutting edge?

In this context, it is important to scrutinise how robust reformulated versions of class theory may be in the light of the predominantly Gesellschaftlich characteristics of modern society. This brings into play the alternative credentials of what has here been called the 'weak' class theory. The intellectual coherence and explanatory power of this idiom is, however, difficult to grasp unless we are prepared to accept that liberalism offers genuine scientific insights into processes of economic inequality, social differentiation, cultural identity, and normative order. Marx's comments on commodity fetishism and the abstract character of liberal-democratic political theory do not represent the last and conclusive word on liberalism, yet they are often rehearsed as if they expressed enduring and self-evident truths. In this context, there is much merit in considering Max Weber's class theory and economic sociology as the classic statement of a liberalistic *Gesellschaftlich* view of class.

Max Weber, market relations and the transition *to* Gesellschaft

Max Weber's work represents a major turning point in the articulation of a 'weak' class idiom. Since there remains some misunderstanding of his position, it is important to clarify its core propositions. In the first place Weber's class theory sets out from a generic theory of the market place – the classic locus of *Gesellschaft* relations – rather than the mode of production. Markets are social institutions in which scarce resources are allocated to meet a variety of ends, through the actions of individuals. The term 'Gesellschaft' means a voluntary contractual association of individuals – and as such is used equally to describe a joint-stock company as a society characterised by voluntary exchange. Weber's conception of the market place derives in large measure from the Austrian neo-classicists, with whom he shared a profound methodological individualism (Holton and Turner 1989, Chapter 2).

The market place is perhaps the classic example of instrumental purposive rationality, in so far as it is constituted as a disenchanted, impersonal realm dominated by the calculation of advantage through cost/benefit. Rather than seeing this merely as a heartless cash nexus, Weber's anti-organicist, non-romantic viewpoint led him to view the market as a modern rational device which is enabling as well as constraining. The differentiation involved in market activities between ends and means, values and technique, enables cost/benefit considerations to be calculated without constant intrusion of ultimate moral considerations. This not only enables the actor to establish the best means to reach a given end but also to choose more rationally between proximate ends. The structure of ends is, however, distributed among individuals rather than communities. With the 'death of God' and the predominance of this-worldly occidental rationalism, we are in a position of having to assert our own values, and then to pursue their successful attainment. No organic community can any longer determine values, and hence there is no objective basis upon which to ground a labour theory of value. Although individuals may come together in voluntary associations, they do so as individuals. This amounts to a radical subjectivism as to the validity of individual ends, but not a subjectivist understanding of the sources of ends. These arise in society. The constraints on economic action are therefore not merely technical – the problem of how to deploy scarce resources – but cultural: namely, what to choose.

Beyond this, as we have seen, Weber's 'social economics' sees the market place as constituted through power relations. We are not simply dealing with an impersonal but efficacious rational device for allocating means to ends. For the market simultaneously enhances and constrains life chances as a result of inequalities in the distribution of power. For Weber such inequalities are conceptualised as class situations. Without this element of inequality in power there would be no need for class analysis, since different market outcomes could be ascribed either to variations in individual rationality (for example, differences in knowledge and errors of judgement) or to in-built differences in skill.

The lynch-pin of Weber's discussion of market power is the notion of differential life chances that arise as a result of inequalities in powers of ownership and control over marketable resources. The emphasis on individual life chances and individual mobility opportunities is of course entirely typical of a *Gesellschaft* construction of class. Inadequate attention has been given to the life-chance concept by most commentators on Weber. Most commentaries have insisted on a dichotomic classification of class theories centring either on production, or on exchange and/or distribution. Marx's class theory is taken as centring on production, while Weber's centres on exchange and/or distribution (see, for instance, Crompton and Gubbay 1978). There is room for a good deal of confusion here, however, when we try to establish exactly where market relations fit into this dichotomy. [. . .]

Weber's concern for market exchange as more central than production does not exclude a certain common ground with Marx. Both are interested in the significance of market inequalities for the distribution of power and income. Where Weber departs from Marx is first of all in regarding the market as central to class (Marshall *et al.* 1985). Second, Weber manages to do entirely without an objective *Gemeinschaftlich* value theory. In this sense, property rights in the production process, however unequal, need not necessarily be described as exploitative. Third, Weber follows through market-based power conflict in the allocation of resources to production, into distributive patterns of income and access to key life chances (for example, education) that result.

The substance of Weber's market-based theory focuses on the complexities involved in inequalities of power and ownership and control over resources. Two distinct types of inequality are involved. The first centres on the ownership dimension, in which variations in amounts of capital resources owned prescribe different life-chance situations (for instance, rentier versus propertyless worker). Weber's ownership criterion is similar to Marx's. The second dimension of Weber's discussion involves possession of marketable skills, around which commercial class positions form, analytically distinct from ownership class positions. In this second dimension, those with marketable skills, such as managers and professionals, are distinguished from unskilled workers. This has of course provided a major dimension missing in Marx's class theory – namely, the capacity to analyse a middle class of salaried possessors of marketable skills, distinct from both capitalist and working classes. It also pre-figures recent developments in New Class theory (Gouldner 1979). The point to emphasise at this stage is that we are dealing with class positions, not classes as such. For Weber, such positions are arranged gradationally, and involve no necessary sense of dichotomy. This gradational pattern of individual power inequalities in the market place is structured on an inherently *Gesellschaftlich* basis. It leaves room for the analysis of certain market-based inequalities as a function of differing human capital endowments between individuals, rather than manifestations of exploitation of the working-class community. In this respect Weber's analysis is inherently modern, relating to the achievement-oriented pursuit of individual goals.

Weber's concern to link power differentials in production and exchange to distributional outcomes arises because he rejects Marx's polarisation theory of class structure. In this theory private capital accumulation so effectively polarises society that distributional issues become of limited importance. The lot of all workers becomes increasingly homogeneous as advantages of skill and localism are undermined by the global structural determinism of capital. Judged by Marx's *Gemeinschaftlich* standards, the qualitative characteristics of the capitalist totality are thoroughly alienating. There is no interest in individual fates, as such, nor in the qualitative resources at the disposal of individuals within the market place; hence the failure to leave any theoretical space for the analysis of social mobility as it is affected by the distributional dimensions of market inequality. Marx similarly leaves no space for an understanding of private consumer strategies, as they relate to saving and to the purchase of life-enhancing goods and services, such as homes, means of transport, travel, and so on.

Beyond this, Weber treats the problem of class-like *Gemeinschaft* formation as a contingent rather than necessary product of social change and historical development. 'Social classes' with some kind of solidaristic identity may form at points where sets of individuals share common mobility chances within a range of market opportunities. The four social classes Weber located in early twentieth-century Europe were:

(a) the working class;
(b) the petty bourgeoisie;
(c) the propertyless intelligentsia and specialists;
(d) the classes privileged through property and education (Weber 1978:305).

Although Weber does not develop the discussion of social classes very far, the logical inference to be drawn is that there are at least two minimum conditions for social class formation:

1   common mobility chances of moving among a limited set of class positions;
2   power differentials blocking mobility into other positions.

In this way, Weber's social classes occupy a contingent and therefore somewhat precarious place in the social structure. Further structural changes in economic development may change opportunities for social mobility, leading to the possible corrosion of existing social classes and the possible development of new ones. There is no logical reason to guarantee that social classes will persist, and absolutely no place for teleological accounts of history in terms of the 'necessary mission' of particular classes.

The final dimension of Weber's account of class concerns the much misunderstood relationship between class, status, and party. (For clarification, see Giddens 1973:41–52.) Commentators on Weber are now rather less prone to render this tripartite set of terms as class, status and power. It is quite clear from the texts that Weber's intention was to distinguish between class, status, and party, not as differing bases of stratification, but rather as alternative bases for the distribution of power within a community. [. . .]

For Weber, the theoretical underpinning of this anti-reductionist multi-dimensionality is the axiomatic proposition that individuals have both material and ideal interests, and that neither is epistemologically privileged. In this respect, it is equally possible for class positions in the labour market to be dominated by status interests (for example, racial and ethnic labour-market closure) as for status divisions to be used to protect powerful class interests by strategies of divide-and-rule. In this way class and status may in certain circumstances be complementary. [. . .]

Marx–Weber comparisons do not provide the sole vantage-point from which to assess Weber's impact on class theory, since they take insufficient account of attempts to extend and refine the Weberian legacy. The most important recent attempt of this kind is the extension of Weber's concern with market inequalities and with the distributive consequences of the market for class structures, into the areas of housing and consumption (see Rex and Moore 1967, Dunleavy 1979, Saunders 1978, 1981, 1984, 1987, 1990a). This line of argument represents a major extension of *Gesellschaftlich* versions of class theory – the weak class idiom – and a major setback for the attempt to defend an intermediate class idiom, able to retain as much of the strong class *Gemeinschaftlich* idiom as possible. [. . .]

Concluding remarks

The robustness of the strong class idiom has disintegrated in the last forty years. On an intellectual level, this process owes something at least to Weber's cryptic but influential articulation of a weak *Gesellschaftlich* conception of class. The weak class idiom has not, of course, gone unchallenged. Yet the attempt to stabilise an intermediate or 'strong-as-possible' class idiom has been purchased at the cost of an abandonment of the labour theory value, and, in some cases, the harnessing of rational choice theory to class analysis.

Even Giddens's (1973) more modest proposal to centre class analysis on the problem of transformation from economic class relations to social class formation seems increasingly redundant. As the full maturity of *Gesellschaftlich* relations is secured within contemporary consumerism and the extension of individual citizenship rights, there seems little place any more for social classes in the neo-Weberian sense of class communities.

This leaves us with the continuing debate as to whether class analysis should be re-formulated as the analysis of social stratification via inequalities in the occupational structure (for a strong statement of this option see Goldthorpe and Marshall below, Ch. 7). This genre of research has been immensely important in furthering understanding of changes in the life-chances of individuals in terms of social mobility patterns. However, as Crompton (1993:116–17) points out, what the debate around the work of Goldthorpe and his associates is really about is not social class as such, but 'long-term developments in the employment structure', 'the inheritance of occupational inequality', and 'the relative significance of occupation as a variable in attitude research'. The conclusion that follows, as Holton and Turner (1994:801) have indicated, is the over-identification of class with occupational measurement, 'at the expense of wider dimensions of economic power and social action'. Class is thereby reduced 'to a statistical aggregate with only indeterminate relations to actual consciousness or action'.

All this is not to deny the salience of social conflict within the market economy or within structures of political authority. Yet this generally takes the form either of managed conflict between organised interest groups (for example, trade unions, organised employers and the state); or non-class protests by social movements over the environment, women's rights and so on. All this appears to make class an increasingly redundant issue, except in the weak sense as a means of delineating forms of economic power relations which generate and reproduce inequalities.

Note

1. Exerpts (with minor authorial revisions) from Chapter 6 of *Max Weber on Economy and Society* by R. J. Holton and B. S. Turner published by Routledge & Kegan Paul, London, 1989.

CHAPTER 2

Are social classes dying?[1]

Terry Nicholls Clark and Seymour Martin Lipset

New forms of social stratification are emerging. Much of our thinking about stratification – from Marx, Weber and others – must be recast to capture these new developments. Social class was the key theme of past stratification work. Yet class is an increasingly outmoded concept, although it is sometimes appropriate to earlier historical periods. Class stratification implies that people can be differentiated on one or more criteria into distinct layers, classes. Class analysis has grown increasingly inadequate in recent decades as traditional hierarchies have declined and new social differences have emerged. The cumulative impact of these changes is fundamentally altering the nature of social stratification – placing past theories in need of substantial modification.

This paper outlines first some general propositions about the sources of class stratification and its decline. The decline of hierarchy, and its spread across situses, is emphasised. The general propositions are applied to political parties and ideological cleavages, the economy, the family, and social mobility. These developments appear most clearly in North America and Western Europe, but our propositions also help interpret some of the tensions and factors driving change in Eastern Europe, the Soviet Union, and other societies.

We broadly follow Marx and Weber in understanding social class as social differentiation emerging from structured socio-economic life changes of distinct social categories of persons. Social classes can emerge from differential access to the means of production (as Marx stressed) or to trade or consumption (as Weber added). Class consciousness may be said to emerge if these social categories develop distinct subjective outlooks, culture and behaviour patterns. [. . .]

If one looks closely at class theories in recent decades, it is striking how much class has changed. This is not immediately obvious since most theorists claim direct descendance from Marx and Weber. But many have in fact fundamentally altered the concept of class towards what we term *the fragmentation of stratification*. Consider some examples of class theory and social stratification. Dahrendorf (1959:157–206) stressed that many lines of social cleavage have not erupted into class conflict. For a Marxian revolution, the working class should suffer immiseration and grow more homogenous; capitalists should join in combat against them. But Dahrendorf points instead to the 'decomposition of labour': workers have become more differentiated by skill level – into skilled, semi-skilled and unskilled. Unions often separate more than join these groups. Perhaps even more important is the expansion of the 'middle class' of white-collar non-manual workers. Such a middle class was largely ignored by Marx; it was expected to join the capitalists or workers. Instead it has grown substantially, and differentiated internally, especially between lower-level salaried employees and managers. Dahrendorf might have abandoned the concept of class, but instead retained the term while redefining it to include all sorts of groups in political or social conflict: ' "class" signifies conflict groups that are generated by the differential distribution of authority in imperatively coordinated associations' (Dahrendorf 1959:204).

Many writers have, like Dahrendorf, retained terms from Marx, while substantially changing their meaning. Erik Wright (1985:64–104) has sought to capture some of the same changes as Dahrendorf. He does so by developing a 12 category 'typology of class location in capitalist society' that includes: 1. bourgeoisie, 2. small employers, 4. expert managers, 5. expert supervisors, 8. semi-credentialled supervisors, and continues up to 12. proletarians. It explicitly incorporates not just ownership, but skill level, and managerial responsibility. It is striking that Wright, a self-defined Marxist, incorporates so much post-Weberian multi-dimensionality. [. . .]

These analyses stress changes in work-place relations. Yet social relations outside the work-place are increasingly important for social stratification. If proletarians are visibly distinct in dress, food and life style, they are more likely to think of themselves, and act as a politically distinct class. In the nineteenth and early twentieth century, this was often the case, as novels and sociologists report. The decreasing distinctiveness of social classes is stressed by Parkin (1979:69), who holds that this brings the 'progressive erosion of the communal components of proletarian status'. Specifically, 'the absence of clearly visible and unambiguous marks of inferior status has made the enforcement of an all-pervasive deference system almost impossible to sustain outside the immediate work situation. It would take an unusually sharp eye to detect the social class of Saturday morning shoppers in the High Street, whereas to any earlier generation it would have been the most elementary task.'

The same tendency toward fragmentation emerges from assessments of political leadership and power. The elitist and hierarchical assumptions that lie behind ruling class analysis as developed by Marx, Pareto and Mosca have been increasingly weakened. When Hunter's *Community Power Structure* appeared in 1953, it confirmed the view of many social scientists that upper class power elites ruled. But over the next three decades, this class domination view was supplanted by a pluralistic, multi-dimensional conceptualisation. The paradigm change did not come easily: it cumulatively evolved from some 200 studies of national and community power, accompanied by considerable debates about power elites and class domination (cf. Dahl 1961, Clark 1975, Clark and Ferguson 1983). Stressing historical changes, Shils (1982:31) suggests that by the late twentieth century 'these reflections seem to lead to the conclusion that Mosca's conception of a political class is no longer applicable in our contemporary societies'.

Should the social class concept be abandoned? In a 1959 exchange, Nisbet suggested that class 'is nearly valueless for the clarification of the data of wealth, power and social status in the contemporary United States' (1959:11). Commenting on Nisbet in the same journal, Bernard Barber and O. D. Duncan both argued that his position had not been substantiated, and that a sharper analysis and evidence were necessary. This was over 30 years ago. Yet today class remains salient in sociologists' theories, and commentaries. We do not suggest it be altogether abandoned, but complemented by other factors. [. . .]

Many stratification analysts used class analysis longer and more extensively than empirically warranted due to their focus on Europe. Analysts of American society are often defensive, suggesting that America is somehow 'behind' Europe. Marxists were among the most outspoken in this regard, but not unique (e.g. Wilson 1978). However, things changed as new social movements emerged in the 1970s and 1980s. The United States then often seemed more a leader than a laggard. This seemed even more true in the dramatic changes of the late 1980s as the former communist societies, led by Eastern Europe, sought to throw off their central hierarchical planning and move toward free economic markets and political democracy.

What do these changes imply for theories of stratification? A critical point is that traditional hierarchies[2] are declining; economic and family hierarchies determine much less than just a generation or two ago. Three general propositions state this argument:

(i) *Hierarchy generates and maintains rigid class relations. The greater the hierarchical (vertical) differentiation among persons in a social unit, the deeper its class divisions tend to become.*

Since the degree of hierarchy will vary with a society, we add:

(ii) *The greater the hierarchical differentiation in each separate situs[3] (or separate vertical dimension, e.g. economic institutions, government organisations, and families), the most salient are class-defined patterns in informed social relations, cultural outlooks, and support for social change, such as support for social movements and political behaviour.*

(iii) *Conversely, however, the more the hierarchy declines, the more structured social class relations diminish in salience. And the larger the* number of situses which evidence declining hierarchy, the less salient are class relations in the society. As class conflict declines, there may be less conflict, or conflict may be organised along different lines (for instance, gender). Not all hierarchies generate counter-reactions. There must be sufficient acceptance of democratic processes to permit opposition to surface. And the more that legal structures, the media, and other institutions, permit or enhance the articulation of social conflict, the more can anti-hierarchical themes spread and win social support. [. . .]

We now consider separate situses of social stratification in terms of our three general propositions. In each situs we consider some of the specific dynamics by which social classes have declined. The cumulative effect, across situses, is emergence of a new system of social stratification.

Politics: less class, more fragmentation

Political behaviour is an ideal area to assess changes in stratification. It was central to Marx and Weber, it is highly visible today; it has been studied in detail; it permits tests of competing hypotheses, Lipset's *Political Man* stressed class politics in its first edition (1960). But the second edition (1981, especially pp. 459 ff.) focused on the declines in class voting. A striking illustration of this change is in the results from the 1940s to 1980s on the Alford Index of Class Voting. This index is based on the percentage of persons by social class who vote for left or right parties. For instance, if 75 per cent of the working class votes for the left, and only 25 per cent of the middle class does so, the Alford index score is 50 (the difference between these two figures). The Alford Index has declined in every country for which data are available (see Lipset 1981, updated in Clark and Inglehart 1991). [. . .]

What is replacing class? The classical left–right dimension has been transformed. People still speak of left and right, but definitions are changing. There are now two lefts, with distinct social bases. The traditional left is blue-collar based and stresses class-related issues. But a second left is emerging in Western societies (sometimes termed New Politics, New Left, Post-Bourgeois, or Post-Materialist), which increasingly stresses social issues rather than traditional political issues. The most intensely disputed issues for them no longer deal with ownership and control of the means of production. And in many socialist and even communist parties (in the 1970s in Italy, in the 1990s in Eastern Europe) supporters of these new issues are supplanting the old.

Political issues shift with more affluence: as wealth increases, people take the basics for granted; they grow more concerned with life style and amenities. Younger, more educated and more affluent persons in more affluent and less hierarchical societies should move furthest from traditional class politics. [. . .]

These trends are congruent with the 'post-industrial' trends identified by Daniel Bell and Alain Touraine, and the 'post-materialist' (earlier termed 'post-bourgeois') patterns identified by Ronald Inglehart (1990) – stressing 'self-actualisation' via aesthetic intellectual and participatory concerns. Scott Flanagan (1980) suggests a shift from traditional consciousness to libertarian consciousness. But one should not overstate the changes: Alan Marsh, analysing British data, finds that 'materialists' and 'post-materialists' do not differ in their concern for having enough money, which both share. The post-materialists, however, 'are distinguished by their relative youth, wealth, education and by their concern for ideology' (Marsh 1975:28). [. . .]

Economic organisation changes: sources of a new market individualism

One simple, powerful change has affected the economy: growth. And economic growth undermines hierarchical class stratification. Affluence weakens hierarchies and collectivism; but it heightens individualism. With more income, the poor depend less on the rich. And all can indulge progressively more elaborate and varied tastes. *Markets, ceteris paribus, grow in relevance as income rises*. But as such complexity increases, it grows harder to plan centrally; decentralised, demand-sensitive decision-making becomes necessary. These contrasts particularly affect(ed) centrally-planned societies like the Soviet Union. But they operate too for firms like General Motors or US Steel.

Many private goods come increasingly from more differentiated and sub-market-oriented small firms, especially in such service-intensive fields as 'thoughtware', finance and office activities. By contrast huge firms are in relative decline, especially for traditional manufacturing products like steel and automobiles. Some 2/3 of all new jobs are in firms with 20 or fewer employees, in many countries (Birch 1979). These small firms emerge because they out-compete larger firms. Why? Technology and management style are critical factors.

The more advanced the technology and knowledge base, the harder it is to plan in advance and control administratively, both within a large firm and still more by central government planners. Technological changes illustrate how new economic patterns are no longer an issue of public versus private sector control, but bring inevitable frustrations for heirarchical control by anyone. As research and development grow increasingly important for new products and technologies, they are harder to direct or define in advance for distant administrators of that firm, and even harder for outsider regulators or political officials seeking to plan centrally (as in a Soviet five-year plan, to use an extreme case). Certain plastics firms have as much as one third of staff developing the chemistry for new products. Computers, biological engineering and robotics illustrate the dozens of areas that are only vaguely amenable to forecast and hence central control.

A major implication for social stratification of these economic changes is the decline in traditional authority, hierarchy and class relations. Current technologies require fewer unskilled workers performing routine tasks, or a large middle-management to coordinate them, than did traditional manufacturing of steel, automobiles, etc. High tech means increasing automation of routine tasks. It also demands more professional autonomous decisions. More egalitarian, collegial decision-making is thus increasingly seen as a hallmark of modern society, by analysts from Habermas and Parsons to Daniel Bell and Zbigniew Brzezinski, and to consultants in business schools who teach the importance of new 'corporate culture' – as illustrated by *In Search of Excellence* (Peters and Waterman 1982), the number one non-fiction best-seller in the United States for some time, and widely read by business leaders in the United States and Europe. Even Soviet scholars as early as 1969 noted 'a sweeping qualitative transformation of productive forces as a result of science being made the principal factor in the development of social production' (Richta *et al.* 1969:39). The occupations that are expanding are white-collar, technical, professional and service-oriented. The class structure increasingly resembles a diamond bulging at the middle rather than a pyramid. Higher levels of education are needed in such occupations; the numbers of students pursuing more advanced studies has rapidly increased in the past few decades.

The larger the extent of the market, the less likely are particularistic decisions (preference for family members, city residents, or nationals) likely to prevail. Local stratification hierarchies are correspondingly undermined as markets grow – regionally, nationally and inter-nationally. The force of this proposition has grown in the 1970s and 1980s with the globalisation of markets for manpower, capital and sales. Big and small firms have experienced major consolidations – enhanced by the growth of multinationals, the 1970s oil boom and subsequent bust, leveraged buy-outs, the rise of the Eurodollar market, and world-wide trade expansion. The growth of the US economy has been fuelled by massive in-migration, especially from Mexico, Latin America and Asia. More immigrants came into the United States in the 1980s than in any decade since before World War I. These factors combine to undermine the familistic-quasi-monopolistic tradition of business hierarchy and class stratification patterns.

A slimmer family

Major trends here parallel those in the economy. The traditional family has been slimmed and hierarchical stratification has weakened. Family and intimate personal relations have increasingly become characterised by more egalitarian relations, more flexible roles, and more tolerance for a wider range of behaviour. The authoritarian paternalistic family is decreasingly the model for stratification in the rest of society. Fewer young people marry, they wed later, have fewer children, far more women work outside the home, divorce rates have risen, parents and grandparents live less often with children (e.g. Cherlin 1981, Forse 1986). Paralleling these socio-demographic changes are changes in attitudes and roles concerning the family. Children and wives have grown substantially more egalitarian in a very short period of time. Indeed attitudes towards the family have changed more than almost any other social or political factor in the past 20–30 years, especially to questions like 'Should women work outside the home?' The proportions of wives and mothers working in jobs outside the home have grown dramatically, first and especially in the United States, but in many European countries too.

The family has also grown less important as a basis of stratification in relation to education and jobs. Increased wealth and government support programmes have expanded choice to individuals, and cumulatively transferred more functions than ever away from the family. Families are thus decreasingly responsible for raising children and placing them in jobs. Fewer children work in family firms (farms, shops, etc.). US mobility studies from the late nineteenth century onward report few changes until the 1960s (Lipset and Bendix 1991, Grusky 1986) but major changes since: Hout's (1988) replication of Featherman and Hauser (1978) showed that the effect of origin status on destination status declined by 28 per cent from 1962 to 1973 and by one third from 1972 to 1985. Social mobility studies also show decreasing effects of parents' education and income in explaining children's occupational success. At the same time the independent effects of education have increased.

Conclusion

New patterns of social stratification are emerging. The key trend could be described as one of 'fragmentation of stratification': the weakening of class stratification, especially as shown in distinct class-differentiated life styles; the decline of economic determinism, and the increased importance of social and cultural factors; politics less organised by class and more by other loyalties; social mobility less family-determined, more ability and educational-determined.

Notes

1. Extracted with abridgements from 'Are social classes dying?' *International Sociology* 6:4, December 1991:397–410.
2. By hierarchy we understand the vertical differentiation of individuals and sub-units in terms of specific criteria, such as income, status or power. Hierarchies may be continuous, ranking persons from high to low, but need not include any distinct classes.
3. We adapt the concept of situs from Benoit-Smullyan (1944) and Bell (1973:377), to refer to parallel but distinct sectors of social organisation, each with its partly distinct rules of the game (or culture).

CHAPTER 3

The persistence of classes in post-industrial societies[1]

Mike Hout, Clem Brooks and Jeff Manza

[. . .] The recent paper by Terry Nichols Clark and Seymour Martin Lipset (1991) [see Chapter 2 in this volume] offers an updated version of the declining significance of class argument. They give an unequivocal 'yes' to the question in the title of their essay, 'Are Social Classes Dying?' They echo Nisbet's (1959) claim that class analysis is strictly for historians in asserting that class 'is an increasingly outmoded concept' (above, p. 44), and that new forms of stratification are replacing class. They support these large claims with data selected to indicate that class has less of an effect on political, economic and family outcomes than it used to, and go beyond routine reports that some of the parameters of social stratification are changing to announce the decline of classes and the fragmentation of social stratification. They lament that, 30 years after Nisbet's essay, 'class remains salient in sociologists' theories and commentaries' (above, p. 44), and they seek to bring this state of affairs to an end. Clark and Lipset do say at one point that their goal is not to 'suggest that it (i.e. class) be abandoned altogether, but complemented by other factors' (above, p. 44). The general thrust of their argument, however, is to throw out class altogether. For example, they never indicate in what concrete ways they believe the concept of class remains relevant. It is this general thrust to which we respond.

Clark and Lipset have joined with other writers past and present who leap from data on trends to conjectures about the future. The death and dying metaphors suggest more finality than the data will support. For, while we would be contradicting our own results if we were to deny that there have been trends towards a diminished effect of class on important social indicators, e.g., the openness in mobility (Hout 1988), we see those trends as the outcome of a class-political process that is neither immutable nor irreversible. The past 25 years of class research reveal a mix of upward and downward trends in the effects of class. The mix is confusing for those who view them through the lens of Marxist and functionalist theories that specify the economy as cause and politics as consequence in the political economy of class. The empirical record is becoming clearer and clearer, however, that the causal arrow needs to be reversed. The mix of increasing, unchanging and decreasing class effects reflect the important role of politics in determining such mainstays of class analysis as the class structure itself, the mobility regime and class voting in a society (Esping-Anderson 1990; Heath *et al.* 1991; Erikson and Goldthorpe 1992).

Coming from Seymour Martin Lipset, whose earlier work taught us much about the link between class and political life, this latest challenge to class analysis should not be ignored. Unlike Nisbet, who explicitly dismissed empirical research, arguing that 'statistical techniques have had to become ever more ingenious to keep the vision of class from fading away altogether' (1959:12), Clark and Lipset summarise a wealth of empirical data to make their case. On closer examination, however, we find that much of the evidence they cite is highly selective and cannot withstand critical scrutiny. We are especially troubled by their complete neglect of other evidence which shows the continuing – and even rising – importance of class. Altogether, we believe it is impossible to sustain their conclusion, and in the discussion which follows we seek to show that, while class may be defined and used by social scientists in a number of different ways, the concept remains indispensable. Be it as an independent or dependent variable, sociologists will turn away from class at their own peril.

The persistence of classes

Sociologists did not invent the concept of class. But we have made more out of it than others have, mainly by emphasising the point that it is how one makes a living that determines life chances and material interests. We differ from economists' nearly exclusive focus on the quantity of income or wealth and commonsense conceptions that blend life style and morality with economic and sociological considerations (Jencks and Petersen 1991). The part-time school teacher, the semi-skilled factory worker and the struggling shopkeeper may all report the same income on their tax returns, but we recognise that as salaried, hourly and self-employed workers they have different sources of income and, consequently, different life chances. Clark and Lipset, however, put great stock in life style, citing Parkin's contention that 'the absence of clearly visible and unambiguous marks of inferior *status* has made the enforcement of an all-pervasive deference system almost impossible to sustain outside the immediate work situation' (Parkin 1979:69; our emphasis). To our mind this counters Clark and Lipset's general point that status distinctions are on the rise as class is on the wane.

At various points in their paper, Clark and Lipset seem to equate class and hierarchy, but they are separate dimensions. Hierarchy, in sociological usage, could refer to any rankable distinctions. Class refers to a person's relationship to the means of production and/or labour markets, and it is an important determinant of an individual's income, wealth and social standing. We thus adopt a generic definition of class that we hope is compatible with the contemporary versions of both neo-Marxist and neo-Weberian concepts[2]. Hierarchy or related concepts might be used as an explanation of stratification processes, as in Erikson and Goldthorpe (1992) or Hout and Hauser (1992), but to use the concepts as explanandum and explanans they must be defined independently and the relationship must be spelled out.

Class is an indispensable concept for sociology because: (1) class is a key determinate of material interests; (2) structurally defined classes give rise to – or influence the formation of – collective actors seeking to bring about social change; and (3) class membership affects the life chances and behaviour of individuals. The first concern refers to the intrinsic importance of class. The other two are relevant for 'class analysis' – the investigation of how class affects other aspects of social life. Clark and Lipset state their case – which refers to all three of these concerns – without acknowledging that each raises different sets of issues. As a result of these confusions, Clark and Lipset's argument collapses analytically distinct processes.

Clark and Lipset also confuse trends in society with trends in writing about society. To be sure, our conceptions of class have grown more complex over the years. Marx's initial codification of the importance of whether one works for a living or expropriates a profit from the sale of goods produced by others has been supplemented over the years by additional distinctions, most of which are ignored by Clark and Lipset. In addition to workers and capitalists, contemporary Marxist accounts of class structure recognise professionals and crafts persons, who extract rents on their expertise, and managers and supervisors, who extract rents on their organisational assets (Wright 1985). These are not mere status distinctions, as Clark and Lipset would have it. They are class distinctions because they specify economic roles with respect to labour markets and material interests. Furthermore, in arguing that Wright is forced 'to incorporate so much post-Weberian multi-dimensionality' in his models of class structure (this volume, p. 43), they ignore the underlying logic of Wright's analysis of the mechanisms of exploitation. Contemporary Weberian theories of class also admit to complexity without negating the existence of classes. Weberians focus on the closure strategies that professionals and skilled workers use to influence labour markets to their collective advantage (Parkin 1979, Goldthorpe 1987:39–46, Erikson and Goldthorpe 1992:42–3, Manza 1992) and the internal labour markets that select managers and supervisors (Parkin 1979, Kalleberg and Berg 1987). While sociologists' models of class are a lot more complicated than they used to be, complexity alone does not imply that class is dead or dying.

Clark and Lipset's conclusions about the decline of class in post-industrial societies hinge on the claim that 'traditional hierarchies are declining; economic and family hierarchies determine much less than just a generation or two ago' (above, p. 44). However, hierarchy is never defined and the assumed link between hierarchy and class in their formulation is at best vague. In moving back and forth between a materialist analysis of class to the vaguer concept of 'hierarchy', Clark and Lipset are tacitly shifting the terrain of debate away from class *per se*. This conceptual slippage makes it easier for them to conclude that classes are dying. Their emphasis on hierarchy is also potentially misleading in that forms of hierarchy could decline without any change in class structure or the general importance of class for systems of stratification or political behaviour. They persistently conflate class-based inequalities with non-class forms of stratification. Perhaps as a consequence, Clark and Lipset conveniently ignore some of the most salient aspects of class inequalities in contemporary capitalist societies. First, they completely ignore the remarkable persistence in the high levels of wealth controlled by the bourgeoisie in these societies. The pattern of the amount of wealth controlled by the richest 1 per cent of the populations of different capitalist societies seems to be remarkably consistent and seems to hold across different societies (for comparative data see Wolff 1991; on US, Levy 1987, Phillips 1991; on Britain, Shorrocks 1987; on Sweden Spånt 1987. See also Bottomore and Brym 1989, Zeitlin 1989 and cf. Scott, this volume). Secondly, they ignore the capacity of wealth-holders to influence political processes, either directly through financial contributions, intra-class organisational and political networks and government agencies, or indirectly through control over investment decisions (Clawson, Neustadt and Scott 1992, Domhoff 1990, Useem 1984, and Bottomore and Brym 1989 on direct control; and Block 1987, 1992, Lindblom 1977 on indirect control). Lastly, educational institutions play an important role in transmitting privilege from one generation to another (see Baltzell 1958, Domhoff 1970, Useem and Karabel 1986, Marceau 1977, Bottomore and Brym 1989).

Private fortunes are still predicated on ownership of the means of production. During the 1980s when inequality of wealth and earnings was growing in the United States and elsewhere, the private fortunes at the forefront of resurgent inequality were in almost all cases built through ownership. High-tech champions like Gates, merchandisers like Walton and developers like Trump got rich because they owned the means of production. Arbitragers collected high fees and executives were 'overcompensated', but they gained more from ownership of shares of stock than from their wages and salaries (Crystal 1991).

One important test for class analysis is the demonstration that some classes have material advantages over others. If classes are dying, then we would expect incumbents of different classes to earn similar amounts, i.e., all of the income or earnings inequality should be within classes. In fact class differences in earnings are statistically and substantively significant. This was shown, for example, by a recent telephone survey of American adults over 18 years old[3] in which both of the leading class schemes in the current literature – Wright (1985) and Erikson and Goldthorpe (1992) – were used. Wright's capitalist class were at the top of the earnings distribution and his bottom class – workers – at the bottom. The ratio of earnings from top to bottom was 4.2:1 for men and 2.5:1 for women. Wright's class scheme explained 20 per cent of the variance in earnings. Adjusting for sex, education, age and hours worked mediated some of the class differences, but the adjusted means showed significant variation. The Erikson–Goldthorpe scheme also shows a pattern of significant variation. The ratio of the top class's earnings to the earnings of their lowest class was 4.9:1 among men and 3.6:1 among women. The ratio of between-class variance to total variance in the Erikson–Goldthorpe scheme was 1.7. From both class schemes it is clear that changes in the class structure have not eroded the important effects of class on earnings.

The growth of the proportion of the population that is middle class and the proliferation of middle classes has also not negated the persistence of income inequality (Smeeding 1991) and the growing proportions of the populations of industrial societies that are living in extreme poverty. The broad outlines of this 'new poverty' (Markland 1990) are becoming increasingly clear (Wacquant 1993; cf. Jencks and Petersen 1991, Townsend et al. 1987, Mingione 1991, Engbersen 1989). The existence of long-term joblessness or occupational, marginality among sectors of the populations of these societies, and the growth of low-income areas characterised by multiple sources of deprivation for residents (Massey 1990, Massey and Eggers 1990) does not fit very well with Clark and Lipset's claims about the decline of 'traditional hierarchies'.

In general, the persistence of wealth and power at the top and growing poverty and degradation at the bottom of contemporary class structures suggests that Clark and Lipset's conclusions about the impending death of classes is premature. In the United States, the country which we know best, it is becoming increasingly common in urban communities for privileged professionals and managers to live in secluded enclaves and suburbs (often behind locked gates) or in secured high-rise condominiums, while marginalised sectors of the population are crowded into increasingly dangerous inner-city areas (a trend discussed at length by the new Secretary of Labor in the United States, Robert Reich, in a recent book – Reich 1991, Davis 1991). As long as such conditions prevail, we are sceptical that sociologists would be wise to abandon the concept of class, whatever other evidence might be adduced to show that the importance of class is declining.

Are social classes dying? No

The evidence presented above should be enough to sustain our thesis that class divisions persist in post-industrial societies. But Clark and Lipset base their critique less on the existence of class divisions than on the supposed decline in the effects of class in three 'situses' (politics, the economy and the family) in these societies. We shall show that, even on their own terms, Clark and Lipset's empirical evidence cannot support their conclusions about the declining significance of class.

Politics

To demonstrate the declining significance of class in the political arena, Clark and Lipset attempt to show that class voting has declined. Their evidence is based on the claim that 'the Alford Index [of class voting] has declined in every country for which data are available' (above, p. 45). Four observations about their data undermine these assertions, however.

First, their reliance on the Alford Index as the proper measure of class voting is highly dubious. [. . .] [See Goldthorpe, this volume, pp. 200–1, for an extensive discussion of this and related issues (Eds).] Second, [in the Alford Index – Eds] cross-national differences raise serious doubts about their propositions that 'hierarchy generates and maintains rigid class relations' (Clark and Lipset, above p. 44). Problems with the Alford Index notwithstanding, reasonable estimates of class voting are likely to show Sweden as the nation with the strongest association between class and voting (among the five countries considered by Clark and Lipset) and the United States as the weakest. And yet, with respect to income inequality, Sweden is the most egalitarian country among the five by most indicators and the United States the least among the five (Esping-Anderson 1990). Parkin (1971), Korpi (1983) and Esping-Anderson (1990), among others, have advanced the converse proposition that Sweden's class politics have produced the social policies responsible for Sweden's low levels of inequality. Not only are the data inconsistent, but the causal order between egalitarianism and class voting is reversed.

Clark and Lipset seem to assume an unmediated connection between class and voting, ignoring completely the decisive role of unions, social movement organisations and political parties in shaping the conditions under which voters make choices. When parties and other political organisations are organised around class, high levels of class voting can be expected. Przeworski and Sprague's (1986) analysis of the dynamics of social democratic parties based originally on working-class votes suggests that the strategic decision of these parties to weaken their class-based appeals to seek middle-class votes – a trend celebrated in Lipset (1990) – has had a profound effect on the social bases of their political support. If workers' parties abandon or compromise their specific interests, does it mean those interests no longer exist? We say 'no'. Class interests may remain latent in the political arena, but this does not mean they do not exist.

Clark and Lipset flesh out their case for the declining significance of class for politics by arguing that the traditional left/right cleavages characteristic of democratic capitalist societies have increasingly given way to more complex, multidimensional political ideologies. Such a claim shifts the focus from class as a determinant of political views to class or class inequalities as an object of public opinion. Clark and Lipset repeat the assertion that there are now 'two lefts', one based on the economic demands of subordinates classes, the other stressing 'social issues' (above, p. 45; Lipset 1960 (1981): 501–1). From this disjuncture of economy and society, they wish to infer that the class content of political struggles and public debate is declining. However, this contention is not supported by either the data they cite or by the existing research literature. For example, Weakliem's (1991) research on the dimensionality of class and voting casts doubt on the empirical adequacy of Clark and Lipset's interpretation of political trends. Weakliem finds that, while a second (plausibly post-materialist) dimension of politics is necessary to explain the relationship between class and party identification, it applies equally well to older and younger cohorts. The similarity of cohorts contradicts the claim that complexity is new, and Weakliem's crucial finding that 'all classes have been moving towards the post-materialist left' in his analysis of voting trends in Italy, the Netherlands and France (1991:1350) leads us to reject Clark and Lipset's assertions about the 'two lefts'. In any case, the emergence or re-emergence of 'new' political issues, such as gender or the environment, does not mean that they are sufficient to displace or reconstitute fundamental dimensions such as the left–right split in politics.

The complexities of political strategies and tactics make the distinction between class as a causal agent and class or inequality as an object of discussion absolutely critical. Merely because an issue is not directly couched in terms of class or traditional left–right politics does not mean that class is irrelevant to understanding it. Luker's (1984) research on the world-views of pro-choice and pro-life activists exemplifies an issue which – while not ostensibly about class – turns in part on the contrasting class interests and experiences of the activists. What if some 'new' social issues have become the object of political struggles and public debate in part because they resonate with peoples' traditional left–right political heuristics (Sniderman, Brody and Tetlock 1991)? Could it be that controversies over affirmative action or the extension of rights to new categories of citizens (such as the disabled) gain their ideological strength from being about 'old' (class) issues, such as equality or social democracy? [. . .]

In short, Clark and Lipset's evidence on class politics is incomplete and unconvincing. They have failed to make the case that class is declining in importance for politics. Class never was the all-powerful explanatory variable that some intellectual traditions assumed in earlier periods; class was always only one source of political identity and action alongside race, religion, nationality, gender and others. To say that class matters less now than it used to requires that one exaggerate its importance in the past and understate its importance at present. Class is important for politics to the extent that political organisations actively organise around class themes. Hence, in some periods the political consequences of class may appear latent, even if the underlying logic of class is unchanged. We would suggest that the same is true of other sources of social inequality. Race and gender, for example, have always been important to the social fabric of American society, but they have not always been central loci of political organisation and struggle. We believe that on balance, however, the evidence shows that class remains important, and that Clark and Lipset fail to demonstrate that class voting and traditional political values have declined.

Post-industrial economic trends

Clark and Lipset argue that 'economic growth undermines hierarchical class stratification' (above, p. 46). They argue markets are growing in relevance as a consequence of rising incomes, and that 'decentralised, demand-sensitive decision-making' is growing to meet ever more complex consumer demand (ibid.). While huge firms are in relative decline and smaller niche-oriented ventures are increasing in at least some countries (Sabel 1982, Piore and Sabel 1984), we question whether any of the other claims they make in this section can stand up to critical scrutiny.

We first note that Clark and Lipset's claims about the growing 'marketness' of capitalist societies in comparison to earlier periods is very difficult to sustain empirically (Block 1990:56–66), and no substantial evidence is provided by these authors. Further, it ignores completely the steady and spectacular growth of the state throughout the course of the twentieth century in all industrial societies (Esping-Anderson 1990).

Even if Clark and Lipset's claims about growing marketness were true, there is good reason to question their analysis of how this affects class-based stratification. For example, they note that most good job growth in recent years has taken place in small firms (above, p. 46, citing Birch 1979). But they fail to point out that smaller firms are rarely able to offer their employees all of the income, benefits and job security of larger firms and that most unstable, low-paying jobs are located in small firms (Gordon, Edwards and Reich 1982, Edwards 1988, O'Connor 1973, Stolzenberg 1978).

Clark and Lipset then argue that more advanced technologies make it 'harder . . . to plan in advance and control administratively' and that these economic changes are leading to a *decline in traditional authority, hierarchy and class relations* (above, pp. 46–7; emphasis in the original). Their discussion of technology takes the most optimistic conceivable scenarios as reality, ignoring the more complex institutional patterns actually emerging in post-industrial societies. The use of new management styles in response to the appearance of high technology is heavily dependent on the context in which it is embedded (Zuboff 1988, Shaiken 1984). In many firms, managers resist any transfer of authority to lower-level employees, even if the new 'smart machines' make possible a democratisation of decision-making within firms (Zuboff 1988). Far from eliminating class struggle, the introduction of new technology and management styles often creates new forms of class conflict. The jury is still out on the fate of hierarchy in post-industrial firms.

Finally, Clark and Lipset argue that economic growth is undermining 'local stratification hierarchies as markets grow – regionally, nationally, internationally' (above, p. 47). Mills (1946) effectively countered such observations nearly half a century ago by arguing that the gulf between decision centres in metropolitan skyscrapers and the dispersed loci of production and consumption was yet another layer of stratification, not a pattern that 'combine[s] to undermine the familistic-quasi-monopolistic tradition of business hierarchy and class stratification patterns' (above, ibid.), as Clark and Lipset would have it (cf. Featherman and Hauser 1978:482–94, Hodson 1983, Harrison and Bluestone 1988).

Family

Clark and Lipset argue that the 'slimmed' family in post-industrial society has 'increasingly become characterised by more egalitarian relations . . . [as] hierarchical stratification has weakened' (ibid.). While the patterns they refer to in support of these arguments (greater freedom of marriage and divorce, greater opportunities for women to work in the paid labour force, and the decline of extended family arrangements) are clearly important, they provide no evidence that the 'slimmed' family is a more egalitarian one. The modern family is a good deal more complex than Clark and Lipset imply (Connell 1987:120–5). Research on contemporary family life suggests that while egalitarian beliefs are more widespread than in earlier periods, a clear gender division of labour remains in place in most families (Hochschild 1989). In the United States, for example, the evidence overwhelmingly suggests that the rise in female-headed 'slimmed' families with the liberalisation of divorce law has led to rising rates of poverty in female-headed families (Thistle 1992:Ch. 4, Weizman 1985). For the urban poor, the 'slimmed family' celebrated by Clark and Lipset is a major source of poverty and inequality (Wilson 1987). This is attributable in part to the positive association between husbands' and wives' occupations that increases differences among families even as differences within families decrease (Bianchi 1981, Hout 1982).

Under 'family', Clark and Lipset also address recent changes in social mobility, arguing that 'the slimmer family determines less the education and jobs of individual family members and that 'social mobility studies show decreasing effects of parents' education and income in explaining children's occupational success' (citing Featherman and Hauser 1978 and Hout 1988). However, Clark and Lipset fail to take due note of the sources of those changes. It is true that class origin affects students' progress through the educational systems of most industrial societies less than it used to, but the cause of diminished educational stratification is not less class-based selection but less selection of any kind at the early transitions where class matters most (Mare 1980, 1981). Replications of Mare's results for the United States in 15 industrial societies show that only Sweden, Hungary and the former Czechoslovakia had real declines in class-based selection (Shavit and Blossfeld 1992, Raftery and Hout 1993). In Hungary and Czechoslovakia political party tests replaced class selection; only Sweden saw a real growth in the openness of the educational stratification process.

Likewise, falling class barriers to social mobility cannot be attributed to 'affluence' or other indirect forces. The expansion of higher education in the United States – a class-conscious policy designed to benefit youth of lower-middle and working-class origins – has brought down class barriers to achievement (Hout 1988). It works because through this century a college diploma served to cancel the effect of social origins on occupational success. By making college accessible to working-class youth, the expansion of higher education in the United States removed class barriers for those who took advantage. Elsewhere, different mechanisms affected mobility. In Sweden, the social democratic welfare state assured more equal access not only to universities but also jobs in desirable occupations (Esping-Anderson 1990: 144–61). In Hungary, political tests for professions and managerial positions guaranteed a dramatic weakening of class barriers during the first generation of communist rule; it slacked after the first generation (Wong and Hauser 1992). Where class-conscious action does not organise opportunity, as in Ireland (Hout 1989:Ch. 11), class barriers are unshaken – even by industrialisation on a scale that might be said to lead to an increase in 'affluence'. Policies that did expand equality of opportunity have in any case now been eroded by 'taxpayers' revolts' and diminished economic growth and, although it is too early to show, should eventually lead to a re-emergence of class barriers to mobility.

Conclusion: classes are not dying

Class structures have undergone important changes in recent decades, with the rise of post-industrial societies. The birth of new sources of inequality does not imply the death of the old ones. In arguing that Clark and Lipset have failed to show that social classes are dying, we do not wish to imply that there have been no changes in the class structure of advanced capitalist societies, or in the association between class and other social phenomena. The manual working class has declined in recent decades in most countries, while the proportion of the labour force working in the service sector has increased. Such changes are important; they tell us that the nineteenth-century models of class are no longer adequate. Yet moving to more complex, multidimensional models of class does not imply that classes are dying. The persistence of class-based inequalities in capitalist societies suggest that in the foreseeable future the concept of class will – and should – play an important role in sociological research.

While the research evidence on the persistence of class as a factor in life chances and politics is abundant and convincing, explanations for that persistence are not. As a profession we have documented the parameters of class relations to a high degree of precision, while simultaneously demolishing the older theories that framed our work. We have discovered that class structures are more complex than Marxist and other theories that assign class structure a causal role in the evolution of societies and less subject to the calming effects of affluence that modernisation theories posit. The theoretical question for the next decade is 'Why is class so complex and why is it dependent on politics instead of determinative of politics?' As citizens and sociologists we would very much like to live in a world in which class inequalities have disappeared. But – to paraphrase Gramsci – class society is not yet dying, and truly classless societies have not yet been born.

Notes

1. Extracted with abridgements from 'The Persistence of Classes in Post-Industrial Societies', *International Sociology* 8:3, September 1993; 259–77.
2. We wish to avoid distracting from our main point (that class continues to affect social stratification and politics) by discussing the ongoing debates among class theorists over how best to understand class conceptually and in contemporary societies.
3. For data and further details see the original journal article on which this extract is based and Hout, Wright and Sanchez-Jankowski (1992) [Eds].

CHAPTER 4

The dying of class or of Marxist class theory?[1]

Jan Pakulski

'Are Social Classes Dying?' (Clark and Lipset 1991) [see Chapter 2 in this volume] has touched a raw nerve. Any argument about the weakening or demise of class will trigger controversy. Yet such an argument is long overdue, and should be made more persuasive in the light of both the social transformations in what is labelled the 'advanced West' and the experience of the East European revolutions. It is not only that these processes prompt us to question the relevance of the old concepts and theories, the Marxist class theory in particular; they also make the task of questioning easier by reducing the ideological divide between the West and East. The class debate is no longer conducted from the trenches, and it involves a growing number of East European sociologists newly liberated from ideological and censorship constraints.

The Clark and Lipset article opens the way for such a debate. It points to declining hierarchies, a declining rigidity of class divisions and, above all, a declining impact of class location on political attitudes and behaviour in the areas of politics, economic organisation and family relations. It concludes with a thesis on the 'fragmentation of stratification' which, in the eyes of the authors, reflects the 'decline in traditional authority, hierarchy and class relations' and consequently a decline in the explanatory value of class analyses, especially for political behaviour. It is not an entirely new argument; the notion of 'non-egalitarian classlessness' has a venerable tradition, especially in America where affluence, intense mobility and, above all, the apparent weakness of class ideologies, class organisations and class politics, provided a fertile ground for criticisms of Marxism.

In their reply, Hout *et al.* (Chapter 3 in this volume) offer a vigorous defence of class as a key determinant of organisation of material interests, life chances and collective action. While agreeing that 'class structures have undergone important changes in recent decades, with the rise of post-industrial societies', they reject the 'death of class' claim, and argue for 'the continuing – and even rising – importance of class'.

Although Clark and Lipset's arguments on social change are poignant and persuasive, their conclusions as to the utility of the class concept, and the theoretical frameworks in which these conclusions are coated, need elucidation. Because of the often bland nature of these conclusions, they pose a danger of shifting attention away from the key issues of social theory and social change and into an area of semantic conventions (what is class? what does 'death' mean?). Hout *et al.*'s rejoinder seems to respond more critically to these semantic conventions in Clark and Lipset's arguments, and less to the authors' key claims about the changing nature of social inequalities and political cleavages in advanced societies, and the theoretical implications of these changes.

In order to re-focus the debate, I would like to make a distinction between three issues at stake: first, the analytical clarity and utility of the concept of class; second, the relevance of Marxist class theory; and third, the often conflated issue of the importance of the old 'industrial classes' understood as historical actors.

The meaning of class: Conceptual stretch and semantic pluralism

The concept of class suffers from what Sartori (1970) diagnosed as 'conceptual stretch'. Its denotation (coverage) has extended, mainly due to indiscriminate application, at the expense of its clarity and precision. Stretching debilitates research and paralyses theorising by transforming the former into an equivalent of driftnet fishing. Stretched conceptual nets scoop indiscriminately into one container very diverse aspects of social reality and transform class theory into the 'theory of everything'. Another unfortunate consequence of conceptual stretch is that class means different things for different people. There is nothing necessarily wrong in this semantic pluralism, as long as it does not lead scholars to talk past each other. Unfortunately, this seems to be the case in the current debate. Clark and Lipset gloss over some more recent re-formulations of the Marxist class theory (e.g. Wright 1985), but they are quite clear in what they mean: they identify 'class' and 'class stratification' with the persistence of 'distinct layers', as well as class-defined patterns in informal social relations, cultural outlooks, and support for social change, such as support for social movements and political behaviour. In this context, they point to the decline of hierarchies and the fragmentation of inequalities, as well as to the well diagnosed trends in class and partisan dealignment. To them, these processes suggest the 'death of class' (with a question mark). Hout *et al.* respond by choosing quite different semantic conventions and a different concept of class. They define class as 'a person's relationship to the means of production and/or labour markets', which implies that classes exist as long as individuals differ in the sources of their economic subsistence/wealth.

Such a concept of class can hardly serve in engaging the Clark and Lipset arguments about the fragmentation of stratification and dealignment. Classes exist – by the definition suggested by Hout *et al.* – in all modern societies.

Instead of debating the relative merits of these quite different concepts of class, I would like to suggest a brief typological clarification illustrated in Figure 4.1. In the mainstream Marxist tradition, the concept of class is linked with property relations and is used to *explain* social conflicts and social change. Such a concept and usage – let us call it 'generative/explanatory' – typically focuses on economic roles, stresses the polarity and conflict, and ignores the issues of class boundaries. Classes mark objective positions in the societal production processes and what most Marxists see as 'objective and antagonistic' interests, which are attributed to these positions. It is these structurally imputed conflicting interests that are seen as the main propellant of historically important collective conduct, even if they are not always well articulated in the consciousness of social actors. If they do articulate – and many Marxists see the rise of 'class consciousness' of workers as inevitable – classes transform into historical actors capable of concerted action and, ultimately, revolutionary change. Thus within the 'generative' concept-user camp one can find a division between structuralist objectivists, who see class mechanism (labour *vs* capital) as the principal conflict generator (e.g. Althusser 1971), and actional subjectivists who identify classes with collective actors challenging the status quo in a radical way, regardless of the socio-economic positions of the challengers, the forms of the challenge or the identities of the actors (Touraine 1985). For the former, classes are ubiquitous but typically hidden from an 'empiricist' gaze; class conflicts permeate social reality but reveal themselves only to those who use the right method of analysis (that is, presuppose their existence). For the latter, classes are also ubiquitous but more tangible: they appear whenever solidary groups form and challenge the dominant values, norms and institutions.

Figure 4.1   A typology of class concepts

	GENERATIVE/EXPLANATORY	CATEGORICAL DESCRIPTIVE
OBJECTIVE	structural mechanism	economic/occupational category
SUBJECTIVE	socio-political actor	socio-cultural category

In contrast to the 'generative/explanatory' ones, the 'categorical/ descriptive' concepts of class serve to outline patterns of social inequalities. Classes are units of stratification – inequalities in societal power, economic life chances, occupational prestige, etc. – but they do not necessarily form the bases of identification and conflict (as is the case in the generative approaches). This way of conceptualising classes typically draws inspiration from the Weberian tradition, although Weber's (1978) careful analytical delineations (e.g. between classes, status groups and parties) are not always respected by those in the categorical/descriptive camp.

The objectivists in the categorical/descriptive camp see class as determined primarily by such tangible assets as wealth, income, occupation, education or by the combination thereof (e.g. Broom and Jones 1976). The subjectivists (one may call them 'socio-culturalists') focus on inequalities reflected in the consciousness and identity of actors, on socio-cultural aspects of social inequalities and their correlates – values, norms, life styles, etc. – all seen in the context of persistent and intergenerationally reproduced socio-cultural hierarchies (e.g. Bourdieu 1984). For the 'subjectivists', these hierarchies imply meanings; they are seen as reproduced through symbolic means, and they are studied with the 'humanistic coefficient'.

This typology is rather basic, but sufficient for an argument I am trying to develop, namely, that the first step in the current debate should involve a conceptual clarification. In particular, the notion of class as a unit of the inequality system should be disentangled from class understood as a basis of identification and conflict. With that, the assumption of a necessary correspondence between these four notions of class needs to be addressed in a more systematic way.

The theoretical importance of class: causes and connections

Clark and Lipset are guilty only of misplaced criticism. What they criticise – in my view, quite correctly – is the relevance and utility of the *Marxist* concept of class with its theoretical and analytic framework. Three elements of this framework are (explicitly or implicitly) questioned by Clark and Lipset: (i) its economic determinism and reductionism: the notion that property relations are the key determinant of social inequalities, divisions and conflicts; (ii) the notion of strong causal links between socio-economic and socio-cultural inequalities, and between inequalities, social identification and political action; (iii) the 'logic of capitalism' argument assuming the cumulative nature of class inequalities, the simplification of the class structure, the rise of class consciousness, and the intensification of class conflict.

While these aspects of Clark and Lipset's arguments are persuasive, albeit hardly original, their criticism of the Weberian tradition, especially its relevance for the analysis of stratification and conflict in the industrialised West, is much less convincing. In fact, Clark and Lipset quote with approval the 'neo-Weberian' analyses of Dahrendorf, Giddens and Parkin, and endorse what may be considered as the distinctive elements of the Weberian perspective:

(i) the notion of the 'multidimentionality' of stratification (classes, status groups, parties/interest groups); (ii) the emphasis on the complexity and fragmentation of classes (including the proliferation of 'middle classes', the formation of closure-based 'social classes', and the importance of 'income classes'); (iii) the relative independence between socio-economic inequalities, socio-cultural inequalities (status groups) and socio-political inequalities, as well as between inequalities in general on the one hand, and consciousness *cum* action on the other. Indeed, the well known Weberian arguments on the decomposition of classes, etatisation of political conflicts (e.g. Dahrendorf 1959, 1988), marketisation, social closure (e.g. Parkin 1979) and the importance of status identification and 'status politics' (e.g. Turner 1988) seem to fit Clark and Lipset's diagnoses quite well.

Hout *et al.*'s rejoinder also poses some problems. Although the authors acknowledge that '[c]lass structures have undergone important changes in recent decades, with the rise of postindustrial societies' they insist on retaining some key elements of the Marxist class concept, and they ignore the issues that are central for Clark and Lipset: that of the *fragmentation* of stratification and *relative importance* of class inequalities and class conflicts. They claim that 'social class organises material interests'. However, the fact that there are many other, perhaps equally important, 'organisers of material interests', and that so many contemporary conflicts revolve around 'ideal interests' (viz. the 'new politics' in the advanced West, conflicts in Russia, Bosnia, Georgia, Middle East, Iran) is not considered at any length. Further argument for the indispensability of class is seen in the fact that 'structurally defined social classes *occasionally* give rise to collective actors that bring about social change' [italics mine – J.P.]. However, the key question of *how occasionally* that happens is, again, left largely unexplored. It is quite obvious that sometimes people do act on the basis of their economic interests – hardly any social scientist, including Clark and Lipset, would deny that. The point is that the evidence of partisan and class dealignment in the industrial West, plus the evidence of non-class (ethnic, religious, racial, regional, etc.) cleavages and conflicts in industrialised and industrialising societies, weakens the argument of Hout *et al.* on the indispensability/centrality of class. Finally, the third theoretical argument in defence of the concept of class (defined in terms of a person's relationship to the means of production and/or labour markets) is that 'social class membership affects the life chances and behaviour of individuals'. Again, the key questions posed by Clark and Lipset are, first, how strongly class membership affects life chances, identity and behaviour, compared with, say, status group, generation, ethnic group, occupational category, or religious minority; and, second, how strong is this influence now, compared with the past. These questions are not systematically addressed by Hout *et al.*

The supporting evidence brought by Hout *et al.* raises many questions. They point to the persistence of income and wealth inequalities – which is not denied by Clark and Lipset (and, for that matter, by anyone in the field). They show that there is a significant variation in US earnings between classes, when the latter are measured by Wright's (1989b) 12-class scheme. There is no doubt that this 12-class scheme is an improvement over Wright's (1985) earlier 6-class scheme. Doubtless, a 24-class scheme would be even better. The question, however, is at what point such 'class maps' become indistinguishable from occupational status maps and what advantage or improvement they offer.

The decomposition of classes in the industrialised West

The very fact that a leading Marxist scholar like Wright is compelled to multiply classes on his 'class maps' in order to capture complex empirical configurations seems, if anything, to support Clark and Lipset's contention about the fragmentation of stratification. A more systematic addressing of such questions should reveal not only the changes signalled by Clark and Lipset, but also some other aspects and mechanisms of the 'fragmentation of stratification' and 'decomposition of classes'. In the industrialised West, these recent changes involved:

(i) The proliferation of small property ownership

Massive privatisation programmes undertaken in the last decade by most Western governments, regardless of their partisan colouring, resulted in a proliferation of small property and further blurring of the (crucial for the Marxists) divisions between propertied and non-propertied categories. In Britain, for example, over 40 per cent of the state sector has been privatised, more than one million public housing tenants have become owners, and the proportion of share owners grew from one-twentieth to over one-fifth of the population (e.g. Naisbitt and Aburdene 1990). Self-employment has been growing rapidly in all advanced societies, and the concentration of capital has been declining (OECD 1992). Extension of superannuation and pension schemes – typically invested in industrial stocks – also contributes to this blurring. If continued, this proliferation *cum* blurring may overshadow the impact of the spread of joint stock companies in the first half of this century.

(ii) The credentialisation of skills and the professionalisation of occupations

These further weaken the old class divisions, especially the owner-worker dichotomy (e.g. Parkin 1979). Some analysts suggest the formation of a new distinctive 'knowledge class' whose members are seen either as potential rulers (e.g. Bell 1973) or as the main challenger to the industrial bourgeoisie (e.g. Berger 1987:66–9).

Others see professionalisation as an alternative to a class mode of social structuring (e.g. Perkin 1989).

(iii) Weakening state regulation, both internal and international

In the past, state interventions combined quasi-mercantilist protection with pro-market internal regulation and welfare redistribution. The impact of these measures on social inequalities and patterns of conflict has been well documented. The impact of the more recent drive towards expansion of civil rights and open trade still awaits analysis. However, some of its consequences are already diagnosed, and they point to further erosion of class divisions. The expansion of civil rights – especially the 'special status rights' of numerous categories, such as native peoples, racial minorities, women – links life chances with politically defined and legally protected entitlements. This, as Turner (1988) and Waters (1989) suggest, further fragments stratification patterns, and generates new cleavages and conflicts. Class organisations such as trade unions lose support (Golden and Pontusson 1992). Simultaneously, the unravelling of corporatist deals and the globalisation of markets provoke backlash in defence of state protected privileges which typically cut across the old class divisions. For example, the owners, managers and workers in the Australian car industry form a coalition in defence of protective tariffs – in defence, that is, of profits, salaries, wages and jobs.

(iv) Increasing consumption and consumption orientations

While Clark and Lipset point to the importance of affluence, one may stress the impact of mass consumption on changing mass values and orientations (Inglehart 1977, 1990, Inglehart and Flanagan 1989). It should be noted that the recent expansion of mass consumption occurs at least as much due to the increases in earnings as to the lowered prices of consumer goods. This generates a tension between the interests of people as consumers (in lowering the cost of production and prices) and the interest of people as producers (in securing high wages/salaries). It is this tension that may lead to the well documented weakening of the traditional class-party alignments (e.g. Crewe and Denver 1985, Dalton 1988, Dalton et al. 1990).

(v) The formation of 'imagined communities' under the impact of the mass media

Perhaps the most striking aspect of class decomposition occurs through the formation of what is referred to as non-class 'imagined communities' (Anderson 1983). Although they had always been prominent, these communities seem to proliferate now: people start to regard themselves as members of communities of shared concerns (e.g. Greens), habits (e.g. non-smokers), tastes (e.g. vegetarians) or some ascriptive characteristics (e.g. blacks, women). Such imagined communities provide identities, encourage a sense of solidarity, and prompt a common action to a larger extent than it was in the past. While the proliferation of these imagined communities is well documented, their impact on the old identities, including the class identities, is less thoroughly scrutinised.

(vi) The mobilisation of 'new social movements' and 'new politics'

Finally, one of the celebrated topics in contemporary political analysis is the upsurge of political activism studied under the label of 'new social movements' and 'new politics'. The point is that this activism does not mobilise class members, ignores the traditional class issues and class-related organisations, and generates political cleavages which cut across the old class-related left–right spectrum. Neither the composition of the 'new movements constituencies' nor the character of the publicised issues and styles of activism can be analysed in class terms (e.g. Pakulski 1993). Instead, Baker *et al.* (1981), Dalton (1988) and Abramson and Inglehart (1992) point to the importance of generational divisions in new politics; other analysts opt for such concepts as 'status blocs' (e.g. Turner 1988), and 'civil society' (e.g. Cohen 1985).

To sum up, a current review of class analyses called for a serious revamp of the old class concepts, 'passed by' the developments in the real world (Myles and Turegan, Chapter 13 in this volume). A study of identity (conducted in Australia) concluded that 'the discursive salience of class for identity is almost minimal' (Emmison and Western 1990:241); another Australian study of inequality and political activism ended with the conclusion that political conflicts, and political activism in general, are only marginally affected by class location and class identity (Graetz 1992:157). These findings cast serious doubts on the utility of Marxist class theory.

Stratification and conflict in communist societies

One of the cruel ironies of history is that the attempts to realise in practice Marx's doctrine undermined the credibility of Marx's class theory and the utility of the Marxist concept of class. The experience of state socialism – its formation, functioning and collapse – cast serious doubts as to the strength of the causal connection between property and market relations on the one hand, and the patterns of social inequalities and social conflicts on the other. First, all state socialist societies developed conspicuous inequalities and clear stratification patterns, in many respects similar to the Western patterns, without large-scale private property and market relations. Second, all of them experienced strong conflicts and, most embarrassingly for the Marxist class theory, they collapsed in revolutionary upheavals.

What is more, the conflicts and the revolutionary mobilisations which preceded the 'velvet revolutions' reflected more 'ideal interests' than economic positions and 'material interests'. The revolutions helped to revive such alternatives to class concepts as 'civil society', 'political community' and 'generation' (e.g. Pakulski 1986). Third, the conflicts that followed the collapse of communism and the disintegration of the Soviet and Yugoslav 'quasi-empires' do not fit the class scheme either. They revolve around the issues of nationality, ethnicity, religion, locality and state sponsorship. The revival of property rights and the market have not led to the re-formation of class divisions, conflicts and cleavages. Class theories, in other words, appear to be of little use for the analysis of inequalities, conflicts and change in communist and post-communist societies. Attempts to adapt the 'class perspective' resulted in further conceptual stretch and/or abandonment of the Marxist class theory (Radaev and Shkaratan 1992).

Thus, as far as the experience of the rise and fall of communism is concerned, the Marxist class theory is dead. It has been an embarrassing demise, because of the sheer scale of the failure to account for the patterns of stratification and change in a major type of modern society. The class theory failed to account for what was arguably *the most important social transformation of this century*. [. . .]

Classes as actors: the demise of the old industrial classes

Another dimension of Clark and Lipset's article – not always clearly separated from other arguments – concerns the weakening of the *old* class actors: the industrial bourgeoisie and the working class. The latter, in particular, has been seen as *the* class actor, and most of Marxist theorising on classes, politics and social change in general, in fact, concerned the industrial proletariat. Therefore the waning of the working class – its fragmentation, weakening of identification, dealignment, etc. – has often been seen as the waning of class-actor in general.

The evidence of this waning – in terms of socio-economic, socio-cultural and socio-political distinctiveness, as well as of consciousness, identity and solidarity – seems to be indisputable. There are also good theoretical accounts in Dahrendorf (1959) and Bell (1973) to Gorz (1982) and Hindess (1987). Instead of repeating their arguments, I would like to highlight some general points.

Although the articulation of industrial classes, as Marx rightly suggested, accompanied all cases of capitalist industrialisation, the degree to which the classes formed distinct socio-cultural entities and political communities varied significantly. Britain was the celebrated case of strong and multidimensional articulation; but North America, Central-Eastern Europe and South East Asia did not experience such strong and all-pervasive articulations (Berger 1987:Ch. 7). While the concentration of workers in heavy industries (especially shipbuilding, steel, railways and mining) was the first necessary condition of class articulation, other conditions were political in the broader sense. In particular, the process of emergence of trade union and socialist parties, and their subsequent incorporation into corporatist structures of governments, entrenched class by providing it with a clearly articulated organisational, ideological and programmatic 'superstructure'. It is this 'superstructure' of class, rather than its economic structural basis, that made the working class such an important historical entity. It is also the dismantling of this superstructure that marks what one may call the demise of class politics.

Let me comment briefly on the less well diagnosed and more recent processes which eroded the institutional and ideological 'superstructure' of class. The processes of institutionalisation and organisation in the early twentieth century contained politically the processes of occupational differentiation and proliferation by articulating occupational interests and aggregating (channelling and funnelling) them into broad trade union and party-political platforms. This led to the 'nationalisation of classes' (that is, internal market regulation plus the imposition of liberal legal-political frameworks), the spread of corporatist deals, and the extension of welfare entitlements. The corporatist deals, in particular, helped to construct and cement the social entities, modes of action and patterns of inequalities which have been associated with the contemporary notion of 'class'. This institutional cementing coincided with economic crises and intense political and ideological conflicts in the first half of this century. Corporatist inclusion helped to defuse these conflicts; it resulted not only in the institutionalisation of class but also in the 'domestication' of class conflict (Lehmbruch and Schmitter 1982, Schmitter and Lehmbruch 1979).

However, all these political containment measures have also increased tensions between the ongoing socio-economic differentiation, which eroded the unity of class, and political organisation, which reconstructed class unity. Thus classes were (re)constructed politically and ideologically at the time when the structural-economic content (that is, the commonality of life chances and interests) was rapidly evaporating. Collapse of the traditional heavy industries (shipbuilding, railways, mining), combined with accelerated occupational differentiation, proliferation of non-manual occupations in the burgeoning tertiary sector, and intensified mobility, started to undermine the corporatist structures. They turned into increasingly empty shells maintained more by bureaucratic inertia and political patronage than by the broad community of economic interests. What is diagnosed as 'new politics' – the loosening of corporatist deals, partisan dealignment, de-unionisation, mobilisation of the 'new social movements', and proliferation of quasi-interest groups – are the symptoms of this erosion and dissolution of 'class-actors'. The label 'death of class' seems to encapsulate these changes quite aptly.

Conclusions

Clark and Lipset single out political cleavages, economic organisation and family as the key arenas of change and suggest that this change – subsumed under the label of 'fragmentation of stratification' – reduces the political significance of class. What 'dies' (in Clark and Lipset's parlance) is mainly the old industrial classes: the old socio-economic divisions, the old institutional actors representing these divisions, and the old forms of identification that reflected them. With these processes the theoretical and analytical edifice of Marxism loses much of its grounds. However, one may argue that the demise of the old industrial classes and the theoretical exhaustion of Marxism do not necessarily mean the abandoning of 'class' understood as one of many analytical categories in stratification and conflict analysis.

This point has of course been made repeatedly by Goldthorpe (e.g. 1987), and more recently by Marshall *et al.* (1988) and Goldthorpe and Marshall (below:Ch. 7). However, while they opt for a 'humble' version of class analysis – with no reductionist theory of history and political action – they still insist on maintaining class in the centre-stage privileged position in social analysis. This central – if not monopolistic – role they give to class is incompatible with multidimentionality of Weberian analysis.

If it is to be preserved, the concept of class has to be radically separated from the Marxian theory and eschatology, and it has to lose its privileged status as *the* key sociological concept. This, as suggested here, may mean a revival of the Weberian social analysis which, unlike neo-Weberian 'class analysis', sees the social fabric as always combining a warp of class with a weft of status and a rich embroidery of associative-party relations.

Note

1. Abridged. Originally published as 'The Dying of Class or of Marxist Class Theory?' *International Sociology* 8:3 1993:279–92.

CHAPTER 5

Succession in the stratification system: A contribution to the 'death of class' debate[1]

Malcolm Waters

The 'death of class' debate turns on the simple issue of whether or not class exists and is in part about the conceptualisation of class itself. Class can be conceptualised in Marxisant terms as a system of collective actors, generated within industrial capitalism by radical differences in property ownership, that struggle against each other to fix property relations in terms of mutually exclusive interests. Some authors insist that class, thus defined, remains the central and vital element in contemporary society (e.g. Hout *et al.* above, Ch. 3, Miliband 1989, Wright 1985). But class can also be conceptualised as simple socio-economic inequality, an approach which involves a conceptual stretch, to include not only property ownership but any pattern of inequality derived from employment relations and location in the labour market (e.g. this volume, Chapters 3 and 7). This division of opinion opens up two possible claims about the demise of class as a significant social force. One might argue that class disappeared altogether when it was tamed within the configuration we call the welfare state. Alternatively, one can take the extreme position that class, however defined, has a reducing or minimal social impact.

This paper takes a radical and theoretically speculative position in this debate. It does not argue that the concept of class should be abandoned, nor does it side with the view that the concept should be detached from its Marxist origins and stretched so that it is purely empirical and contingent. Rather it argues that the possible bases of stratification are multidimensional and that in the class-party-status triplet, Weber signalled the most significant possible of these. Furthermore, stratification orders exhibit patterns of competition, domination and succession over time. Class was the dominant stratification pattern only under nineteenth-century Western capitalism and since then we have witnessed not the 'death of class' but its subordination to other stratification orders. During much of the twentieth century the predominant order has not been focused on private property and production but on the state and organisational systems. Under current circumstances, however, predominance is shifting away from the state and organisations to cultural items and processes, to idealised communities that focus on life styles and value-commitments.

It follows that the idea of a class-registrated society should be restricted to a particular historical configuration in which collective actors determined by production relations struggle within that arena for control of the system of property ownership. Employment relations or labour market position may continue to have salience in determining social rewards outside this configuration. However, in many if not most instances these will be determined by factors other than property ownership, including organisational position, skills and credentials or the social worth of value-commitments. Under such an argument the history of industrial-capitalist societies might be conceived not as the history of struggle between classes but as a history in which there is competition and struggle between *orders* of stratification. The bulk of this paper is a development of this idea.

Succession in the stratification system

The idea that there are multiple stratification orders that can succeed one another in terms of social predominance comes originally from Weber:

> Commercial classes arise in a market-oriented economy, but status groups arise within the framework of organizations which satisfy their wants through monopolistic liturgies, or in feudal, or in *ständisch*-patrimonial fashion. Depending on the prevailing mode of stratification, we shall speak of a 'status society' or a 'class society'. (Weber 1978:306–7)

Weber's argument about succession in the West might be elaborated as follows. Pre-modern societies were dominated by feudal estates, legally and religiously sanctioned status groups, that monopolise material, cultural and political privileges. The estate system was disrupted by the rise of rentier and commercial classes that attempted to usurp these privileges by establishing markets. The estates and the new classes existed alongside each other in early modern society, engaged in a contest between alienability and heritability of property, and between status and contract as the basis of exchange. Thus we witness a shift from 'estatist' (*ständisch*) society to class (*klassenmabig*) society. Within this second formation, new status groups sought to establish themselves on the basis of property ownership, occupation, ethnicity or other categories of social membership. In so far as they were successful, they moderated the extent to which society was structurated into classes by the market.

This paper suggests the possibility of four contingent stratification orders based on shifting patterns of domination and subordination between three commonly recognised social spheres or realms, the economic, the political and the cultural.

1   In an *estatist society* the three realms are fused together so that no single one can be held to be in domination. The strata, estates, are engaged in diffuse and localised relationships that simultaneously embrace production relationships, political authority, moral esteem, and consumption privileges.

2   A *class society* is arranged into patterns of domination and struggle between interest groups that emerge from the economic realm. In the familiar terms of Marx, the classes will be property owners and sellers of labour power. The dominant class can capture the state and maintain itself as a ruling class by rendering the state weak. In so far as the subordinate class undertakes collective action it will be rebellious or revolutionary in character aimed at dislodging this ruling class by the abolition of private property. Culture is divided to match class divisions, into dominant and subordinate ideologies and into high and low cultures.

3   A *command society* is dominated by the political or state sphere in which the significant strata can be conceptualised as power blocs. It is typically dominated by a single unified bloc, a political-bureaucratic elite, that exercises power over one or more subordinate mass blocs. These blocs may be factionalised horizontally into formally opposed parties. The elite will comprise either a party leadership or a corporate leadership integrating party leaders with the leaders of other organised interest groups including economic and cultural ones. The elite uses the coercive power of the state to regulate the other two spheres. The state can dominate the economy by the conversion of private into public property, although this need not be a complete accomplishment. Classes, in turn, organise themselves in political rather than industrial terms by establishing links with parties. Meanwhile, the cultural realm can be unified under the state umbrella or under the aegis of state-sponsored monopolies. It can thus be turned into an industrialised or mass culture.

4   In a *status-conventional society*, stratification emerges from the cultural sphere. The strata are lifestyle and/or value-based status communities. They can form around differentiated patterns of value-commitment, identity, belief, symbolic meaning, taste, opinion or consumption. Because of the ephemeral and fragile nature of these resources, a stratification system based on conventional, status communities appears as a shifting mosaic which can destabilise the other two spheres. The state is weakened because it cannot rely on mass support, and the economy is weakened (in a social power sense) because it cannot control either its workers or its markets. Each situs is deconcentrated by a prevailing orientation to values and utilities that are established conventionally rather than by reference to collective interests.

The pattern of succession should by now be apparent. Weber has given us the first step. An estatist society experiences a primary pattern of differentiation in which, for whatever reason, classes and market institutions emerge. A second succession occurs when the dispropertied working class successfully captures the state or invades and establishes a significant power position within it. The state is reorganised and strengthened by power blocs and the parties that represent them as they extend their regulative influence throughout the society. A third succession then becomes possible, in which status-groups which must be cultivated as clients and political supporters of the state, are able to undermine it and to establish social domination on the basis of control of cultural valuables. Each emergent phase in the succession process does not eclipse the strata given by the previous phase. Class does not disappear in a command society but is reorganised and, indeed, reproduced through the state. Equally, in a status-conventional society, classes and blocs remain as culturally ordered entities (cf. Lockwood 1986:12).

We can now examine each of these shifts substantively, reserving most attention for the shift which may be under way in the contemporary period. The main intention here is not to provide a historical sketch but to show that the transformation from one order to another is the consequence of crisis and subsequent reorganisation. The principal substantive focus is on the capitalist West, although the argument also applies to the formerly socialist East.

From estate to class

Feudalism, the principal European instance of estatist society, is based on a fusion of stratification arrangements integrating four social resources: labour, land, the means of violence, and religious legitimation. Its origins lie in a protection racket established by mounted warriors over local tribal populations. Warriors appropriated land from peasants and offered military 'protection' to them in exchange for a labour-service tenancy. Subsequent elaboration of this pattern of exploitation led to the development of a hierarchy of land tenancy and service exchange that connected the peasant to the monarch. The system received religious legitimation in so far as the monarch was understood to have received the kingdom as God's tenant. . . . Because all land derived ultimately from God, tenancy arrangements were fixed in the religious ritual of *hommage*. Feudal society was therefore stratified into three estates – nobility, peasantry and clerisy – although only the first two were really important. Estate membership was fixed at birth so that estates were closed, endogamous, and heritable. The boundaries were established in custom, law and religion, and they were sanctioned by the use of force.

For most of the history of feudalism, the centralised state was weak and sat more firmly in the hands of the knights who directed agricultural production, raised armies, and supported priests, than with the monarch. The state was simply a federation of aristocratic landholdings loosely integrated by an idealised and religiously sanctioned pattern of tenancy. Such fragile federations could only hold together so long as there was a unified pattern of religious legitimation. By the seventeenth century this ceased to apply and the European societies were afflicted by civil wars between aristocratic elements divided along religious lines (Kossallek 1988). The typical resolution was to strengthen and extend the power of the monarch and thus to establish an absolutist state. Here the aristocracy was integrated around the monarchy which became the sole source of secular law and governed with the aid of a professional bureaucracy and military (Mann 1986:476).

In some circumstances, however, collective actors formed in other situses could exploit aristocratic weakness. [. . .]

An economic system based on trade, and eventually on manu-facturing, gave rise to at first a mercantile and then an industrial bourgeoisie which could stand opposed to aristocratic and monarchical power. As Anderson (1979:142) affirms, the development of the English absolutist state under the Tudors and Stuarts was 'cut off by a bourgeois revolution' in the mid-seventeenth century. The English bourgeoisie succeeded in 'constitutionalising' the monarchy in 1688. Bourgeois revolutions took a different tack elsewhere (e.g. America 1786, France 1789) but the effects on the estate system were similar.

The emerging bourgeoisie sought to liberate trade and industrial production from state and religious control and thus from the control of the aristocracy. It sought to establish new institutions: alienable private property; contract; formally free wage labour; the commodity form; money; and open markets. In order to achieve this the aristocracy was ejected from the state (e.g. English Reform Act 1832) or eliminated entirely (e.g. French Revolution 1789). Its privileges in agricultural trade were curtailed (e.g. repeal of the English Corn Laws 1846) and its diffuse hold on agricultural labour was loosened (e.g. English Poor Law Amendment 1834; American emancipation of slaves 1865). Under nineteenth-century liberal capitalism the state progressively withdrew from the economy and civil society. It did not own property, as did the absolutist monarchies, but rather extracted revenues on a fiscal basis. Because the bourgeois class was so effective in subordinating the proletariat in industrial contexts, the state used these revenues mainly to co-ordinate bourgeois collective action for military and trading purposes. [. . .]

Cultural developments followed a similar pattern. . . . Much of this occurred beyond the restrictions of aristocratic sponsorship in those newly secularised sites of bourgeois cultural reproduction, the universities. The universities, among other institutions, managed to fix hierarchically differentiated patterns of taste and style into what have become known as high and popular culture. Neither the classical traditions nor the avant-garde were accessible for the subordinated proletariat. Culture then was similarly class divided.

From class to command

From here the issues become much more contentious because much of the theoretical literature on stratification often makes a claim for the continuing salience of class. The contrasting view advanced here is that a significant shift away from class occurred in many societies towards the end of the nineteenth century. In summary, a rise in the importance and power of the state relative to the economic production contributed to a displacement of the bourgeois class as the dominant collective actor.

In seeking to identify the nature of the crisis we might well agree with the vulgar Marxist view about the capitalist tendency to self-destruction. Nineteenth-century liberal capitalism can be argued to have been overturned by a sequence of events prescribed by its own demands. Without going into great detail, its survival depended on the cultivation of mass political loyalty, mass economic commitment, and mass technical skill in a disempowered proletariat. However, enhancing these resources had the precise consequence of proletarian empowerment, and so the reproduction of classes entered an expanding cycle (Stewart *et al.* 1980:277). The working class acquired material, technical and organisational-political resources that enabled it to challenge the bourgeoisie.

In the West, at first this challenge was mounted within the economic-industrial situs itself but here the working class was defeated. Its trade unions were unable to depose the bourgeoisie and indeed the existence of these labour organisations was itself threatened. Liberal capitalism was thus faced with a stalemate and appeared to grind to a halt. The capitalist class had exhausted all possibilities for exploitation and control using the means available to it within the system of production. Meanwhile, unable to exact change, all the working class could do was to withdraw its labour.

The intact working-class organisations made a lateral switch, transferring their attention to party politics, seeking to capture the state and thus in effect to solve the crisis. In so far as they were successful, they transformed the society in the direction now commonly referred to as 'organised capitalism' (Hilferding 1910 (1981), Lash and Urry 1987, Offe 1985) or 'corporatism' (Lehmbruch 1977, Schmitter 1974). Because the working class had by this time become relatively powerful it was, within this configuration, able to extract early compromises with parties representing the bourgeoisie.

Before we examine the complex and pluralistic patterns of command that emerged in the West we can turn briefly to some pure 'statist' outcomes where the working class was so weak and disprivileged that it was obliged to capture the state by means of violence. The best known examples of these state-monopolised societies are the Soviet Union and its satellites, the People's Republic of China, such smaller socialist states as Cuba, Vietnam and North Korea, the former fascist states of Germany, Italy and Spain, and some contemporary Asian statist societies including Indonesia, Pakistan and Singapore. Arguably, statist social organisation of this type is waning but there are still numerous other contemporary examples and probably between a third and a half of the global population still lives under such regimes. In each case, the state uses coercion and/or regulation in a direct process of organisation of economics and culture. The organisation and symbolisation of the state in each case is coterminous with the organisation of the political party that controls it. Pakulski (1986:18–20) has coined the term 'partocratic' for such systems, because they emphasise 'commitment and political-ideological "expertise" rather than administrative or technical expertise' (1986:19). [. . .]

In the West, the bourgeoisie was able to force a compromise with the working class within what Crook *et al.* (1992:84–5) call a 'grand armistice'. This armistice was accomplished under the aegis of the state which emerged as a trans-class or class-neutral power centre. The state thus received a legitimacy boost and was able to extend its influence into welfare and cultural arenas in which it had not previously operated. And importantly, the state incorporated big business and organised labour into a single power nexus. For the bourgeoisie this meant acceptance of state intervention and regulation of the economy, and even its partial nationalisation, in return for the preservation of some of the rights and most of the material benefits of private capital ownership. In its turn the working class accepted subordination in the economy in return for an incrementalist political reform programme focusing on improved material security. In the West then, while class was not totally reorganised, it was increasingly subordinated to a system of power blocs committed to control of the state.

However, the extent of state development was not consistent throughout Western societies. In particular the USA has always been less corporatist than Western Europe and Japan. This may be because, although the Civil War destroyed the quasi-feudal society of the South, most of American society was not post-feudal. In Europe and Japan estatist relationships had been incorporated into class arrangements and had the effect of reinforcing and reproducing them through the development of class cultures. [. . .]

Under corporatist or organised capitalism, the state was expansive and interventionist, even in the USA. . . . [Its growth] led to the emergence of three political strata: a bureaucratic-political elite that controlled the distribution of state resources and established privileged access to consumption; a less autonomous and privileged category of public service workers; and a lower stratum of state-dependent citizens. Similarly, monopoly capitalism restructured classes into three parallel strata: company executives and senior managers; white-collar and primary-sector manual workers; and marginalised labour, often manual service labour. Together, the public and private sector hierarchies tended toward horizontal integration into three blocs: (i) a bureaucratic-political-managerial elite (BPME) comprising those holding a disproportionate share of power in the organisations that dominate society (called the 'power elite' by Mills 1959, the 'service class' by Renner 1978 and Goldthorpe 1982); (ii) an 'incorporated (or middle) mass' of public and private sector white-collar workers and primary labour-market manual workers, receiving an approximate balance of rewards and exploitations, and contributing its loyalty, its labour and its taxes to the state-organised system through factionalised mass parties and labour organisations; (iii) and a marginalised, exploited and ghettoised, 'excluded mass' (or 'underclass') of state dependents and marginalised employees, especially including women and members of ethnic and racial minorities, that, to a considerable degree, stood outside the system of political authority and support. [. . .]

From command to convention

In the current historical configuration, the pattern of state-articulated blocs is breaking down. Nowhere has the failure and dismantling of the state been as pronounced as in the statist societies of Russia and East Europe. But we will concentrate upon the breakdown of the Western corporatist state configuration which has undergone an internally generated 'crisis of the state' that parallels the internally generated crisis of private capitalism that occurred at the end of the nineteenth century. Crook *et al.* (1992:92–4) gives as causes: (i) the escalation and elaboration of demands from claimant groups that do not have marketable capacities beyond the ability of the state to meet them; (ii) an increasing impersonality of power that obscures the locus of responsibility; (iii) the cultivation of political support by educational enhancement that in turn leads to a popular focus on post-materialist values that stand opposed to the state; (iv) the development of administrative systems to the point where they consume more resources than are delivered to claimants; and (v) the disruption of the market by regulative measures designed precisely to ameliorate its failures.

As a result the state is losing its force, its functions and its effectivity in three directions (cf. Crook *et al.* 1992:97–104): (i) it is being decentralised to more autonomous localities and ethnically homogeneous regions; (ii) it is being aggregated with other states at a regional or global level; (iii) it is experiencing the differentiating effects of marketisation and privatisation.

(i) As the state declines as a central focus of meaning and management, blocs and parties are decomposing. The challenge to the BPME and the incorporated mass is primarily cultural. The BPME accomplished its legitimacy by means of technical credentialism and ideology – it ruled because of merit or breeding. This legitimacy has been challenged by the rise of the status-group known as 'yuppies' (Lash 1990:18–25), a challenge that was precisely cultural in character. Yuppies used post-modernist culture to elevate elements of mass culture to elite status and to widen and massify the audience for elite cultural performances. We have an emerging 'post-culture' of choice and variability in which no particular configuration can claim privileged status. This cultural switch occurred at the same time as the organisational base of the BPME began to break down with the attenuation of the state and moves towards downscaling in the industrial sector.

Equally the incorporated mass has been subjected to internal differentiation but here on the basis of ascriptive characteristics. It has traditionally been organised around the political and economic participation of male breadwinners. This political solidarity has been attacked by the emergence of the claims of minorities excluded by gender, age, or ethnicity. Male industrial and white-collar workers have retreated to become just another status group, focused on maximising consumption, rather than a leading element in a consensus between blocs. In many societies their party political allegiances have therefore shifted to the right. Furthermore, the general focus on consumption has decollectivised individual consciousnesses and induced an unwillingness to engage in interest-group action. Behind these indicators lies an emerging distrust of party politics and a decline in bloc solidarity. This decline in bloc solidarity is most evident in interest-group formation among private-sector manual workers. The level of unionisation (the proportion of the labour force that is unionised) is declining in most Western societies as is the level of strike action. In the USA labour unions have virtually disappeared as a factor in public life.

The success of the working class in invading the state under a command stratification order was eventually, then, to pave the way for its own marginalisation. It had succeeded in institutionalising that set of universalistic practices called citizenship (Marshall 1973). Originally these had applied to the core sector of male workers who were members of charter ethnic groups. However, citizenship institutionalises equality of opportunity and therefore allowed claims from outside this core. We have therefore witnessed the emergence of collective action based on gender, age, ethnicity, race, sexual preference and physical disability. These collective actors are cultural communities, temporary alliances of people with common character- istics that transcend their specifically social milieux and that are linked to each other by identity, or perhaps by mass-mediated images.

The emerging vehicles for collective action are the new social movements. New social movements can be distinguished from traditional political parties in so far as they stand opposed to the state rather than seeking to capture it, and from 'old' social movements in so far as they stand opposed to the corporatist-bureaucratic-technicist (i.e. state-centred) value paradigm. Rather they adopt non-organised methods that seek to raise consciousness by the mass mediation of value positions that are highly universalistic, pro-human, and rights-oriented. The rise and impact of these new social movements, which include civil rights, ecological, peace and feminist movements, in the West since 1960, has been little short of spectacular. In Europe, active support for them stands at about 20 per cent of the population while public sympathy stands at 60 per cent (Crook *et al*. 1992:141), levels which can only be the envy of the traditional political parties. Moreover they have forced a shift in the public-policy arena away from issues of interest articulation and towards universalised value-issues.

The decline of the state entails a general liberation of stratification from social-structural milieux so that it becomes precisely cultural rather than social, focusing on life style rather than life chances, on consumption rather than production, and on values rather than interests. The emerging pattern of stratification will be fluid and shifting as commitments, tastes and fashions change. It will approximate a multiple mosaic of status communities rather than a small number of enclosed social capsules. Membership of any community will depend not on a person's location in systems of production or control but on status accomplishments, patterns of social worth, established in the spheres of value-commitment, the control of symbolic resources, location in circuits of discourse, and sumptuary behaviour. This pattern of membership will be contingent on mass participation, activism and access to cultural resources as well as to display and profligacy in the consumption of material products.

Such status formations will often be the equivalent of what Anderson (1983) describes as imagined communities. They will involve neither an actuality of shared situation nor dense interpersonal networks but will be established through mass communications and the mass media. Mass mediated simulations are vehicles that allow people who have never met to regard themselves as members of communities with common ascriptive characteristics, or political concerns, or consumption tastes, that is to have a sense of fellowship and shared identity. The literature on 'post-modernism' and 'post-modernisation' emphasises the way in which status symbols dominate patterns of inequality: 'Within "consumer society", the notion of status, as the criterion which defines social being, tends increasingly to simplify and to coincide with the notion of "social standing". Yet "social standing" is also measured in relation to power, authority and responsibility. . . . What is specific to our society is that other systems of recognition (*reconnaissance*) are progressively withdrawing, primarily to the advantage of the code of "social standing"' (Baudrillard, 1988:19). Equally Featherstone emphasises the cultural dimension: 'We are moving towards a society without fixed status groups in which the adoption of styles of life . . . which are fixed to specific groups have been surpassed. This apparent movement towards a post-modern consumer culture . . . would further suggest the irrelevance of social division and ultimately the end of the social as a significant reference point' (1987:55–6).

These conventional communities need carefully to be distinguished from earlier forms of status arrangement. They are not legally or religiously determined as in the case of estates and castes, nor are they ascribed like gender or ethnicity, nor indeed are they similar to 'socio-economic status' which might be regarded as the cultural or communal aspect of classes of blocs. Rather they are distinctly elective and communitarian and their effect is to destabilise and disintegrate these more 'determined' cultural arrangements. The process can be illustrated by reference to two of the most apparent of such arrangements, ethnicity and gender.

In class societies ethnicity was vigorously denied by both the dominant economic classes: by the bourgeoisie because it could threaten the centrality of commodified relationships, and by the working class because it was divisive. (Marx, for example, dismisses the historical significance of ethnic groups as '[R]emains of national-ities, mercilessly trampled on by history' (cited in Parkin 1979:31)). In command societies, ethnicity was reorganised and politicised. The only valid ethnicity was that which coincided with the nation-state. Alternative ethnicities were subjected to assimilation, integration, suppression, forced emigration or even genocide. However, under the current transformation ethnicity is returning as a new power that is helping to undermine both class and state. This is most manifest in the ex-statist societies formerly known as Czechoslovakia, the German Democratic Republic, Yugoslavia and the USSR. Here state formation is being subordinated to ethnic allegiances, as well as to value-commitments in relation to market democracy. However, the cohesion of Western European states is under similar threat from ethnic nationalities in, for example, Catalonia, Euskadi, Flanders, Lombardy, Scotland and Ulster. Third-world states are also frequently vulnerable to ethnic conflict.

Transformations in gender status follow a similar pattern (Brenner and Ramas 1984, Waters 1989). In class societies women are excluded from the production relationships that determine class membership and confined to a domestic sphere. In command societies, social and cultural reproduction is regarded as rather too important an activity to be left to the individual decisions of families and organised by the state as 'health, education and welfare.' Under current circumstances, however, gender is taking on an altogether more elective quality so that the distinction between what is masculine and what is feminine is becoming blurred – gender can not be read from occupation or from the domestic division of labour in the way that it once could. More importantly the genders are becoming more internally differentiated by sexual preference, career orientation, child-bearing pattern, and so on.

We can now return to the general issue of how culture can undermine state and class. Mass action and the mobilisation of public opinion through the mass media effectively can tame the state. States can no longer rely on stable political support deriving from milieux and therefore must cultivate it. Similar processes can be inspected in the economy. As a consequence of what is called 'post-Fordism' and 'flexible specialisation' managerial and labouring functions are becoming reintegrated, confounding traditional industrial distinctions (e.g. Kern and Schumann 1984). Industry is becoming 'culturalised', focusing on decision, discretion, knowledge and information, rather than on technology, bureaucracy and control.

Conclusion: the future of stratification

Is it possible to specify a general trend that runs through these processes? The most suggestive analysis is Beck's notion of the detraditionalisation of industrialism. Beck argues that what we have heretofore described as modern society is in fact post-feudal, it retains traditional components including the ascriptions of gender and kinship roles and, more relevantly, class cultures and solidarities. On this argument, if industrialism were truly modern, class identity would not be secure and class membership would not be reproducible across generations. For him the class system is experiencing a surge of individualisation manifested in mass unemployment, industrial restructuring and deskilling. These force people 'to choose between different options, including to which group or subculture one wants to be identified with' (1992:88). Contemporary society is beset by parallel process of individualisation and societalisation. The former is manifested in the fact that the individual becomes the unit of the social reproduction of inequality, the latter in an increasing tendency for individuals to join cause in the pursuit of 'new socio-cultural commonalities' (1992:90). The outcome is his paradoxical 'individualised society of employees'.

The above discussion of status-conventional society should indicate that, while the general thrust of Beck's argument is correct, society should be viewed as increasingly composed of ephemeral but communitarian status groups rather than total individuals. The force of detraditionalisation might be better expressed as the 'perfectional-isation of the market'. We are generally rather too quick in assuming that Marx's statements about the commodification of labour or Weber's that classes are phenomena of the market means that access to social rewards had indeed been completely marketised with the onset of capitalism. All that these statements meant was that markets had been initiated but not that they were in any sense perfect. The subsequent shift from class to command diminishes still further the force of the property barrier in access to social rewards. Mobility chances were dramatically increased by the long chains of administrative and managerial command established in large-scale organisations. (Of course, it did become possible to monopolise what Wright has called 'organisational assets' but the distribution of such assets was much wider than under owner-managed bourgeois capitalism.)

In the emerging status order, however, abilities, performances and value commitments receive a reward determined by the cultural economy and are not embedded in closed arrangements. The effects of ascription and habitus are progressively separated from life styles, value-commitments, consumption patterns, patterns of discourse, and group memberships. These are now becoming a free-floating currency of social stratification that is displacing both property and the capacity to command. This pattern promises to develop even further as informatic linkages become more intensive and extensive, opening up new possibilities of communication and group formation. In a society in which discourse was instantaneously available with any other inhabitant of the planet the force of status communities would be overwhelming. Thus, the emerging status-conventional society emphasises the choice, flexibility, openness and variability that many have associated with a post-modern culture.

Note

1. Abridged. Originally published as 'Succession in the Stratification System: A Contribution to the "Death of Class Debate"'. *International Sociology*, 9:3 1994. An earlier version under the title 'From Class to Party to Status' was presented to a conference on *Class Status and Party at the Fin de Siècle* at the University of Leicester, England, 9–11 July 1993. Earlier versions have also been presented in the Sociology Discipline, Flinders University of South Australia, and in the Research School of Social Sciences, Australian National University. This paper is part of a research project on *The Death of Class* being undertaken at the University of Tasmania and ANU in conjunction with Jan Pakulski and Gary Marks. I am grateful to many colleagues for comments but particularly to Jan Pakulski and David Lockwood.

Part Two

British Sociology and Class Analysis

Class structure, class position and class action

As we noted in the Introduction, attention to class and debates about it are especially significant in British sociology and its prominence has sometimes been taken as a demonstration of the peculiarity of British society rather than the salience of class analysis to the wider discipline of sociology. Most British scholars would, however, have rejected that view until recently. The appearance in 1989 of Pahl's lively and polemic essay in the relatively esoteric pages of the *International Journal of Urban and Regional Research*, however, encouraged a vigorous debate in which a surprising number of well known figures have also been prepared to challenge the British orthodoxy and 'mainstream' class analysts have felt themselves on the defensive. The strength of feeling may reflect the defence of careers and professional identity, but a more likely explanation is the political situation in Britain itself as Thatcherite administrations introduced a more abrasive form of social order and forced the Labour Party, whose problems have always influenced British class analysis, into a revisionist look at its soul.

As the papers reprinted here show, the British debate has been more focused on a specific range of issues than that contained in Part One of this book. Pahl's original discussion set out from the problem of class explanation, albeit in a rather sweeping way (and even though it hinted, in a passage not reproduced here, at a number of substantive post-modernist themes). The major thrust of Pahl's arguments does seem to be to attempting to move beyond traditional distinctions between structure and action in social theory and to redirect class analysis along the general theoretical lines advocated by Giddens in his theory of 'structuration'. The work and statements of the historian E. P. Thompson are cited as embodying the same ethos.

Pahl's article attracted a swift rebuttal (Marshall 1991) and this, together with Pahl's brief reply (1991) stimulated lively discussions at subsequent conferences and seminars. We reprint here the celebrated defence of class analysis by Goldthorpe and Marshall which appeared in 1992, in *Sociology*, the main journal of the British Sociological Association, together with a reply in the same journal by Pahl.

After denying any links with – in effect – the 'strong' propositions of Marxist class theory, Goldthorpe and Marshall's arguments appear simply to be about the substantive issue of whether class exists in contemporary societies or not. However, these authors are writing from a view of sociology and social research method which views the locus of an explanation to be in its power as a predictor of empirical associations as revealed by quantitative data. They thus write from a position of hostility to the purely conceptual agonisings about class to be found in some of the other chapters of the book. Pahl's response, in fact, is to charge Goldthorpe and Marshall with proposing a class analysis that has no theory of class at all.

Between that reply and Scott's commentary on the exchange we have interposed an essay by Rosemary Crompton on class and gender which is highly pertinent. Crompton also opts for a strategy of abandoning the structure/action distinction altogether. Her chapter begins with a review of feminist critiques of class analysis and of the long-running parallel controversy in British sociology about the allocation of women to classes in the class schema used by Goldthorpe and Marshall. Offering her own typology of different levels of class analysis, she argues, contrary to an earlier position, that the gendered nature of social practices is such that it has to be built into the very conceptualisation of class at *all* levels.

Scott's commentary seeks to combine the issues in this debate into a general defence of Weber's original class theory and in particular his separation between the analysis of class position and *social* class analysis. With this distinction much of the altercation about theory in class analysis can, he thinks, be resolved. Likewise, the debate about the unit of analysis in class research – whether it be the individual or the household – can be resolved in the same way. Scott therefore rejects Crompton's conclusions.

CHAPTER 6

Is the emperor naked? Some questions on the adequacy of sociological theory[1]

Ray Pahl

There is in sociology a too-frequently used structure-consciousness-action theoretical chain which starts from the material and existential circumstances of people in specific contexts, moves through a common awareness of the exploitation or disadvantage inherent in such contexts, and leads on to forms of social action which would, finally, achieve the removal, amelioration or diversion of the offending social institution, oppressive relations or whatever. The essence of this chain of social action is summed up by the mantra:

Structure → Consciousness → Action (SCA).

The basic idea is that there is something *inherent* in the social and economic circumstances of categories or, even more usually, *classes* of people that leads them, apparently with deterministic logic, to acquire a radical consciousness of their oppressed, deprived or exploited situation. Once such a consciousness takes a hold, the assumption is that it becomes a force for change (rather than, say, a fatalistic resignation) and this force manifests itself in political or violent action leading to social changes which then lead to the removal of the conditions that initially caused the distress. It is a model that is based on the collective organisation of power from below, whereby subordinated classes or categories usurp the power or decisions of superordinates. 'Consciousness' appears as an intervening variable in the model and should not necessarily be assumed to be completely determined by structure in a mechanistic manner. Yet the links in the chain are rarely seen as problematic.

In what follows I will argue that the missing links in the chain of structure, consciousness and action have not been found and that in particular, class as a concept is ceasing to do any work in sociology. Clearly I intend to provoke argument and to stimulate debate: my intention is to be critical yet constructive. Lest some assume that it is only sociology that feeds on its own self-doubts, I think it is encouraging to see that other disciplines are showing signs of questioning conceptual categories they had previously taken for granted. In the field of economics, for example, some recent internal criticisms appear to me to be absolutely devastating. Lester Thurow's (1983) demolition of economists' theories of the labour market seems to me so convincing that I find it hard to see how it is possible to continue to write about labour markets as if nothing has changed. In what follows, I make a start on doing the same for sociology as Thurow has done for economics. Emperors who have no clothes (or at least far fewer than they assume) should say so before the little boys notice. . . . I make no apologies for my polemical stance.

Structure, consciousness and action in class analysis

The SCA model is used at a number of levels – explicitly or implicitly. In recent urban analysis, for example, it has been applied to groups of squatters, gays, single parents, people living close to industrial plants emitting high levels of toxic waste and, indeed, any social group or category in specific urban or rural environments that feels that it is being oppressed, discriminated against or put upon in some way. Analysts of 'urban social movements' that 'emerge' from these situations often evoke SCA as a way of 'theorising' their descriptive accounts. But they do so usually implicitly, for as Pickvance (1977) has reminded us, the mechanisms and processes whereby as 'social bases' the squatters, the polluted, etc. turn into a 'social force' (that is an urban 'social movement' of some sort) are highly complex and these are not made clear by the analyses in question. Their authors rarely do comparative studies of apparently similar social bases or localised disadvantaged populations elsewhere, in order to enquire into the specific circumstances or processes that transform those in one context into a social force, while those in another remain stewing in their oppressors' noxious juices or whatever. Such studies as have been carried out in the urban context tend to emphasise idiosyncratic factors – such as a particularly able administrator or charismatic political leader whose presence activated those in one context only, who then benefit arbitrarily in comparison with those equally deprived elsewhere. Thus we are no further forward in our understanding of the links between S, C and A.

The flexibility of the model, however, also allows it to be applied at the level of the nation-state – for example, when the 'working class' in a given social formation is expected to take history into its own hands and move from common consciousness to revolutionary action. The model can also be applied to groups of nations such as the European Community, OECD or OPEC and, indeed, to the 'communist bloc' and the third world. Here differences within social formations are assumed to be over-ridden by differences between them, but at this level of abstraction the detailed processes transforming social forces into social action have become so soggy that anyone with an agile mind can bend them to suit a diversity of purposes. However, the model is less often invoked to account for top-down revolutions (USSR today?) or social change originating at the top of the social structure ('Thatcher's Britain'?). The assumption is that S produces C more readily among the powerless than the powerful but it is not clear why this should be so. The SCA model has acquired a tradition of romanticising the underdog and neglecting the interests of and cleavages in the dominant class. However, to be fair, this is simply a tradition and is not inherent in the model *per se*. It is arguable that consciousness of structural position is more easily perceived by those in dominant positions.

Those who implicitly or explicitly use this model rarely recognise that the links in the chain S–C–A have not been adequately theorised. The model is seen as unproblematical when, as Lockwood (1981) has shown, it is based on notions of a theory of action which, in practice, does not exist and also indicates that Marx, from whom the model derives, had an inadequately formulated theory of action.

Class: new research and old dogmas

Doubts and difficulties in relation to the SCA model have been explored in the sociological literature over the past decade. (Some of the most useful contributions – including the Lockwood article – have been published in Rose 1988.) As a result the concept of class has also come under serious scrutiny by a number of authors, particularly by certain feminist critics in such a way as to cast doubt on its unproblematic use as a key explanatory variable.

As Marshall and his colleagues (1988) show, it is very difficult to devise a single set of class categories which can accommodate the models and assumptions of diverse practitioners in the field. E. O. Wright in America and John Goldthorpe in the UK have both laboured long and hard to devise a scheme which might have some general validity. They have each produced a plausible set of categories for their respective countries but, sadly, they do not appear to be congruent. Fifteen per cent of Wright's managers and supervisors are classed as routine manual and non-manual employees by Goldthorpe. Marshall *et al*. (1988) note that there is 'considerable disagreement between the two classifications' and they conclude that 'the two schemes are simply incommensurable' (p. 27). It is odd that they did not expect to find this. Of course both Goldthorpe and Wright will claim that they had different purposes in mind and so there is no reason why their schemas should coincide. There can be no 'true' number of classes: the actual number put forward in any given analysis will depend on the problem that is being addressed.

Sadly, empirical researchers do not always specify their problems before they go seeking for classes. Those who wish to make the concept of class do some work for them would presumably like to fit it into the SCA model by using it to define the S. It is of little analytical value to report that poor people are working-class, when poverty is a fundamental defining element of the social class category itself. There is evidently considerable danger of circular reasoning so that socio-economic conditions produce 'classes' which are then used as an explanation of the same socio-economic conditions. Analytical distinctions related to a putative class structure are of interest only if such distinctions lead to greater understanding. The reason why sociologists concern themselves with embourgeoisement or proletarianisation is not because they are concerned simply with refining a classificatory scheme, but because these social processes, if they exist, are assumed to lead to significant social change through evolutionary or revolutionary processes. Hence, what matters is not whether there are shifts in occupational prestige or in the distribution of earnings and wealth but how such putative shifts work out in terms of consciousness and action.

We inevitably return to the familiar SCA model. Sociologists who busy themselves with allocating individuals, households, occupations or distinctive employment relations into categories or who attempt to measure the inter- and intra-generational flows between such categories are stuck at the stage of analysing structure, the S of the model, which may or may not have consequences for consciousness and action.

There is a general assumption that those with poorer access to socio-economic resources prefer to vote for a political party that will offer them more and those who are, or who perceive themselves to be, better-advantaged will attempt to hold on to what they have or what they think they have. Political sociologists have for long taken this simple notion as the basic foundation of class-based politics. However, many argue that in a society that perceives itself to be richer, such a division is becoming less significant in comparison with particularistic goals and values based on locality, race, religion, gender and nation. This evidently shifts the argument away from the categorisation of individuals, families and households by their attributes to a categorisation according to their attitudes and values. It would obviously be convenient if there were a congruence between the two, so that social attitudes could be read off from economic positions. Since that does not seem to work empirically, traditional class analysts are in more than a little trouble.

One way out of the difficulty is to impute false consciousness to those who for reasons of race, religion, gender, short-term affluence or whatever, fail to recognise their 'true' interests. The elitist and inside-dopester aspects of such theoretical tricks are now less acceptable in their social community than they once were, thanks to the clearer articulation of feminist, nationalist and other ideological positions. Failing such an escape route based on 'real' or 'latent' interests, investigators have been obliged to pay more attention to the notion of 'identity' or the way people actually report seeing themselves individually and collectively. This approach has led advertisers and market researchers to devise various typologies based on 'life styles', creating a large armoury of neologisms to reflect what they claim is a new social reality. The emphasis has shifted from groups to individuals, from classes to categories and from producers to consumers. People's market behaviour (their life styles) is said in a tautological way to define their market behaviour. Collectivities in the class war are replaced by individuals in an 'open market'. This shift in social imagery from the military to the market seems likely to affect the way that sociologists see the world: but it does not follow that the social world has changed as much as the language used to describe it. These shifts in language emphasise the links between life style and action and largely ignore structure altogether. Life style categories are based on clusters of common attitudes gathered from regular surveys. They are ad hoc and pragmatic and do not derive from any clear theoretical orientation but they seem to provide a better guide to what people will do with their money than categories based on socio-economic groupings. So market researchers have abandoned class for empirical, not theoretical reasons: it simply does not work. Clearly these life-styles categories are not useful in analysing deprivation which is directly related to poverty, but the market economy is, in any case, less interested in the poor. Those with money and access to credit are segmented according to market researchers' labels and these constructed life style types are self-perpetuating. If some people are encouraged to adopt a distinctive style of consumption as a way of presenting their particular identity they will have a vested interest in justifying and maintaining it, so the categories could be self-perpetuating once well enough established. However, there is also a need to develop new markets for new products and so there will be a tendency for putative innovators to undermine emerging identities based on life style and to establish new ones. Hence the typologies and categories may well be short-lived.

The relationship between these life-styles categories and political attitudes is unclear and the voting behaviour of those who perceive themselves to be not among the poorest can be expected to be volatile. In the traditional language, it is in the 'class interests' of employees – whether managers or manual workers – to get the best economic deal going. Yet to assume that certain categories (managers) will align with 'the interest of international capital' out of ideological commitment to capitalism is as naive a belief as to assume that others ('the workers') will oppose those interests because of an ideological commitment to the overthrow of the system. Such broad ideological commitments are likely in practice to be subordinated to the practical and pragmatic considerations of good access to health, housing, education and credit-based consumption of goods within a nation state. The relations of production are internationalised but the consumption of goods – wherever they were produced – is perceived to be a local or national matter. This would explain the importance of consumption interests as a force in electoral politics.

In summary, then, class as force for political and social change is problematic, since the links in the SCA chain are inadequately theorised and there is little empirical indication that the model has much relevance in practice. Secondly, as a classificatory device class does little to help us understand the life styles of the privileged and adds nothing to the brute facts of poverty when considering the other end of the social structure. Finally, it is apparently well-nigh impossible to operationalise the concept in order to make international comparisons.

Origins of the contemporary faith in the universal value of class in sociological explanation

A number of reasons may be adduced for the weak position of class as an explanatory tool in contemporary analysis. First, class analysis was developed by people in the UK in the nineteenth century when the concentration of manufacturing industry and the more transparent structure of the relations of production made the connections between a bourgeoisie and a proletariat more obvious and both state intervention and state employment were of negligible importance. Secondly, the nation state appeared to be a more coherent entity so that the prospect of seizing control of the state by a revolutionary class seemed rather an exciting and practical way of gaining substantial and lasting benefit for the ascendant class.

The empirical situation in the last few years of the twentieth century is evidently very different. When those employed in manufacturing industries decline to about one-fifth of the labour force the 'traditional' manual worker inevitably declined in numerical importance and new technical and service workers became an expanding proportion of the occupational structure. Of course these new categories, whatever their superficial status, even as managers of various sorts, may be just as subordinate to the needs of capital as their nineteenth-century forebears. However, it simply does not seem like that to them and such perceptions cannot be wiped away as so much false consciousness. A class model based on manufacturing is bound to fit rather uneasily on a services-based economy.

Furthermore, the globalisation of economic relations both economically through multi- and transnational corporations and politically through such organisations as the European Community have made the state a rather anachronistic arena in which the proletariat can struggle with the bourgeoisie. Any sensible national proletariat in Europe would do well to make solidaristic overtures to its opposite numbers in other countries if it wants to be more than a spectator in the creation of the 1992 unified market. The bourgeoisie, on the other hand, might have rather more to lose from the weakening of the state's control over its economic life. Alternatively the bourgeoisie might itself see greater advantages from international pacts and linkages, since they have more to gain from larger markets and access to cheaper labour. The exact balance sheet will probably vary from nation-state to nation-state. Given this uncertainty about where the natural arena for practical class activity might be, it is not surprising that other forms of identity and social consciousness are coming to have greater practical relevance.

Class as catch-all concept undermines its potential usefulness

I am not, of course, saying that we should forget about class: I am simply stating that if the concept does so little useful work for us we should cease behaving as if it does more. It is little good clinging to it in the naive belief that if we hold on to it hard enough it will eventually come to be of central analytical value once more. The statement that, for example, the mortality rate is higher for working-class people than for middle-class people is probably conflating a number of quite distinct processes that should be kept analytically distinct. The differences observed may be related to poor housing, inadequate diet, particular conditions of employment and a variety of other cultural and economic circumstances. Introducing class into the analysis suggests some advantage in social understanding which is spurious and misleading and reflects more than logic or reasons.

If the term class is used in the context of a theory of social change whereby consciousness develops and leads to action – a class in itself becoming a class for itself – then evidently we are back to the problem of the links in the SCA chain. If, on the other hand, we are using a class as a handy labelling device or proxy in order to make cross-national comparisons of disadvantage, then we return to an unsatisfactory and inconclusive argument about definitions. Finally, if we are concerned with ameliorating the lot of the disadvantaged in order to limit variations in mortality to age and gender alone – as is increasingly the case in Scandinavian countries – then we are not interested in slogans but need to understand the precise relations between income, housing conditions and so forth and the causes of death. The term 'class' adds nothing to our understanding at the empirical level since in both Scotland and Finland, say, those in similar class situations have, literally, different life chances.

It is a sad paradox that those on whose behalf the concept of class is most frequently invoked have the least opportunity and capacity to use it as a mobilising force. When, however, the interests of a powerful class fraction such as financiers or corporate oligarchies are affected, then such categories are very effective in mobilising their collective power through a variety of strategies. Certainly, they would strongly resist the suggestion that they were acting in class terms and would consider the use of the term unnecessary and probably offensive. Sociologists might again believe that they were adding something to the analysis by categorising the process in terms of class consciousness. However, it is again difficult to see what, specifically, is added to the analysis by so doing. The attempt by, say, city financiers to resist the intrusion of categories based on legal, political or industrial power that may wish to impose constraints or limits will be defended in other more or less specious terms: they will argue that the national interest is coterminous with their interests, that the basis of the attack or intrusion is misguided or misplaced and so forth. But this is unlikely to convince even the least sceptical of journalists. The sociologists' insistence in bringing class into the analysis raises expectations about what is to be gained from paying attention to such analysis which, if not satisfied, results in the scornful dismissal of the subject for being overcommitted to meaningless jargon.

Lest I be misunderstood, I must make it absolutely clear that nothing I have written so far should be taken to imply that capitalism does not produce a class society. The differences between castes, estates and classes are fundamental and comparative sociology will continue to be based on such distinctions. Modern capitalist society is based on an inherent conflict of interests between capital and labour and each in turn, is fractioned within itself. This I take to be axiomatic. My purpose in casting doubt on the practical usefulness of class is not to say that the concept does not have a value at a higher level of analysis in comparative and historical sociology. However, its frequent incantation is often misplaced and otiose and the concept has been debased through inappropriate and uncritical usage. My position is broadly similar to that put forward by E. P. Thompson a quarter of a century ago:

> Sociologists who have stopped the time-machine and, with a good deal of conceptual huffing and puffing have gone to the engine room to look, tell us that nowhere at all have they been able to locate and classify a class. They can only find a multitude of people with different occupations, incomes, status-hierarchies, and the rest. Of course they are right, since class is not this or that part of the machine, but the way the machine works once it is set in motion – not this interest and that interest, but the friction of interests – the movement itself, the heat, the thundering noise. Class is a social cultural formation (often finding institutional expression) which cannot be defined abstractly or in isolation, but only in terms of relationship with other classes: and ultimately the definition can only be made in the medium of time – that is, action and reaction, change and conflict . . . class itself is not a thing it is a happening. (Thompson 1965:357)

Theory in much sociological reporting is in danger of becoming a conventional appendage – rather like the Marxist-Leninist preamble to technical papers published by Soviet social scientists in the days before *glasnost* and *perestroika* [. . . .]

Does the foregoing imply that I have effectively argued out sociological theory from urban and regional analysis? I think not. Paradoxically I believe I have argued it back in. My contention has been that scholars have behaved as if the links in the SCA chain were self-evident. Once it is understood that such links have yet to be discovered an important programme of research designed to advance theoretical understanding can be opened up. From informal social networks through families, kinship links and the whole range of formal and informal associations of civil society people are engaging in voluntary solidaristic and collective activity for a variety of goals. These informal groupings and associations have played an important role in the recent political changes in the USSR and they remain a latent force in many countries where the traditional lines of political cleavage are crumbling (Yanitsky, forthcoming). Overwhelmingly these social groups are issue-oriented and territorially based.

Now whether these informal associations are the stuff out of which the links in the chain can be forged is hard to say. At present work on such associations, locality-based groups and networks is not directly focused to the theoretical lacunae in the SCA model. However, there is no reason why this should not be done. Perhaps in the responses to my provocation those working on these topics will be encouraged to make explicit their specific theoretical contributions to the body of social theory centring on the SCA and class mode of analysis. . . . Let us clad the Emperor.

Note

1. Extracted with abridgements from 'Is the Emperor Naked? Some Comments on the Adequacy of Social Theory in Urban and Regional Research', *International Journal of Urban and Regional Research*, 13:4:1989 709–20. I was initially stimulated to work on this issue by an article by David Lockwood (1981) focusing on the missing links in a chain of reasoning central to much work in the Marxian tradition. I am happy also to acknowledge my indebtedness to Anthony Giddens who has consistently addressed the central problematic of action and structure and has done more than most to resolve many of the difficulties through his formal theory of 'structuration'.

CHAPTER 7

The promising future of class analysis[1]

John H. Goldthorpe and Gordon Marshall

What are the prospects for class analysis? Of late, the enterprise has been widely dismissed as unconvincing and unproductive by prominent critics writing from a variety of different standpoints. Our own work has been a frequent target. In the present paper, however, our primary aim is not to reply to such charges on our own behalf, but rather to uphold the kind of class analysis that our work can be taken to represent – since it is our contention that its promise is far from exhausted.

The paper comprises two parts. In the first, we seek to clarify the nature and purpose of class analysis as we would understand it, and in particular to distinguish it from the class analysis of Marxist sociology. This is necessary because some critics – including Hindess (1987), Holton and Turner (1989), and Sørensen (1991) – have not, in our view, made this distinction adequately, while others, most notably Pahl (1989, Chapter 6 in this volume), have failed to make it at all. In addition, several instances can be noted of authors who, having lost faith in the Marxist class analysis that had once commanded their allegiance, or at least sympathy, now find evident difficulty in envisaging any other kind. Gorz (1982), Hobsbawm (1981), Bauman (1982), Lukes (1984), and Offe (1985) are obvious examples.

In the second part of the paper we then go on to make the case for the continuing relevance of class analysis, in our own conception of it, by reviewing findings from three central areas of current research. Here we seek to take issue more specifically with the assertions made by Pahl (above, p. 89) that, in modern societies, 'class as a concept is ceasing to do any useful work for sociology', and by Holton and Turner (1989:196) that we are now 'in a situation where the persistence of the class idiom is explicable in terms of the metaphorical character of class rhetoric than any clear intellectual persuasiveness.'

Class analysis, in our sense, has as its central concern the study of relationships among class structures, class mobility, class-based inequalities, and class-based action. More specifically, it explores the interconnections between positions defined by employment relations in labour markets and production units in different sectors of national economies; the processes through which individuals and their families are distributed and redistributed among these positions over time; and the consequences thereof for their life chances and for the social identities that they adopt and the social values and interests that they pursue. Understood in this way, class analysis does not entail a commitment to any particular theory of class but, rather, to a research programme – in, broadly, the sense of Lakatos (1970) – within which different, and indeed rival, theories may be formulated and then assessed in terms of their heuristic and explanatory performance.

It may be asked, and critics have indeed done so (see, for example, Holton and Turner 1989:173), why such a programme should be pursued in the first place. We would think the answer obvious enough. The programme is attractive in that it represents a specific way of investigating interconnections of the kind that have always engaged the sociological imagination: that is, between historically formed macrosocial structures, on the one hand, and, on the other, the everyday experience of individuals within their particular social milieux, together with the patterns of action that follow from this experience. These are precisely the sort of interconnections that, in Wright Mills's (1959) words, allow one to relate biography to history and 'personal troubles' to 'public issues'. From an analytical stand-point, the programme also promises economy of explanation: the ability to use a few well-defined concepts such as class position, class origins, class mobility or immobility, in order to explain a good deal both of what happens, or does not happen, to individuals across different aspects of their social lives and of how they subsequently respond.

But *a priori* there is only attraction and promise. Whether the research programme of class analysis proves worthwhile – is progressive rather than degenerative – must be decided by the results it produces. No assumption of the pre-eminence of class is involved. To the contrary, it is integral to the research programme that specific consideration should also be given to theories holding that class relations are in fact of diminishing importance for life chances and social action or that other relations and attributes – defined, for example, by income or consumption, status or life style, ethnicity or gender – are, or are becoming, of greater consequence.

It ought to be readily apparent that class analysis, thus conceived, differs significantly from the class analysis of Marxist sociology. Nevertheless, in polemicising against – or despairing of – the latter, several critics have evidently supposed that they were providing the quietus of class analysis *tout court*. Before proceeding further, therefore, we think it important to spell out four elements, in particular, that class analysis as we would understand it does *not* entail – although they are found in most Marxist versions.

First, our conception of class analysis entails no theory of history according to which class conflict serves as the engine of social change, so that at the crisis point of successive developmental stages a particular class (under capitalism the working class) takes on its 'mission' of transforming society through revolutionary action. Critics have tended to suggest that such a theory is actually or potentially present in class analysis *per se* (see e.g. Pahl Chapter 6 in this volume, Sørenson (1991: 73) and Hindess (1987:2–4) even claims to find a historicist position in *Social Mobility in Great Britain* Goldthorpe (1987: 28–9; cf. however, Heath *et al.* 1991:Ch. 5). But in fact, among those sociologists who have been actively engaged in what we would regard as the research programme of class analysis, a strong opposition to all such historicism, whether of a Marxist or a liberal inspiration, can be found – despite the fact that the programme is not one of a formally organised kind and there is room within it for significant areas of controversy (see, for example, Goldthorpe 1971, 1979, 1992, Korpi 1978, Marshall *et al.* 1988:Ch. 10, Esping-Anderson 1990:Ch. 1, Haller 1990). The emphasis is, rather, on the diversity of the developmental paths that nations have followed to modernity and on the very variable – because essentially contingent – nature of the part played in this respect by class formation and action.

Secondly, class analysis as we understand it implies no theory of class exploitation, according to which all class relations must be necessarily and exclusively antagonistic, and from which the objective basis for a 'critical' economics and sociology can be directly obtained. Although exponents of class analysis in our sense would certainly see conflict as being inherent within class relations, this does not require them to adhere to a labour theory of value, or indeed any other doctrine entailing exploitation as understood in Marxist discourse. Nor must they suppose, as is suggested by Sørensen (1991:73), that what is to the advantage of one class must always and entirely be to the disadvantage of another. In fact, much interest has of late centred on theoretical discussion of the conditions under which class relations may be better understood as a positive-sum (or negative-sum) rather than as a simple zero-sum game. And this interest has then been reflected in substantive studies in a concern with the part that may be played by 'class compromises' in, for example, labour relations or the development of national political economies and welfare states (cf. the papers collected in Goldthorpe (ed.) 1984b).

Furthermore, arguments advanced from a liberal stand-point, whether by functionalist sociologists or neo-classical economists, to the effect that class inequalities are, through various mechanisms, conducive to the greater welfare of all would be seen as calling for empirical investigation rather than mere ideological rejection. And, in turn, the results of such investigation would be recognised as directly relevant to any moral evaluation of class inequalities than might be made. In this regard, the influence of Marxist theories of exploitation would be surely far less than that of the 'difference principle', as formulated by Rawls (1972).

Thirdly, the version of class analysis that we would endorse takes in no theory of class-based collective action, according to which individuals holding similar positions within the class structure will thereby automatically develop a shared consciousness of their situation and will, in turn, be prompted to act together in the pursuit of their common class interests. In fact, awareness of developments in the general theory of collective action, from the time of Olson's crucial study onwards, has led those engaged in class analysis as a research programme effectively to reverse the traditional Marxist perspective. Instead of expecting class-based collective action to occur (and then having to resort to 'false consciousness' arguments when it does not), they have concentrated on establishing the quite special conditions that must apply before such action can be thought probable – because rational for the individuals concerned – even where shared interests are in fact recognised. Thus, when Pahl (above, pp. 89–94) represents class analysts as mindlessly repeating the 'mantra' of 'structure–consciousness–agency', with the links in the chain being 'rarely seen as problematic', this is in fact essentially the opposite of what has happened over the last decade or more.

In turn, we may add, the models of class-based collective action which critics such as Pahl or Holton and Turner operate are ones that recent work has largely transcended; that is, either the revolutionary 'storming-of-the-Winter-Palace' model, or the *gemeinschaftlich* model of working-class action based on the local solidarities of work-place or community. If a paradigm case of collective class action for 'post-Olson' analysis were to be given, it would surely have to be that of working classes under neo-corporatist political economies – for example the Swedish – which takes on a quite different, and indeed contrasting, character. Essentially, such action (or, some might wish to say, inaction) consists in workers accepting the participation of their union confederations in governmental policies of wage regulation, and in showing a class-wide solidarity by abstaining from the use of localised or sectional bargaining power, so that their leaders may pursue the more generalised working-class goals of full employment and redistributive social welfare policies, as a *quid pro quo* for wage restraint (see Pizzorno 1978, Stephens 1979, Korpi 1983, Goldthorpe 1984b, Scharpf 1984). From this new stand-point, then, the consciousness–agency link at least is radically rethought: class consciousness, to quote Elster's (1985:347) formulation, is 'the ability to overcome the free-rider problem in realising class interests'.

Finally, class analysis as we understand it does not embrace a reductionist theory of political action – collective or individual – according to which such action can be understood simply as the unmediated expression of class relations and the pursuit of structurally given class interests. At the same time as they have come to a much changed understanding of the consciousness-agency link, so also have many class analysts sought to move to a new view of the relationship between consciousness (or at least consciousness of interests) and structure, again under the influence of more theoretical developments (see, for example, Berger (ed.) 1981). What has been rejected is, precisely, the idea that an awareness of and concern with class interests follows directly and 'objectively' from class position.

Rather, the occupancy of class positions is seen as creating only potential interests, such as may also rise from various other structural locations. Whether, then, it is class, rather than other interests that individuals do in fact seek to realise, will depend in the first place on the social identities that they take up, since – to quote a maxim attributed to Pizzorno – 'identity precedes interest'. And although in the formation of such identities various social processes, for example, those of mobility, will be important, it is emphasised that for class interests to become the basis of political mobilisation, a crucial role must be played by political movements and parties themselves, through their ideologies, programmes and strategies (see Pizzorno 1978, Korpi 1983, Esping-Anderson 1985, Marshall *et al.* 1988:Ch. 7, Heath *et al.* 1991:Ch. 5).

Hindess (1987:Ch. 6) has insisted, with reference to some of the authors cited above, that non-Marxist, no less than Marxist, class analysis remains beset with problems of reductionism in its treatment of politics. However, his case is hardly convincing, since he merely asserts that the authors in question are led into reductionist positions, without anywhere attempting to demonstrate this either by quotation or specific reference. And, further, he offers no reason why non-Marxists, who have no theory of history as class struggle to defend, should be at all attracted to reductionism or have any difficulty in rejecting it outright. Although particular analyses may focus on the part that is played in class formation – or decomposition – by social rather than political processes, this in no way implies that the relevance of the latter is denied. Indeed, the authors to whom Hindess refers have all had occasion to emphasise the autonomy – even the primacy – of the political, as against what they would regard as undue 'sociologism'. (There is, for example, simply no warrant for his (1987:99) statement with respect to Esping-Anderson and Korpi (1984) that 'class interests are seen as objectively given in the structure of capitalist relations' and a diametrically opposing view is central to the argument of Esping-Anderson 1985.)

In the light of the foregoing disclaimers, class analysis in our sense may well then appear as a far more limited project, intellectually as well as politically, than in its Marxist form. And indeed in certain respects it is, most obviously in not deriving from or being directed by any one general theory of class, or in turn aspiring to form the basis of yet wider theories of society or history. To this extent, we would in fact concur with the conclusions reached by Wright (1989b:313–23) in the course of providing a comparison of Marxist and non-Marxist class analysis from the Marxist side. However, class analysis as we would wish to defend it has ambitions that lie in a different direction. While its proponents may adhere to different concepts and theories of class, they aim to put these to the test by pursuing issues of the kind posed at the start of this paper and through research of a methodological standard generally more adequate to their inherent difficulty than that previously undertaken. More specifically, if in the research programme of class analysis the leading concerns are those of examining the importance of class (relative to that of other factors) in shaping life chances and patterns of social action, and of seeking to trace any shifts in this respect that may occur over time, then a number of requirements in conceptualisation, data analysis and data collection alike must be met. Three such requirements at least call for attention here, both because of their inherent importance and because this would appear to have been often insufficiently appreciated by critics.

First, class concepts must be as sharply defined as is operationally feasible, in order to avoid any confounding of class with other factors of possible relevance. Holton argues (above, p. 32) that 'status elements' often enter into 'class discourse', but he gives little attention to efforts made over the last decade or so (from both Marxist and non-Marxist stand-points) to produce class concepts and categorisations of an analytically more satisfactory kind. Pahl (above, p. 91) notes such efforts on the part of Wright and of Goldthorpe but then seeks to devalue them since 'sadly, they do not appear to be congruent'. That this should be the case is, however, in itself neither surprising nor disturbing. What Pahl fails to recognise is that it is precisely a concern of class analysts to evaluate rival conceptual approaches, and that there are indeed sound procedures for so doing (see Marsh 1986, Marshall 1988, Marshall et al. 1988, Marshall and Rose 1990). Class analysts have an obvious interest in determining which categorisations are the most effective in displaying variation in dependent variables under examination – and in part because those who have sought to play down class effects have often drawn on results derived from categorisations that are least satisfactory in analytical and empirical terms alike. Pahl (above, pp. 92–3) here provides a good example, while also suggesting (1991:128), quite erroneously, that it makes little difference which approach is followed (for another instance see Saunders, 1990b:221).

A second requirement is that analyses should be undertaken that are of a genuinely multivariate character and that questions of causal 'texture' should be given careful consideration. For example, if it is contended that the explanatory power of class is waning and has been overtaken by that of, say, differences in consumption patterns or life styles, then such a claim obviously calls for multivariate analysis as the basis for its empirical assessment. It is notable, however, that although both Pahl (above, p. 92) and Holton and Turner (1989:185–92) address this issue – and, in Pahl's case, as if it were in fact already decided against class analysis – neither gives any serious consideration to results from studies in which relevant multivariate analyses have figured.

Again, Pahl in particular sets great store on the argument that the simple demonstration that associations exist between class and dependent variables 'is probably conflating a number of quite distinct processes that should be kept analytically distinct' (above, p. 95). But here he merely opens up a range of issues with which he is, apparently, not very familiar. One is that of just how far in any particular case it can actually be shown – as, say, by causal path analysis – that the effects of class are mediated through specified intervening variables. Another is that of the theoretical significance that should in any event be given to causal factors of a less and a more proximate kind. Contrary to what Pahl (1991:128) appears to believe, even the completely successful 'unpacking' of class in the way he envisages would not necessarily reduce its sociological importance. Thus, no one would suppose that the immediate causes of, for example, low educational attainment, voting Labour, and suffering from chronic bronchitis are all the same. But, in so far as a linkage can be traced back from each of the different sets of immediate causes involved to the location of individuals or families in (let us say) unskilled working-class positions, then the importance of class is enhanced rather than diminished. The pervasiveness of the influence of class is underlined.

A final requirement is that class analyses, and in turn the data on which they draw, must in some way or other incorporate a time dimension. Pahl (above, pp. 94–5) and Holton (above, pp. 34–7) both seek to argue that class is losing its explanatory force in consequence of various current trends of economic and social change: the decline of heavy and manufacturing industry and the rise of services, the break-up of 'traditional' working-class communities, the growth of 'household privatism', and so on. But in so doing they move on from some changes that are reasonably well-documented to others that are not; and, as regards class effects *per se*, they make no reference whatever to findings from cohort analyses or longitudinal or panel studies of the kind that would be necessary to give their position adequate empirical support. Rather, they could be said to provide a good illustration of 'the tendency towards dualistic historical thinking' against which Marshall *et al.* (1988:206) have explicitly warned: that is, a tendency 'whereby a communitarian and solidaristic proletariat of some bygone heyday of class antagonism is set against the atomised and consumer-oriented working class of today' – in a manner, however, that has little basis in either sociological or historical research.

Some illustrative results

In this second part of our paper we draw attention, albeit in a very summary way, to findings from three areas within the research programme of class analysis which, we would argue, any serious critique would need to address – and especially if its ultimate aim were to establish that class analysis no longer has a useful part to play in the study of modern societies. We will discuss in turn class mobility, class and education; and class and political partisanship.

Class mobility

To study social mobility within the context of a class structure, rather than, say, that of a status hierarchy, is a conceptual choice that must be made *a priori* (Goldthorpe 1985a). However, where this perspective has been taken, results have been produced that are of no little sociological significance.

For present purposes, what may chiefly be stressed is that, across diverse national settings, classes have been shown to display rather distinctive 'mobility characteristics' that is, in inflow perspective, in the homogeneity of the class origins of those individuals who make up their current membership; and in outflow perspective, in their degree of retentiveness or 'holding power', both over individual lifetimes and intergenerationally (Featherman and Selbee 1988, Featherman, Selbee and Mayer 1989, Mayer *et al.* 1989, Jonsson 1991b, Erikson and Goldthorpe 1992:Ch. 6). Thus, for example, the service classes, or salariats, of modern societies tend to be highly heterogeneous in their composition but tend also to have great retentiveness both intra- and inter-generationally. In comparison, working classes are more homogenous in composition, and farm classes far more so. Both these classes reveal; lower holding power, especially in inter-generational terms. In other classes, such as among the petty bourgeoisie and routine non-manual employees, the combinations of homogeneity and of work-life and inter-generational retentiveness are different again.

Such mobility characteristics can be shown to have a twofold origin. First, they reflect that classes – defined in terms of employment relations within different sectors of national economies – tend to follow rather distinctive trajectories, or 'natural histories', of growth or decline in relation to the structural development of these economies in a way that strata defined in terms of status or prestige do not. Secondly, they reflect the fact that different classes tend to be associated with specific 'propensities' for immobility or mobility independently of all structural effects. This last finding, it may be noted, is one made possible only by technical advances in the analysis of mobility tables, which have allowed the crucial conceptual distinction between 'absolute' and 'relative' rates to be drawn (cf. Hauser *et al.* 1975, Hauser 1978, Goldthorpe 1987).

That classes can be shown to display such distinctive mobility characteristics would then in itself suggest that they are capable of being defined in a way that is more than merely arbitrary, and that the 'boundary problems' which some critics have sought to highlight are a good deal more tractable than they seek to imply. Certainly, one may question the grounds of assertions such as that made by Holton (above, p. 33), that it is 'very hard to aggregate the multiplicity of class positions into categories, without having recourse to evaluative cultural criteria'. (Note that we are *not* here arguing in favour of the procedure, advocated by Breiger (1981) and others as essentially 'Weberian', whereby class boundaries are *actually determined* on the basis of mobility analyses. Whether or not this approach can claim any serious endorsement in Weber's work, it is, in our view, excessively empiricist and likely to lead to major interpretative problems.)

Furthermore, it is in terms of class mobility characteristics that class formation can be assessed at its basic 'demographic' level

(Goldthorpe 1987); that is, in terms of the extent and the nature of the association that exists between individuals or families and particular class positions over time. And this in turn may be seen as determining the potential for classes, as collectivities, also to develop distinctive subcultures and a 'capacity for socialisation', which are themselves the key prerequisites for class identities to be created (Featherman and Spenner 1990) even though, to repeat an earlier point, the importance of political factors must always be recognised as well. In other words, an approach is here provided, and is being actively pursued, for investigating processes of class formation, or decomposition, through systematic empirical inquiry. It is not supposed, in the manner of dogmatic Marxism, that class formation is in some way historically scheduled. But neither, in the manner of Pahl or Holton and Turner is it assumed that in modern societies class decomposition is a quite generalised phenomenon. And, as we have indicated, the evidence thus far produced does indeed point to the existence of a situation of a clearly more complex kind.

Class and education

The countervailing force that has most often been cited in arguments claiming that the influence of class on individual life chances is in decline is that of education. According to those theories of industrial society which could, in Holton and Turner's phrase, be seen as posing 'the challenge of liberalism' to class analysis, the very 'logic' of industrialism requires both that the provision of, and access to, education should steadily widen, and further that educational attainment should become the key determinant of success in economic life. In turn, then, it is expected that the association between class origins and educational attainment will weaken, while that between educational attainment and class destinations strengthens, and itself mediates (and legitimates) most of whatever association between class origins and destinations may continue to exist (see, for example, Kerr *et al*. 1960, Blau and Duncan 1967, Treiman 1970, Kerr 1983). In other words, there is a progressive movement away from a 'closed' class society towards a meritocratic society of a supposedly far more 'open' kind.

However, in the light of the research results that have so far accumulated, support for this liberal scenario can scarcely be thought impressive. Long-term changes in the interrelations between class and education of the kind envisaged turn out in most national societies to be scarcely, if at all, detectable (see especially Shavitt and Blossfeld (eds) 1992). Moreover, a further major problem is raised by another cross-nationally robust finding from the side of mobility research: namely, that relative rates of intergenerational class mobility typically show a high degree of temporal stability (Erikson and Goldthorpe 1992:Ch. 3). In the case of Britain, for example, at least four independent analyses have revealed little change at all in such rates over the course of the present century – and certainly none in the direction of greater fluidity (Goldthorpe 1987:Chs 3 and 9, Hope 1981, Macdonald and Ridge 1987, Marshall *et al.* 1988:Ch. 5). Thus, even if it could be established that social selection has become more meritocratic, there is little indication of this having had any effect in producing more equal class mobility chances.

In the British case, where research on this issue has been perhaps more extensive than elsewhere, it was initially suggested by Halsey (1977) that although some evidence of a 'tightening bond' between education and work-life success was apparent over the middle decades of the century, this had been offset by widening class differentials in educational attainment, accompanied by little or no reduction in the strength of the 'direct' effects (those not mediated via education) of class origins on class destinations. In the light of subsequent research based on more extensive longitudinal data and more refined analytical techniques, the claim of actually widening class differentials in education would seem difficult to uphold [Editorial note: see also Heath and Clifford, Chapter 16 in this volume]; and the issue has rather become that of whether these differentials have remained essentially unaltered or have in some respects shown a degree of narrowing (Heath and Clifford 1990, Jonsson and Mills 1993). Much turns on just how educational attainment is measured. But what then also emerges is greater doubt about the supposed secular tendency for educational attainment to become more important as a determinant of destination class. Increasing occupational selection by merit, at least in so far as this is defined by educational credentials, is not easy to discern (see Heath, Mills and Roberts 1991, and Jonsson 1991a for similar results for Sweden).

In sum, the evidence for education operating as a force of 'class abatement' remains slight. Rather, what is suggested by the research to which we have referred is that a high degree of resistance can be expected to any tendency favouring a reduction of class inequalities via 'meritocracy'. If education does become somewhat more important in determining work-life chances, then members of relatively advantaged classes will seek to use their superior resources in order to ensure that their children maintain a competitive edge in educational attainment; or, as Halsey (1977:184) puts it, 'ascriptive forces find ways of expressing themselves as "achievement".' Alternatively, and as seems perhaps the more likely occurrence, if class differentials in educational attainment are to some extent diminished, then within more advantaged classes family resources can be applied through other channels, in order to help children preserve their class prospects against the threat of meritocratic selection (see Marshall and Swift 1992). We do not, we would stress, seek to argue here that class inequalities can never be mitigated through changes in educational systems and their functioning: only that there is no reason to suppose, as liberal theorists would wish to do, that this is likely to occur as the automatic and benign outcome of social processes that are in some way inherent in the development of industrial societies. Indeed, among those who still believe that some association can be shown between industrialism and growing equality in educational attainment and relative mobility chances, the connection is now regarded as deriving not from developmental necessity but rather as the contingent outcome of a variety of factors including political ones. (See, e.g., Treiman and Yip 1989, Ganzeboom, Luijkx and Treiman 1989; though cf. Müller and Karle 1990, Jones 1991 and Erikson and Goldthorpe 1992).

Class and political partisanship

[. . .]

[**Editorial Note:** At this point in the original text of 'The Promising Future of Class Analysis' Goldthorpe and Marshall went on to discuss the third of the research areas which they thought should be addressed by those who wish to establish 'that class analysis no longer has a useful part to play in the study of modern societies' (p. 104 above), namely class and politics. A paper by John Goldthorpe, specially prepared for this volume, containing more up-to-date material and addressing itself particularly to the arguments of Clark and Lipset above appears below as Chapter 15. Goldthorpe and Marshall's original discussion has therefore been omitted here.]

Conclusion

We have sought in this paper to respond to recent critiques of class analysis on two principal grounds. First, we argued that critics have not adequately distinguished between class analysis in its Marxist versions and class analysis understood and engaged in as research programme. Various objections that may be powerfully raised against the former simply do not apply to the latter. This is scarcely surprising, given the extent to which class analysis viewed as a field of empirical sociological inquiry freed from entanglements with the philosophy of history and 'critical theory' did in fact develop as a reaction against Marxism. Secondly, we have attempted to show, by reference to three central topics, that the research programme of class analysis has in fact yielded results permitting a flat rejection of the claims of Pahl and of Holton and Turner that class as a concept no longer does useful work, and retains only a rhetorical and not a scientific value. In this connection it is worth noting that we have cited a large quantity of *recent* works exemplifying class analysis as we would understand it, which, for whatever reasons, received virtually no mention from these critics.

Finally, we may note that the two main lines of argument that we have pursued do in a sense converge. For Marxists, class analysis was the key to the understanding of long-term social change: class relations and specifically class conflict provided the engine of this change, and the study of their dynamics was crucial to obtaining the desired cognitive grasp on the movement of history. However, class analysis as a research programme is not only a quite different kind of intellectual undertaking from the class analysis of Marxism, but also generates results which give a new perspective on the substantive significance of class relations in contemporary society. A common theme in the research findings now accumulating is, as we have seen, that of the stability rather than the dynamism of class relations. What is revealed is a remarkable persistence of class-linked inequalities and of class-differentiated patterns of social action, even within periods of rapid change at the level of economic structure, social institutions, and political conjunctures. The disclosure of such stability – made possible largely by the advances in techniques of data analysis and in the construction of data sets to which we have referred – would in turn appear to carry two major implications. Most obviously, problems are created for liberal theorists of industrial society who would anticipate the more or less spontaneous 'withering away' of class, and of class analysis likewise. But at the same time the need is indicated for the theoretical concerns of proponents of class analysis to be radically reoriented. They must focus not on the explanation of social change via class relations, but rather on understanding the processes that underlie the profound resistance to change that such relations offer.

Note

1. Abridged. First published as 'The Promising Future of Class Analysis: a Response to Recent Critiques', *Sociology* 26:3, 1992:381–400. The authors wish to thank Geoff Evans, A. H. Halsey and Ray Pahl for helpful comments on an earlier draft of this paper.

CHAPTER 8

A reply to Goldthorpe and Marshall[1]
Ray Pahl

Does class analysis without class theory have a promising future? British sociology has a long tradition of pursuing the aim of linking an individual's life chances to clearly defined social locations. Merely showing an association between variables, however complex and rigorous the methodology employed, has not fitted well into that tradition. Sociologists in the tradition have maintained a conservative attachment to the categories they consider most significant. Thus class and educational achievement have a well-established provenance as acceptable categories to associate with various measures of an individual's life chances.

Those outside the discipline, uninhibited by conventional or theoretical scruples, have explored other variables. In a recent study of the variables associated with mortality two other variables – home ownership and access to a car were added to the two above variables favoured by sociologists. While there were clearly interactive effects, each variable had an effect on mortality partially independent of the others. It appeared that access to a car was the variable most positively correlated with lower mortality. The significance of car ownership was shown to be such that even among non-manual home-owners, those with two cars had lower mortality than those with one (Goldblatt 1990). However, even if these results were able to withstand the most robust methodological and statistical criticisms, few sociologists would be likely to desert their traditional loyalties. Results without theoretical underpinnings would be dismissed as mindless empiricism.

However, if I decided that I wanted to counter an international network of researchers developing a programme focused on car ownership with an alternative proposal, aiming to establish a more promising programme based on height analysis, showing, among other things that taller people tended to reproduce themselves in the occupational structure, have better educational opportunities and vote in a similar way, so that the pattern of advantage of tall people was remarkably enduring but that, of course, I had no theoretical preconceptions, I would expect to get a hard time from sociologists. But Goldthorpe and Marshall do precisely this in their unconvincing defence of class analysis: they claim that 'No assumption of the pre-existence of class is involved' (p. 99 above). However, they acknowledge that they cannot be completely open-minded and 'class concepts must be sharply defined as is operationally feasible' (p. 103), in a context where 'Class analysts have an obvious interest in determining which categorisations are the most effective in displaying variation in the dependent variables under examination' (Ibid.). This then leads Goldthorpe and Marshall to rely heavily on statistical techniques. Such a retreat from class theory prompts me to respond to reinforce my earlier plea, echoing Goldthorpe himself, for the need to substitute critical for wishful thinking in class analysis.

It is important to stress that I wrote my polemical piece 'Is the Emperor Naked?' [. . .] to stimulate a debate among those researching urban and social movements who were accepting uncritically the idea that common consciousness, arising from given material conditions, produced given action – that is, an urban social movement. Many studies of social movements were weak in analysing and interpreting the process of mobilisation and, while Goldthorpe and Marshall are probably correct in seeing the battle long since won in mainstream sociological circles, my remarks still had force in the context in which I wrote them. I was astonished to find what a raw nerve I had touched. [. . .]

In their article Goldthorpe and Marshall present a united front but in earlier writings they appeared to be in some disagreement. It is not clear to me that these differences have been resolved. The ambiguities I find in their joint article depend in part on how, if at all, they have come to terms with these previous difficulties. To these I now turn.

Classes as demographic categories

In his well known study of social mobility, Goldthorpe's first step was to combine occupation and employment status and then allocate the agents thus defined into demographic categories (Goldthorpe *et al.* 1980). The manner in which Goldthorpe did this has been described by Marshall in such a way that implies Marshall is by no means completely convinced. He notes that Goldthorpe

> claims to have assigned an appropriate class standing to each combination of occupational title and employment status 'in the light of the available information from official statistics, monographic sources, etc. regarding the typical market and work situation of the individuals comprised: e.g. on levels and sources of income, other monetary and non-monetary benefits, degree of economic security, chances of economic advancement,

and location in systems of authority and control' (Goldthorpe and Payne 1986:21). In fact we are never shown the 'available evidence in question'. (Marshall 1990:59)

Goldthorpe constructed for his purposes seven demographic categories and then labelled them as classes. However, these 'classes' are not necessarily to be perceived as a hierarchy despite being set out on the page in such a way as to lead unwary readers to think otherwise. Goldthorpe claimed that these seven categories or lumps carry no theoretical implications in their labels: they could just as well be described as robins, linnets, crows, cuckoos and the rest. In his comment on these procedures Marshall acknowledges that

> Not surprisingly many people were (and continue to be) confused by the fact that . . . mobility was understood to go between 'Goldthorpe classes', categories which had no relation whatsoever to those of the earlier Hope–Goldthorpe scale. (Marshall 1990:55)

Goldthorpe apparently rejected using this scale because it did not suit his current job in the work programme. At that time Goldthorpe wanted to move the debate on from the individualist approach of Blau and Duncan (1967) and also wanted to improve upon Glass's distinction between structural and exchange mobility. He doubtless felt it would suit his research objectives better if he had these lumps – which he referred to as a structure – since in this way he could shift the focus from status to 'class'. Furthermore, at that stage, examination of the data apparently suggested that there was a patterning of inter-generational and career trajectories of Goldthorpe's men and their households and a lumpy model fitted that patterning better than a social continuum. This allowed Goldthorpe the opportunity to emphasise 'structural' constraints.

Now, evidently Goldthorpe makes much of the point that these lumps of distinctive work and market situation combinations appear to solidify and to contribute to occupational inheritance. From the point of his *theory*, as I have suggested, the labels given to the lumps are not particularly significant. Lumps exist. There is a social structure and, as they might say, the proof of the pudding is in the eating.

But why do these lumps endure? It is not convincing for Goldthorpe and Marshall to claim that they do because of class, because they make no commitment to any theory of class in their programme. They simply construct certain demographic categories, find that these categories work well for the goals of the programme and then, retrospectively, claim that the correlation or continuities constitute a theory. Such a procedure appears suspiciously like arguing that aggregates of employment relations account for the reproduction of employment relations.

Of course, *if* those in given aggregates of employment relations or lumps, called whatever you like, start to acquire a common consciousness as a result of their common position, then somebody might wish to argue that material conditions and forms of consciousness are related. But Goldthorpe and Marshall now firmly reject a theory of class-based collective action according to which individuals holding similar positions within the class structure will thereby automatically develop a shared consciousness of their situation and will, in turn, be prompted to act together in the pursuit of their common class interests. (p. 100 above).

In fairness to his followers, Goldthorpe ought perhaps to acknowledge more openly that he has changed his mind from the time when he asserted

Since the relationships they embody are ones in which interests and values come recurrently into opposition, class structures are seen as an inevitable source of social conflict which, in interaction with the processes of class formation and mobilisation – the emergence of class-based social-political movements – has served historically as a major vehicle of social change. (Goldthorpe, 1985:467)

I certainly would not wish to give the slightest impression that it is somehow reprehensible to change one's mind. [. . .] However, I find the 'Promising Future' paper hard to come to terms with, since the authors appear to be seeking a position which escapes all theoretical debates and to be concerned primarily with statistical and methodological rigour. By retreating to a 'far more limited project' (p. 102) which simply examines the importance of a constructed variable in relation to other variables, it is hard to see what can be argued about. To repeat what I wrote in my earlier article: I find it difficult to understand how class without theory can do useful theoretical work. When Goldthorpe and Marshall assert that to study mobility within the context of a class structure 'is a conceptual choice that must be made *a priori*' (pp. 104–5) it is not unreasonable for those interested in class as a theoretical concept to want to know more about how such a choice was made.

The authors give the impression of wanting to investigate class formation without the embarrassing trappings of 'dogmatic Marxism': 'an approach . . . is being actively pursued, for investigating processes of class formation, or decomposition, through systematic empirical enquiry' (p. 106 above). This seems to me to use 'systematic empirical inquiry' as a way of avoiding taking up any position in the theoretical debates about class. [. . .]

In the absence of any well articulated theory by the authors, why should they assume that the lumps they define are anything more than proxy indicators of highly complex processes of accumulation and reproduction of advantageous characteristics? The nature of current employment relations seem to be a rather tiny screen on which to project central concerns of sociological analysis. By refusing to theorise their proxy indicators they encourage me to direct my question to them more specifically: is the emperor naked?

Note

1. Selected with minor editorial revision from 'Does Class Analysis Without Class Theory Have a Promising Future?: a Reply to Goldthorpe and Marshall'. *Sociology* 27:2, May 1993. The author would like to thank those who generously found time to comment on earlier version of this paper and in particular to Rosemary Crompton, Jay Gershuny, Chris Pickvance and Peter Taylor-Gooby.

CHAPTER 9

Gender and class analysis[1]

Rosemary Crompton

Much of the sound and fury in the class analysis 'arena' has been caused by people talking past, rather than to each other (Crompton 1993). As I argued in an earlier discussion (Crompton 1989), many of the disagreements relating to class and gender in particular have taken place because of a failure to recognise the distinction between two different approaches to class analysis. On one hand there are relatively abstract theories in which 'classes' are seen as social forces having an impact upon historical developments (for example, as in the theoretical accounts of Marx and Weber). On the other, there are empirical investigations of class structuring, consciousness and action. Prominent within this empirical work are macro-level approaches in which the employed population (sometimes as individuals, sometimes with their families) is grouped into 'classes' according to their location within the structure of employment (what I and others now describe as the 'employment-aggregate' approach).

Abstract historically focused class analyses, I went on to argue, should not necessarily be criticised because of their lack of attention to gender. This is because they are theories relating to *class* rather than to gender as such. However, gender does present a problem for the 'employment-aggregate' approach, given that the structure of employment, upon which such analyses rest, is itself gendered. An apparent failure to recognise this fact had led to extensive criticisms from feminist theorists who had often linked the concepts of class and 'patriarchy' both in relation to history and to contemporary issues such as women's employment (Walby 1986).

It seemed appropriate to return to and revise my earlier concerns, however, in the light of developments in the areas of both class analysis and feminism. I have, in fact, chosen not to follow exactly the same structure of argument, although I shall be covering the same terrain.

It would be difficult to claim that the debate relating to class and gender has been very fruitful since the late 1980s. The position of some of the most prominent contributors to class analysis has been clarified to a considerable extent but the extent of the gulf between some versions of 'employment-aggregate' class analysis and more historical systemic, or processual, approaches to class analysis has become very apparent. The debates of the last few years might have been better understood, if not settled had the advocates of these different approaches recognised this and communicated with each other more effectively.

Feminist debates have moved on as well, albeit away from the terrain which they once occupied along with class analysis. Perhaps because of the retreat from class in sociology more generally, debates within feminism have tended to move away from materialist explanations focusing upon the impact of social structures, and towards a greater preoccupation with the individually and socially constructed nature of masculinities and femininities. I would readily concede – indeed I argued in 1989 – that masculinities and femininities are socially constructed. The concern here, however, is that in acknowledging this point, the significance of structural factors should not in any way be downgraded.

Class and gender in sociology

I will begin by summarising earlier debates. The area of class theory and analysis was one of the first towards which second-wave feminist critiques in sociology were directed (Barker and Allen 1976, Kuhn and Wolpe 1978). This was hardly surprising because until the mid 1980s class and stratification continued to be seen as central to sociology as a whole. However, despite the ferment of theoretical and empirical debate taking place at this time, it is possible with hindsight to recognise that there also existed within sociology considerable confusion relating to understandings of the concept of class, its operationalisation, and empirical investigation.

Until the end of the 1970s, much empirical work on social class in British sociology was taken to be broadly synonymous with studies of men's employment alone (Goldthorpe *et al.* 1969, Roberts *et al.* 1977, Goldthorpe 1987, Blackburn and Mann 1979; see also for the United States Blau and Duncan 1967). In assuming this stance, sociologists were uncritically reflecting the then dominant 'male breadwinner' assumptions relating to the gender division of labour. The 'male breadwinner' model reflected the fact that the development of capitalist industrialism was associated with a particular form of the gender division of labour. In Britain (and in many other countries including the USA), this incorporated the increasing exclusion of married women from the paid labour force together with the development of a particular ideology of 'separate spheres' of masculine and feminine activity (Davidoff 1986, Davidoff and Hall 1987). Women's sphere was that of the home and domestic labour; men's that of paid work and the market; so studies of 'class' focused upon men alone. Thus women's paid employment (if any) was seen as secondary as far as the economic fate of the household was concerned, and women's domestic work within the household was not taken into account at all (Stacey 1981).

However, from the 1970s feminists argued that the lack of attention given to women's domestic labour in the home effectively marginalised their productive contribution to society as a whole. By being treated as virtually invisible, the essential contribution of women was downgraded and treated as less valuable than that of men. Furthermore, the taken for granted 'male breadwinner' assumption seemed to be increasingly out of date given the increasing number of married women who were entering paid employment. It was further argued, therefore, that women should be given a 'class situation' in their own right, rather than being conventionally allocated to that of their nearest male breadwinner; that is, their own work, rather than that of their male partner, should be seen as determining their class situation (Acker 1973, Allen 1982, Stanworth 1984). However, the persistence of occupational segregation (that is, the concentration of men and women into different occupations) seemed to make it difficult, if not impossible, for a class scheme to be devised which is equally appropriate for men and women at the individual level.

Thus the employment-aggregate approach in particular was criticised as 'masculinist'. It was argued that it effectively ignores women's domestic work and denies women a place in the class structure by treating them as male appendages. It does so through the common practice of (a) taking the household to be the unit of class analysis, and (b) taking the class of the household unit to be that of the 'male' breadwinner. Both problems arise in connection with the two most influential programmes of employment-aggregate class analysis of recent years – those of John Goldthorpe and Erik Olin Wright.

Goldthorpe and Wright have both devised employment-based class schemes which they describe as 'relational' – that is, as reflecting the actualities of class relations rather than the commonsense categories of classifications such as those of the Registrar-General (Marshall 1988). Admittedly, Goldthorpe has denied that the construction of his class scheme has any theoretical antecedents (Goldthorpe and Marshall Chapter 7 this volume) but in fact two elements contributed to the location of occupations within the initial version: employment status (whether employed, self-employed, an employee, etc.) and the 'market' and 'work' situation characteristic of the occupation. Goldthorpe's scheme, therefore, has often been described as 'neo-Weberian', following Weber's equation of 'class situation' with 'market situation'. (Another significant influence was Lockwood's *Black Coated Worker* (Lockwood 1958.) This approach treats the occupational order as gender neutral, disregarding occupational segregation. However, there are a number of well-known examples of occupations in which the 'market' situation (understood particularly with reference to the nature of the work, and promotion prospects) associated with an occupation depends crucially upon whether the incumbent is male or female. In such cases, it is argued that men and women cannot be said to share the same 'class' situation, even if they share the same occupational label. Clerical work, the most commonly occurring female occupation, is an obvious example here (Crompton and Jones 1984; for a feminist argument relating to the construction of clerical work as a gendered occupation, see Valli 1986). Goldthorpe's strategy thus appeared to be inappropriate.

The 'unit of analysis' problem derives from the apparently uncritical incorporation of women's subordination in the family within the framework of the 'conventional view'. As has already been noted, the initial (1970s) Nuffield surveys did not sample women except as wives, and the 'class position' of individual women was generally taken to be that of the most proximate male. Goldthorpe argued that this procedure was justified by the fact that the proper unit of class analysis was the household, and that the class position of the family was most reliably indicated by that of the male head of household. Feminist critics argued that this empirical strategy both obscured the contribution made by women within the household, and took into account neither the rapidly increasing levels of women's paid employment, nor the growing number of female-headed households.

In contrast to Goldthorpe, Wright's class scheme was explicitly grounded in Marxist theoretical principles. It was originally devised with reference to job content, and on this basis classified clerical jobs (and therefore the women who occupied them) in 'worker' positions. Furthermore, Wright's approach, in which the individual rather than the family is regarded as the unit of class analysis, might seem to be more appropriate as far as feminist criticisms are concerned. However, Wright's solution to the problem of the female domestic worker is in fact very similar to the strategy employed by Goldthorpe. Women not in paid employment, Wright argued, may be assigned a 'derived' class situation, that is, they take the class position of their 'male breadwinner' (Wright 1989a).

Although, therefore, Goldthorpe and Wright have often been taken to represent very different theoretical approaches to class analysis, there are a number of parallels in their work as far as their approach to gender is concerned. Both have focused upon the topic of women's political preferences, particularly as compared to those of their partners. Indeed, Erikson and Goldthorpe's (1992) defence of the household as the unit of analysis rests in large part upon the empirical finding that women's political attitudes are more closely associated with those of their male partner than their own occupation (or class). Wright argues that while gender is relevant for understanding and explaining the concrete lived experiences of people, it does not follow that gender should be incorporated into the abstract concept of class (Wright 1989a:291). This analytical separation of class and gender may be seen as part of a more general strategy, endorsed by Goldthorpe and Marshall (1992) within the employment-aggregate approach in which the continuing relevance of 'class' is demonstrated by the empirical evidence of 'class effects'.

Erikson and Goldthorpe (1992:Ch. 7) have demonstrated that as measured by the Goldthorpe class scheme, the pattern of women's relative rates of social mobility (i.e. social fluidity) closely parallels that of men. This demonstrates, they argue, that the impact of 'class' on occupational fate is similar for men and women. Thus the differential experiences of men and women in the labour market are a consequence of sex, rather than class, and their approach (including the use of an ostensibly 'gender-blind' class scheme) is justified. This stance closely parallels that of Wright and, interestingly, draws upon the same logic as the defence of abstract 'class theory' described in my own 1989 paper. That is, it is argued that as (employment-aggregate) class analysis is about class rather than gender, then it cannot be criticised for failing to give an account of gender-related phenomena.

Levels of class analysis

Although feminist criticisms have focused upon the division of labour between the sexes, together with the associated structure of employment, it is important to remember that the assumption that classes may themselves be adequately identified within the employment structure represents just one strategy within the sociology of 'class analysis' as a whole. Thus the 'employment-aggregate' approach can be located within the broader sociology of class and stratification as shown in Figure 9.1.

Figure 9.1 Levels of class analysis

LEVEL OF ANALYSIS	METHOD OF INVESTIGATION
(1) Class formation	Socio-historical analyses of change (e.g. Thompson 1968)
(2) Class placement in employment structures	Large data sets aggregating jobs (e.g. Goldthorpe 1987, Wright 1985)
(3) Class consciousness and action	Contemporary case studies of specific groups (e.g. Newby 1977, Savage *et al.* 1992)

What I have been calling employment-aggregate approaches (level 2) typically rest upon large sample surveys gathered at the national level. They proceed as we have seen by assigning individuals to positions within a 'class' scheme (most often on the basis of their job or occupation) and then aggregating these positions into an overall class structure. Wright and Goldthorpe are the best known examples of such work because they have gathered extensive survey data and analysed it with reference to their own sociologically informed 'class' schemes. However, this general strategy towards 'class' is widely employed, not least in empirical discussions of inequality employing 'intuitive' or 'commonsense' class schemes such as those of the Registrar-General (and it should be noted that feminist criticisms have also been directed at these 'intuitive' class schemes) (Marshall 1988, Crompton 1993; for an example of the latter see Reid 1981). In fact, the employment-aggregate approach to class analysis has been described as having become 'hegemonic' over the last decade (Savage *et al.* 1992, see also Cyba 1994). That is, it has been taken to be representative of 'class analysis' as a whole as is shown by the reaction to Pahl's critique (Chapter 7 in this volume).

However, within the wider framework of class analysis as a whole there are also studies of class formation (level 1), which have often been historical, charting the emergence and development of groups having particular characteristics within the capitalist division of labour – for example, Lockwood's (1958) examination of clerical workers in Britain, Renner (1953) on the development of the service class, Boltanski (1987) on the development of cadres in France, and so on. Much early work influenced by second-wave feminism was in fact similarly historical in its approach, recovering and rediscovering the role played by women as workers in both the public and private spheres during the transition to capitalist industrialism.

Studies of class consciousness and action (level 3) have often overlapped with level 1 style studies of particular occupational groups, but here a historical perspective has been complemented by contemporary empirical research – including, for example, quantitative survey analyses of the group in question (Newby 1977). For example, given the crucial location of the white-collar 'middle classes' within class theory, empirical research has often focused upon clerical, administrative, and managerial workers (Crompton and Jones 1984, Smith 1987).

Thus two major strands may be identified within empirical approaches to class and stratification analysis in sociology (Crompton 1993:110). One strand (level 2) has concentrated mainly upon the quantitative analysis of large data sets, the other (levels 1 and 3) is oriented more towards case study approaches using a variety of methods. These different approaches to class analysis in sociology are part of a broader discourse relating to 'class' within the social sciences. In my original paper this was described as a contrast between models of class processes in which structure and action are kept analytically separate (e.g. Dahrendorf) and those (such as Thompson 1968) in which the possibility of this analytical separation is denied (for a recent discussion see Joyce 1995). Some of the disagreements relating to gender and class have taken place as a consequence of the failure to recognise these variations.

In particular, for many of those interested in the exploration of the class/gender interface, a rigid separation of 'class' and 'gender' seemed increasingly inappropriate – particularly in respect of level 1 and level 3 (class formation, and class consciousness and action). The structure of paid work rests upon a complementary structure of unpaid work together with a division of labour which has been constituted on gender lines. Class formation in the employment sphere, therefore, is implicated with the gender division of labour in both the public and private spheres. Feminist sociologists wishing to explore the links between gender and class, therefore, have sought to explore the nature of the changing interaction of the public and the private which had been indicated by the growth of women's employment. The debates associated with the 'employment-aggregate' approach to class analysis did not seem particularly fruitful to those interested in these gender-related issues. The increase in the paid employment of married women and the changes in family dynamics associated with this increase (Leiulsfrud and Woodward 1987) was seen to be one of the major social changes which had taken place in Western Europe and the US since the Second World War. Nevertheless, the employment-aggregate tradition of 'class analysis' had little to say about these phenomena and indeed sought positively to distance itself from them (Erikson and Goldthorpe 1988).

To understand this confusion it is necessary to recognise that the employment-aggregate approach represents only one strand within the complex totality of class analysis. In particular, it is important to remember that although in contemporary societies employment is an invaluable proxy for class position, bundles of jobs and/or occupations are not 'classes' in a sociological sense. Both class formation, as well as class consciousness and action (i.e. levels 1 and 3), depend crucially upon organisations and processes which cannot be adequately investigated or grasped via macro level survey analyses alone. Households, communities and work-places – as well as trade unions, political parties, and other social movements – require analysis and investigation via quantitative and qualitative case studies and ethnographies, as well as sample surveys. In British sociology, there is an important tradition of this kind of empirical work – the 'Affluent Worker' studies of Goldthorpe, Lockwood et al.; Newby's research on agricultural workers; Hindess's work on local politics; Hill's study of dock workers; Crompton and Jones on clerical workers, and so on. This kind of work has emphasised the significance of processes of class formation, as well as the links which may or may not occur between such formations and class consciousness and action.

Such ethnographies and case studies of class formation, and of class consciousness and action, have demonstrated that in reality, class and gender processes are inextricably entwined, rather than separate phenomena. For example, feminist historians have described the manner in which the structuring of class and gender moved in parallel from the beginnings of industrialism; how the bourgeois wife was gradually transformed from a co-worker within the unit of domestic production into the refined and delicate 'angel in the house' (Davidoff and Hall 1987). Similarly, the twentieth century emergence of the 'service class' rested upon a particular structuring of the gender division of labour in both the public and private spheres (Crompton 1989). This *de facto* intertwining of class and gender appeared to conflict with the apparent insistence, within the employment aggregate approach, that class and gender should be (a) regarded as separate phenomena, and (b) that the class situation of women should be seen to reflect that of men.

Nevertheless, although it is possible to be critical of the distortions the employment-aggregate approach introduces into the study of the class/gender interface, it remains an essential element in the study of structured social inequality. I have argued elsewhere (Crompton 1993) that the regeneration of class and stratification analysis requires the re-integration of the three levels identified in Figure 9.1, together with the different methods they characteristically employ. In a similar vein, I would argue that the study of gendered inequality must grasp the same diversity. However, the nature of gender itself adds a further dimension to this complexity, and it is to these problems that we now turn.

Equality and 'difference'

'Equality' and 'difference' describe tensions which have always existed within feminism. If women are the equals of men, should they, therefore, attempt to pattern their activities on those of men as nearly as possible? Alternatively, should the differences between men and women be explicitly recognised – for example, in special protections for women as mothers. This tension between equality and difference has been a constant presence in feminist politics, and in policy developments influenced by feminist ideas (Bacchi 1990). The 'equality agenda' has been one of the major objectives of liberal feminism, and has sought to achieve, as far as possible, an androgenous 'sameness' with men. These objectives have sometimes come into conflict with those of 'welfare feminists', who in contrast have advocated special (or different) provisions for women.

The liberal feminist 'equality agenda' has sought to remove the structural constraints on women's capacities to act in the world. It has always been associated with 'emancipatory politics' (Giddens 1990). Thus it has concerned itself with the enfranchising of women, gaining women's access to higher-level educational institutions and professional training, equal pay and opportunities in employment, and so on. In short, its aim has been to achieve full 'citizenship' for women. The process of gaining equal rights and status for women has been a remarkably protracted one – in Britain, the Equal Pay Act was only brought onto the statute book in 1976, and full access to elite educational institutions (e.g. Oxbridge colleges) and professions came even later. However, in the West, in recent years the process of achieving a formal equality of opportunity for women has been virtually completed.

Nevertheless, despite the success of the 'equality agenda' – and its supposed implementation in the ex-state socialist countries – there remain persisting material differences between men and women. It has always been recognised that many of the institutions to which women have, through the equality agenda, struggled to gain access are themselves profoundly 'gendered' – that is, structured in ways which make indirect discrimination against women more than likely. This is particularly the case in respect of paid employment. The model of employment so painfully established in the 'first industrial nation' (and subsequently followed by others) was one of full-time work and unbroken employment patterns (Thompson 1964). The subsequent struggles of the working class not only reduced the length of the working day but also sought to gain a 'family wage' – that is, a wage sufficient to support a family without the wife having to engage in paid employment. With hindsight, this process might be described as one of patriarchal exclusion (Hartmann 1982), but there can be little doubt that for many of those involved, the family wage was seen as a gain for both men and women (Humphries 1984). Nevertheless, the increasing separation of women from market work and the identification of paid employment as masculine has had important consequences. Many of the rights and benefits accruing to 'citizens', for example, are available to citizen-employees, rather being universal entitlements (Pateman 1988). Even when women gain access to employment, however, marriage, motherhood and conventionally assigned domestic responsibilities often make it difficult for individual women to participate as full-time, lifetime, workers. This has been clearly demonstrated in the ex-state socialist countries. Full-time employment for women was seen as a national duty. However, the difficulties associated with the 'double burden' have meant that the broad contours of occupational, segregation by sex in the ex-state socialist countries were very similar to those of the capitalist West. Indeed, social science research during the era of state socialism indicated that for women (but not for men) domestic responsibilities made it difficult for them to undertake the further qualifications necessary to undertake upward occupational mobility, for example (Heitlinger 1979).

A concern with equality, therefore, has been associated with an emphasis upon the significance of structural constraints in determining the situation of women, and of the necessity for their removal. As discussed in the earlier version of this paper (1989), much of this debate, paralleling the then contemporary debates relating to class analysis, revolved around the possibility of the identification of a patriarchal mode of production, together with a 'system' of patriarchy and associated patriarchal institutions (Walby 1990).

However (and perhaps because of the persistence of gender inequalities despite the widespread removal of these constraints), recent feminist work in the West has developed more of a focus upon the exploration of the structuring of sexual difference. Much of this work has drawn upon cultural and psychological, rather than structural, explanations of the inequalities (differences) between men and women (e.g. Chodorow 1989, Pringle 1988). Indeed, the notion of 'difference' has been highly significant in political debates within feminism. Segal (1987) has argued that this reflects a growing essentialism within feminist politics: 'feminist analysis has moved towards a new emphasis on the inevitability of men's violence and competitive power-seeking . . . an apocalyptic feminism has appeared which portrays a Manichean struggle between female virtue and male vice, with ensuing catastrophe and doom unless "female" morality and values prevail' (p. ix). More seriously, one major outcome of the current focus upon 'difference' is that, as Maynard (1994) has argued, the move away from materialist models and social structural explanations within feminism has had an unfortunate tendency to obscure the persistence of gender hierarchies and inequalities between men and women.

In the study of the inequalities associated with gender, therefore, I would argue that we should neither deny these tensions and contradictions (i.e. between difference and equality-as-sameness), nor feel that we have to choose between them. However, we should develop a sensitivity to the way in which they are manifest in empirical approaches to gender inequality. An emphasis on the removal of structural and legal constraints on women will focus attention on the empirical outcomes following their removal. These outcomes will invariably be measured by the yardstick of sameness – that is, the extent to which the circumstances of women are the same as, or equal to, those of men. The investigation of the processes which have contributed to these outcomes, however, will inevitably emphasise the structuring of the differences between men and women.

A parallel may be drawn, therefore, between the *de facto* fragmentation of the sociology of class and stratification, and the potential for fragmentation in the study of gender inequality. The investigation of the processes of the formation and structuring of significant groups or 'classes', it has been argued, became separated from the study of the 'class' (or occupational) structure by macro-level survey researchers, and mutual incomprehension has been a consequence. In a parallel fashion, there is a danger that the necessary attention paid to and explanation of the processes of gender structuring might result in an excessive emphasis on difference (indeed versions of neo-essentialism would appear to characterise influential sections of feminist academia). As a consequence, 'gender' and associated sexualities sometimes seem to have become fluid and virtually undefinable within academic discourse. However, despite the psychological and cultural nuances of 'gender' and its representations, we should not forget that biological sex remains an essential indicator as far as empirical research into social and material inequalities between men and women are concerned. Direct male/female comparisons are the most useful guide we have if we wish to investigate the extent to which inequalities have been moderated.

In practice, therefore, it is necessary to work simultaneously with both equality and difference in approaching the subject of gender; women are both equal to, and different from, men. In particular, it has been argued that it is important to avoid a polarisation of the debate.

Masculinities and femininities are culturally and psychologically constructed and complete androgyny is unlikely ever to be achieved. At the same time, however, we should not forget that *structures count* and that they have a differential impact on men and women.

Discussion and conclusions

In the previous sections it has been argued first, that class and stratification analysis in Britain underwent a (largely unacknowledged) process of fragmentation of both level and empirical approach during the 1980s. This may be described, in brief, as being between on the one hand, the macro-level employment-aggregate approach, focusing mainly on class (or employment) structures, and on the other, macro and micro socio-historical studies, case studies, and ethnographies of the processes of class formation and consciousness. Second, it has been suggested that something of a parallel phenomenon has been taking place within feminist approaches to the study of gender difference and inequality. Perhaps because of the influence of then-popular Marxist and socialist feminist ideas, much empirical work in sociology influenced by 'second-wave' feminism had, up until the mid-1980s, tended to emphasise the significance of structural constraints and restrictions in explaining the inequalities between men and women – thus the 'equality agenda' was firmly linked to 'emancipatory politics'. However, recent work has tended to focus more upon the way in which the 'difference' between men and women is actively constructed, rather than structurally imposed. These shifts in academic discourse have had their parallels within policy debates – for example, within the language of Equal Opportunities there has been a shift from 'achieving equality' to 'valuing diversity'.

The value of diversity should not be denied. The problem – as feminists have always been aware – is that gender (and racial) differences are ordered hierarchically. Feminist theorists may have inverted this hierarchy in their claims as to the superiority of 'feminine' characteristics. However, the fact remains that 'masculine' characteristics – interpersonal detachment, rationality, attachment to the mechanisms of power and domination – are those which are most likely to be associated with material success. The celebration of 'difference', therefore, may result in the intensification of material inequalities.

Even though the 'women and occupational class' debate may not, on reflection, be seen to have been particularly fruitful, this does not mean that we should cease to explore the significance of the employment/gender interface for the structuring of material inequalities. Access to employment, both in general and more specifically, is central to any explanation of material inequalities between men and women. An increasing number of women are in paid work, but it is commonplace that the extent and type of paid work undertaken by women remains remarkably sensitive to the nature of their domestic situation (this is not the case as far as men are concerned) which is itself a consequence of the assumption that women will take a major share of domestic responsibilities.

Let us return, therefore, to the argument that: 'within the occupational structure, the impact of "class factors" cannot be isolated from gender, which is a central element in the structuring of occupations' (Crompton 1989: 582). This fact was held to constitute a serious problem as far as macro-level occupationally-based attempts to measure the 'class structure' (i.e. 'employment-aggregate' approach) – were concerned, given the problems of distinguishing between 'class' and 'gender' factors in the allocation of occupations to categories within class schemes. As we have seen, the two major practitioners of this approach – Goldthorpe and Wright – have subsequently argued that 'gender' and 'class' can and should be kept separate as far as their investigations are concerned. Logically, their arguments may be sustained, but the practical difficulties remain.

It would appear that, in any case, Wright's heroic attempt to construct a Marxist 'class map' has been successively wrecked upon the shoals of the complexities of the modern employment structure, and sunk in the quagmires of Marxist class theory (Wright 1990). Goldthorpe has continued to defend his position. However, this defence has incorporated above all an emphasis upon stability rather than change, and in taking this approach, significant developments within the occupational structure, such as the increase in the employment of women, have been disregarded. Thus his position has moved even further away from level 1 and level 3 approaches to 'class analysis'. As far as our sociological understandings of the gender/class interface are concerned, this is regrettable.

In contrast, therefore, I would conclude by emphasising the fluid and socially constructed nature of the occupational structure. It is not 'the unproblematic raw material upon which the investigators' class scheme may be imposed. It is an object of investigation, rather than a taken for granted starting point' (Crompton 1989:584). The implications of this stance are that we should focus upon the outcomes of the interaction of 'gender' and 'class' (or employment) factors, rather than attempting to maintain their separateness. The position taken here would argue that, as the boundaries between the 'public' and the 'private', together with their characteristic masculinities and femininities, are increasingly being eroded in the late twentieth century, so this should be reflected in our empirical sociology. This does not mean that we are witnessing 'the end' of class analysis, as some have suggested (e.g. Hall and Jaques 1989, Pahl 1989 – see Chapter 6 in this volume). Rather, it is being argued that the best way forward is to embrace a more flexible approach to the topic as a whole.

Note

1. Chapter specially written for this volume (Eds).

CHAPTER 10

Class analysis: Back to the future?[1]

John Scott

A Weberian programme of class analysis has been defended by Goldthorpe and Marshall in the face of their critics. Contrary to those who argue that class analysis has had its day, they argue that class remains a central structural feature of British society and that class analysis remains central to the sociological enterprise. Pahl's view is that their case is unproven and that if class analysis does, indeed, have a future, then its foundations must be built on firmer ground. Many of the points made by Pahl are, I believe, themselves unfounded, but he is correct to claim that the Weberian programme of class analysis is beset by theoretical problems that demand resolution. My aim in this paper is to highlight the most pressing problems and to suggest ways in which their resolution may be attempted. My argument is that the 'promising future' of class analysis can be achieved only if we go back to the very theoretical foundations of the Weberian programme.

The Weberian foundations

Central to the Weberian approach to class analysis is a distinction between 'class situation' and 'social class'. Although this distinction is not made explicit in Goldthorpe and Marshall's paper, it is fundamental to their argument. Their failure to discuss it explicitly has opened the way for Pahl's critical comments. Class situations (class positions or class locations) are specific 'causal components' in life chances, and Weber holds that 'the kind of chance in the *market* is the decisive moment which presents a common condition for the individual's fate' (1914:928). Goldthorpe and Marshall (see Chapter 7 in this volume) see class situation as involving the two dimensions of market situation and work situation, which are, in turn, defined through 'employment relations in labour markets and production units' (above, pp. 98–9).

There will be a complex kaleidoscope of such economically constituted class situations in any society, and when Weber seeks to discuss the use of class analysis in historical and comparative investigations he turns from class situations to social classes. Where economic class situations comprise specific causal components in life chances, social classes are actual social groupings that may, under certain conditions, form the basis of collective action. A social class, Weber argues, comprises 'the totality of those class situations within which individual and generational mobility is easy and typical' (1920:302). Social classes, then, are clusters of inter-linked economic class situations, and their boundaries can be identified from evidence on intra-generational and inter-generational social mobility, intermarriage, and informal interaction. For Goldthorpe and Marshall, social classes are defined by 'the processes through which individuals and families are distributed' among the various class situations. This conceptual distinction between class situation and social class allows them to argue that social class boundaries can be defined 'in a way that is more than merely arbitrary' (above, p. 105) by the use of sophisticated measures of 'absolute' and 'relative' mobility between class situations. Social class formation, then, is a 'demographic' process: social class boundaries are defined by 'the extent and the nature of the association that exists between individuals or families and particular class positions over time' (above, p. 106).

It is on this basis that Goldthorpe and Marshall have set out their defence of class analysis. They argue that recent criticisms have failed to undermine the research programme of class analysis, which

> explores the interconnections between positions defined by employment relations in labour markets and production units in different sectors of national economies; the processes through which individuals and families are distributed and redistributed among these positions over time; and the consequences thereof for their life-chances and for the social identities that they adopt and the social values and interests that they pursue. (above, pp. 98–9)

A retreat from class

Pahl (see Chapter 8 in this volume) takes no account of these theoretical points, explored in numerous previous publications by Goldthorpe and by Marshall, and he argues that Goldthorpe and Marshall have abandoned any attempt to outline a theoretical basis for their research programme. Central to his concern is the question of how we are to evaluate competing conceptions of class and how their explanatory merits can be compared with those of non-class factors. Pahl's initial objections to the Goldthorpe and Marshall argument are unconvincing. He cites with obvious disapproval what is, in fact, a strikingly uncontentious set of statements. Goldthorpe and Marshall had recognised that 'No assumption of the pre-existence of class is involved' in their work (above, p. 99). This means that in order to test whether class or some other factor is 'the most effective in displaying variation in dependent variables under examination' it is necessary that 'class concepts must be as sharply defined as is operationally feasible' (Goldthorpe and Marshall, above, pp. 99, 103; cited Pahl, above, p. 111). To Pahl this open-minded and sensible empirical approach is, apparently, unsatisfactory, and he sees it as a 'retreat from class theory' (above, p. 111). It is as if Pahl would prefer class analysts to prejudge the relevance of class analysis, to disregard effectiveness in explanation, and to adopt woolly and vague concepts.

The nub of Pahl's paper, however, is addressed to theoretical problems that he also identifies in the previous works of Goldthorpe (1987) and Marshall *et al.* (1988). His discussion of these problems is unfair in its claim that Goldthorpe and Marshall 'make no commitment to any theory of class' and that they 'simply construct certain demographic categories, find that these categories work well . . . and then, retrospectively claim that the correlation or continuities constitute a theory' (Pahl 1993:255–6). As I have already suggested, both writers have placed themselves firmly within the Weberian tradition, in terms of which class situations are constituted through the market and work situations that are defined by prevailing employment and property relations. Pahl is, nevertheless, correct to emphasise that both Goldthorpe and Marshall have, at crucial points, tended to retreat from any explicit theorising of their empirical results. They have sometimes, indeed, seemed to depart from their own theoretical foundations.

Marshall and his colleagues in the Essex study, for example, have quite properly *eschewed* any 'essentialism' in the definition of class, but their *disavowal* tended to negate their own theoretical foundations:

> Since we do not hold with essentialist definitions of class the most important question is, in our view, an empirical one. Which conception of social class best illuminates the nature of collective action, shared life-style and beliefs, and patterns of association? (1988:26)

This is, quite simply, to put the cart before the horse. We do not choose between competing concepts of class simply on the basis of their explanatory power. The task of the sociologist is not to shape definitions by explanatory power, but to arrive at theoretically grounded concepts and then to assess their explanatory power. The explicit strategy advocated by Marshall and his colleagues offers no basis for rejecting alternative definitions of class which might be without theoretical foundation. Nor is Goldthorpe completely immune to this theoretical retreat. When contrasting 'individual' and 'family' based approaches to class analysis, for example, he referred to the choice between the two being made on the grounds of predictive power. He claimed that 'a better prediction of an individual's situation . . . can be obtained if class position is taken as being determined by the employment of the male head of his or her household rather than by that of the individual himself or herself'

(1984b:494). This may or may not be the case, but it is almost entirely irrelevant to the *theoretical* definition of 'class'.

To take an example that is given by Pahl. If it could be shown that categorised measurements of height give a better predictive and explanatory purchase on life style and living conditions than do occupational categories, would Goldthorpe or Marshall reject market and work situation and re-define 'class' in terms of height categories? I think the obvious answer is 'no'. They would reject such a definition of class on strong and compelling theoretical grounds. They would argue that, whatever the explanatory power of the concept of 'height', its effects must be distinguished from those of class. If it turned out that class had less explanatory power than height, then so much the worse for class analysis. Any such empirical finding would, however, provide no grounds for the re-definition of class in terms of height simply in order to save the rhetoric of 'class' analysis. They may, however, also wish to claim that height was itself a proxy indicator for certain aspects of class situation. The life chances that derive from class situation might, for example, include forms of diet and other living conditions that encourage or discourage physical growth, and these advantages may be reproduced inter-generationally.

Some of the stated positions of Goldthorpe and Marshall seem to leave this kind of empirical re-definition of class as a possibility, and this has allowed Pahl to suggest that they have no theoretical basis for their arguments. In fact, Marshall and his colleagues do recognise some of the problems of their strong statement, and they add that they are not 'total relativists where social class is concerned. Our own concept of class . . . is itself theoretically derived' (1988:494). They do not, nevertheless, seem to appreciate the significance of the contradiction between the advocacy of a clear, theoretically derived concept of class and a research strategy that sees the choice between alternative concepts as being a purely empirical matter. Their statement obscures the perfectly valid point that the research programme of class analysis involves the comparison and testing of alternative theories of class 'in terms of their heuristic and explanatory performance' (Goldthorpe and Marshall, above, p. 99) only where these concepts are rooted in a theoretical framework of market, employment and production relations. Anything else is simply not a matter of 'class', unless the intention is to completely disavow any attempt at terminological and theoretical consistency.

The points made by Pahl, then, are not compelling, though he has usefully highlighted the ambiguity in the Weberian research programme. This ambiguity can, however, easily be resolved through a more explicit attention to the theoretical basis of the programme. The major difficulties for the argument of Goldthorpe and Marshall do not, in fact, lie in the areas identified by Pahl. They are to be found in the comments of a number of other critics who have reviewed work associated with the Weberian research programme. These problems concern the demographic formation of social classes from economic class situations, the individual and the family household as units of analysis, and the inter-connections of gender and class. I wish to argue that a sustained discussion of these problems will support a Weberian research programme, but only if its theoretical foundations remain at the centre of attention.

From class situations to social classes

I have shown that the distinction between 'class situation' and 'social class' is at the core of the Weberian approach to class analysis. It is striking, however, that so little attention has been given to the difficulties that stand in the way of operationalising the distinction. Social classes, it will be recalled, are demographically defined clusters of class situations among which mobility is 'easy and typical'. A research programme aimed at the identification of social class boundaries and the construction of a social class map ought, then, to use evidence on inter- and intra-generational occupational mobility, family formation and informal interaction among class situations. The clusters disclosed in such a demographic analysis would comprise the social classes. This strategy has not, however, been adopted in any of the studies undertaken by Goldthorpe, Marshall or their colleagues.

Goldthorpe's (1987) modelling of class situations in terms of 124 groups of 'occupational grading units', for example, was converted into his seven well-known social classes, but the conversion involved no explicit use of mobility data. Goldthorpe simply relies on his professional judgement about these matters. The exercise of professional judgement can, of course, be contested (Penn 1981), but Goldthorpe has very good reasons for adopting this strategy rather than using empirical data. Even with a data set as large as that used in the Nuffield study (10,309 male respondents), a 124-by-124 matrix of class situations will contain many cells with very small totals, and it would be difficult to draw any conclusions about significant demographic links between class situations. Results from such an analysis would be theoretically valid, but empirically unreliable. For this reason, Goldthorpe seems to have concluded that the appropriate procedure is to make an informed professional judgement about the boundaries of social classes and only then to seek a *post hoc* empirical justification by looking at mobility patterns among the social classes that are identified. (In his latest version (Goldthorpe 1985a) Goldthorpe has recognised eleven social classes instead of the original seven. The logic of his approach to the identification of social classes is identical.)

This is undoubtedly, from a theoretical standpoint, a second-best solution, but it is probably the only feasible one, given the scale of the resources that are typically available to social scientists. Unless work on the scale of the Nuffield study could be repeated with some regularity and with a sample many times larger, the ideal solution of a direct empirical examination of demographic processes is unattainable.[2] There is, then, nothing wrong with the exercise of professional judgement about social class boundaries, so long as it is recognised as a proxy for a direct empirical investigation and so long as an attempt is made to use appropriate demographic data to test the robustness of the identified boundaries. This aim can be achieved only if the theoretical basis of the distinction between class situation and social class is kept firmly in mind.

The important thing, then, is to understand the logic of what we ought to be doing and then to attempt the best implementation of the second best solution.

The individual and the family household

Central to much of the debate over women and class analysis has been the contrast between those, such as Goldthorpe (1983), who see the family as the unit of analysis in discussions of class, and those, such as Marshall *et al.* (1988) and Stanworth (1984), who see the individual as the unit. The debate has generated much heat, and it remains unresolved. This may reflect the rather paradoxical fact that *both* of these positions are, in certain respects, correct. I wish to argue that the individual is the basis for allocation to class situations, but the family household, as a demographic unit, is central to social class formation.

Goldthorpe has stated his own position with some force. The family household, he argues, is the unit of reward and fate within the stratification system, and the class position of family members depends upon that of the chief breadwinner. This is, he claims, because 'only certain family members, predominantly males, have, as a result of their labour market participation, what might be termed a directly determined position within the class structure' (1983:468). Other family members, and particularly women, have infrequent or limited participation in the labour market and make no independent contribution to family life chances. Social stratification concerns the fate of whole families, and the life chances of family members are 'derived' from the market and work situation of the 'head'.

The use of the term 'head' of family can, of course, be challenged, but Goldthorpe's usage of this term is to identify what he terms the 'chief breadwinner'. Also the terms 'family' and 'household' are not, of course, interchangeable. Goldthorpe uses the term 'family' throughout his analysis, assuming that non-nuclear family households and other types of households are unimportant. These variations are, in fact, of crucial importance to the demographic formation of social classes.

The real point to be made, however, applies whatever concept of household is used and concerns Goldthorpe's equivocation as to whether the class situation of the chief breadwinner is a *determinant* of household social class or merely an empirical *indicator* of it. Much of his analysis of data suggests the latter, but his explicit statements tend to imply the former. This ambiguity can be resolved only if the Weberian distinction between class situation and social class is taken seriously.

I have shown above that Weber sees class situations as pertaining to individuals: life chances are defined in relation to the individuals who enjoy them. When we are concerned with class situation, then, the 'individual method' of allocation must be used. The family household, however, is a demographic unit and its kinship patterns enter into the demographic constitution of social classes. When analysis is concerned with social classes, how are we to allocate specific individuals to a social class? Marshall *et al.* (1988) advocate the individual approach: if class situation depends upon individual involvement in the labour and capital markets, they argue, then we must also allocate individuals to social classes on the basis of their own class situation. This argument ignores the demographic aspects of class formation and is made possible by a devaluation of the distinction between class situation and social class.

The correct procedures must surely be to follow Marshall and his colleagues so far as the allocation of individuals to class situations is concerned, but to recognise that individuals are, at the same time, typically members of the families and households that form the units of social classes. As all members of a household contribute to its social class position, the ideal solution would be for demographic research to investigate intermarriage along with social mobility and for this to produce results that would specify the social class corresponding to each possible combination of class situations for all household members. This would involve a recognition of the issues addressed by Heath and Britten (1984) in their discussion of 'cross-class' families. It would recognise, however, that all family households are 'cross-class situation', but none are 'cross-social class'.

In practice, such research is not likely to be possible because of the difficulty of obtaining appropriate demographic data. Research must, once again, have resort to the second best solution of taking an *indicator* of household social class. It is necessary to use our professional judgement in order to decide upon an indicator of social class position that yields results that reliably conform to those that would be produced by a comprehensive analysis. It is in this light that the use of one person's occupation may serve as an indicator of the social class of all members of her or his household. Goldthorpe (1984), for example, has relaxed his initial argument about the male 'head' of a family household and has advocated Erikson's (1984) 'dominance' and 'worktime' measures 'as being among the possible ways' (Goldthorpe 1984:494) in which the family household approach could be operationalised. The class situation of the 'dominant' labour market participant in a household, Goldthorpe suggests, may be a reliable indicator of the social class of the whole family household. The use of this indicator must, however, be justified on empirical grounds, and this remains an unresolved task for class analysis. Whatever the outcome of the search for an indicator of social class, the theoretical foundations of the Weberian programme remain: individuals occupy class situations, but family households enter into the formation of social classes.

Gender and class

The debate over gender and class is, perhaps, the most important of all the issues raised in the Weberian programme. Central to this debate is the question of whether it is possible to separate 'gender' from 'class' variables. This question underlies much of the confusion between individual and family household approaches to class analysis. Indeed, Marshall and his colleagues use the interdependence of gender and class as one of the supporting arguments for their adoption of the individual approach to class allocation. They argue that 'class systems are structured by sex in ways that clearly affect the distribution of life-chances, class formation, and class action among both women and men alike' (1988:73).

The sphere of employment is not gender-neutral. Occupational segregation by gender results in the rewards of certain occupations being lower than others simply because they are regarded as 'women's work' – rewards are determined more by 'the nature of the likely incumbent' than by the technical content of the job (Crompton 1993:93, Scott 1986). Crompton's recent review of the relevance of this to class analysis concluded that existing schemes of occupational classification are unacceptable bases for the allocation of individuals to class situations as they fail to recognise the specific features of female employment (Crompton 1993:118). These schemes are not pure measures of the market and work situation of job occupants; they also reflect the social consequences of the personal attributes of the occupant herself or himself. This fact has led many to conclude that an awareness of the gendered nature of markets has to be built into our very conceptualisation of class.

Despite the obvious interdependence of gender and employment, I wish to argue that this conclusion is unfounded. Restrictions on the market as a result of the gendered nature of employment involve the intrusion of a *status* element into the operations of the market, and a Weberian programme of research should be based upon a clear conceptual distinction between class and status. Weber held that class situations 'will become most clearly efficacious when all other determinants of reciprocal relations are . . . eliminated in their significance' (1914:930). The fact that this 'elimination' has not taken place in a particular system of stratification is no reason to abandon the very conceptual distinction that allows us to understand the interdependence of gender and the market. In saying this, I am not, of course, holding that 'status' factors exhaust the relevance of gender to social stratification or that gender categories are 'status groups' (Lockwood 1986). The point is that the gendering of employment may be understood as reflecting status divisions rooted in gender. (The point cannot be developed here but the issues of class analysis that arise in relation to gender also arise in relation to age and ethnicity.)

The point is not to reject occupational classifications and what Crompton (1993) has called 'employment-based class', but to refine them. It is important that we try to analytically distinguish the elements of 'market' and 'work' situation from the gender and other status elements that modify them in particular circumstances. This task is not easy, as the gendering of employment is all-pervasive. Such processes can rarely, if ever, be observed in their pure form, but this is in the very nature of the Weberian methodology of the ideal type. Any judgement about the relative importance of class and status factors and about the role of market processes *per se* in the life chances of individuals may be difficult to make, but it is essential that it be attempted. Sociologists must make the analytical distinction of 'class situation' from 'status situation' and must use available evidence to seek valid and reliable ways of operationalising the distinction. That a distinction is difficult to make is no argument for abandoning it; it should be a spur to further attempts to refine it.

Conclusion

There is, indeed, a future for class analysis, and a way to steer through many of the debates that have beset stratification studies over the last decade or so, but the advance towards this future must be on the basis of a clear theoretical framework. Going back to the Weberian distinction between class situation and social class, I have argued, provides the securest basis for future advance. This theoretical framework is implicit – and often explicit – in the various works of Goldthorpe and Marshall, but their failure to pursue its conceptual implications has opened the way for critics of the Weberian programme and has meant that they have not provided compelling answers to their critics. I have tried to suggest the directions in which a Weberian programme of research must move in order to resolve its theoretical lacunae and to establish a firm empirical basis for class analysis.

Notes

1. Originally published as 'Class Analysis: Back to the Future'. *Sociology*, 28:3, 1994.
2. Even if it could be assumed that the data would be evenly spread across the cells of the matrix, an investigation of 124 class situations would require a sample of more than 300,000 to ensure 20 people in each cell. It would require a sample of more than three quarters of a million to ensure 50 people in each cell. As the existence of social classes would mean that the data were *not* spread evenly across the whole matrix, a much larger sample would be required for a properly grounded statistical analysis.

Part Three

Researching Class

Class research and class explanations

By this point in the book it should be clear that there is no real possibility of dismissing class research in sociology in principle and at a distance. To understand its limitations and strengths a thorough familiarity with the diverse types and findings of class analysis is required. The aim of the chapters in Part Three is to give significant examples of such work. Apart from their intrinsic informative value, what each of the chapters shows is that in practice the simple separation between 'strong' and 'weak' forms of class analysis breaks down. Most authors are working with an extremely complex and subtle understanding of 'class'.

In Chapter 11, John Westergaard, whose works are written from a broad empirically based Marxist perspective, achieves a sweeping survey of the extent of inequality in Great Britain. He argues, however, that a similarly detailed look at most other highly industrialised societies would come up with comparable findings. Nor should his work be simply thought of as merely describing economic inequality. His chapter is an impressive attempt to demonstrate that class relationships in fact take explanatory priority over other sources of division and that the critics of class analysis are themselves guilty of rather gross explanatory simplifications.

Whereas Westergaard works with a very broad definition of the term, however, John Scott in Chapter 12 focuses on class as (capital) 'ownership interest' in order to deal with the vitally important issue of exactly how economic power is structured in late-twentieth-century industrialism. He persuasively argues that there is no evidence at all for the thesis of the separation of ownership from control and that it, along with equally simplistic Marxist models should finally be laid to rest. In fact, there is considerable variability in patterns of capitalist development across the globe.

The need to abandon simple 'unilinear' theories of class and capitalism is also a theme of the extract from Myles and Turegun's review of comparative research on class. The early part of the original article from which it is taken covered similar terrain to Scott's chapter but in less detail. We take up their discussion at the point where it begins to look comparatively at several other pivotal issues in recent class analysis. These authors too are working with a conception of class that would lead away from a narrow 'positional' (in effect weak) view of class, arguing that such an approach has missed out on understanding the direction of socio-economic change.

In Chapter 14, Lydia Morris describes a case study in labour market analysis in particular focusing on unemployment and the so-called underclass. Given that 'market situation' figures so centrally in Weberian theory it is curious that few neo-Weberian class researchers have attempted labour market investigation of this sort. She disturbingly concludes that occupational class schemas are not very illuminating in the face of the complex factors behind long-term unemployment.

Chapters 15, 16 and 17 have all been specially written by members of Nuffield College, Oxford, England. All three authors work closely together and understand class as 'measured class situation' using the schema of class measurement devised by John Goldthorpe – whose name, as we noted in the Introduction, has become synonymous with neo-Weberian class analysis. Goldthorpe himself addresses the supposed decline of class-related voting, which, as he points out, many critics use rather misleadingly as an indicator of class identity. The catalyst to this paper was a reply by Clark and Lipset in *International Sociology* (Clark, Lipset and Rempel 1993) to the papers by Hout *et al.* reprinted above (Chapters 3 and 4). In it Clark, Lipset and Rempel repeated the claim of class dealignment in political behaviour and supported their views with a certain amount of fresh data. Goldthorpe uses an even wider range of comparative data to challenge their arguments. He concludes that the 'death of class' debate is about competing conceptions of social science rather than about socio-political realities. Anthony Heath and Peter Clifford describe the results of a new and up-to-date study of the trend in class differentials in education in Britain. Their paper illustrates well the sophisticated distinctions and techniques used in this style of data analysis and in particular the crucial distinction between relative and absolute class differentials. Lastly, Geoffrey Evans returns us to the guiding theme of class in a post-communist world. He addresses the question of the emergence of class in the former communist countries, presenting data from a large and unique sample drawn across nine countries.

CHAPTER 11

Class in Britain since 1979: Facts, theories and ideologies[1]

John Westergaard

This chapter is about a puzzle. On the one hand, the facts about class – in Britain and a number of other western countries – show that inequality has widened quite dramatically since about 1980. Yet, over just this same period, fashionable theories and influential ideologies have appeared to say almost the opposite. While rich and poor have grown further apart, both predominant ideology and social theory have set out to dismiss this; or to argue that it does not matter anyway. If we are to believe the commentators, politicians and academic theorists who have set this tone in current debate, class inequality has lost social, moral and political force.

I shall try to do three things. First, I want to challenge these class-denying theories and ideologies, by summarising the facts which weigh against them. Second, I want to untangle the false assumptions which go into those theories and which have helped, as I see it, to blind theory to fact. Third, I want to consider some of the social reasons and forces behind today's class-denying ideologies.

I shall concentrate on Britain, because I know Britain best, yet the USA could have served equally well. There too, divisions between poverty and wealth, concentrated power and widespread lack of power, have widened in recent years, as economic uncertainty has set in more deeply. Yet there, too, the place of class in social theory has become still smaller than ever in debates about theory, ideology and policy. Or I could have gone to the opposite end of the political range among western countries – to Sweden where only 10–15 years ago the leading question in both theory and politics turned on labour movement hopes to 'socialise' the national economy, and further to reduce class divisions. That debate seems rather a forgotten dream in Sweden now. Though the evidence suggests an incipient widening of inequalities, there too the current politico-economic climate tends to set class disparity aside. So my theme is at least western-wide, though I shall use Britain to illustrate it in detail.

I also need to make a preliminary comment about what I mean by 'class'. I take the term to signify a set of social divisions that arise from a society's economic organisation: from its arrangements for command over, and benefit from, the deployment of scarce resources. People, then, may be said to be in different classes in so far as they occupy – and generally continue to occupy – distinct and unequal places in that economic organisation. This in turn means places in the orders both of production and of distribution. I add the latter point to make clear that I am not concerned here with any subtleties of conceptual distinction between, say, Karl Marx and Max Weber. If Marx emphasised place in production, he was after all equally intent upon the effects in distribution – this by way of surplus appropriation versus labour exploitation. And if Weber emphasised place in distribution, when he wrote about the unequal 'life chances' of people in different classes, he also saw those inequalities as the result primarily of differences of place in production. Moreover, Marx and Weber shared in essence a crucial distinction between two aspects of class. This is the distinction between class as an economic category and class as a socio-political group: between what Marx (in *The Poverty of Philosophy*) saw as class-in-itself and class-for-itself. Though Weber coined no set terms for the distinction, he like Marx took the logic of class analysis to put identification of category by way of conditions in life before exploration of group formation to possible political effects. I shall do the same here.

In my conception, then, class structure is first of all a matter of people's circumstances in life as set by their unequal places in the economic order. In that sense class structure has recently hardened in Britain. Thereafter – but only thereafter – comes the question of whether, and how, this hardening of class–as–category may translate into political or quasi-political group divisions. It will be part of my argument that fashionable class-denying theory and ideology commits two errors, among others. It blurs the distinction between the two issues of economic category and of political group-formation. And it naively infers, from new complexities of political group formation, an erosion of economic-categorical class which is contrary to fact.

The historical background

In order to show just how contrary to fact this inference is, let me start with a short sketch of the history of class inequality in Britain: before the changes from the 1980s, and back to the 1940s. I take the 1940s to begin with, because that decade was a turning point. The Second World War and its end brought a new socio-political settlement, in Britain as in many other countries. Under first a coalition government, and then a Labour government which at the time met only limited resistance of principle from the Conservative opposition, policy was directed to 'social reconstruction'. This meant two things especially. One was Keynesian – guided public management of the economy, to help growth and to keep both business profits and labour employment high. The other was extensive reform of public welfare provision, which was intended to guarantee everybody a basic low-minimum income, even if unemployed, sick or retired; to give all children free schooling to the best level of their individual abilities, and help towards higher education for the most able; and, most radically perhaps, to make medical care a free public service for all citizens. Some bits and pieces were added to the reform package in the next three decades; a few were taken away; and, from around 1960 especially, governments of both main parties came on the whole to take a more active part in steering the economy, by way of attempted 'corporatist' co-operation with business and trade-union leaders, in the hope of sustaining economic growth while holding back price and wage inflation. As in other countries, the ups and downs in these three-cornered relationships between state, capital and labour made for tensions of class structure, and for disputes over shares in the national economic cake. But in Britain, at least, tripartite corporatism made for no significant and lasting new change; and the main features of the 'class compromise' of the 1940s stayed until the 1970s.

This was evident in the effects on patterns of class inequality. From the start, the pre-war shape of things was changed to give advantages to ordinary workers and the poor. Also, organised labour gained new muscle in the labour market, and more voice in public affairs. Extreme poverty became rarer – and also less visible – than before the war. Inequalities of real income between classes, and between different levels within classes, became smaller. However, this change of balance did not continue beyond the 1940s. Although assuming a new and more moderate shape than before the war, class inequalities were not significantly further compressed over the 1950s, 60s and 70s. (See in general Westergaard and Resler 1975.) By the mid-1970s ownership of private wealth was still highly concentrated with just 5 per cent of the adult population holding nearly 40 per cent of the full total and very much more of personally owned shares in business capital. (Central Statistical Office, *Social Trends* 22, HMSO, 1992:table 5.21.) Inequalities of real income overall, and between different class – and occupational – groups, stayed fairly steady in relative terms over these three decades; and taxation by itself did little to change the pattern, mainly because progressive income tax was countered by regressive tax in less direct forms. Welfare benefits did boost real incomes proportionately more for the poor than for the rich; but studies in 'rediscovery of poverty' from the 1960s on showed many people still living on the margins of, or even below, the officially guaranteed minimum level (Townsend 1979). And the reforms of educational provision – first in the 1940s, with a second set in the 1960s – proved, against all these continuing inequalities, to have little force to reduce class disparities of individual opportunity (Halsey *et al.* 1980, Goldthorpe 1987, Heath and Clifford this volume). Even differences in the risks of death between people of different classes stayed broadly constant in relative terms (Townsend and Davidson (eds) 1982).

The word 'relative' here is important. These thirty years or so were years, generally, of economic growth. Most people had some share in this growth and at all levels of the class structure found their conditions and chances in life improving in absolute terms. It is on this count especially that things have changed since about 1980. Economic growth has faltered; and the vulnerable British economy has suffered two long recessions in just over a decade. Meanwhile, class inequalities of condition in Britain have actually widened again with the result that in the last 10–15 years as a whole many people have been excluded from substantial shares in such economic growth as has still taken place.

The shift from about 1980: causes

There are two sets of immediate causes behind this dramatic change: economic on one hand and political on the other. The first set has involved a series of shifts in economic activity, world-wide and increasingly visible since the mid-1970s. Growth has become more uneven, both over time and across the globe. The older 'imperial' capitalist economies of the West have faced increasing challenge from Japanese, and now also from other East-to-South East Asian, business enterprise. Changes have accelerated in the pattern of division in production, and in markets for finance and services, for commodities and labour. Developments in the transnational organisation of capital have continued to outstrip, by far, the still largely nation-bound organisation of political and collective labour defences. Lastly, much of the world moved into a downward phase of the long-term cycle or 'wave' of economic activity from the mid – or late – 1970s and recovery is still uncertain (e.g. Tylecote 1992).

For many and complex reasons, the British economy has been particularly exposed to risk from all this. So, secondly, reactions in British politics and policy have shown a distinctively sharp edge of their own (despite the many parallels with developments in other Western countries). At the General Election of 1979, a government led from the radical right flank of the Conservative Party came to office – and has stayed. That is why my title sets 1979 as a watershed year. For the first time in some 35 years, there was now a government seriously and openly committed to challenging the socio-political 'class compromise' of the 1940s born of post-war social reconstruction.

The effects of this political sea-change on class structure proved stark. Government policy since 1979 has been directed to widening the scope for private business initiative in freed markets. The main means to this have included: legal curbs on trade union power; thinning out previous measures for protection of low-paid labour; deregulation in other forms; privatisation of once-public enterprises; reductions in direct taxation to foster initiative; and a general reliance on market competition for growth and for industrial discipline. Simultaneously, radical-right ministers and their advisers have sought to hold back public expenditure, especially for welfare provision (though, significantly, not to dismantle it wholesale); and to encourage private provision in such fields as housing and retirement pensions and to a degree also in medical care.

The consequence has been dramatically to sharpen the pattern of 'class as category', as policy has deliberately aimed to increase economic inequality. True, this has been an instrumental aim rather than an end-in-itself. The declared ends of the shift in policy have been to promote long-term economic growth; and to extend individual choice and personal responsibility. But increased disparity of earnings, profits, pensions, real incomes overall is explicitly accepted as a necessary means to those ends; and wealth is celebrated as a reward for successful personal business enterprise. What is rather surprising, however, is that apostles of this policy have at the same time anxiously tried to deny or ignore the harsher consequences for the many people who, by virtual necessity, have shared little or nothing from such success.

A good measure of these consequences is the distribution of real incomes. I will start with wages and salaries from full-time employment – for which detailed figures are available. They show that, from 1980 to 1990, earnings among the top tenth of white-collar employees rose in real terms by about 40 per cent. Increases were proportionately smaller for nearly every step down the pay-ladder: for manual as well as non-manual employees, for women as well as men. Even the best-paid tenth of blue-collar workers saw their real wages rise at only about half the top white-collar rate. Moreover, against the latter 40 per cent or so increase, the blue-collar median wage rose by little more than 10 per cent over the full ten years; while the poorest-paid tenth among blue-collar men gained hardly anything in real terms. (Calculations from basic data on weekly pay before tax in the official New Earnings Survey 1990, part A, table A.15.1. Retail Price Index, all items, used to convert 1980 pay figures to 1990 values.) These are plainly divisions by class in a very familiar sense; and the class gaps have widened right across the range.

Let me take next the distribution of gains and losses from changes in taxation together with changes in public welfare benefits. A comprehensive estimate for much the same period, here 1979 to 1989, shows some net gains for most households (Johnson and Stark 1989). But it shows no gains for many of those households with only basic state pensions or unemployment benefit to live on; and these, of course, are people who were generally at low levels of the labour market when, earlier, they did have work. By contrast, of the aggregate net gain from changes in tax and public welfare over the ten years, nearly half the total (46 per cent) went to just the richest tenth of all households. Most of the rest went to those in the next few deciles down. And the entire 60 per cent of households from above 'middle income' to the very poorest got, between them all, only a 20 per cent share in this distribution of the proceeds from re-gearing of the public money system. One-fifth only to the poor and middling three-fifths together, little short of half to the one-in-ten best-off – this, or something like it, is a recurrent pattern of experience over the past decade and more.

Now put all this, and also property-incomes, together to get a picture of what has happened to shares in real income from all sources. Estimates differ somewhat according to details of the mode of calculation; yet the broad results are now incontestable. From 1979 to 1991 real incomes rose by over 60 per cent among households in the top-decile income bracket, and by more than 40 per cent for the next best-off 10 per cent of households (ministerial answer to parliamentary question, *Independent*, 11.10.1993). But the gains became steadily smaller lower down the scale. Even in the decile bracket just below mid-point, real incomes increased by only a little over a fifth during the 12 years; and among the poorest 10–20 per cent gains were marginal at best, or real incomes actually fell (Department of Social Security 1993; see also Townsend 1991, and Jenkins 1991). So two facts stand out. First, there has been a sharp new polarisation of incomes. The share of the poorest one-in-five households in all income fell from 10 per cent in the late 1970s to 7 per cent in the late 1980s. The share of the richest one-in-five grew from 37 per cent to 44 per cent: now over six times the share of the poorest, and this after adjustment for difference in household composition (*Social Trends* 1992:table 5.19). It is perhaps not surprising, then, that there has been evidence also of some widening of relative class differences in death rates over the period (Whitehead 1987). Secondly, however, it was not just the poorest who lost out. Substantial growth of affluence has been limited to people at or near the top. At least right up to 'middle incomes', gains in real income were small; and for all but the richest, shares in the total of real income fell. The point is important for a matter I shall come to later.

A second test of my argument concerns the distribution of property. Here, you might have expected some trend the other way, for government policy has favoured wider ownership of housing, and some wider ownership of shares in business through sale of previously public enterprises. But no: overall, stakes in private property of all kinds have in fact become more concentrated; not less (*Social Trends* 1992: table 5.21). So, for example, the richest 5 per cent of the adult population owned 36 per cent of all personal marketable wealth at the beginning of the 1980s; at the end of the 1980s their share was up to 38 per cent, and excluding the value of housing their share rose from 45 per cent (at the turning point of a previous downward trend) to 53 per cent by 1989 [. . . .][2]

So much for a summary of the recent hardening of class inequality in Britain. Behind these trends lies a shift in the structure of class power and class politics, which I shall discuss later. But let me first consider those shifts of current sociological theory and perception which claim that class analysis has lost its point.

Controversies about the social salience of class

The theme of class and its wide ramifications has long been central to British sociology; and work in this and related fields has constituted a major British input into progress of the discipline internationally. However, criticism of the salience given to class in British social enquiry is not a wholly new phenomenon. The 1950s-to-1960s speculation about postulated 'embourgeoisement' was an earlier instance to similar effect and the stimulus was similar on both occasions. In the 1950s-to-1960s, as in the 1980s-to-1990s, the Labour Party as the formal standard-bearer of the working class had lost three or four elections in a row, and revisionist theorists and commentators drew a similar conclusion. If Labour loses votes, they argued, it must be because the working class is disappearing; and if the working class is disappearing, then class division must be dissolving. This conclusion is a simple inversion of vulgar Marxist determinism, which infers 'class for itself' directly from 'class in itself'. Counter-Marxist revisionism, just as vulgarly, infers a dissolution of 'class in itself' from what it takes to be a disappearance of 'class for itself'. Both, equally, confuse class as division by economic category with class as political-group mobilisation. Both are simplistic: one assumes that working-class radicalism must follow from working-class subordination; and the other assumes that lack of working-class radicalism must reflect a disappearance of working-class subordination.

But I cannot dismiss the new revisionism merely by making this conceptual point. I need to consider the arguments more closely and, above all, empirically. As surrounding chapters in this volume illustrate, the real question is whether or not class is fast losing salience because other divisions now override it; or because class now divides only an isolated minority of poor people from a mass majority of affluent people. The two kinds of argument overlap and intertwine. But I will nevertheless deal first with arguments that postulate new divisions which cut across class.

Some may, loosely, be described as 'demographic' in kind. It has been argued, for example, that division by age is now a more important source of economic inequality than division by class. In particular, so it is said, old people make up a large proportion of the poor. True enough, over 40 per cent of the poorest one-in-five households in Britain, for example, comprise people retired from work (*Social Trends* 1992). But the conclusion does not follow. For one thing, from the 1980s (the crucial period for the purpose of the argument), the relative share of old people in poverty has actually fallen, not risen. This is, quite simply, because the new harsh labour market has swollen the aggregate numbers of unemployed and low-paid employed people who are now poor. But more importantly, old age by itself does not bring poverty anyway: it does so only in circumstances which are set by class structure. The people who risk being poor when they are old are those, by and large, who have retired from wage-earning jobs – in Britain, even from skilled jobs in blue-collar work, or from white-collar jobs in routine grades – because these jobs have given them few or no pension rights on top of the low minimum they get from the state. By contrast, people who retire from salaried careers get generous pensions; and their pensions, of course, are the higher, the nearer their careers came to the top of the occupational hierarchy. Pension arrangements remain, in fact, strongly class-divided (see e.g. Office of Population Censuses and Surveys, *General Household Survey* 1988, HMSO, 1990). Class inequality after working life matches – even tends to exceed – class inequality during working life.

So much for the argument by reference to age. Yet another argument in 'demographic' style tries to explain much of the inequality of incomes observed between households as a function, not of class differences, but instead of differences in household composition – hence a reflection of different 'income needs'. In fact this argument, in simple form, has no application to the figures I gave earlier to show a sharp growth of inequality in households incomes from around 1980, for those figures had mostly been standardised to eliminate precisely the effects of differences in size of households, and in number and ages of children, on 'income needs'. But there is still another line to that sort of argument. This notes the steep rise in employment of married women, which has continued now for thirty years or more – not least in Britain, where nearly three in every four wives of working age are in the labour market today. The argument then goes on to assert that inequalities in income between families come now not so much from the 'class' of work that earning family-members have, as from the effective number of earners in the family. It is decisive, so the argument here runs, whether the wife works full-time: or whether she works only part-time (as do about one half of all working wives in Britain); or whether she has no paid work at all. So the argument concludes that personal or family 'strategies' in life are coming to displace class in determining household income. (See Pahl 1984, and above p. 93.)

Again, however, the conclusion does not fit with factual evidence. Of course, the number of earners does affect family income; but the result, if anything, is to strengthen the impact of class rather than to weaken it. (See Bonney 1988a and 1988b; also Dex 1985.) First, to take the argument historically, paid employment among married women has increased more in the 'middle and upper' classes than in the working class. This is mainly because many working-class wives had some kind of paid work already earlier – at a time when most middle and upper-class families still upheld the convention that wives ought to stay at home (cf. Westergaard and Resler 1975:Part 2, Ch. 6). So new 'dual earning' has boosted middle- and upper-class household incomes more, over time, than it has boosted working-class incomes. Second, the result in fact is that – unlike in the past – dual earning is now rather more common among married couples in the middle and upper strata than among working-class couples. The differences are not great; but their effect, once again, is to widen class disparities rather than to narrow them.

The third point is that these differences seem to reflect class disparities in opportunity. The evidence here is softer. But it suggests, not surprisingly, that upper- and middle-class wives are relatively well-placed to exercise some choice about whether and how to take paid work. By contrast, when working-class wives take only part-time work or have no employment at all, it is often because they have no realistic alternative. They have not the means to travel far from home to work; the range of work they can find locally is limited, and liable to be of an ill-protected part-time sort; public provision for child-minding is scarce; and the poorer families can lose more by state-benefit losses than they would gain from a wife's low wage. So the very scope for personal or family 'strategies' is itself class-dependent: it looks narrower down the class scale than up it.

Gender division

To talk about women's employment is to begin to talk about a larger issue, the relation of class inequality to gender inequality (cf. Crompton and Mann (eds) 1986; Crompton, this volume Ch. 9). It has been a major line of revisionist theory to postulate that class division is much less salient now, because gender division cuts across it. Inequality between the sexes is not new, of course. But, so the new revisionism says, gender inequality is the more visible and potent now, when women have increasingly challenged it; and when, especially, the great majority even of married women in Britain are in the labour market for most of their working-age lives – and there, all the more visibly, are exposed to practices and conventions that disadvantage women *vis-à-vis* men at all levels of the market.

One sign of women's disadvantages *vis-à-vis* men is that women, generally, have lower real and effective incomes. This reflects the multiple handicaps they suffer both in the labour market and outside it: handicaps from continuing job and pay restrictions, and from continuing conventional definitions of women's roles as inherently private and domestic. It also, perhaps curiously, reflects one advantage which women have over men. More women than men survive into old age and they die later; and in the working class, old age continues to carry a high risk of poverty from lack of adequate pensions. But just as class inequality here interacts with gender inequality, so it does more widely. Division by gender is indeed a potent dimension of equality. It is conceptually distinct from division by class, and certainly not confined to capitalist societies. But in practice the two twine together, to reinforce the effects of class rather than to go against them.

I have already given one example. This is the fact that upper- and middle-class wives have found rather more freedom of choice to challenge the constraints of domesticity than their working-class 'sisters', so-called. But let me take the point further. Once in the labour market, women confront just the same inequalities of class as do men. Disparities of pay and conditions of work are, by and large, as sharp among earning women as among earning men, according to the 'class' of work done. Opportunities for advancement and the risks of demotion differ at least as much among women as among men, according to the individual's level of work and point of origin in the class structure. The difference is that, at every level, women are usually worse off than their male counterparts. Level for level of work their pay tends to be poorer; their pensions, if any, tend to be much lower; their opportunities for careers are much more restricted; their confinement to routine-grade work, and their risks of demotion, are greater; and they are far more liable than men to have part-time work only. (For a little of the voluminous evidence for these points, see *Social Trends* 1992:table 4.8; Marshall *et al.* 1988:tables 4.6 and 4.9; Goldthorpe 1987.) Yet none of this involves any sort of suspension of the force of class structure on economic life. The class structure of the labour market for women parallels that for men. It is in a sense the same structure except – crucially – that women are pressed into its routine-grade slots a good deal more than are men.

To sum up, you could put the point of logic I draw from these facts like this. When women have paid work, as most now do in Britain, they mostly find jobs well below the upper rungs of the class structure of work: still more so than men. That signifies a continuing, though now somewhat easing, subordination of women to men. But it equally signifies a continuing structure of class. I have still, however, to put in one last link in my chain of argument. What if the work that married women do is, in class terms, unconnected with their husbands' work – or even tends to 'compensate' for it? What if wives in career posts are quite often married to men in blue-collar jobs; or vice versa? Then, surely, class inequalities would even out, when measured by family circumstances?

The answer is quite simple: this can happen; but it happens only quite rarely. Thus some two in every three wives who have 'service class' work are married to men who themselves are professionals, managers or the like; hardly any have blue-collar husbands. True enough, if you use a three-group classification of work – 'service class', intermediate and core working class – you then find that there are many dual-earning couples of apparently 'mixed class': around 50 per cent of all dual-earning couples in Britain today. This has implications for the question just where the main boundary lines fall in the class structure. But in at least some 4 in every 5 of these ostensibly 'mixed-class' marriages, the mixture arises only because one partner is in 'intermediate-class' place – most often the wife, with a lowish-grade 'white-blouse' job of quite limited prospects. This large routine-job category of female work draws on women married to men in all three class groups, if with distinctions within the category which are not yet well mapped. But marriage between partners in wholly contrasting types of work – service versus core working-class – is rare; and, in statistical terms, the employment class of wives correlates well with that of their husbands. (For the main data summarised here, see Goldthorpe 1987 and Marshall *et al.* 1988; cf. also McRae 1986.) There is, then, no general breach of class division on this score. Once again, inequality by gender interacts with inequality by class: the one has not displaced the other.

Other divisions

Revisionist theory points also to other divisions often now said to override class. About ethnic division – division by skin colour especially – I can be very brief here. People of black and brown skin are indeed distinctly handicapped in Britain today: there are new and nasty lines of racial inequality. But those lines have in no way supplanted the lines of class inequality. For one thing, racial division – on this score much like gender division – comes to expression in good part as low placement of its victims precisely in the economic order of production and distribution: that is in the structure of class. For another, despite such common discrimination against them, the 'coloured minorities' in Britain still stretch across too many occupations to constitute a single economic category. They are also culturally divided; and black-skinned people of Caribbean origin are more concentrated in lower-grade positions than brown-skinned people of South Asian and East African origin. Thirdly, their numbers – some 5 per cent of the total population – are in any case too few to give the British class structure that prominent imprint of ethnic division which is distinctive, say, of American, let alone of South African, class structure. (There is a large literature on this subject. For one cogent analysis, see Solomos 1989.)

But revisionists have postulated yet another kind of division which, they claim, increasingly puts old-style class division out of joint. This is division, so to speak, by patterns of consumption. The argument here is that the real contrast in life circumstances now comes between a majority of people who have enough private resources to give them fair power over their own lives; and a minority of people who lack such private resources, and instead have to depend on generally poor public provision. Revisionist theory in this manner has pointed, in part, to the growth of private pension schemes; of private health insurance on top of national health provision; of private motor-car ownership. But it has pointed particularly to the fast growth of private ownership of housing. (See especially Saunders 1990a, also Saunders and Harris 1990, and Dunleavy and Husbands 1985.)

Certainly, private ownership of housing spread still faster in the 1980s than before. Today in Britain some two in every three households either fully own their own homes or are buying them on long loans, and the figure is above 40 per cent even among unskilled blue-collar workers. Yet it does not follow that old-style class division is giving way to division between a majority of home-owners and a minority of tenants (mainly tenants in public housing). After all, relatively poor home-owners own relatively poor and low-price homes. They receive less tax relief from the state to help them pay for their homes in consequence (see e.g. *Social Trends* 1992:table 5.11). They are at higher risk of losing their homes when, as in recession, they cannot keep up mortgage payments. In general, 'consumer power' from private resources remains highly unequal power, when overall private resources – that is to say, real incomes – remain highly unequal, and have grown more unequal over the years since about 1980. Consumer power, after all, is money power: quite simply, the rich and the comfortably off have much more of it than ordinary wage-earners, let alone the poor who are out of wage work. Ownership of housing confers no general immunity from these wider disparities of 'consumer power'; and these disparities in turn continue, as before, to come from the structure of economic class. (For a study whose conclusions go against equation of home ownership with a postulated new consumer sovereignty, see Forest *et al.* 1990.)

Underclass segregation versus mass affluence?

Talk about emancipation through new consumer empowerment often goes together with a view that accepts some of the evidence for increased inequality, but none the less regards its signalling a dissolution of old class divisions. In their place, a new division is supposedly emerging between a minority, the 'underclass', cut off either by moral depravity or by economic deprivation, and the rest of society. The 'rest of society', it is said, consists of a classless mass-majority united in more-or-less common experience of growing affluence. There is then one line of division left; but this is a new line, which divides only the indigent or the poorest from everybody else. There are, according to such fashionable assumptions, no comparable lines left above that which will matter much over time ahead: no line of lasting importance, for example, between regular rank-and-file wage-earners and salaried executives or professionals in high-set careers; no line, of great concern at least, between these categories in turn and elites right at the top by way of privilege and power. I need to look at conjecture of this sort more closely, both because it subsumes several of the themes in other current counter-class thinking; and because here is the point where, most visibly perhaps, academic social theory and more widely pervasive public commentary have overlapped with each other, in partly common tune with the shift of economic and political climate from the late 1970s.

One of the various versions of 'underclass talk' (Westergaard 1992) takes present-day poverty to be essentially a cultural phenomenon, which has grown as an 'underclass culture' has spread (Murray 1990). The carriers of that culture are people who do not want to work: unemployment, according to this thesis, is largely self-chosen. They are people who choose to live outside regular marriage – who therefore bring up their children in the poverty of lone parentage, and pass on their irregular life style to those children. They are people prone to habits of delinquency and criminality. They are people who have been corrupted into irresponsible dependency on public welfare provision. There is, however, a large array of factual evidence to show that the vast majority of unemployed people want to have paid work, but cannot find it; that single-parenthood, while growing, is spread across the class structure, and so has variable consequences for family economic circumstances; that delinquency and crime have multiple causes and, while class-skewed, tend to arise from poor material opportunities rather than create them; and that, when the poor depend on public welfare provision, they do so not by choice but by force of circumstance. It is both false and arbitrary to assert that unemployment, marriage instability, delinquency and subsistence on state benefits somehow make up a single package which, in turn, constitutes a self-chosen style of life. Underclass talk in this 'moral turpitude' version revives the old notion of a 'dangerous class' below respectable society and turns a blind eye to the evident and predominant structural causes of poverty. (See e.g. Bagguley and Mann 1992; Mann 1992; cf. Walker 1991.)

This version has politically right-wing genesis and appeal. Not so a quite different version of underclass theory which I call the 'outcast poverty' version. This, realistically, posits structural causes of poverty; and, in political terms, it has centre-to-left resonance. Its underclass are poor not by choice, but indeed by force of circumstance (see e.g. Field 1989, Halsey 1987, Townsend 1993). But, it says, these people are no longer just the most deprived among a larger working class. They are people more or less permanently excluded from the world of wage-earning work; or they are only on the fringes of that world. They are increasingly outcast from society because, bereft of regular and dependable employment, they have little or no part in the growth of 'affluence' which more or less all others are said to enjoy in common. And there is some good sense to these descriptions – up to a point. However you may define poverty, the numbers of the poor have grown greatly since about 1980. I have already outlined the reasons why and the solid evidence for them. It certainly means that inequalities are sharper now within the working class, as well as above it.

But it is quite another matter to say that what was the working class no longer really exists, because it is now deeply split between a distinct and growing isolated underclass on one hand and a much larger number of people in regular work on the other who, even if nominally wage-earners still, are increasingly 'middle-class' and increasingly indistinguishable from the categories once regarded as above them. Take the first point first. It could be that people outside work or on its fringes are now near to living in a separate, deprived and outcast world of their own. Polarisation might eventually go that far. This is a matter for empirical enquiry, though the empirical evidence so far lends the idea little support. Retired workers, for example – who make up over 40 per cent of the poor by any definition of poverty – are hardly a class that is distinct from the active but pension-right poor wage-earners they once were themselves. There is more individual movement within the working-class world than the thesis implies: movement between unemployment and employment; between skilled and non-skilled wage-earning work (e.g. Goldthorpe 1987, Westergaard et al. 1989). And there is much commonality of circumstances too, at least in Britain, between skilled and non-skilled labour (Erikson and Goldthorpe 1992, Marshall et al. 1988, e.g. tables 4.6 and 4.9; cf. also evidence summarised earlier about occupational pension provision). Again, though labour markets are to a degree segmented, recent studies show no simple pattern and no clear general trend to increased segmentation (e.g. Gallie 1988).

That part of the argument which postulates a new distinct segregation of the workless and the poorest workers is, then, conceivable as a hypothesis but, so far at least, it seems not to be true. Far more trouble comes when this notion is linked to the idea that, above the hypothetical underclass, old divisions of class now matter less and less. This second idea has hinged especially on a belief that, under the new dispensation from about 1980, more or less all people except the poor have come to share, more or less commonly, in growing prosperity (e.g. Halsey 1987, Saunders 1990). But that belief is demonstrably, and seriously, wrong. As I showed earlier, real earnings and real incomes increased only quite modestly in the 1980s, even for people at and around the middle of the range. The majority of the population either actually lost out, or gained at rates well below that statistical average which is often spuriously cited as evidence of dramatically enhanced mass affluence. This 'national average' is, of course, a statistical artefact; and it was high only because the wealth of the prosperous – of many executives, managers, well established professionals and, most of all, people in the top circles of business and finance – increased enormously. This has been the extreme, and the most potent, aspect of a general polarisation in economic class structure.

Top-class privilege and power

I have said enough already about the growth of economic privilege at the upper end of the scale since about 1980 – around 50 per cent boom in top-quintile real incomes, for example. (Prize gains at the very peak of wealth are concealed from sight in most comprehensive statistical series, and are known best from ad hoc reports of directors' salaries, share options and the like.) Power has also grown at the top; and not just in the sense that extra privilege can be assumed to bring extra power with it anyway. The power of private business has grown, of course, as free market policies intended. To take just one instance, business representation in the governance of public education and health has been consistently stepped up; and, more generally, business-style prescriptions for 'cost-efficiency' have spread widely in the conduct of public-sector affairs. Moreover, 'free' markets are in practice markets led by inexorable trends to oligopoly if not monopoly, notwithstanding government declarations in favour of widened competition; and sale of once-nationalised industries has, at best, converted public monopolies into private oligopolies. Though very small enterprise did grow in the 1980s, leading capital power remains concentrated in large corporations. In Britain, it is concentrated especially in the hands of the major financial institutions, centred in the City of London; and it is their activities – rather than those of the fast declining manufacturing sector – which have yielded the richest gains in money at and near the top.

The trade unions have been firmly ruled out of the junior consultative role which they had during the period of 'tripartite corporatism'. This 'lock-out' is an inherent feature of the free-market drive against 'labour monopolies', and against bureaucratic centralisation of leadership power within the unions. In the process, the *de facto* consultative role of private business in public government has become all the greater, if less visible because less dependent on formal procedures. The key representatives of business for this purpose are a small network of top people from top corporations and institutions.

These corporations and institutions, including insurance companies and pension funds, are now the major shareholders in private business. The power which the people in their top circles wield comes from the mass of corporate assets whose strategic deployment they lead rather than from their own personal wealth, though that wealth is large because of high executive salaries, directorial and consultant fees, dealer commissions and expense allowances, as well as substantial private shareholdings and capital gains. Except in the case of a few 'newspaper headline' tycoons, the power they wield – in markets and through understanding with government – is in large part 'impersonal'. (See especially Scott 1986, 1991 and below, Chapter 12.) But it is high power none the less. It is power for personal and family advantage as well as to more diffuse capital and class benefit.

It is power, moreover, quite beyond the reach of the general run of executives, managers and professional specialists below them, most of whom have drawn tangible gains from the recent polarisation of real incomes, albeit on a more modest scale than the small group of grand commanders in private business. This 'top class', with their families, may still number less than 1 per cent of the population, even if we add to their number large rentiers; high officials in government (central rather than local government) who move to a degree in the worlds both of public service and private enterprise; and top establishment professionals (as well as star entertainers) who have acquired large wealth and some opinion-shaping influence if hardly commensurate power. Even by a looser count, top-class numbers are too small, and their sources of power and privilege are too intricate, for them to be separately identified in most sample surveys or the general run of statistical series. They have always tended to vanish from sight there. Their visibility has been still further obscured by the shift of ideological climate from the late 1970s, and by the concomitant revival of class-dissolution theory. (This greater concentration of power is evident also from new trends in the centralisation of the state's authority, in closer linkage with increased representation there of business interests – though I cannot elaborate on this point here.) Overall, then, the class structure shows sharper divisions than before over the whole range; not just in the 'lower' reaches, as underclass theory implies.

Politics and Labour decline

We are still left with a puzzle: when class division 'in itself' has sharpened, why does class division 'for itself' seem to have faded? Britain has a long history of class politics, though of moderate character. How then has a Conservative Party led from the radical right been able to win four successive elections, in harsh economic circumstances? True, the Conservatives have not won a full majority of votes: only some 44 per cent at most, against an aggregate majority of votes for opposition parties. Yet Labour's share of the poll fell disastrously to 28 per cent in 1983, this at a time of high unemployment: and even in 1992 the figure was up only to some 34 per cent against still nearly 42 per cent for the Conservatives. One prevalent theory, for a time, was that Labour's collapse signalled an end to class division in voting patterns. This has proved misleading. Examination of detailed survey data (especially Heath *et al*. 1985) has shown that, measured in relative terms, class differences in party support have stayed much the same as before: not so distinct as in Scandinavia, for example; but as relatively distinct in Britain of the 1980s as they were in Britain of the 1950s to 1970s.

So Labour's weakness has not come from a collapse of all class politics. It has come, first, from the fact that the number of blue-collar workers has been steadily falling for a long time and it was they who, historically, formed Labour's main base. Yet the point only raises further questions. The circumstances of many non-manual workers – those with 'jobs' rather than 'careers' – are little better than the circumstances of manual workers. And though women in routine-grade white-blouse jobs are often married to men in better class positions, this is still not enough to explain Labour's general failure to appeal very much beyond the blue-collar world. Second, Labour's appeal to the old blue-collar working class has actually waned, not waxed as one might have expected from the economic polarisation of recent times. In fact, over the years around 1980 votes swung away from the party in all classes. The swing left the relative differences in Labour support much as before; but at lower levels throughout, and drastically so in 1983. The party partly recovered in 1987 and 1992, yet to results well short of the continuing Conservative lead? Why?

Survey evidence suggests that Labour lost votes most first – in 1979 and then badly in 1983 – through widespread disillusionment over (i) its 'capacity to govern'; (ii) the evident failure of its corporatist economic policies; (iii) the eruption of strikes at the tail-end of Labour's period in government office; and (iv) subsequent internal party disputes. (Cf. e.g. Heath *et al*. 1985, Dunleavy and Husbands 1985, Westergaard *et al*. 1989.) But explanation of this kind arguably only skims the surface. Why in turn was Labour so greatly vulnerable to a mood of disillusionment, especially when, as I shall show, popular sentiment against the hardening of class inequality is widespread and growing? Here it might seem after all is some potential for the resurgence of class politics around an agenda set to challenge the established concentration of power and privilege. Why no so far?

Conjectures abound. One, though much disputed, is that the party has never firmly set out to challenge established concentrations of power and privilege. It has been largely a reformist rather than a radical party – as working-class parties in Western Europe generally have become. Their long-term support, too, has tended to slip. If there are clues here, they point – in my own view – to the processes by which class politics has become 'institutionalised'. In such processes, historically, class conflict was formally admitted to the political scene, and came to form the recognised main theme around which parties mobilised. But it also came to be institutionally regulated and moderated in consequence. Compromise, first pursued as a tactic, became usually an end almost in itself. Reform was sought because it was easier to achieve, and could bring some tangible benefit, without head-on challenge to the established order. But as head-on challenge dropped generally from sight, and as reform came closer to its limits without it, the class substance of institutionalised politics tended to drain away. Rival parties contested for the 'middle ground', for 'floating voters', still confident that they could retain the support of their original class constituencies none the less. And the parties came to base their claims increasingly on purported instrumental competence in governance, more than on principled and long-term pursuit of class-constituency interests. So politics became, and is now commonly seen as, 'dull', even when not mean-spirited or corrupt. And as politicians and parties have lowered their sights, voters at large have come to expect little of them; and to vote, when they vote, just in pragmatic manner.

In Britain this has fitted quite well with one radical-right doctrine: that governments should do much less of what they once did and let markets do much more. The radical right has also, of course, been well placed to cash in on long-standing Conservative claims to superior competence in governance, when governance means management of established order: the Conservatives are, after all, the party of 'practically minded' business. True, the radical right has pursued its own brand of class politics with much vigour, to the effect of economic polarisation; and voters generally are well aware of this, despite Conservative disclaimers. But, through the 'institutionalisation of class politics' which I have just tried to outline, many voters may now have little faith in political opposition as a means to reverse the effect.

Disillusionment with politics and politicians, then, has spread wide; and opinion surveys generally confirm this. That, I suggest, has damaged Labour and the left more than Conservatives and the right, because the former have empty hands unless their politics can effectively change the order as it is. When the Conservative Party continued to lead the voting field even 1992, it was probably on the basis of quite pragmatic considerations: in part because, as the party of business, it was still – if curiously – trusted to be more competent in economic management than Labour; in part because enough voters, who favoured higher taxes on the wealthy, were still worried that higher taxes might reach down to themselves.

Opinion surveys also show, however, that support continues to be widespread – especially in the working class, but in significant respects also among professional if not business groups – for the kinds of principle which Labour historically has represented: for union defence of employees against employers; for extensive public welfare provision; for 'fairer shares', and some progressive redistribution to curtail wealth and power at the top. The evidence on this front is remarkable, to the effect that the radical right have not won 'hearts and minds' for their social philosophy. (For relevant opinion survey data, see successive issues of *British Social Attitudes*, ed. R. Jowell *et al.*, also, e.g. Heath and McMahon 1991, Taylor-Gooby 1991, Marshall *et al.* 1988, Westergaard *et al.* 1989.)

Most people, then, appear to want to see 'fairer shares'. And although many are sceptical about the means to that end, popular conceptions are nevertheless quite out of line with fashionable social theory and right-wing ideology. This at least seems the case so far.

Note

1. This chapter is an abridged and slightly revised version of three lectures given in December 1992 at Hitotsubashi University, Tokyo. The lectures were published, in English, in the *Hitotsubashi Journal of Social Studies*, Vol. 25, 1993; and in Japanese translation with additional commentary (translator and editor, Masao Watanable), by Aoki Press, Tokyo, 1993. I am grateful to the journal editors, book publishers and Professor Watanabe for their support and agreement to publication of this abridgement. A much extended version of the same arguments forms Part III of J. H. Westergaard, *Who Gets What?* Cambridge: Polity Press, 1995.
2. Passages I have omitted in the process of abridgement include some which discussed trends in social mobility, and the vacuity of notions of 'classlessness' conceived merely as 'opportunity' without reference even to equality of opportunity.

CHAPTER 12

Patterns of capitalist development[1]

John Scott

The mainstream of stratification research seems to have experienced a loss of confidence in its central concept, the concept of 'class'. Nowhere is this loss of confidence more marked than it is in the case of the study of dominant classes. Announcements of the death of class have been preceded by obituaries for capitalist classes. There has always been some reluctance among mainstream researchers to recognise the existence of dominant, propertied classes, rooted in the ownership and control of capital, but a kind of surrogate research on 'elites' was, until the 1970s, a mainstay of stratification studies. (See, for example, the research in Britain of Cole 1955, Guttsman 1963, Bottomore 1964, Stanworth and Giddens 1974). Since the mid-1970s this kind of research has all but disappeared and in many countries it has been left to one or two isolated researchers to keep the issue alive.

This lacuna in stratification research reflects a conceptual failure in class analysis. Theorists and researchers alike, for all their ritual obeisance to Marx and to Weber, have failed properly to conceptualise the relationship between property ownership and class structure. This has made it all but impossible for them to understand the real implications of the restructuring of property relations that has occurred since the late nineteenth century. While Marx and writers in the Marxist tradition appreciated that the joint stock company and the system of finance capital had altered the basis on which capitalist classes were structured, critics of Marxism drew contradictory and somewhat naive conclusions. These changes, they claimed, had led to the demise of the capitalist class.

Daniel Bell (1961, 1973), for example, spoke for many when he drew on the research of Berle and Means (1932) and concluded that a 'separation of ownership from control' had eliminated the capitalist class and had replaced it with a new class of salaried managers. Property was simply irrelevant to class structure. (See also Parsons 1949, Kerr *et al.* 1960). This 'managerial revolution' was seen as an inexorable consequence of the 'logic of industrialism'. Many who rejected the structural functionalism on which this argument was based accepted, nevertheless, that property ownership no longer needed to be considered in class analysis and that no further research on capitalist classes was necessary (Dahrendorf 1959).

There is now sufficient evidence to show that the naive conclusions that were drawn from the early work of Berle and Means were unfounded and that the issues of ownership and control are far more complicated than is generally assumed (Zeitlin 1989, Scott 1985). This evidence seems to have by-passed the mainstream of stratification studies, which have either continued to ignore or – at best – pay lip-service to the idea of a dominant class or 'elite'; or, as I show elsewhere, they have thoroughly confused the important differences between the concepts of class and elite (Scott, 1996). A reconsideration of the implications of property-holding for class structure is long overdue. Such a reconsideration will, furthermore, highlight a number of issues that are pertinent to the wider question of the supposed 'death of class' and which have barely been considered in the voluminous debates on that claim.

If this issue is to be reconsidered, however, it must be done on the basis of a proper understanding of the complexities that are involved in capitalist development over the last 150 years. This period has seen a transition from forms of personal possession of capital to increasingly impersonal forms of possession. Individual and family owners have been supplemented and, increasingly, replaced by corporate and institutional owners. Control is 'depersonalised', located in anonymous structures of power rather than personal hands. But this transition has taken a number of different forms. Structural functionalist theorists, 'conflict theorists', and Marxists alike have tended to assume the existence of a unitary pattern of capitalist development. Structural functionalists have tended to generalise this unitary pattern from the American experience, while Marxists have tended to generalise from the German case. What must be recognised is that there are a number of different routes from personal to impersonal possession, reflecting different trajectories of industrialisation. Societies have different starting points, follow different paths and, therefore, develop in different ways, and our theories must take account of these variations.

This is not, however, an argument for historical uniqueness. Behind the diversity in forms of capitalist enterprise can be discerned a limited number of patterns that can be conceptualised as ideal types for comparative investigation. It is possible to identify four 'established' patterns of capitalist development: the Anglo-American, the German, the Japanese and the Latin. There are also two 'emergent' patterns to which I wish to give particular attention. These are the post-communist and the Chinese. The names should not, however, be taken to imply a cultural determinism but are merely convenient descriptive labels for patterns that, for a variety of reasons, actually occur within particular cultural contexts. Each pattern is organised around specific mechanisms of capital mobilisation, and their reproduction or transformation is a result of the potentials and limits built into these mechanisms.

The Anglo-American pattern of capitalist development shows a transition from entrepreneurial mechanisms of capital mobilisation, as found in relatively small-scale family concerns, to the institutional mechanisms characteristic of large-scale production. Financial institutions such as pensions funds and insurance companies increasingly replace personal wealth as the source of business finance. The German pattern centres around the mobilisation of capital through a banking mechanism that makes long-term credit available to large industrial enterprises. The Japanese pattern of capitalist development involves a clustering of enterprises into tightly integrated groups within which capital is circulated from one enterprise to another, moving it from less to more profitable uses or to a long-term investment strategy. This clustering mechanism initially took a vertical form in which company groups were subject to family control, but it subsequently developed into a horizontal form. The Latin pattern of capital mobilisation, the last of the established patterns, has involved what I call a corporate web. The shareholdings of families, banks and investment companies intersect to form complex patterns of control that allow the continuation of family influence within a more depersonalised system of investment funding.

These four established patterns are those that have arisen within the core of the capitalist world-economy. Outside the core a number of other patterns have emerged as economies have industrialised, but in this paper I have highlighted what I have called the post-communist and the Chinese patterns. The post-communist pattern of a truck mechanism involves haggling, bargaining and barter and has developed from the former communist systems as they are turned in a capitalist direction. The Chinese pattern, on the other hand, involves a fraternal-provenance mechanism and is found in the 'new' economies of East Asia.

My purpose in this paper is to highlight the aspects of these contrasting patterns of capitalist development that are most pertinent to class analysis and to sketch out some of the implications that they have for theorising and researching capitalist classes.

Established patterns of capitalist development

The Anglo-American pattern has been studied most fully in Britain and the United States, although the pattern is also found in Canada, Australia and New Zealand (Scott 1985:Chs 3–5, 1986, Scott and Griff 1984). British industrialisation was largely undertaken by small-scale, self-financing enterprises, and the individuals and families who ran them resorted to the banking system only for short-term credit. As a result, the banks played no active role in industrial development (Ingham 1984). Expansion, when and where it occurred, involved the amalgamation of enterprises into larger family controlled undertakings.

American industrial development followed a similar pattern, though the sheer size of the American economy meant that enterprises were forced to expand beyond the limits of family capital. The New York banks played a leading role in providing additional capital, but they did not displace family shareholders (Chandler 1990:57-8; see also Chandler 1963, Lash and Urry 1987:69). The former owners became majority or minority controllers, and investment bankers joined industrial boards in large numbers. The investment banks limited their role to the provision of short-term finance, few of them taking long-term shareholdings in companies. As a result, the influence of bankers was short-lived, and it declined as the large enterprises established themselves (Mizruchi 1982). New capital came, instead, from the growing number of investment companies, insurance companies and pensions funds, which became the principal owners of company shares and which took a short-term orientation towards their investments.

The industrial problems of the inter-war years led bankers in Britain to become more closely involved with industrial concerns, but this was merely a temporary response to their financial difficulties, and the banks withdrew from industrial reconstruction as soon as possible. In neither Britain nor the United States was entrepreneurial capital replaced or supplemented by long-term banking capital. In both countries it was financial 'institutions' – insurance companies, pensions funds, and so on – that played the central role in the transition towards a more 'organised' form of capitalism.

The outcome of the growth of institutional shareholding in Britain and America has not been a separation of ownership from control of the kind that was anticipated by Berle and Means (1932). The dominance of the big financial institutions in share capital has meant that 'controlling constellations' can hold up to 50 per cent of the shares in large enterprises. The result is what I have elsewhere termed 'control through a constellation of interests' (Scott 1985). The impersonal financial interests that dominate corporate ownership are formed into loosely structured and overlapping constellations that dominate the share capital of particular enterprises. These constellations do not form cohesive controlling groups, but they do exercise a significant constraint on managerial autonomy and they are a major force in corporate decision-making (Scott 1990a, 1993a). Institutional shareholdings and directorships interweave to form complex networks of intercorporate relations in which bank directors stand at the heart of an 'inner circle' of business decision-makers (Useem 1984). There are not, however, the kind of business groups or financial empires that were anticipated by some writers on finance capital (Villarejo 1961, Perlo 1957, Rochester 1936, Menshikov 1969). The predominance of these constellations of institutional interests in the Anglo-American system has led to particular patterns of short-term investment that contrast markedly with the more long-term patterns of investment found in other systems.

Capitalist development in Germany, Austria and much of Central Europe took a very different pattern that I have termed the German pattern and that is found in its clearest form in Germany itself. The weakness of the German bourgeoisie and the state of agriculture in the nineteenth century forced the Prussian state to encourage the involvement of foreign capital in industrial development. This was intended to allow indigenous sources of capital the time to ready themselves, and new banks were organised to lead this process (Kitchen 1978). These so-called 'universal banks' combined long-term industrial investment with short-term banking, and so channelled surplus funds into industry. Through the flotation of companies, the provision of credit, and the holding of substantial shareholdings, they dominated company boards and played a major role in corporate affairs (Chandler 1990:416–17, Landes 1969: 205, Gille 1970).

The merging and syndicating of banking produced a pattern of interweaving shareholdings that put the big banks in a dominant position in the German economy by the time of the First World War (Tilly 1986, Milward and Saul 1977:47, Henderson 1961:62ff, Kocka 1980:90, Tilly 1974). Each bank had minority holdings in large industrial enterprises, and each enterprise was generally allied with more than one bank (Scott 1987:215). The banks were a hegemonic force in the economy, standing at the apex of a vertically structured industrial system.

A similar pattern of capital mobilisation developed in Austria and Switzerland, and it also prevailed through much of Central Europe until the inter-war period. One observer (Teichova 1992:18) has even claimed that Austria, not Germany, should be seen as the exemplar of universal banking, and it was certainly the opinion of Hilferding (1910) that Austria was the clearest case of bank hegemony. In Austria, however, state involvement in banking increased during the 1930s and the influence of the state after the Second World War laid the foundations for Austria's distinctive corporatist political structure. The state banks in Austria have been closely allied with a state holding company for industry, and the whole network of intercorporate relations has a hierarchical structure (Zeigler, Reissner and Bender 1985).

In Germany itself, the banks alone remained the dominant force in the economy. The big three German banks have interests and influence in many of the largest enterprises in finance, heavy industry, mining and utilities (Zeigler, Bender and Biehler 1985, Franks and Mayer 1992, Scott 1985:126–31), and in Switzerland the big three banks play a similar role in relation to financial and multinational enterprises (Rusterholz 1985).

The third established pattern of capitalist development to consider is the Japanese. In this pattern, enterprises have been clustered together into cohesive business groups. While the pattern is clearest in Japan, a variant of it can be found in contemporary South Korea (Hamilton and Biggart 1988). The Meiji modernisers in Japan aimed to build a world role for the country through the creation of strong and powerful business groups (Allen 1972, Lockwood, W. 1968, Hirschmeier 1964, Morishima 1982:94). These private business groups – the so-called *zaibatsu* – became the major force in the Japanese economy, each group operating in all the principal industrial sectors and being united under family control and through common trading arrangements. The Japanese banks, themselves integral members of the various groups, concentrated almost exclusively on the provision of long-term finance to industrial concerns. Each *zaibatsu* bank mobilised funds from within its group and channelled them into other group ventures (Tominomori 1979).

This pattern of rapid industrialisation through a vertically structured clustering mechanism persisted in Japan until the end of the Second World War. After the American occupation, and despite an attempt by the American authorities to destroy the clustering mechanism, the system was reconstructed on a new basis. The *zaibatsu* families had been divested of their shareholdings, but former *zaibatsu* enterprises re-established their connections with one another as more horizontally clustered formations. These new groups – the *kigyoshudan* – take the form of tightly connected corporate sets that are linked through reciprocal shareholdings, trading links, banking links, and interlocking directorships (Scott 1985:142–51, 1986:Ch. 7). Within each business group there is a decentralised and impersonal 'alignment' of enterprises that is the basis of an 'insider' system of corporate control.

What I call the Latin pattern of capitalist development makes its clearest appearance in Belgium, though it is also characteristic of France and Italy. It is, in some respects, a hybrid of elements from each of the patterns so far described, but it involves a distinctive structure of capital mobilisation that I term the 'corporate web'. In both Belgium and France, industrial development was very slow throughout the nineteenth century (Fohlen 1970). The stock exchanges were too weak to support autonomous capital expansion, and long-term banking of the kind found in Germany played no significant role (Milward and Saul 1977:118, Gille 1970:280–81, Palmade 1961). In both France and Belgium, the maintenance of family control was, even more than in Britain, the overriding goal, and families turned to the banks only for small supportive investments (Gerschenkron 1962:12–13).

In this situation, firms that expanded did so by seeking partners who would not threaten the continuation of family control. Banks formed investment holding companies or themselves acted as investors, taking small strategic stakes in a range of companies and thereby spreading their risks. Industrial families, in turn, took stakes in the investment companies in order to ensure that they would not play too powerful or independent a role. The investment companies enlarged the pool of capital, but they were not agents of control in their own right. Their own capital was owned by intersecting bank and family shareholders, and wealthy families retained stakes in the various enterprises in which the investment companies invested. This complex interweaving of shareholding participations constitutes the corporate web.

In France, Belgium and Italy, investment holding companies have been the focus for the mobilisation of capital from connected families, and their interweaving shareholdings have created loose enterprise groups (Allard *et al.* 1978). The French intercorporate network became organised around Suez and Paribas into a characteristic web structure (Swartz 1985, Scott 1985:131–42), the state holding companies IRI and ENI played a similar role in Italy (Chiesi 1982, 1985), and in Belgium the Société Générale de Belgique is all-pervasive (Cuyvers and Meeusen 1985, De Vroey 1973).

Emergent patterns of capitalist development

I have concentrated on describing the four established patterns of capital mobilisation that can be found in those economies at the core of the capitalist world-economy. In this section I will discuss, more briefly, two emergent patterns outside the core that are playing a crucial role in the transformation of that system. These are the post-communist pattern found in Russia and Eastern Europe, and the Chinese pattern found in East Asia and mainland China.

The communist system of the former Soviet Union centred on a mono-organisational state apparatus of state planning (Rigby 1990) that developed Russian industry in a non-capitalist direction. The collapse of this system left the controllers of industrial enterprises with the problem of evolving appropriate methods for raising capital. In doing so, they have drawn on the heritage of the communist and pre-communist periods and created a distinctive 'post-communist' system.

The post-collapse policy aimed at building a capitalist market economy resulted in a new system of capital mobilisation, rather than an emulation of any existing system. The disintegration of the planning and command system left industrial enterprises isolated from the central agencies that had formerly regulated them. The 'industrial nomenklatura' continued to control many of the enterprises that they had long managed, but they built new economic structures using the established practices of bargaining and inter-enterprise bartering. In the absence of an overarching framework of planning and command, an 'anarchic' structure of economic relations developed (Burawoy and Krotov 1992). Capital mobilisation centres on a 'truck mechanism' in which access to capital and investment opportunities depend upon ad hoc bargains, rather than straight commercial exchange. Access to bank credit, supplies and outlets depends upon the bargaining abilities of directors and managers, not on the commercial viability of particular projects. This truck mechanism has been buttressed by new forms of ownership and control in 'privatised' enterprises. The existing management in enterprises have generally been able to acquire majority and controlling minority holdings, and this control allows them to secure credit, supplies and outlets by establishing liaison shareholdings with other enterprises and agencies (Clarke 1992:14).

The future of the post-communist pattern of capital mobilisation is uncertain. It is unclear whether the truck mechanism will allow a stable system of capitalist development to be established. It may turn out to be a fragile and temporary response to the immediate problems that resulted from the collapse of the planning system. Communist China still operates with a formally communist political system, but there are signs there, too, of the emergence of new forms of capitalist development. In this case, however, there are striking parallels with the 'Chinese' business patterns that are already in existence in the newly industrialised countries of East Asia.

This 'Chinese' pattern is found in the overseas Chinese economies of Taiwan, Singapore, Malaysia and Hong Kong, where rapid industrialisation occurred on the basis of long-established mechanisms of capital mobilisation supported by strong facilitative states. In Chinese business families, wealth is divided among all the sons of the owner, and this 'fraternal' division of property sets definite limits to capital accumulation, as large businesses must be organised as loose overlapping groups of separately owned enterprises that are linked through the purely personal bonds of kinship. On the death or retirement of a business founder, the fragmenting effects of the system of inheritance prevent the business from continuing to expand (Wong 1985). The experience of migration from the mainland to the overseas Chinese communities has reinforced this pattern. Those of a similar provenance on the mainland have been regarded as especially trustworthy business partners and are relied on in co-operative ventures (Wong 1991, Redding 1990). Combining kinship and other personal links into a fraternal-provenance mechanism of 'trust' means that substantial business ventures can be built. In the long term, however, such co-operative ventures are limited as the fragmenting effects of the fraternal mechanism make themselves felt.

This mechanism of capital mobilisation has, however, been the basis of rapid industrialisation in the post-war period, and the overseas Chinese societies may be in the early stages of a transition from personal to impersonal possession. In Taiwan, for example, a strong state sector was built in banking and key industrial sectors. Large private businesses developed with the sponsorship and encouragement of the state, and with the state sector now forms the leading element in the economy (Numazaki 1986, 1991, 1992, Hamilton et al. 1987). Traditional Chinese business practices were nurtured and became a powerful economic force. In Hong Kong, wealthy Chinese families were able to use profits from urban property development after the 1960s to enlarge their businesses through stock exchange flotations and the purchase of former colonial companies (G. Wong 1991). Through the fraternal-provenance mechanism, these families could take advantage of their property earnings and could break the power of foreign capital. It is uncertain whether they can avoid eventual fragmentation, although there are indications of change in the network of intercorporate relations. Interlocking directorships among the top Hong Kong companies became both more extensive and more inclusive during the 1980s, but they also became less cohesive and less centralised (G. Wong 1991), a move that brought Hong Kong business closer to the pattern of private business found in Taiwan.

The economic reforms in the People's Republic of China established 'special economic zones' and 'open cities' along the south and east coast and, supported by foreign capital from Hong Kong, Taiwan, Korea and Japan, the Shanghai stock exchange has become an important focus for industrial development. The return of overseas Chinese families to business activities on the mainland has re-introduced the fraternal-provenance mechanism that proved so successful in other parts of East Asia. Central control remains important, but the establishment of capitalist enclaves and the extension of this principle to the rest of the country during 1992 involved a strategy of combining an increasingly capitalist economy with a centralised and authoritarian state. The model followed by the Chinese leadership has been Taiwan, where a strong state facilitated economic growth and consumer affluence.

Class situations and social classes

I have outlined the results of investigations into changing patterns of property holding and capitalist business in order to suggest the complexity that is involved in considering the fate of the propertied classes since the nineteenth century. While there has been, in all the major capitalist economies, a move away from the classic forms of personal possession associated with entrepreneurial capital, this has not involved any straightforward separation of ownership from control, and moves towards more impersonal forms of possession have not followed a single unitary pattern. Propertied class formation continues to be significantly shaped by persistent variations in patterns of capital mobilisation. Some of the implications of this variation can be sketched.

The situation is clearest in the countries that have followed the Anglo-American pattern, where there is at least a certain amount of existing research to draw upon. The rise of institutional capital in Britain and America has been associated with a differentiation of capitalist class situations and command situations. ('Command situation' is used in this context to refer to positions of authority in the economic sphere; see Scott 1996 for further discussion.) Entrepreneurial class situations still occur in large enterprises, but these increasingly involve mechanisms of majority or minority control and an accommodation to institutional capital. Executive class and command situations play a key role in other large enterprises, and especially within the financial institutions themselves. The dispersal of company shareholdings that has taken place over the course of the century has generated many more rentier class situations, where life chances depend upon portfolio investments in a wide range of securities. In these rentier situations, executive situations and, to a lesser extent, entrepreneurial situations, economic interests are increasingly system-wide, rather than being restricted to particular enterprises, and the life chances of the occupants of these situations depend upon the operations of the financial institutions.

The occupants of these class and command situations are demographically clustered into a single, cohesive social class. Capitalist social class formation is no longer such a direct and straightforward process as it was in the nineteenth century, the rise of institutional capital having resulted in a partial separation of the mechanisms of capital reproduction from the mechanisms of class reproduction. The dominant social class is formed through links of career recruitment and mobility, common schooling and university attendance, intermarriage, and the various informal patterns of interaction that, in Britain, have been described as comprising an 'old boy network'. (For Britain see Scott 1991 and 1993b. For the United States see Domhoff 1983, Mintz 1989, Baltzell 1958, 1964. For Canada see Brym 1985, 1989.)

In the countries characterised by the Latin pattern, the corporate web has allowed family capital – and a degree of family control and family influence – to persist on a greater scale than is the case in the Anglo-American pattern. Entrepreneurial class situations remain a central feature of big business, despite the increased importance of executive situations in the large investment holding companies and non-family enterprises (Martinelli and Chiesi 1989). Here, too, there has been a partial separation of the mechanisms of capital reproduction and class reproduction, as Bourdieu (1973) and Bourdieu and Passeron (1970) have emphasised in their investigations into the part played by cultural assets alongside economic capital in the formation of a dominant social class in France (see also Marceau 1977, 1989a). The social class of the 'patronat', with its stronger entrepreneurial and family basis, seems more willing to recognise its class character and, even, to accept the designation 'bourgeois'.

Propertied class formations in the German and Japanese patterns have been far less studied, and a major research programme remains to be undertaken. The survival of the successors of the great entrepreneurs in Germany has occurred within a framework that is dominated by those in executive situations in banks and large industrial enterprises (Spohn and Bodemann 1989). In Japan, the dominance of the *kigyoshudan* and those who occupy their executive situations has greatly reduced the opportunities for large-scale entrepreneurial capital. Despite the importance of petty bourgeois situations in small-scale enterprises, large-scale entrepreneurial capital is a relatively minor feature of the Japanese economy. In neither Germany nor Japan is much known about rentier capitalists with wide-spread investments. The fate of the former *zaibatsu* families who had to convert their direct shareholdings into other financial securities, for example, is unknown to researchers. Similarly, mechanisms of social class formation are less clear, though the role of the big four universities in the career placement and class cohesion of executive capitalists is clear. The extent of the overlap with occupants of other class situations through mobility and other forms of demographic circulation is simply unknown (see Morioka 1989).

The propertied social classes of the emergent systems of capitalist development are the least well-studied of all. The overseas Chinese societies have only recently moved towards relatively impersonal forms of possession, and it is unclear whether this move can be sustained. As a result, entrepreneurial capitalist situations predominate and the reproduction of social classes is still quite directly linked to the mechanisms of capital reproduction. The situation in mainland China is particularly uncertain, as the drive towards capitalist industrialism involves the intrusion of a significant amount of foreign capital and raises the possibility that entrepreneurial and other capitalist class situations may be tied to external interests in a 'comprador' structure. The rise of comprador class situations is also a distinct possibility in the post-communist societies, though their lines of development are far from certain. The demise of the ruling elites in the Soviet Union and other communist countries has been associated with a fragmented structure of class and command situations, and there has been some discussion, albeit on the basis of limited evidence, of new 'entrepreneurs', 'nomenklatura', and former black market 'mafia' groups as the principal capitalist class situations of the nascent Russian economy (Kryshtanovskaya 1993). What is certain, however, is that processes of social class formation are remarkably weak, and no single dominant social class has yet been formed. There may, at best, be fractional social classes around the various distinct class situations, but whether commentators have correctly identified the major lines of division is unclear without more detailed research, which is very difficult to undertake.

These sketches of class situations and of social class formation have been, at best, suggestive and are not intended as definitive statements. My aim has been to outline the major areas in which research is required. The apparent certainties of the 'managerial revolution' must finally be put to rest, patterns of propertied class formation must be directly investigated. Far from supporting the idea of 'the death of class', research on structures of capital ownership and business organisation suggest the continuing existence of fundamental class divisions. A comprehensive research programme awaits the attention of sociologists concerned with patterns of power and domination in the contemporary world.

Note

1. Specially written for this volume, this paper draws on a larger project concerned with identifying and explaining variant patterns of capitalist development and corporate control. An earlier version of part of it was presented at a conference in Leicester in 1993 to mark the career of John Rex. I am grateful to the conference organisers, Richard Jenkins and David Mason, and to other conference participants for their comments on that paper. I have also benefited greatly from discussion with Gilbert Wong on a number of issues.

CHAPTER 13

Comparative studies in class structure[1]

John Myles and Adnan Turegun

[. . .] Our goal is to examine the empirical legacy that developed out of the theoretical and methodological agendas of class analysis and comparative methods in the 1970s and 1980s. Debate over theory and method are fruitful to the extent that they give birth to new questions to guide empirical research. The agenda-shaping debates of the 1970s gave birth in the 1980s to a considerable research enterprise ranging from in-depth historical case analysis to cross-national comparative surveys. Our focus here lies almost exclusively on those studies that examine the variants in the class structure of the developed capitalist democracies. In the body of the paper we highlight what has been learned from this endeavour and our aim is mainly descriptive. In the conclusion, we turn our attention to the limits of (now) conventional methods of class analysis.

As the Fordist world of wages, employment contracts, and social programmes began to unravel in the 1980s, the inability of both class analysis and conventional stratification studies to account for, or even detect, this transition became apparent. This failure of the 'positional approach' (Parkin 1971) common to both traditions indicates that reformulation – both theoretical and methodological – is now in order. Furthermore, this comparative literature has shown that the universalising statements of the early and mid-twentieth century [. . .] were built on, and limited to, particular trajectories of capitalist development. [. . .]

[Editorial Note: In the original article on which this chapter is based, the authors begin their discussion with a consideration of comparative research on patterns of capital ownership and development, covering a similar range of material to Scott in the previous chapter and reaching comparable conclusions regarding the ownership and control controversy. The relevant section of Myles and Turegun's article has been omitted for reasons of space.]

The return of the petite bourgeoisie

Until recently, the safest ground for universalism has been the fate of the petite bourgeoisie in any such trajectory. For classical sociology, Marxian and Weberian alike, the story of the petite bourgeoisie was a foretold one. Independent producers who own and operate their own means of production would fight a losing battle under the conditions of an industrial economy. The predicted gradual erosion of the petite bourgeoisie's economic bases was attributed to the increasing polarisation of property relations, in Marx's words the concentration and centralisation of capital. The petite bourgeoisie was a phenomenon of the past, not the future. As a sociologist trying to bridge Marx and Weber, Mills (1951:14, 28) aptly summarised classical sociology's stance on the issue when he declared that the centralisation of property, ending the 'union of property and work', sounded the death-knell of the old middle classes which had been 'clogging the wheels of progress'.

The resounding performance of the advanced capitalist economies, especially after the Second World War, took more and more people out of the ranks of the rural and urban petite bourgeoisie into the ranks of both the working class and the new middle class. Consequently, the petit-bourgeois share of the labour force declined, though variably across the nations, during most of the post-war period. For both Weberians (Bechhofer and Elliott 1968, 1976, 1978, 1985) and Marxists (Burris 1980), this development marked the removal of the petite bourgeoisie from the main axis of class relations in advanced capitalist societies.

However, towards the close of the 1970s with the post-war boom at an end, sociologists of various persuasions began to rethink the traditional view and to question long-established conceptions on the historical trajectory and social position of the petite bourgeoisie including their marginality to capitalism, technological backwardness, economic inefficiency, and uninterrupted decline (Curran and Burrows 1986, Scase and Goffee 1982). A central theme of the 'reformed' perspective was the ideological, political, and economic functions of small commodity production in the reproduction of advanced monopoly capitalism. This would accordingly set the research agenda in the late 1970s and early 1980s.

Those who saw contemporary economies as divided into the 'traditional' and 'modern' sectors concentrated on the mechanisms of articulation and integration between the two. In her studies of Italy and France, the only major European economies which contain a sizeable petit-bourgeois population, Berger (1980, 1981) tried to make sense of the resilience of the small-scale traditional sector in terms of its functions for the large-scale modern sector – the production of high-demand goods that large firms do not produce, the cushioning of the economic impact of hard times on the modern sector by reducing unemployment, and providing the (modern) economies of a rigid kind with flexibility through subcontracting. Political factors were also given a role. The Gaullist parties in France and Christian Democrats in Italy have historically been protective of the class of small producers for both short-term electoral and long-term alliance purposes (see also Weiss 1984 for Italy).

Portraying the petite bourgeoisie as a passive resource readily used by the larger forces of the society is not obviously a radical break with the traditional perspective. But now the self-induced dynamics of small production were also highlighted. In the case of France, for instance, beginning with the Poujadist movement of artisans and shopkeepers in the 1950s, the petite bourgeoisie succeeded in extracting a number of financial concessions from governments. And due to the historical prestige it has enjoyed among consumers, French artisanal bakers were able to defeat 'industrial bread' at the market level (Bertaux and Bertaux-Wiame 1981). Another example of successful petit-bourgeois mobilisation against government policies was the mushrooming of right-wing populist parties in Scandinavia (except Sweden) during the late 1960s and early 1970s. Propelled by a sense of the erosion of the petite bourgeoisie's economic bases, these parties sought and managed to influence the policies of the mainstream parties (Hoff 1982).

The 1980s proved to be a turning point in the petite bourgeoisie's (mis-) fortune, both socially and academically. Neo-conservative governments which came to office with an unambiguous anti-labour and pro-business agenda targeted the small business sector as a 'test case' of their market-based initiatives in policy and, most conspicuously, ideology. It was against this political background that a new generation of studies on the petite bourgeoisie began to appear. The central theme of the new stream of research was the arrest of the decline in self-employment or, more arguably, the resurgence of the petite bourgeoisie. And implicitly, this amounts to nothing less than a claim that the centralisation, if not concentration, of capital has come to an end.

In the past two decades the decline of the 'old' middle class and small capital in general has reversed in many capitalist economies. Two trends demonstrate this fact. The first is a rise in self-employment in countries as diverse as Canada, the United States, the United Kingdom, Italy, Belgium, Finland and Ireland (Steinmetz and Wright 1989, OECD 1992). Until the mid-1980s, truly dramatic growth rates in self-employment levels were limited to the Anglo-American democracies – Australia, Canada, the United States and the United Kingdom – all of which embarked on ambitious programmes of neo-liberal economic restructuring that favoured the growth of small enterprise. But since the mid-1980s even social democratic Sweden has witnessed a remarkable rise in self-employment from 4.5 per cent of the non-agricultural labour force in 1985 to 7 per cent in 1990 and among men from 6.1 to 10.2 per cent (OECD 1992). Until the 1980s, rapid employment growth in the public sector had been the foundation of Swedish full employment policy (Esping-Anderson 1990). Since then, greater emphasis has been placed on local employment programmes and small business start-ups, a strategy that has enhanced the space for small-scale capital in Sweden (Johanisson 1989).

The second trend illustrating the changing fortunes of small capital is the rising share of employment in small firms and a decline in average firm size. By the mid-1980s the OECD (1985) had noted declining firm size in Austria, Belgium, France and Japan, and when only manufacturing is considered, in Denmark, Luxembourg and the United Kingdom as well. By the end of the 1980s, substantial downsizing had been noted in both Canada (Wannell 1991) and the United States (Granovetter 1984, Davis and Haltiwanger 1989, Brynjolfsson *et al.* 1989).

These developments suggest nothing less than a reversal of the long-term trend towards the centralisation of capital and a resurgence of the petite bourgeoisie and small capital. Not surprisingly, reactions to these developments have been cautious. In Britain, for example, many of those who are officially classified as self-employed do not meet the usual criteria of self-employment, such as autonomy in the work-place or the ownership of the means of production; they are in fact contractual workers (Dale 1986). In the United States, a significant portion of the officially self-employed (especially in service occupations) experience subproletarian conditions in terms of income, social security, skill, and autonomy (Linder and Houghton 1990). Since official classification methods are not able to make an unambiguous distinction between the self-employed and employees, corporations may register employees as self-employed to avoid taxes and social payments. Nevertheless, as Steinmetz and Wright (1989) observe, self-employment growth in incorporated business – the most likely site of real petit-bourgeois expansion – has been more rapid than in unincorporated business where the marginal self-employed are likely to be found.

Progress in identifying the causes of this reversal and its national variants has scarcely begun. Traditionally, self-employment has grown as a short-term cyclical response to recession and high unemployment. National studies suggest that this is the case in some industries, such as construction trades, but overall the counter-cyclical effects of increasing unemployment on self-employment have been declining (Sharpe, 1983, Steinmetz and Wright 1989). Rainnie (1985) offers a classical Marxist explanation for this 'relative retreat' of the process of concentration and centralisation. When large firms found themselves in a crisis situation during the late 1970s, the argument goes, they began to experiment to avoid the high wages, union militancy, and high costs of innovation, by fragmenting some of their operations into smaller units and by 'contracting out' others to small firms. However, it has been pointed out that this corporate strategy of downsizing and development (e.g. franchising, licensing and subcontracting) can account for only part of the small-business revival (Shutt and Whittington 1987).

In the now abundant literature on post-Fordism (e.g. Piore and Sabel 1984), the resurgence of small capital is associated with the end of the Fordist model of mass production. The emergent and increasingly successful technologies, it is argued, combine skilled labour with general-purpose machinery to produce small batches for specialised markets (Brusco 1982, Brusco and Sabel 1981). Economies of scope, not of scale, are now the order of the day (but see Murray 1983, 1987). The shift to services – especially consumer and business services – is a contributing factor. But again it is clear from national studies that this accounts for only a small share of the total shift in self-employment (Steinmetz and Wright 1989) and declining firm size (Wannell 1991). Brynjolfsson *et al.* (1989) show that increased investments in information technologies result in a decrease in vertical integration and greater reliance on market transactions to obtain inputs and distribute outputs. In short, the reduced transaction costs brought about by new technologies bring a shift from 'hierarchies' to 'markets'.

If the causes of this development are ambiguous, the consequences for workers are more apparent. Those employed in small firms tend to have lower wages, fewer benefits, are less likely to be unionised, and tend to have higher turnover rates – issues to which we return in our conclusion.

In search of the new middle class

Few questions in modern sociology are as disputed as those surrounding the 'new middle class'. Who is in it? What are its boundaries? What is its future? In post-war sociology, the dividing line was frequently drawn between white-collar and blue-collar workers using conventional and relatively simple occupational classifications. The 'working class' was composed of factory workers, truck drivers, and other blue-collar wage-earners who did 'manual' work.

Managers, school teachers, even clerks and secretaries – 'non-manual' employees who worked for salaries rather than wages and in offices and stores rather than on the shop floor – made up the new and expanding middle class. For Mills, White Collar provided a more than adequate title for his major study of middle-class life in post-war America.

With the passage of time, the boundaries of the new middle class were conceptually whittled away. The armies of (largely female) clerks, secretaries, retail sales and service workers are no longer accorded 'middle class' status by the majority of either conventional or Marxist sociologists (but see Gagliani 1981). By virtue of their typical earnings, job requirements and position in the 'relations of ruling' of the contemporary enterprise, they are more likely to be counted among the lower echelons of a new post-industrial proletariat instead. At the other end of the spectrum, those corporate executives who exercise traditional entrepreneurial functions of investment and allocation (strategic decision-making, to use Chandler's terms) are now typically counted among those who exercise 'real economic ownership', that is, as a fraction of the ruling class or bourgeoisie.

By the 1970s virtually all class theorists – Marxist and Weberian – had converged on the centrality of two broad strata for understanding the class structure of advanced capitalist societies: the growing army of mid-level corporate officials engaged in the day-to-day administration of the modern firm on the one hand, and the professional and technical 'knowledge workers' who have become virtually synonymous with post-industrialism on the other. Just how to treat the latter group was a matter of considerable contention. For the Ehrenreichs (Ehrenreich and Ehrenreich 1979), these employees became part of the 'professional-managerial class', for Goldthorpe (1982) part of the 'service class', and for Poulantzas (1975), part of the 'new petite bourgeoisie'. In Wright's (1978) initial class schema, the new 'knowledge workers' outside the traditional axis of managerial authority were allocated to a 'contradictory class location' – semi-autonomous workers – while in his later version (Wright 1985), the credentials of the 'expert class' are seen as a new basis of class exploitation.

Irrespective of theoretical predilection, both groups had to be taken seriously if for no other reason than numbers: together, 'new middle class' administrative, professional and related occupations made up between a quarter and a third of the labour force in the developed capitalist economies by the beginning of the 1980s. And despite the plethora of case studies showing processes of 'deskilling' in particular occupations and the expansion of low wage 'junk jobs' in the service sector, 'new middle class' positions continued to grow disproportionately to the rest of the economy through the 1970s and 1980s.

In what could be counted as a 'first generation' of comparative studies to discuss national differences in the size of growth of the new middle class, authors such as Burris (1980), Livingstone (1983), Carboni (1984) and Ornstein (1983) followed the expedient of adjusting occupational distributions, routinely published by the International Labour Organisation, to approximate a definition of the 'new middle class'. These studies pointed to the fact that the United States and the United Kingdom, countries that 'have occupied a dominant position within the capitalist world economy' (Burris 1980:167), were also where the new middle class had attained the most significant dimensions. Just as the decline of the old middle class was associated with the transition from feudal-agrarian to a capitalist-industrial economy, the rise of the new middle class could be understood as 'the product of developmental tendencies specific to the advanced stage of monopoly capitalism' (Burris 1980:164). Especially notable was the large size of the managerial strata. Carboni's estimates (1984:136) showed the United States and Britain with 10.5 per cent and 9.4 per cent of the labour force in management occupations, respectively, compared to 3 per cent to 5 per cent in most other countries at the end of the 1970s. Sweden, a late industrialiser, was also notable for its relatively large new middle class – indeed the largest in Burris's estimates, but this was entirely due to the large number of professional and technical employees. This was a result, as Burris agreed (1980:172), of 'four decades of Social Democratic rule' which has created a labour market dominated by health, education and other state welfare services.

These authors offered a variety of plausible interpretations for the patterns they observed but lacked any data to evaluate their claims. Drawing on Hymer's (1972) classic essay, Burris argued that the high percentage of managers in the United States labour force reflects the concentration of the administrative, planning, and research functions in the metropolitan centre of an American-dominated multinational economy (see Johnson 1982). For Livingstone (1983:62), the fact that Canada had fewer managers than the United States reflected Canada's position as a 'secondary imperialist formation' and net importer of foreign capital. For Burris and Carboni, Great Britain's relatively large managerial strata was a residue of both its imperial past and its continued importance as an international financial centre.

In contrast, Bowles *et al.* (1983) argued that America's high administrative overheads are largely a result of American forms of labour control that emphasise intensive supervision and regulation of workers. In the United States, they argue, the accelerated growth of the administrative component of the American economy after the Second World War reflects increasing intensity of supervision over American workers, a response by employers to growing resistance on the shop floor.

Esping-Anderson (1990) added a distinct 'post-industrial' twist to these views. Because the public welfare state is underdeveloped in the United States, the corporate welfare system must compensate. More managers are required to administer the huge and complex fringe benefit programmes that constitute America's private 'welfare state'. And because the United States lacks a well developed system of labour exchanges and work-training institutions, American firms require very large personnel departments to recruit and train labour.

To adjudicate among these interpretations with occupational data was impossible for the simple reason that occupational codes tell us little about what people actually do in their jobs. A minimal requirement for understanding why American workers appear to be 'overmanaged', for example, is knowledge of what so-called managers actually do when they manage. Are they engaged in making high-level policy decisions (Burris), regulating workers (Bowles *et al.*), or administering corporate welfare and training programmes (Esping-Anderson)?

Many of these difficulties were overcome by a 'second generation' of comparative studies initiated by E. O. Wright at the University of Wisconsin which, rather than relying on the vagaries of occupational titles, used a complex set of direct behavioural measures to determine what people do in their jobs.[2] In addition to the usual self-reported occupational titles, respondents in the Comparative Class Structure Surveys (CCSS) were asked detailed questions about their involvement in organisational decision-making, the forms of authority they exercise over other employees, and their place in the organisational, hierarchy (see Wright, Costello, Hachen and Sprague 1982).

The advantages of directly measuring what people do in their jobs was illustrated by one of the first studies to emerge from this set of cross-national surveys. In a comparison of Sweden and the United States, Ahrne and Wright (1983) demonstrated that the American labour force was indeed 'overmanaged', not because America has more senior executives administering the American multinational empire, but because American employers hire more labour to supervise and regulate the activity of other workers. In a follow-up study that included Canada, Black and Myles (1986) were able to show that this American pattern – the 'American Way' – was also characteristic of those sectors of the Canadian economy traditionally controlled by American capital and organised by American unions, namely, manufacturing and resource extraction. In financial, social and other services, the class organisation of the Canadian work-place resembles that of Sweden.

These studies also demonstrated that the other side of the 'middle class' – Wright's 'semi-autonomous employees' – were proportionately twice as numerous in Sweden as in the United States, but not simply or even mainly because of Sweden's large public sector and developed welfare state. Rather, employers in all sectors of the Swedish economy employ disproportionately more 'knowledge workers',[3] and such employees are less likely to be involved in exercising authority over other employees. The United States does have a large 'new middle class' by international standards, but the reason for this lies in its distinctive 'industrial relations' system, not its position in the world economy or because of its underdeveloped welfare state. Indeed, contrary to the evidence derived from ILO occupational data, Clement and Myles (1994) have shown that as one narrows the definition of what is meant by a manager to include only higher level executive positions, national differences virtually disappear. Even with Wright's broader definition of management, Holtmann and Strasser (1990) show a rather narrow range of variation, with managers making up between 12.2 per cent and 14.8 per cent of the employed labour force.

Despite improvements in measurement quality, the Comparative Class Structure Surveys quickly proved limited in their ability to account for the differences they identified. Because of their cross-sectional, design, explanation was limited to differences that could be accounted for by compositional differences in industry mix or the level of state employment. Such avenues were quickly exhausted because country-specific patterns tend to dominate mere compositional effects. The result, as in the first generation of studies, was reversion to plausible but ad hoc historical interpretations for which there was little direct evidence. Australia, for example, has as many supervisory employees as the United States and even more managers (policy-makers), a fact attributed to an historical attraction to 'bureaucratic' solutions to economic problems (Boreman *et al.* 1989).

Great Britain and the United States show the greatest resemblance in their class structure (as the ILO data also suggest) despite radically different patterns of economic growth and development in the twentieth century (Holtmann and Strasser 1990:19).

Post-industrialism, women and working class

One of the oddities of the class debates of the 1970s and early 1980s is that theoretically there was more concern with drawing class boundaries (who was in the middle class, who was not) than with explaining the results once the boundaries were drawn. Several consequences followed from this preoccupation. First, once the data were gathered, there was little in the way of theory to guide empirical investigations of class structures. Second, there was even less concern with national differences and changes in the composition of the working class who for the most part were defined as a residual category once non-working (and especially 'new middle') class positions were identified. During the 1980s, however, all this began to change. Under the rubrics of 'post-Fordism' and 'post-industrialism', attention returned squarely to issues related to the dynamics of class structure in general and its consequences for the working class in particular. In this context, the question of gender as a class issue could no longer be ignored.

The stereotypical worker who emerges from the pages of the history of industrial capitalism was a male, blue-collared worker employed in the production of goods (mining, manufacturing, construction) and their distribution (railways, trucking, shipping). He was typically employed by a capitalist firm, not the state, and was the raw material from which the labour movement was formed. The relative and now absolute decline of the industrial (male) working class is a result both in the material division of labour and in the social composition of the people employed by capital. The first of these changes has to do with the shift of employment from the production of things to the production of services; the second is a result of the massive entry of women into the paid labour force.

Drawing on Baumol (1967), Esping-Anderson (1993) postulates three potential outcomes for the working class of the 'post-industrial' economies. As high productivity in manufacturing releases labour, the service sector's capacity to generate new jobs is limited because of low productivity growth. The first possibility, as a result, is a rise in unemployment, declining labour force participation, and the growth of an 'outsider' class of welfare state clients. A second possibility is government-subsidised employment, primarily in the form of welfare state jobs in health, education and social services. The third possibility is that service employment will expand in the private sector because of low wages that correspond to productivity differentials between sectors.

The main consequences of these alternative scenarios will be experienced by women who make up the majority of service workers. In the first – low employment – scenario, women bear the brunt of low labour participation rates; in the government-led wage subsidy model, they will have high participation rates but also high levels of job segregation in social services; where low wages are the main source of service growth, they will be concentrated in low-paid personal services.

Welfare states and labour unions play key roles in shaping which outcome is likely to occur. Service-intensive welfare states, such as Sweden, will tend to the high-employment government subsidy model; transfer intensive welfare states such as Germany will tend towards the low employment, 'outsider class' variant. In countries such as Canada and the United States, with weak labour unions and less developed welfare states, the low-wage, high-employment model can be anticipated.

Using reconstruction of micro-data from national censuses, Esping-Anderson (1993) is able to show rough correspondence between his theoretical expectations and the occupational and industry composition of the working class for six countries. Germany, a transfer-intensive welfare state, has had much slower service sector growth than elsewhere, comparatively few unskilled workers in either goods or services, low female participation rates, and a very large 'outsider class'. Sweden and Norway have high levels of service employment as a result of a large, unskilled, and predominantly female work force in the welfare state and high levels of sex segregation. North America's 'flexible' (i.e. low-wage) labour markets also have high levels of service employment, and a highly developed, low-wage, consumer service sector. Britain, Esping-Anderson concludes, straddles the German and North American models: slow to post-industrialise, but biased towards the low-skill low-wage American consumer service model.

But the implications of all this for the future of the working class are less than clear. Country-specific studies included in the Esping-Anderson volume show there is little indication that a new 'post-industrial' proletariat is taking form except in Britain. Unskilled service employment in both North America and Scandinavia mainly provides entry-level jobs for the young who typically move on rather quickly to more traditional 'working-class' occupations in blue-collar occupations (for men) and clerical employment (for women). Germany has low mobility out of unskilled service work but comparatively few unskilled service jobs. Only in Britain is there a large, relatively stable, unskilled, and post-industrial proletariat emerging.

The future of class analysis

As class analysts, whether Marxist (Wright 1985) or Weberian (Erikson and Goldthorpe 1992), were developing new data bases appropriate to comparative studies of class structure and class mobility during the

1980s, the real world passed them by. Irrespective of the variety of methods and typologies these authors adopted, all reached the same conclusions concerning emergent trends in class structure. Traditional proletarian jobs in manufacturing were declining and the shift to services was dominated not by low-end fast food workers but by high-end managerial, professional and technical occupations. To put matters simply, all of these studies converged on the claim that 'good' (read 'middle class') jobs were on the rise and 'bad' (proletarian) jobs were in decline (Block 1990, Boyd 1990, Esping-Anderson 1990, 1993, Goldthorpe 1987, Mayer and Carroll 1987, Myles 1988, Wright and Martin 1987). By virtually all of the conventional sociological yardsticks, emergent trends in Western labour markets appeared to be taking us towards a post-industrial Nirvana and the demise if not the disappearance of the 'working class' as we know it. As Esping-Anderson (1993:225) concludes: 'there is little doubt that the kind of polarization depicted by traditional class theory has lost much of its face validity'.

Outside of the small world of sociology, however, matters looked very different. As Levy (1988) showed for the United States, patterns of upward economic (not occupational) mobility had declined dramatically since the 1960s both between and within generations (for Canada, see Myles, Picot and Wannell 1993). The rapid growth in real living standards that characterised the post-war boom and created Goldthorpe's famous affluent worker (better known in popular North American parlance as the 'middle class') had come to an end. During the 1980s, attention turned to the 'declining middle class' (Kuttner 1983), a result of growing polarisation in wages and earnings in Europe, North America and Australia (Gottschalk and Joyce 1991, Gottschalk 1993) and, to a more modest extent, welfare state cutbacks in some countries (Fritzell 1992). Downsizing, contracting out, expanded use of 'just-in-time' and temporary workers began to affect not just low-wage service personnel but professionals and mid-level managers as well.

Gottschalk and Joyce (1991), using the Luxembourg Income Study data base for the 1980s, show rising inequality and polarisation in wages and salaries for Australia, Canada, France, Germany, Netherlands, Sweden and the United Kingdom and the United States. All countries showed below average growth or declines in wages in the lower deciles and above average growth (or below average declines) for the upper deciles. In a five-country study from the same data base, Fritzell (1992) shows that the growing wage inequality (the main source of growing inequality in family income) was exacerbated by changes in the tax-transfer system (welfare state cuts) in Sweden, the United Kingdom and the United States, but largely offset by welfare state transfers in Canada and Germany. The most dramatic shift in the earnings profile occurred in the United Kingdom where the 'middle' (those earning between 50 per cent and 150 per cent of median earnings) declined from 62 per cent to 43 per cent.

All of this came as a great surprise to economists who had become accustomed to the stable patterns in the structure of income inequality that prevailed from the end of the Second World War until the 1970s (Danziger and Gottschalk 1993:3). Progress in identifying the causes for this shift has been slow, however, more a matter of chipping away at prevailing popular explanations and eliminating theories (deindustrialisation, demographic shifts) that are inconsistent with the data (see Danziger and Gottschalk 1993, Gottschalk and Joyce 1991). Only in the case of Sweden is there a clearly identifiable 'smoking gun', namely, the breakdown of centralised wage bargaining after 1983 (Hibbs 1990, 1991).

This disjuncture between the conclusions of conventional socio-logical studies of class and actual trends in wages and other job characteristics since the 1970s poses a number of theoretical and empirical conundrums. Unlike economic theory, in which rewards and life chances are seen to accrue to persons and their human 'capital', sociologists have always insisted that rewards are attached to positions (Parkin 1971:13). The class system or the structure of inequality is defined by the distribution of positions, and the only remaining issue is to identify the process by which persons are recruited to fill these positions. For Parkin (1971:18): 'The backbone of the class structure, and indeed of the entire reward system of modern Western society, is the occupational order.' Marxisant versions of this 'positional' account differ only by virtue of the way 'positions' in the structure of empty places are defined. But as Levy (1988) clearly shows, occupational mobility is a poor indicator of economic mobility either intergenerationally or over the life course. And one of the earliest lessons learned from the 'declining middle' research is that changes in occupational structure (the distribution of positions) are a poor guide to changes in the distribution of wage and earnings (compare Rosenthal 1985 with McMahon and Tschetter 1986).

The failure of class-based positional models to identify key shifts in economic mobility and the structure of inequality is especially problematic for so-called neo-Weberian class models (e.g. Goldthorpe 1987) in which 'life chances' figure prominently in the definition of classes and there is a presumption that 'classes' cause inequality. Neo-Marxist orthodoxy has generally insisted on separating the definition of classes defined by production relations from class definitions that include living standards (the sphere of consumption). But the general failure of neo-Marxist class models (Wright and Martin 1987) to detect the polarisation of the 1970s and 1980s and instead to insist along with everyone else that trends in class structure point to a general deproletarianisation of labour in advanced capitalist economies must pose some theoretical discomfort. As it has turned out, Braverman's (1974) scenario of class polarisation was correct at the level of consumption, not at the level of production relations as he anticipated. And ironically, it is a former consultant to the Republican Party, Phillips (1993), who has built on these developments to provide the more provocative account of the historical implications of America's shifting 'class structure'.

Post-war North America and then Europe saw the emergence of a high-wage working class protected by public, corporate and union policies to stabilise both wages and employment. The result was to eliminate for many the 'cycle of poverty' (Rowntree) traditionally associated with the working-class life course. For workers, Rowntree's life cycle of poverty was replaced with what might be called the 'Fordist life cycle' (Myles 1990) characterised by relative stability of both jobs and income over the ups and downs of the business cycle and the individual life source. Since the 1970s the search for labour flexibility has begun to unravel post-war employment relations and with them have gone the class and stratification implications the sociologists once felt secure reading off occupational hierarchies and class maps. For the most part, wage polarisation and growing labour market insecurity have grown within not between classes during the 1980s. As a result, the familiar positional approach – the 'backbone' of empirical class analysis – has lost some of its analytical power for explaining much that is consequential to class theory, whether Marxian or Weberian. This hardly means that class analysis is dead. Instead, it calls for new analytical tools to capture the class character of late twentieth-century capitalisms.

Notes

1. Abridged. Originally published as 'Comparative Studies in Class Structure'. *Annual Review of Sociology* 20, 1994, 103–24.
2. Designed explicitly to measure national differences in class structure, a 3-country data file (including the United States, Sweden, and Finland) became available in the early 1980s, followed by a 5-country file (adding Canada and Norway) and at the end of the decade a 10-country file (now adding Great Britain, the former West Germany, Australia, Denmark, and Japan). These data are well known and have been described in detail elsewhere. A useful introduction to the project can be found in Wright (1995) and to the debates it engendered, in Wright (1989).
3. Those familiar with the debate on Wright's class typology will be aware of the especially contested nature of his category of 'semi-autonomous' workers. Two points were at issue: first, the theoretical status of the category as a separate (contradictory) class location; and second, the measurement properties of the procedure used to identify such jobs. As a result of a special supplement to the Canadian version of the survey, Clement and Myles (1994: Appendix II) were able to demonstrate that the latter concern is unwarranted. The procedure used to identify semi-autonomous employees in Wright's original survey provides a valid, indeed rigorous, procedure for identifying 'knowledge workers', a category of workers characterised by high levels of self-direction and jobs with high levels of cognitive requirements.

CHAPTER 14

Classes, underclasses and the labour market[1]

Lydia Morris

In recent years there have been a number of deep-seated changes in the British economy. Levels of male employment have fallen dramatically, the gender composition of the work-force has altered, and there have been shifts in emphasis from full-time to part-time employment, from male to female labour, from manufacturing to services, and from secure to casualised work. My own research over much of this period has been concerned to document the social impact of such changes, through an examination of the work experiences of those populations most directly affected. It has been something of a puzzle for me that social class, the concept which most overtly and directly addresses issues of structured inequality, has seemed of little relevance to this work. In part this is because I have been centrally concerned with changes concentrated within a broadly defined working class,[2] but also because these changes have themselves served to undermine conventional approaches to class analysis (see Morris 1995).

High levels of unemployment, non-standard employment patterns, and dual employment for married couples all raise problems for approaches to social class based on a sole or principal earner. More significantly, any social class schema derived from a static model of occupational structure will be poorly equipped to address the nature and effects of rapid labour market change; the structure and the relative positions it represents are themselves in flux. I hope to illustrate some of these points by a focus on the specific debate surrounding the notion of the underclass, and in the light of some related empirical data.

The popular assumption when male unemployment began its sharp rise was that in many homes women would be taking over from men as principal earners in the household. After all, there had been a substantial rise in the labour market activity of *married* women throughout the 1970s and 1980s. 'Role reversal' was in fact only a minority response to male unemployment for reasons by now well documented (for review see Morris 1990, Irwin and Morris 1993), and instead we are seeing a process of 'social polarisation'. This term was adopted by Ray Pahl (1984) to refer to a pattern in which employment has come to be concentrated in some homes and completely absent from others; a two-earner/no-earner divide. The phenomenon was part of the basis for his view that social class is no longer the best vehicle for analysing social structure. Whether a household has any employed members at all was thus argued to be more important than the particular occupational ranking of any one of them (Pahl 1988). A more extreme reaction to the same phenomenon has been the adoption of the notion of an 'underclass' to capture the nature of change in our social structure, although definitions and explanations are hotly contested.

Conflicting notions of the underclass

Towards the end of the 1980s in Britain there was an upsurge of interest in the concept of the 'underclass'. A good deal of the surrounding debate was political in nature, driven by fears of social unrest among disaffected youth, and by claims that the welfare state had been over-generous, creating a 'dependency culture' which was at least partially responsible for high levels of unemployment. Such ideas have already been debated extensively in an American literature of much longer standing and Wilson (1987) reviews the US discussion to date, offering his own definition of the 'underclass':

> Included in this group are individuals who lack training or skills and either experience long-term unemployment or are not members of the labour force, individuals who are engaged in street crime and other forms of aberrant behaviour, and families that experience long-term spells of poverty and/or welfare dependency. (p. 8)

He then makes two related distinctions: the polarisation between conservative and liberal views, and the corresponding opposition between cultural and structural explanations.

The conservative perspective embraces a cultural explanation, rooted in the idea of socialisation into a counter-culture or sub-culture of dependency (Murray 1984). In this respect it shares much with the culture of poverty thesis (Lewis 1968). A structural approach emphasises long-term unemployment as a failure of the economy, and argues that welfare provision, far from inducing dependency, offers inadequate support. It has, however, been argued (Gans 1990) that the term 'underclass' has become so hopelessly polluted that it should be dropped, and Wilson (1991) takes up this argument by submitting the term 'ghetto poor' and calling for 'a more concentrated focus on research and theoretical issues and less fixation on disputed concepts or labels' (p. 5).

There has, however, been an additional dimension to the debate in Britain, which relates directly to some of the problems confronting class analysis. Unemployment has always posed a problem for classificatory schema based on occupational groupings, and the notion of the underclass has been taken up by some in an attempt to deal with the problem as, for example, in Runciman's (1990) article 'How many Classes are there in Contemporary British Society?'

Runciman's objective is not in any sense explanatory, and this is an issue I return to later; he is concerned with definition alone, placed in the broader context of class analysis. Beneath the conventional six class schema (one upper, three middle and two working classes), Runciman argues that there is a seventh to whom the term 'underclass' may be applied:

> But the term must be understood to stand not for a group or category of workers systematically disadvantaged within the labour market but . . . where benefits are paid by the state to those unable to participate in the labour market at all. (p. 388)

Members of this group are seen as being 'typically the long-term unemployed' (p. 388); though the *potentially* broader definition given by Runciman prompts questions about the classification of those more conclusively outside the labour market by virtue of age, disability, etc., who might seem to belong to a separate category.

Runciman's principal criterion for representing divisions *within* the working class is 'marketability', though this may combine with aspects of 'ownership' (or tools) or 'control' (of entry) in the case of skilled workers (p. 387). In his view the long-term unemployed are among those 'unable to participate in the market', and are placed in a residual class location by virtue of their lack of success in the competition for work. The 'underclass' is thus defined by Runciman in relation to the occupational structure, but on the basis of either ineffective or non-participation. A similar approach has been adopted by others, and is for example contained in Smith's definition:

> The underclass are those who fall outside (the) class schema because they belong to family units having no stable relationship with the mode of production – legitimate gainful employment. (Smith 1992:4)

A broader approach to defining the underclass emphasises more generalised labour market disadvantage as underlying its (alleged) existence (cf. Wilson 1991). So, for example, Giddens (1973) writes that:

> The 'underclass' is composed of people that are concentrated among the lowest paid occupations, or are chronically unemployed or semi-employed, as a result of a 'disqualifying' market capacity of a primarily cultural type. (p. 465)

Here Giddens is abstracting from a predominantly US literature which places explanatory weight on cultural factors, a view also adopted by Murray in his recent observations in the UK (1990). Murray, however, wishes to emphasise family circumstances and particularly the significance of single parenthood in generating a subculture of dependence. The definition offered by Giddens differs from this approach in resting entirely on position in the labour market, albeit with some reference to a cultural dimension. By implication, therefore, he shares Runciman's focus on 'marketability', though unlike Runciman he makes no reference to a formalised class schema.

Giddens's definition of the 'underclass' has been taken up by Gallie (1988), whose interest also hinges upon position in the labour market and is closely connected to the speculation and debate in recent years about 'flexible' employment. Gallie's concern is with the potential for class formation in the sense of collective self-awareness. His conclusion is that the population groups affected by flexible working patterns are predominantly female, and too disparate to provide any foundation for distinctive sub-cultures, while for the long-term unemployed social withdrawal and heterogeneity reduce the possibility of a collective identity emerging – either through political action or sub-cultural norms. In other words, the structural location for an underclass exists, but the cultural underpinnings do not – this very point could of course be made about other class groupings.

Implicit in these contrasting approaches to the notion of the underclass is the question of at what duration of unemployment 'no stable relationship' with paid work is deemed to exist; and how this condition stands in relation to unstable employment? It is not clear that these questions can be resolved by the theoretical construction of a new class location rather than by empirical investigation into discontinuity in labour force experience, and the changing structure of employment. In fact, the more general question raised by such debate but not quite made explicit is how class analysis can deal with labour market change, and specifically changing employment structures.

Unemployment in Hartlepool

To explore these problems further reference is made to data collected in Hartlepool from a random sample of three distinctive groups of male workers: Group A: those suffering continuous unemployment for at least the last 12 months; Group B: those in continuous employment with the same firm for at least the last 12 months; Group C: those recruited to employment within the last 12 months, who at the time of interview might be either employed or unemployed.

The definition of this last group was intended to maximise the chances of detecting the existence of a group of male workers who typically experienced frequent and involuntary job changes. If such a group exists a recent job start would probably have been preceded by frequent entrances to and exits from employment such as to constitute a 'chequered' job history (cf. Harris 1987). This possibility was investigated by the completion of an employment history for all groups, covering the period 1979 to 1989, and including questions about means of access to jobs and reasons for their termination.

A crude indicator of difference between the sample groupings is the total number of job episodes contained in the 11-year work histories. From this data alone it is clear that the recent recruits (group C) were, over the total 11-year period, likely to have held more jobs than either of the other two groups. About 70 per cent of the recent recruits had held four or more jobs in their 11-year history, in contrast to less than a quarter of group B (stable), and less than one tenth of group A (unemployed). Almost half of group C workers had held six or more jobs in the period considered, often interspersed with periods out of work.

The first step is to consider just how far conventional social class designations can take us in understanding these differences. For example, it is quite possible that the contrasting experience of the three sample groups is simply a product of their different 'social class' positions.[2] Since the focus at this stage of analysis is on sources of labour market vulnerability the long-term unemployed are classified with reference to their stated 'main line of work'.

A number of points of interest emerge from the class composition of the sample groups, the most obvious being the familiar concentration of unskilled workers among the long-term unemployed: 15.3 per cent of all the unskilled in the sample had never worked in their 11-year history, in contrast to roughly 2 per cent for classes IIIm and IV. The unskilled also make up over half of those who have never moved out of unemployment into work, and little over one third of those who have. Yet the long-term unemployed do not constitute a homogeneous group; 32 per cent are skilled manual workers (and 19 per cent semi-skilled), albeit much less likely to have served an apprenticeship than those in the other groupings. The circumstances of the long-term unemployed thus largely, *but not exclusively*, reflect their social class designation by main line of work, and their lack of formal craft qualifications. In this context social class is an important key to understanding long-term unemployment, and whether unemployment *per se* should have a separate class designation is not clear.

The difference between groups B (secure) and C (insecure) pose more of a problem, and cannot similarly be linked to contrasting social class positions. Both groupings are made up of predominantly skilled manual workers, but the insecure group shows a much greater vulnerability to job loss and unemployment, albeit short-term. The fragmented pattern seems to result from a combination of repeated redundancy and temporary employment. Once out of work then a person is likely to become prone to redundancy in firms which operate on a 'last in first out' basis, and also to become a likely candidate for temporary employment for which the competition is lower than for secure jobs.

The composition of the three sample groupings suggest that social class distinctions neither capture nor explain the nature of the contrast between the secure and insecure workers, which persist even across the manual/non-manual divide. While class designation does reveal an important aspect of long-term unemployment – which the notion of the underclass threatens to obscure – it also tends to conflate different employment histories and trajectories, and is not so easily applied to those who have never worked.

The limits of social class designations

To summarise the argument so far, the concept of the underclass has been used by various writers to refer either to the long-term unemployed, to a more broadly defined group suffering labour market disadvantage, or to a benefit-dependent population, a definition based on state dependence. This last definition misleadingly combines groups both active and inactive in the labour market. While the data on male work histories does show a clear distinction between the long-term unemployed and those with fragmented work histories, who cannot legitimately be grouped together, the difference between them is largely a factor of social class; the long-term unemployed fall predominantly (but not exclusively) into the unskilled (class V) category, in contrast to insecure workers who are predominantly skilled. If long-term unemployment is a feature of this class position it seems inappropriate to assign it to a separate class location, that of the underclass. To separate those affected from their position when in work is to disguise the source of their vulnerability.

Against this argument is the fact that the long-term unemployed group is not homogeneous in class terms, and their classification by 'main line of work' does not convincingly accommodate those who have never worked. As to workers suffering insecure employment, social class position is not sufficient to distinguish between them and those more securely placed, partly because both groups fall predominantly into class IIIm, and partly because the differences remain, even within other class categories. There is some evidence of a cohort effect, and the propensity for broken employment tends to decrease with age. However, the characteristic differences between the groups remain *within* age bands, despite the greater vulnerability of young workers. Even above age thirty well over one third of workers from groups B and C combined have employment histories which may be characterised as fragmented.

One further question regarding the relationship between non-stable employment and class designation is the extent to which job moves may be seen as embracing career development, or 'mobility' (defined here in terms of movement across Registrar-General social class groupings). If a social class represents common life chances then we would expect to find similar trajectories following from a specific designation. In general terms there is some evidence of mobility in the sample as a whole with reference both to their own starting position, as indicated by first job on leaving school, and with reference to their father's class position.

The prospects of mobility can be assessed comparatively for the stable and insecure groupings, and here we find that the chances of advancing upon starting position (first ever job) are good for *both* groups, though higher for the less frequent changers.[3] Conversely, a significant proportion of both groups experience some deterioration in their position. Thus, the experience of fragmented employment can encompass very different trajectories, representing both upward and downward movement, and does not appear of itself to constitute a class position. The picture is further complicated by comparisons between 'insecure' and 'secure' workers, for although they are largely similar when classified by current occupation, the two groups have distinctively different employment histories and prospects.

The pattern for the insecure group is certainly not indicative of advancement through deliberate and calculated movement, for evidence of *involuntary* job change with fragmented employment is very powerful; 29.2 per cent of those with four or more jobs in their 11-year history made no *voluntary* departures from work, and only 8.2 per cent made no *involuntary* departures. This compares with 68 per cent of those with 3 or less jobs who made no *involuntary* departures. When combined with an associated experience of unemployment (85 per cent of the insecure group), the pattern suggests that with or without some progressive movement the fragmented employment detected in the current research represents a distinctive position of disadvantage, but not one easily captured by social class designations.

Implications for class analysis

Brown (1982) has pointed out the limitations of a cross-sectional approach to the analysis of class structure, and argued that work history data is necessary in order to identify the contrasting experiences of employment, sub-employment and long-term unemployment. Thus, as we note above, at any given point identical occupational positions can represent moments in very different employment histories, (cf. Stewart *et al*. 1980, Prandy 1990) as indeed can unemployment. Two additional and related problems are highlighted by our data; not only do social classes expand and decline over time with economic change, but employment trajectories also change.

Job mobility in Hartlepool once represented a viable career option; it now almost inevitably entails significant periods of unemployment. Thus while it is true that we can only fully capture the nature of social stratification by incorporating a life-course view, the very structures in which an individual's employment experience is located are subject to change over time. The nature and distribution of vulnerability which results from these changes present a problem for any snap-shot picture of the class structure, for the structure in which such trajectories are located is itself undergoing change, and the relative positions any schema may represent are never fixed.

Thus, the emergence of a group designated the 'underclass' is only the most obvious manifestation of more complex and far-reaching change, and the notion is itself unhelpful. If defined in terms of state dependence then the category embraces too many groupings – the retired, the unemployed, single parents – who have nothing else in common. But to restrict the label to the unemployed disguises the source of their vulnerability as (disproportionately) unskilled workers.

But there are further, more damaging problems for class analysis, and these are illustrated by the data on insecure employment. Static social class schema are not designed to illuminate the dynamics of the labour market, and the effect of this is that class designations are of little use to those who wish to examine the nature and effects of recent economic change. To do so would require a more dynamic approach to social and economic relations, one aspect of which concerns the structuring and restructuring of employment. Another is the process whereby some workers find work and others do not, which takes us back to certain aspects of the underclass debate.

Informal aspects of social structure

'Cultural' approaches to unemployment (e.g. Murray 1990:17) have focused on individual 'attitudes', such as the absence of a will to work, which is often seen as a defining feature of the underclass. For example, Murray (1990), extending his work on the American 'underclass' (1984) to the UK, argues:

> Definitive proof that an underclass has arrived is that large numbers of young, healthy, low income males choose not to take jobs. (p. 17)

> An unknown but probably considerable number of people . . . manage to qualify for benefit even if in reality very few job opportunities would tempt them to work. (p. 18)

A counter-argument is put forward by Wilson (1987, 1991) writing in the USA. He argues that economic decline is the principal explanation of long-term unemployment, exacerbated by spatial and social concentrations of the unemployed.

> The central predicament of inner-city ghetto residents is joblessness reinforced by a growing social isolation in impoverished neighbourhoods, as reflected, for example, in the rapidly decreasing access to job information network systems. (Wilson 1991:9)

Informal networks of association have been rather more the terrain of anthropologists than of sociologists, and where they do feature in sociology it is usually with reference to some specific aspect of social interaction, rather than in connection with social structural divisions. Arguably social networks make manifest a dimension of social structure which is not accessible through either a snap-shot analysis of individuals' employment status, or even a somewhat broader household perspective. Yet it remains to explore how informal patterns of association interact with other social divisions, and whether they themselves constitute a significant component of structured inequality. Social networks of informal association and exchange represent an underexplored aspect of social and economic life, which may offer an important key to understanding the dynamics of social structural change. To explore this question further we must first determine the extent to which the different groupings investigated by this study tend towards mutual association, or even social segregation.

Social segregation

The association of unemployment in domestic partnerships has long been acknowledged as a symptom of social polarisation. Data from the Hartlepool research show considerable variation by sample group in the employment status of the female spouse, ranging from 13.2 per cent in employment for group A (long-term male unemployment), to 71.0 per cent for sample group B (secure male employment). At the extreme positions of male long-term unemployment and male secure employment, the two-earner/no-earner division is more marked than is apparent in national statistics, probably because the national data do not separate out long-term from short-term unemployment (for discussion see Irwin and Morris 1993).

It has for some time been known that unemployment tends to be concentrated within nuclear family households (Payne 1987) but data from the Hartlepool survey suggest that such concentration is also to be found within the extended family. The long-term unemployed men (group A) seem to show a tendency towards segregation in terms of both the level of employment and unemployment to be found among close male relatives: 35.2 per cent of close male kin were *unemployed* at the time of interview as compared with 15.8 per cent of the group in secure employment (group B), and 19.2 per cent for the insecure workers (group C). Similar contrasts, though not so marked, are found when we look at the levels of *employment* for close male kin resident in Hartlepool, and the contrasts were repeated when male respondents were asked to name up to three close friends, giving their employment status.

Household and kinship concentrations of unemployment were found to be compounded by spatial concentrations, and the three sample groupings in this study show markedly different residence patterns. The long-term unemployed rely to a very great extent on local authority accommodation, while the employed population are predominantly in owner-occupied housing. Because of the arrangement of the housing stock in the town this translates into a distinctive spatial pattern, with high concentrations of unemployment in particular areas. One of Pahl's early conclusions in research on the Isle of Sheppey (1984:309) was that neighbouring households with broadly similar qualifications in terms of skill and experience could find themselves in contrasting positions. The data from Hartlepool, however, reveal a distinct spatial dimension to social polarisation. As a result any casual patterns of social contact are thus disproportionately likely to be with others in similar circumstances, and we are likely to find concentrations of unemployment within social networks.

In summary, then, the long-term unemployed tend to live on public-sector housing estates with high levels of unemployment, tend to have partners who are also unemployed, to show concentrations of unemployment in their extended networks, and to name close friends who are also unemployed. These patterns are not to the total exclusion of the employed population but there is certainly a strong tendency towards mutual association. It remains to spell out the implications of these concentrations and what remains of this paper will consider the significance of informal job search.

Informal job search

Data on job search show that informal networks play a central role in recruitment through the exchange of information and influence. Just over half of all jobs in the work history data were accessed by informal methods. There are two possibilities to investigate here; first that the information resources embodied in informal networks affect the propensity to find work, and second that different means of access to employment will have different implications with regard to security.

The Hartlepool data reveal three almost equally significant sources of information: relatives, old friends and acquaintances. The findings are interesting when considered against Granovetter's hypothesis on the strength of weak ties (1973). His contention was that weak ties are more important than strong ties for job search because it is the breadth of the field covered rather than the quality of the tie which is important. This seems to be contradicted by the data above which suggest that the close ties of relatives and friends are more important than those of acquaintances. The explanation for this may be that when competition for jobs is high, i.e. in areas where the level of unemployment is high, then a system of preferential channelling may assert itself. This would mean that job information would be more likely to be passed on selectively than dispersed broadly and readily. It may also be that Hartlepool, being a relatively close knit community, shows a higher incidence of 'strong ties' than might otherwise be the case.

It is not simply the relationship between the job seeker and the informant which is of interest, however. Success for the job seeker is very much more likely in cases where the informant is employed at the place where a vacancy arises. A similar finding is revealed when we ask whether the informant put in a good word for the applicant, and where they did then the application was more likely to be successful. Thus, those best placed in the search for work are people with a broad network of employed friends or relatives, but especially if they are in a position to speak on behalf of the candidate. Yet we know from the data presented earlier that the long-term unemployed are necessarily at a disadvantage in this process.

The other distinctive point to emerge from the data on job search concerns the insecure group. While there is a generally high reliance on informal recruitment in the Hartlepool labour market, it is of particular significance in the histories of insecure workers. For them informal recruitment is linked to temporary employment in a manner not apparent for the other groupings. This suggests an explanation of the broken employment pattern which shows an age and skill related influence, but is most strongly linked to the types of jobs made available through respondents' own particular social networks of information. In other words, the world of social contact which grows up around insecure employment does much to reproduce the pattern, just as the concentration of unemployment in the networks of the jobless tend to confirm their disadvantage.

Conclusion

A number of recent changes in employment structures have seemed to present a challenge to class schema based on occupational groupings. Long-term unemployment is one manifestation of change, and the argument here has been against the creation of a new class location (such as the underclass) to accommodate this position. This paper has instead broadened the focus on changing patterns of employment to consider the varied trajectories of secure, insecure and unemployed workers. In doing so some rather more fundamental problems for class analysis have been revealed; notably the varied histories of workers who at different times have occupied the same 'class' position, and the changes in the occupational structure itself which underly these different trajectories.

The significance of informal networks of association has been demonstrated in relation to job search and recruitment, such that the long-term unemployed with reduced workplace contacts suffer considerable disadvantage. The role of social networks, the changing structure of employment, and more particularly, the interconnection between the two suggest that a dynamic approach to social structure may be more revealing in times of change than a narrowly focused concern with refining static class schema. Such schema seem only to offer a starting point for the investigation of labour market dynamics.

Conventional approaches to social inequality, by the occupational ranking of either individuals or even by some composite household indicator, need then to be complemented by both a consideration of the dynamics of labour market change, and also by a consideration of the informal processes in which social structures are embedded. Such processes can serve both to reproduce disadvantage and to mediate economic change, and are thus of particular relevance for the ongoing debate about the extent and nature of an 'underclass' in British society. Attempts to identify the boundaries of such a class, however, run up against the changing structures and trajectories of employment, and the broader problems they raise for class analysis.

Notes

1. Chapter specially written for this volume. The research reported was financed by the ESRC (grant number R000231381) whose support is gratefully acknowledged.
2. Here I am principally interested in divisions within a broadly defined working class, which encompasses 80 per cent of the total sample. The analysis uses the Registrar-General's classification of occupations.
3. Some caution must be exercised here, for the upwardly mobile are most likely to have started in unskilled positions and progressed to a skilled job, while those with no movement either up or down will include a large proportion of skilled workers.

CHAPTER 15

Class and politics in advanced industrial societies[1]

John H. Goldthorpe

The significance of social class in the politics of modern nations is an issue of long-standing controversy. A hundred years ago, it held a central place in the 'debate with Marx', in which many of the great founders of sociology and of political science were engaged. And, today, the issue of class and politics is still one that provokes vigorous and complex argument. However, in order fully to appreciate this latest phase in the controversy, it is important to recognise that for several decades following the Second World War a period of relative consensus intervened. In this period, a broadly similar understanding of the relationship between class and politics could in fact be shared by analysts of widely differing ideological persuasions.

The essentials of this consensus, formed chiefly under the influence of the work of Lipset and Rokkan, were the following (see esp. Lipset and Rokkan (eds) 1967). On the one hand, it was accepted that, as the Western world had industrialised, fundamental changes had occurred in lines of social cleavage. Divisions deriving from processes of 'nation-building' and state formation – for example, ones grounded in religion or region – had tended to decline in political importance, while the importance of divisions based on class had steadily grown. In 'mature' industrial societies, political organisation and political partisanship were in fact largely class-based. On the other hand, it was also accepted that although class conflict had often played a part in the creation of liberal democratic polities, such conflict did not necessarily – or even typically – lead in turn to the revolutionary overthrow of such polities. Rather, liberal democracy provided an institutional context within which class-based political action might be contained, yet at the same time allowed an effective expression. Thus, Lipset (1960) could write, from an American liberal stand-point, that the participation of citizens in the electoral politics of Western nations represented 'the democratic translation of the class struggle'; and more than twenty years later Korpi (1983) could entitle *The Democratic Class Struggle* a work examining the possibilities, as seen from the left wing of the Swedish Social Democratic Party, for a non-revolutionary transition to socialism.

It is the breakdown of this post-war consensus that is now at hand. While the consensus prevailed, most of the objections that were raised against it came from unreconciled Marxists, who remained firm in the belief that 'bourgeois democracy' was a sham which working-class revolution would, sooner or later, sweep away. But, from the 1980s, a challenge of a quite different character has gained in strength. What is now maintained is that, at least in the more advanced societies of the late twentieth century, the political importance of class is on a decisively downward curve. The contention is not simply that class cleavages and conflict can no longer be seen as 'the engine of history' – as the source of collective action that creates epochal change. What is further held is that even at the level of the everyday, and especially of the electoral, politics of liberal democracies, the influence of class on individuals' attitudes and allegiances is steadily waning.

However, while arguments to this effect have been advanced with growing frequency in recent years, it must be noted at the outset that, in their more detailed content, these arguments vary a good deal. Although the 'decline of class' is an increasingly common theme, quite diverse explanations of this decline are in fact proposed. At least four different positions can be identified.

First, it has been claimed that, at the present time, the main lines of social cleavage are, once more, being redrawn. Just as religious and regional divisions earlier gave way to those of class in determining the broad pattern of political alignments, so class is now giving way to new forms of cleavage that are characteristic of advanced industrial or 'post-industrial' society. For example, it is held that important divisions – with evident political implications – are emerging along *sectoral* lines, and in regard both to production and consumption. Conflicts, actual or potential, arise, on the one hand, between those who are employed in the public as opposed to the private sectors of the economy; and, on the other hand, between those who rely on public as opposed to private provision in such respects as health, housing, education and transport (e.g. Kitschelt 1994; for Britain see Dunleavy 1980, Dunleavy and Husbands 1985 and Saunders 1984, 1990a).

Secondly, one has the argument that in the more advanced societies of today individuals' social structural locations, *however* defined, are becoming of less importance in shaping their political outlook than are their general belief and value systems. Previously, a close connection might be supposed between, say, class position and ideological position. But now such connections are weakening, among younger generations especially, as material interests become less compelling and as belief and value systems become more autonomous. In turn, then, the old bread-and-butter issues of politics give way to the 'new agendas' of 'post-materialism', which centre on such issues as personal liberty, women's and minority rights, the environment, etc. In this regard, the most influential work has been that of Inglehart

(Inglehart 1977, 1984, 1990; Ingelhart and Rabier, 1986. Cf. also Eder 1993).

Then, thirdly, there are those who maintain that the impact of class on politics is declining primarily because of a process of change in the nature of political action itself. The citizens of advanced societies are increasingly making political decisions on the basis of a rational assessment of particular issues and policies, rather than responding more or less automatically in ways that might be predicted either from the social positions they hold or from some overarching ideology to which they are committed. For example, it is claimed that in elections voters are now beginning in a genuine sense to *choose* which party they will support, in the light of the prevailing circumstances, instead of voting more or less unthinkingly for the 'natural' party of their class or political creed. And, thus, far greater variation – or 'volatility' – can be seen, from election to election, both in the strength of party support and in its social composition (see especially Rose and McAllister 1986; also various contributions in Franklin *et al.* 1992).

Fourthly, and finally, the emphasis may be placed simply on the decline of class *per se*. In modern societies, it is argued, class is ceasing to be a major determinant of life chances, life styles and collective identities, and its influence on politics is therefore weakening *along with* its influence in virtually all other aspects of social life. Advancing industrialism or emerging post-industrialism not only create greater wealth overall and a more equal distribution of material resources but, in addition, more equal opportunities for economic and social advancement. Old ascriptive hierarchies break down and social selection becomes increasingly based on individual merit, while at the same time the decline of former solidarities of community and work-place encourage men and women to pursue their own individual projects. In turn, then, the very rationale for thinking and acting politically in terms of class membership is progressively undermined. Of particular interest is the change in Lipset's position (in Chapter 2 above) from that described earlier (see also Pahl, above, Chapters 6 and 8).

In these differing accounts there are of course various complementary elements – but a number of contradictory ones also. In various respects, their exponents are in disagreement with each other. It is, for instance, difficult to reconcile arguments that new structural cleavages have superseded those of class with arguments that claim the end of 'cleavage politics' of any kind. However, the aim here is not to proceed with further exegesis, critical or otherwise. It is, rather, to challenge the *initial* thesis that each of the arguments presented above is intended to uphold: i.e. the thesis that in the economically advanced societies of the late twentieth century there is a comprehensive and secular tendency for the class basis of politics to be eroded. In raising this challenge no attempt will be made to rehabilitate the post-war consensus previously referred to – which could be thought, if anything, to have *exaggerated* the importance of class in the politics of the *mid*-twentieth century. Nor will it be maintained that the relationship between class and politics in modern societies reveals no changes of any kind. The attempt will rather be to show that these changes are too complex, and also far too variable cross-nationally, to be captured by *any* single thesis that is couched in quite general and 'developmental' terms.

Flogging a very dead horse

To begin with, one may observe that many of those who now take up the theme of the decline of class politics seem set on conducting 'the debate with Marx' all over again – and that this is not at all helpful to their case. The main empirical claim would appear to be that in modern democracies there is little sign of class-based political action that is of a revolutionary or even of a determinedly radical character. Labour and social democratic parties now form an integral part of the established political system and no longer view themselves as the organisational spearheads of transformatory social movements, while communist parties have become largely ineffectual and, since the collapse of the Soviet bloc, have often just disappeared from the political scene.

Now with all of this, one may readily agree. The Marxist theory of class and of the class determination of politics has undoubtedly been undermined, and by events still more than by social research. However, very little then follows for the matter in hand. Marx's theory of class is not, and never has been, the *only* one on offer. It is here worth remembering that many of the great figures who, as mentioned at the start, engaged with Marx at the time when to debate with him had real relevance, did not reject the concept of class as such – nor its significance for political analysis. Think only of Max Weber, Vilfredo Pareto or Josef Schumpeter. It should not then be too difficult to recognise that many – probably most – of those who today believe that class remains a key factor in the politics of advanced societies are themselves *not* Marxists. They operate with different – and, they would maintain, more sophisticated – understandings of how class inequalities are formed, of how these inequalities are subjectively experienced and of how this experience is in turn reflected in politics.

It ought, then, to be obvious that the case for the decline of class politics cannot be made simply by pointing to the failure either of Marxist theory or of Marxist practice. Nor, moreover, is there much merit – or even logic – in another argument that has been advanced by those who are preoccupied with the critique of Marx. That is the argument that if, today, a more refined form of class analysis is indeed required than that provided by Marx, then this in itself *implies* that the political impact of class is less than it once was. Thus, for example, Clark, Lipset and Rempel (1993) in a response to Hout (Chapter 3 this volume) acknowledge that analyses of the class structures of modern societies are now available that go far beyond such crude dichotomies as 'bourgeoisie' and 'proletariat'. But, they contend, to abandon such Marxist categories in favour of ones that recognise a more differentiated, less polarised, class structure is in itself to concede that class membership has become 'less politically salient' (c.f. also Holton, above, Chapter 1).

However, what could be more convincingly argued is more or less the opposite of this position. That is, that only when one has an understanding of class that is appropriate to the complexities of modern societies will it be possible fully to comprehend the kinds of relationship that now prevail between class and politics. And, one could go on, it is largely *because* commentators such as those cited have difficulty in appreciating class analysis other than in its Marxist versions that they fail to see the extent to which class politics persists. In other words, a rather strange paradox may be suggested. Those who maintain the thesis of declining class politics are led to do so because they cannot themselves escape from ways of thinking about class – and about politics – that are too much influenced by the Marxism that they so obsessively attack.

Since this is perhaps a rather difficult point to accept, it may be helpful to develop it in more specific terms. One of the principal claims advanced by those who argue for a decline in class politics (Clark, Lipset and Rempel included) is that over recent decades the association between class and vote in Western democracies has steadily weakened. To support this claim, a resort is typically made to the 'Alford Index' of class voting (Alford 1962, 1963). This index is one easily calculated from social survey data: that is, by taking the percentage of the working class who vote for left-wing parties and then subtracting from this the percentage of those not in the working class who vote for such parties. The larger the index, the stronger, it is supposed, is the class–vote link.

The Alford Index has for long been known to have serious statistical deficiencies (cf. Hout, Brooks and Manza 1995a). However, what, for present purposes, is of greater significance is that the index directly reflects, and is indeed entirely dependent upon, the idea of a simple class dichotomy – working class *versus* a residual non-working class – taken together with a corresponding party dichotomy – left *versus* a residual non-left. If such a Marxisant approach is rejected, and more than two classes, or more than two kinds of party, are recognised, then the Alford Index simply cannot be used.

It is, furthermore, of interest to observe that essentially the same limitation applies with the alternative index of class voting devised by Rose and McAllister (1986), to sustain their argument that voters are now 'beginning to choose'; and, again, that a dependence upon the same dichotomies of class and of party underlies the seemingly more sophisticated methods followed by Franklin and his associates (1992) in their comparative study of electoral change in Western democracies, in which a weakening in almost all forms of cleavage politics is alleged. The analyses presented in these latter studies, it should be said, are no less open to technical objections than those that rely upon the

Alford index.[2] But the point of main relevance here remains the crude conceptual treatment of both class and party that is entailed – which may itself very easily lead analysts into drawing quite mistaken substantive conclusions.

For example, where no more than a dichotomy of working class/non-working class is recognised, major problems necessarily arise over the class allocation of various 'intermediate' groupings – such as self-employed artisans, foremen and supervisors, technicians, or routine workers in services – whose members together make up a quite substantial component of modern electorates. With more refined forms of class analysis, it is possible for these groupings to be treated in a theoretically differentiated way; and, it turns out, the distinctions that are made often do matter a good deal for the issue of class and party support. Thus, it has been found in several nations that self-employed artisans, along with other 'own account' workers, have a particularly high level of *right-wing* voting – often in fact higher than that which prevails among white-collar employees (for Britain, see Heath *et al.* 1991: Ch.5). Consequently, if such self-employed individuals are included along with manual wage-earners in the working class, as usually happens with dichotomous schemes, then a quite misleading impression will be gained of the political heterogeneity of this class and, in turn, the strength of the class–vote link is likely to be underestimated.

Likewise, where attention is concentrated simply on support for left, as opposed to non-left, parties, it becomes difficult to assess the influence on class voting patterns of relatively complex party structures – and of changes therein. If, for instance, in a multi-party system, a new right-wing party were to arise with quite homogeneous class support – say, a 'tax revolt' party backed chiefly by higher-level salaried employees and the petty bourgeoisie – then this development could easily be overlooked, and even if it led to class voting being intensified. That is, merely because it occurred within the residual, non-left range of the political spectrum, in contradiction with the underlying supposition that class voting is of interest only as a phenomenon of the left.

Finally in this connection it is relevant to note that what also lies beyond the scope of all merely 'two-valued' treatments of the class–party link is the question of *non*-voting and of *its* relationship to class. In several cases, however, most notably, perhaps, that of the USA (on which see further below), this question is one that any serious analysis of the social bases of electoral politics must take fully into account.

This, then, is the burden of the more negative part of the critique that may be made of the thesis of class politics in decline: that those who seek to uphold this thesis do so largely on the basis of simple, and indeed conceptually inadequate, dichotomies of class and of party, and by then focusing their attention primarily on the working class and on left voting. It is found preferable, it would seem, to continue with an implicit, if not explicit, attack on Marxist class theory – which is surely flogging a very dead horse – rather than to attend to the analytical developments that are required if the relationships that actually do prevail between classes and parties within modern democracies are to be more profitably examined.[3]

Against class dealignment – some recent findings

In the remainder of this paper the aim is to pursue the critical argument in a more positive fashion. A number of illustrations will be given of findings from recent research which does actively seek to raise conceptual and technical standards in electoral sociology; and, as will be seen, these findings in fact provide ample empirical grounds for questioning the idea that a progressive weakening of the class–vote link represents a *generic* feature of the politics of advanced societies. The studies to which reference will be made have several features in common. First, they abandon class dichotomies in favour of more differentiated categories. Secondly, they take into account voting for all parties and also, where relevant, non-voting. And thirdly, instead of relying on indices of an essentially ad hoc kind, they seek to test different hypotheses about class voting by embodying these in formal statistical models. Of course, by concentrating on the relationship between class and *vote*, the question of class and *politics* is being considerably narrowed down. However, the proponents of the thesis of 'class politics in decline' have themselves largely based their arguments on the supposed weakening of the class–vote link – in so far as these arguments have been given any clear empirical reference at all.

The first illustration comes from the British case, where the issue of class and party has perhaps been for longest disputed. A process of 'class dealignment' in British politics was initially claimed after the General Election of 1959, when Labour lost for the third time running. The working class, it was held, no longer provided Labour with the same solid support as previously. Then, when Labour defeated the Conservatives at elections in the 1960s and 1970s, a different twist was given to the argument: the emergence of a new kind of middle-class 'leftism' was now suggested. But, finally, with Labour's four successive defeats at the polls from 1979 onwards, the idea of 'the end of working-class politics' was again taken up. In attempted explanations of these differing phases and forms of class dealignment, it may be added, versions of all of the theories previously reviewed have at some point or other been invoked (see e.g. Abrams, Rose and Hinden 1960, Sarlvik and Crewe 1983, Robertson 1984, Franklin 1985, Rose and McAllister 1986, Butler and Kavanagh 1992). However, in more recent years, the entire debate on class voting in Britain has been transformed as a result of a major programme of research undertaken by Heath and his associates. This has involved the systematic reanalysis of data from the full series of British General Election Surveys that have been carried out after each election from that of 1964 to that of 1992 – nine elections in all (see especially Heath, Jowell and Curtice 1985, Heath *et al.* 1991, Heath *et al.* (eds) 1994, Heath, Evans and Payne 1995). The two findings of key significance to have emerged from this research are the following.

First, when appropriate statistical techniques are applied to the data, it is apparent that there has been *no* steady tendency for the net association between class and vote to weaken over the period in question. A rather sharp decline in class voting does show up between the elections of 1964 and 1970, but this decline was not maintained and, after 1970, only trendless fluctuation in the level of class voting can be discerned.[4]

Secondly, then, Labour's failure in recent elections cannot be attributed to any *specific* weakening in the political solidarity of the working class. It is true that, since 1979 especially, workers have been clearly less likely to vote for Labour than before. However, such a tendency to desert Labour has in no way been confined to the working class but is apparent throughout the electorate. What is indicated is that Labour has just been a rather unattractive party 'across the board' – and also that 'third' parties, that is, the Liberals and others, have tended to increase their appeal. Furthermore, Labour has suffered from the fact that the working class, in the sense of the body of manual wage-earners, has been declining in size in Britain, as in all other advanced societies. Thus, even though there has been no particular defection of the working class from Labour, there are simply fewer and fewer manual workers in the electorate to vote for Labour as their 'natural' party.

In addition, one other finding of present interest may be obtained from the data-set that Heath and his colleagues have assembled. That is, that class voting in Britain, at least since the 1970s, is more or less as strong on the right as it is on the left (Goldthorpe 1996; cf. Evans 1993a). For example, the propensity for Conservative voting among the service class or 'salariat' of professionals, administrators and managers or again among the petty bourgeoisie is almost as marked as is the propensity for Labour voting among the working class. It can, it is true, also be shown that from the 1970s through to the election of 1992, the Conservatives enjoyed, *in addition to* the support of those classes for whom they represent the 'natural' party, a clearly higher level of 'non-class' appeal than Labour within the electorate at large (Goldthorpe 1996). Nevertheless, the idea that Labour can be set in contrast with the Conservatives as being a distinctively 'class' party must be thrown into serious doubt.

The second set of findings to be noted derive from research being currently undertaken by Hout and his associates of voting in United States Presidential elections from 1956 to 1992 (Hout, Brooks and Manza 1995b). There are good grounds for believing that in the USA the influence of class on vote has been, historically, at a lower level than in European nations (Nieuwbeerta and De Graaf 1996) – and especially relative to the influence of such other factors as region, race and ethnicity. None the less, the thesis of class dealignment in voting has also been applied to the USA, and the research project in question is specifically aimed at testing its validity in this case.

The main conclusion reached thus far is that, just as in British electoral politics, no steady tendency is apparent for the net class–vote association to weaken; again, there is merely trendless fluctuation over the three-and-a-half decades that the analyses cover. Two supplementary findings of obvious importance are, however, also reported.

First, while there is little evidence of class *de*alignment in voting, processes of class *re*alignment would appear to be in train: that is, processes which, while leaving the overall *level* of class voting unchanged, none the less imply some shift in the *pattern* of association between class membership and party support. In particular, a tendency is revealed on the part of routine non-manual employees – that is, workers in lower technical, clerical and service occupations – to give increasing support to Democratic candidates while, however, skilled manual workers show some movement, albeit of an erratic kind, towards greater Republican voting.

Secondly, it is confirmed that, in the American case, non-voting, just as much as voting, is class-linked, and rather stably so. Members of the working class, in the sense of manual wage-earners, are clearly less likely to vote in Presidential elections than are members of all other classes. Furthermore, differences in non-voting as between skilled and non-skilled manual workers would appear if anything to be diminishing – that is, skilled workers have in recent elections become almost as likely not to vote as non-skilled workers. This finding helps bring out a general point that has been often overlooked in the debate on class voting: that the extent of such voting depends not only on features of the class structure but on features of the *party* structure also. Thus, class voting – as opposed to non-voting – might well be higher in the USA if there were actually a working-class party for workers to vote for. As two other American investigators, Vanneman and Cannon (1987), have observed, non-voters in the US are in their class composition very similar to Labour voters in Britain, but, they conclude, 'the United States has no leftist party . . . so workers sit out'.

A third instructive illustration of recent research findings is provided by a comparative study carried out by Weakliem (1991) of electoral politics in three European nations, France, Italy and the Netherlands. Weakliem analyses data on class and vote for these nations, taken from repeated surveys over the years 1973 to 1985. His concern is again that of examining the thesis of declining class politics – but with special reference to one of the more detailed underlying arguments that were earlier noted: that is, the argument that class is a declining force in modern politics because, among younger generations especially, 'new agendas' are emerging that are not primarily related to class interests. In this case, as Weakliem observes, the class–vote link is seen as being loosened through the tendency of left-wing parties to take up 'post-materialist' rather than old-style 'class' issues. In this way, they gain in appeal for affluent white-collar voters who are the main bearers of post-materialist beliefs and values – but at the cost of alienating some of their more traditional supporters in the working class, who may then move to the right, attracted, say, by populist rhetoric.

In the outcome, Weakliem's findings in regard to class voting are much in line with those previously considered. In France, Italy and the Netherlands, just as Britain and the USA, there is little evidence of class voting being in progressive decline. Rather, class cleavages in party support appear to fluctuate around a fairly level trend. Moreover, while there is evidence of a post-materialist 'dimension' in the electoral politics of all three nations, this remains generally weaker than the materialist 'dimension' which reflects class interests – and even among voters in younger age-groups (cf. on the related issue of 'gender politics', Evans 1993b). In other words, the importance of 'new agendas' is easily exaggerated.

Furthermore, Weakliem's analysis allows him to put forward an explanation of why post-materialism has failed to reduce the level of class voting in the manner anticipated. This is because, in so far as post-materialist ideology has strengthened, it has done so *across all classes alike*. Thus, the fact that left-wing parties have pursued post-materialist issues has not, in itself, led to a significant loss of working-class, relative to non-working-class, support. Rather, left party support may have helped post-materialist beliefs and values to develop within the working class.

The fourth, and final, instance of research to be discussed concerns what may appear to be a rather special case, that of the Irish Republic. Irish electoral politics have indeed been regarded as quite exceptional in that it has proved difficult to find any clear social bases for party support (see especially Whyte 1974). The two main parties in the Republic, Fianna Fáil and Fine Gael, have their origins in the Civil War of 1922–3, and subsequent support for them has appeared to be largely a matter of family tradition that, over time, has come to have an essentially symbolic significance. However, recent research by a number of Irish sociologists and political scientists has led to some revision of this view.

To begin with, more refined forms of class analysis have revealed a greater degree of class-linked voting than was previously supposed, even if still well below the general European level. Further, though, and more interestingly, there are indications that in recent Irish elections the influence of class on party support has been growing. In particular, Fine Gael is beginning to look more like a centre-right party with distinctive appeal for the expanding salariat, while the previously insignificant Labour Party is coming into greater electoral prominence on the basis of chiefly working-class support (see e.g. Mair 1979, 1992, Laver, Marsh and Sinnot 1987, Breen and Whelan 1994). What, in other words, would seem to be happening is that at last, after some seventy years, symbolic politics are on the wane and class interests are beginning to pattern party support somewhat more strongly.

Ireland can then count as another national case where the thesis of the decline of class politics scarcely applies. However, its significance might perhaps prove be a good deal wider than this. The Irish case, taken as one of *the decline of symbolic politics*, may prove to be of particular relevance to our understanding of the development of the new, post-communist democracies of central and eastern Europe. Here, too, the electoral politics that have followed immediately on the creation of new democratic systems have contained a largely symbolic element, reflecting divisions in the pre-democratic period and in the struggle to throw off foreign domination. And the Irish example does indeed suggest that such symbolic politics may have great durability. But it further suggests that, sooner or later, the influence of material, and especially class, interests are likely to be felt. During the decades ahead, then, at least the ethnically less fragmented nations of central and eastern Europe – and assuming, of course, that they keep their democracies intact – may provide instances of just the opposite of class dealignment: that is, of nothing less than a reassertion of electoral politics as primarily the democratic translation of the pursuit of class interests and of the conflicts thus engendered.

Conclusions

Three points may thus be emphasised. First, if Marxist approaches are to be abandoned, the concept of class should be alternatively understood – and rendered operational. (One approach which has influenced several of the empirical studies referred to above is Goldthorpe 1987:Ch. 2; cf. Erikson and Goldthorpe 1992:Ch. 2, Evans 1992, 1993c, 1994). The thesis of declining class politics can then be directly challenged on the basis of current research of greater conceptual and technical refinement than that on which the thesis itself has been maintained.

It is not, it must be stressed, an implication of the research and analysis that have been considered that sustained class dealignment in electoral politics *never* occurs. To the contrary, there appears to be good evidence now emerging that something of this kind did indeed take place over the post-war period in both Norway (Ringdal and Hines 1996) and Sweden. (An analysis of Swedish data is currently being undertaken by the present author and Robert Erikson and indicates a decline in the level of class voting at least in the early post-war period.) Further cases may well be documented. However, what the illustrations provided do indicate is that the decline of class politics cannot be seen as a quite general tendency that is in some way 'built into' the developmental logic of modern democracies. The far more typical finding is that, in the short term, the class–vote link shows a good deal of fluctuation in its strength and, on a longer-term view, displays either stability or a trend of only a very uncertain kind.

Secondly, although class dealignment is not an integral feature of the politics of modern societies, class realignment may be reckoned as a far more probable occurrence. That is to say, without the level of class voting necessarily weakening overall, the pattern of class–party linkages is susceptible to change. The actual forms that are taken by such realignment may be expected to display considerable cross-national variation, since realignment is likely to result more from changes in party structure – and party strategies – than from changes in the class structure directly. The arguments reviewed at the start of this paper would all appear to underestimate not just the persisting force of class as a factor in democratic politics but, further, the readiness and capacity of political parties to respond purposively to the development of class structures in order to maintain and increase their electoral support.

Thirdly, research of the kind illustrated should be seen as that which points the way for the future. It is not research undertaken in the interests of Marxism, nor yet of anti-Marxism. It aims to go beyond this now quite sterile confrontation. What those who engage in such research have chiefly in common is a commitment not to some political world-view but rather to a particular conception of social science (cf. Goldthorpe 1990). Central to this is the insistence that, whatever may be the motivations, political or otherwise, that underlie a research enterprise, the attempt must be made to conduct it according to the best available methodological standards – *and* that such standards *can* be specified. In its current phase at least, the debate on class and politics is perhaps as much about whether or not such a conception of social science is to prevail as it is about socio-political realities.

Notes

1. Specially adapted and revised for this volume, this paper is based on a lecture given to the Hellenic Political Science Association in February 1994, a version of which was subsequently published (in translation) in the *Greek Political Science Review*. I am indebted for helpful conversations to Geoffrey Evans and Paul Nieuwbeerta.
2. Rose and McAllister's index shares with the Alford Index the basic flaw that it is not 'margin insensitive'. This means that when these indices are used to assess trends in class voting, measurement of the class–vote association itself is confounded with the effects of changing marginal distributions in successive class-by-party tables. In the case of Franklin and his associates, the fact that they persist in working with a merely dichotomous dependent variable – i.e. left/non-left voting – should then have led them to the use of logistic, rather than ordinary least squares, regression.

3. Exception should here be made of certain authors who have of late attempted to offer a defence of the thesis, or at least a reasoned response to its critics, by taking seriously the conceptual and technical issues that they have raised. For example, Nieuwbeerta and De Graaf (1996) examine the effect on estimates of trends in class voting of moving from dichotomous to more elaborate class categories; but are forced by their comparative strategy to retain the simple left/non-left party division.

4. Weakliem and Heath (1996), using Gallup data that extend back to 1935, find that class voting in Britain actually peaked between 1945 and 1950; between 1935 and 1945 it appears to have been at a rather lower level than after 1970. Unfortunately, the degree of reliability of the Gallup data seems to be difficult to determine.

CHAPTER 16

Class inequalities and educational reform in twentieth-century Britain[1]

Anthony Heath and Peter Clifford

Educational reform has had many objectives – the socialisation of the lower classes into civic responsibility, the increase of economic efficiency, the extension of meritocracy and the reduction of inequalities between the classes. It is the last of these which has been most amenable to empirical research and which has been a major focus of sociological endeavour. In Britain we now have a unique series of major national surveys from which we can chart the history of class inequalities in education over the course of the present century, and we can in principle relate any changes in class inequalities to such major educational reforms as the 1907 Free Place Regulations, the 1944 Education Act and the 1965 circular (10/65) from the Department of Education and Science which initiated the replacement of a selective system of schooling with comprehensive schools (Silver 1973). The present chapter updates our previous work in this area (Heath and Clifford 1990) by incorporating the results from the most recent national survey of 1992, thus permitting a reliable assessment of the impact of comprehensive reorganisation.

Educational researchers had great hopes of the 1944 reforms, since they established free secondary education for all. The financial barriers, which many believed had restricted working-class access to grammar schools, were swept away. Thus David Glass, the senior author of the first national study in 1949, was in no doubt that the 1944 Act would 'greatly increase the amount of social mobility in Britain' (Glass 1954:22). 'Given the diminishing importance of economic and social background as a determinant of the type of secondary education a child receives, social mobility will increase, and probably increase greatly' (p. 24). Glass accepted that 'Not for another forty years or so shall we be able to see how this new, far more revolutionary expansion of educational opportunity has altered the degree of social mobility in the community' (p. 21) but he believed that 'It is at least already evident that, proportionately, far more "working-class" children are now going to grammar schools and are thus overcoming the first hurdle in the path to university or professional education and to occupations of relatively high social status' (p. 21).

There have been somewhat similar hopes of the comprehensive reorganisation that was set in train by the DES circular 10/65. Reorganisation had many objectives, but certainly one of them was that the pupil intake to a school should 'represent a fuller cross-section of the community' (Scottish Education Department quoted in McPherson and Willms 1987). We might expect that class differences would decline if pupils from different backgrounds were educated in the same school environment rather than segregated in secondary modern and grammar schools. Certainly, McPherson and Willms, and other sociologists too, have assumed that a major objective, and a likely consequence, of comprehensive reorganisation was that 'the association of [educational] attainment with social class should fall' (McPherson and Willms 1987:512).

The 1944 and 1965 reforms will certainly have had many other educational consequences, but in this paper we focus on the question whether they were successful in reducing class inequalities in education. Essentially, our question is whether children who passed through the schools after the implementation of these reforms were less divided by social class in their educational experience and attainments than were those groups who went through immediately prior to the reforms. We therefore use our series of national surveys to check the trends over time in the relationship between education and social class.

To be sure, there may be many other reasons, quite aside from educational reforms, why class differences might be declining over time. Clark and Lipset; (Chapter 2 in this volume) for example, ask whether social classes are dying, and answer in the affirmative. They, and other scholars, have argued that the social divisions between classes have become progressively more blurred – partly perhaps as the result of increased affluence, greater geographical and social mobility, cross-class marriages and the decline of the traditional working-class communities centred around heavy industry (cf. Crewe 1984). The debate about the withering away of class has been particularly heated in political sociology where class differences in voting behaviour have been vigorously debated (Heath *et al.* 1985, Crewe 1986, Heath *et al.* 1987). The social changes which the political scientists have postulated should in principle affect class differences in education just as much as they affect class differences in voting behaviour. However, for our purposes in the present paper the crucial point is that these social processes might be expected to be gradual and continuing ones ('glacial' trends as Crewe rightly suggests), whereas, the educational reforms of 1907, 1944 and to a lesser degree those of 1965 might be expected to have led to sharper breaks in the trends. In the educational sphere, therefore, we need to look for discontinuities in the trends at the times of the major reforms. It might also be useful to compare the magnitude of the trends. If there have been common social processes, blurring class divisions, in both the political and the educational spheres, while there have been additional processes brought about by educational reform, then we should expect to find a greater overall reduction in class inequality in education than in voting behaviour.

Sources of data

The national surveys on which we rely are the 1949 mobility survey (organised by a team from the LSE), the 1972 mobility survey (organised by a team from Nuffield College, Oxford), and the British election surveys of 1983, 1987 and 1992 (organised by a team from SCPR and Oxford University). These are all national stratified probability samples. In the 1949 study, the issued sample consisted of 10,000 names of people aged 18 years and over living in England, Wales and Scotland, drawn from the 'live' cards maintained in the various local offices of the national registration system, the primary sampling units being local government administrative districts (for further details of the sampling see Gray and Corlett 1950); 7,751 completed interviews were obtained, but substitutes were then selected and the final achieved sample contained 9,296 respondents.

In the 1972 study the issued sample was 16,563 male electors aged between 20 and 64 and resident in England and Wales. The sample of names was drawn from the electoral registers and clustered within 417 primary sampling units (groups of wards and parishes). This initial sample was used both as a sample of individuals and as a sample of households and institutions from which further individuals not on the electoral registers could be selected. The final achieved sample was 10,309 male respondents. (For further details see Goldthorpe 1987).

The British election surveys of 1983, 1987 and 1992 were designed by the same team and carried out by the same research institute (SCPR). In all three the sampling frame was the electoral registers of Great Britain. The issued sample in both 1983 and 1987 was of 6,000 people, clustered within 250 polling districts, and the achieved samples were 3,955 and 3,826 respondents respectively. (For further details see Field 1985.) The 1992 survey differed in that Scottish residents were oversampled in order to permit a detailed study of Scottish voting behaviour. In the current paper we weight the sample so that the proportion of Scottish residents in the survey corresponds to the actual proportion in the electorate as a whole. The weighted sample size in 1992 was 2,855. Given their fundamental similarity in design and procedures, we are able to pool these three election surveys, yielding a combined sample size of 10,636.

Comparing datasets collected over the course of nearly half a century is by no means unproblematic. As we have just seen, there are differences between the three datasets in size, age range, sex, place of residence, the sampling frame used, the mode of its use and the response rate. In addition, there are inevitably procedural differences in surveys carried out at substantial time intervals and conducted by different fieldwork agencies. In principle it is a straightforward matter to control for age, sex, and place of residence, but there is no easy way to control for the differences in sampling, fieldwork and coding procedures. It follows that it would be unwise to make direct comparisons between the results of the three datasets. To chart the history of class inequalities, therefore, we adopt the strategy of comparing birth cohorts within surveys rather than making comparisons between surveys.

Cohort analysis is not itself free from problems. In particular, mortality and migration mean that older cohorts in a given survey may differ in relevant ways from younger cohorts. We cannot be sure that, for example, members of the 1890–9 birth cohort who survived to be sampled in Britain in 1949 will be representative of those educated in Britain at the turn of the century. We cannot therefore conclude that all differences between cohorts reflect real changes over time in the education of schoolchildren. However, since the age ranges of the surveys overlap, we can check whether the birth cohorts which they have in common show similar trends.

We should also note that it has become increasingly common for people to acquire educational qualifications as mature students after they have left school. This could affect the comparisons between birth cohorts: people from the older birth cohorts will have had more time in which to acquire qualifications.

Class inequalities in pre-war Britain

In the first part of the century access to selective secondary schools was the key educational issue. The 1907 Free Place Regulations (made under an Act of 1902) allowed that fee-paying secondary schools could receive a higher rate of grant from the Board of Education provided that 'a proportion of school places shall be open without payment of fee to scholars of public elementary schools who apply for admission, subject to the applicant passing an entrance test of attainments and proficiency' (Board of Education 1907). The regulations specified that the proportion of free places should be 25 per cent, but the actual proportion gradually increased so that by 1931 45 per cent of children in English secondary schools held free places (Halsey, Heath and Ridge 1980:25). R. H. Tawney, writing in the early 1920s, summed up the recent history of English secondary education as follows:

> The number both of pupils and school places in 1922 is . . . all too small. But, inadequate as they are, they represent something like an educational revolution compared with the almost complete absence of public provision which existed prior to 1902. (Tawney 1922:20)

In the 1930s, however, the growth of free places was reversed. In 1933 the Board of Education initiated economy measures, reducing staff and salaries, increasing fees, lowering the income level of eligibility for maintenance grants, and converting free places into 'special' places. In essence the special places became means-tested. As Floud reports, 'the result was to widen the gap between the demand for and supply of places in the schools and to increase the sacrifices demanded of those parents in the lower status categories whose children might be offered secondary education' (Floud 1954: 109).

A cohort analysis of the 1949 survey enables us to trace the impact of the educational revolution brought about by the 1907 regulations. We base our analysis on the tabulations reported by Jean Floud in Chapter 5 of Glass (1954). A simplified version of her key table is presented here as Table 16.1.

Floud distinguished between secondary modern (a misnomer since secondary modern schools were a post-war invention), grammar (in which she included technical schools) and boarding schools. The numbers in the sample attending boarding schools are too small for useful analysis and so we have combined these with the grammar (and technical) schools. The resulting category can be termed 'selective secondary schooling'. Some kind of selection procedure, whether academic or financial, was involved in recruitment to these schools, which provided a route to professional, technical and managerial jobs. They can be distinguished from non-selective schools, largely elementary schools in the pre-war period, which were attended by the bulk of the school population and which typically led to working-class jobs (see Hall and Glass 1954: Table 1).

Floud divided the adult sample into five birth cohorts. The oldest (1889 and before) cohort would have been entering secondary education up to the turn of the century, well before the 1907 Free Place Regulations came into effect. The youngest (1920–9) cohort would have been entering secondary education in the 1930s when free places had reached over 40 per cent.

Floud also divided the sample according to father's social status, as measured by the Hall–Jones scale (see Hall and Jones 1950 and Macdonald 1974).[2] She collapsed this seven-category scale into the following four:

Higher non-manual: Hall–Jones categories 1–3, which include professional, administrative, managerial and higher grade non-manual occupations;
Lower non-manual: H–J category 4, which includes 'inspectional, supervisory and other non-manual, lower grade';
Skilled manual: H–J category 5, which includes skilled manual and routine grades of non-manual occupations;
Semi- and unskilled manual: H–J categories 6 and 7.

Floud's interpretation of her results was that 'the differential advantage' of males from the higher-status backgrounds declined over the first part of the century. However, the conclusions that we draw from Table 16.1 depend on how we measure 'differential

Table 16.1 1949 study: selective schooling

		% in each birth cohort attending selective secondary schools				
Father's status category		1889 or earlier	1890–9	1900–9	1910–19	1920–9
Males						
1–3	Higher non-manual	32	45	36	44	54
4	Lower non-manual	10	17	13	23	26
5	Skilled manual	2	5	7	10	11
6, 7	Semi- and unskilled manual	3	2	1	4	9
All		10	14	11	17	19
N		670	540	748	767	764
Females						
1–3	Higher non-manual	38	37	34	50	50
4	Lower non-manual	14	13	12	19	22
5	Skilled manual	5	4	7	11	14
6, 7	Semi- and unskilled manual	2	0	1	3	5
All		12	11	11	16	17
N		857	605	832	907	974

advantage'. One straightforward measure is the absolute difference between the status categories. For example, in the oldest cohort, 32 per cent of males from higher non-manual backgrounds attended selective secondary schools, compared for example with 2 per cent from skilled manual backgrounds, a difference of 30 percentage points. This difference tended to increase over time, so that by the youngest of Floud's cohorts it had reached 43 percentage points.

The absolute difference tells us about the similarity between the educational experience of the different status categories. Thus, among the oldest cohorts, the statuses were similar in their education – few children from any background went on to receive a selective education. But by the time of Floud's youngest cohort, the gap had widened. The majority of children from lower-level backgrounds still attended non-selective schools but for the first time a majority (albeit a small one) of children from the higher categories attended grammar or boarding schools. The educational experience of the status categories had diverged.

While the absolute difference is in many ways an informative measure, sociologists have recently tended to use a second measure when investigating class inequalities. (See for example Shavit and Blossfeld (1993.) This measure is the odds ratio, and in effect it measures the relative success of the classes or status categories in the competition to achieve certain destinations and to avoid other destinations.[3] Thus in Floud's oldest cohort, 32 per cent of males from the higher non-manual backgrounds obtained selective secondary education whereas the remaining 68 per cent of boys from these backgrounds failed to obtain selective schooling. For this status category, then, the odds were 32 to 68, which can be expressed as 1:2.1.

For boys from skilled manual backgrounds, the odds were much poorer: only 2 per cent achieved selective schooling while 98 per cent failed to do so. Their odds were thus 2 to 98 or 1:49. A useful way to compare the status categories, then, is to compare their odds of achieving selective schooling. In this case the higher-status category had much more favourable odds than the skilled manual category – their odds were over twenty times better (1:2.1/1:49 = 23.1). We should note that an odds ratio of 1 indicates that the two groups in question have exactly the same relative chances, but that there is no upper bound to the magnitude of an odds ratio.

The odds ratio has a number of convenient mathematical properties, but for us the crucial point is that it can be used as a measure of the relative success of two groups in the competition to achieve some desirable position. It is quite different from our measure of the absolute difference, which simply tells us how similar the two groups are. As we have seen, two groups can be quite similar, in that few members of either group get into grammar schools; but there might none the less be huge differences in the relative success of the two groups in competing for the few places available. Moreover, over time it would be quite possible for the two groups to become more similar in their experience, but to diverge in their relative success, or vice versa.

In practice, over the pre-war period covered by Floud's analysis, the status categories seem to have become more different in their experience of selective schooling but more similar in their relative competitive success. To illustrate the trends over time in competitive success, consider the higher non-manual:skilled manual odds ratio for males. This moved from 23:1 in the oldest cohort successively to 9:1, 5:1, 4:1 and 5:1 in the later cohorts. This does seem to fit rather well with the pattern of educational reforms: there was a major equalisation of competitive chances early in the century (although one that may have started before the 1907 Free Place regulations came into effect) with a reversal of the trend among the youngest cohort, who would have been exposed to the consequences of the 1933 economy measures.

We should not, however, draw any firm conclusions from inspection of a single set of odds ratios. There are many different odds ratios which we could calculate from Table 16.1, and all of them will be subject to sampling variation. In particular there were very small numbers of children from manual backgrounds in the sample who attended selective schools, and many of our odds ratios will therefore have quite large confidence intervals. We therefore turn to loglinear modelling. This is a statistical technique which enables us both to consider the full set of odds ratios and to take account of sampling variation.

We begin by testing the null hypothesis that there was no change in the relative success of the status categories in the competition to obtain selective secondary schooling. We therefore formulate a loglinear model which allows schooling to depend on father's status and birth cohort but which holds the relationship between father's status and selective schooling constant over time. (We also explored whether there were any gender differences but were unable to detect any statistically significant ones. We therefore combined the data for males and females.) In effect, this model takes account of the changing number of places in selective schools and of any changes in the status distribution of fathers, but postulates no change in the relative chances of people from different status origins getting to selective secondary schools.[4]

Fitting this model of 'constant relative chances' to the data of Table 16.1 we do not obtain a satisfactory fit. In other words it is rather unlikely that the discrepancies between the survey data and the model could be explained by sampling variation. (The likelihood ratio chi square is 22.0 with 12 degrees of freedom, $p = 0.037$.) We therefore have to reject the null hypothesis of 'no change' in relative chances.

The statistical analysis, therefore, tells the same general story as the upper non-manual:skilled manual odds ratio did: the data are consistent with the hypothesis that the status categories converged in their relative success in the competition to obtain selective secondary schooling. Of course, a purely statistical analysis of this sort cannot tell us what the causal mechanism was. At most we can say that the evidence is consistent with the idea that the 1907 Free Place Regulations reduced the competitive disadvantages under which the lower status categories had previously suffered. But it is also consistent with other notions – such as a general blurring of class divisions. Unfortunately, for this very early period we do not have data on such things as trends in class voting or trends in class inequalities in health, which might tell us whether or not the equalisation was unique to the educational sphere. However, the timing of the equalisation does seem to point in the direction of a causal role for the 1907 Free Place Regulations.

The effects of the 1944 Act

The 1944 Act provided free secondary education for all, and therefore finally swept away the financial barriers that had restricted access to state selective schools, although of course it left the independent sector unchanged. At the same time, secondary education was reorganised into the so-called tripartite system of grammar, technical and secondary modern schools. These three types of school were intended to have parity of esteem and the 1943 White Paper, *Educational Reconstruction*, proposed that 'so far as humanly possible, all children should receive the type of education for which they are best adapted' and children should be selected 'not on the results of a competitive test, but on an assessment of their individual aptitudes largely by such means as school records, supplemented, if necessary, by intelligence tests, due regard being had to their parents' wishes and the careers they have in mind'. In practice, however, selection was largely based on the competitive '11 plus' examination.

To investigate the effect of the 1944 Act we must compare the educational experience of cohorts educated before and after the Act. The major source of data which enables us to do this is the 1972 mobility survey (Goldthorpe 1980, Halsey *et al.* 1980). As with the 1949 study, respondents were asked for biographical information on their social backgrounds, educational and occupational histories.[5]

John Goldthorpe's analysis of the 1972 material has shown that the post-war period was marked by substantially higher rates of upward class mobility than had characterised the pre-war period surveyed by Glass and his associates (Goldthorpe *et al.* 1978). The post-war period (up to 1972) saw a rapidly changing class structure, professional and administrative jobs expanding in number while semi-skilled and unskilled manual jobs contracted. There was in consequence a substantial net upward mobility, and the overall level of mobility (upward and downward combined) was somewhat higher than in the pre-war period (Heath 1981).

In theory such an increase in upward mobility need have nothing to do with educational reform. It could simply be the outcome of the changing shape of the occupational structure. The reforms of the 1944 Act, in contrast, might be expected to change the terms of the competition for such jobs, i.e. they might be expected to reduce the relative advantages of children from professional backgrounds in comparison with those from, say, working-class backgrounds in the competition for professional jobs. Goldthorpe's conclusion, however, was that relative mobility chances, as defined in this way and measured by odds ratios, had not changed significantly.

Goldthorpe's conclusions were not based on a direct comparison between the 1949 and 1972 data sets, since it proved impossible to replicate Glass's procedures for identifying status categories (Ridge 1974). It derived instead from a log-linear analysis of the relationship between fathers' and sons' classes in successive birth cohorts of the 1972 study. Goldthorpe and his colleagues tested what they called the 'constant social fluidity model'. This model (which is analogous to the one we used in the previous section) allows the class distributions of fathers and sons to vary over time, but postulates that the association between father's and son's class remains constant. This model yielded an excellent fit to the data (with chi square of 11.19, 12 degrees of freedom, $p = 0.51$. See Goldthorpe *et al.* 1978:456). In other words, over the period covered by the 1972 study, it appeared that relative mobility chances for men from differing class origins had remained unchanged.

217

It could be argued that the patterns of relative mobility evident in 1972 had been largely shaped by processes of educational and occupational recruitment in force before the war and that the 40 years which Glass felt were necessary for an adequate assessment of the 1944 reforms had not yet elapsed in 1972. However, comparison of the educational experience of young men educated before and after the Second World War offers little encouragement to Glass's hopes and little support for his expectation that, following the 1944 Act, the importance of social and economic background would diminish as a determinant of the type of secondary education that a child received.

Table 16.2 shows the relationship between class background, secondary schooling and birth cohort in the 1972 study. The same birth cohorts are used as in Floud's analysis of the 1949 material, but, as we noted above, it did not prove possible to replicate the measure of status used in the 1949 study. Instead the seven-class schema devised by John Goldthorpe for the 1972 study has been used (with some minor revisions). This scheme is based on two separate criteria – occupation and employment status. It distinguishes between higher and lower grade salaried classes (covering professional, administrative and managerial occupations), three intermediate classes (routine non-manual, the petty bourgeoisie, and foremen and technicians), and the skilled and semi-skilled or unskilled working classes. Two categories of secondary schooling are also distinguished: non-selective (including secondary modern and comprehensive) and selective (including technical, grammar and private). The definition of technical schools (which were a rather heterogeneous category in the inter-war period) was much wider than Floud's and this accounts for the discrepancy between Tables 16.1 and 16.2 in the overall proportions attending selective secondary schools. Our concerns in this paper, however, are with the relationships between the variables rather than the overall totals attending selective schools (which can be better estimated from the official returns from the Department of Education and Science).

Consider, first, the relationship between birth cohort and access to selective schooling. We see that there was an increase in the proportions from all class backgrounds attending selective schools in the 1920–9 and 1930–9 birth cohorts, the figure rising from 26 per cent in the oldest cohort to 35 per cent and then peaking at 40 per cent. The proportion fell back, however, in the 1940–9 cohort to 35 per cent – the level of 20 years earlier. This pattern is almost certainly a consequence of the fact that the baby boom of the immediate post-war years was not accompanied by a comparable increase in the provision of places at selective schools, while the 1930–9 cohort was relatively privileged owing to its small size. In effect, the competition for places became tougher and hence the proportions of children from all class backgrounds succeeding in the competition declined.

The 1930–9 birth cohort can be thought of as a transitional cohort (many of whom will have begun their secondary education during the war years). In assessing the impact of the 1944 Education Act, it

Table 16.2 1972 study: selective schooling

		% in each birth cohort attending selective secondary schools			
		(males)			
Father's class		1910–19	1920–9	1930–9	1940–9
I	Higher service	69	77	86	74
II	Lower service	57	70	77	62
III	Routine non-manual	34	54	51	47
IV	Petty bourgeoisie	35	41	49	41
V	Foremen	22	34	38	33
VI	Skilled working	19	25	30	21
VII	Semi- and unskilled working	15	23	27	23
	All	26	35	40	35
	N	1802	1969	1880	2231

is the experience of the 1940–9 cohort, who received their secondary education in the heyday of the tripartite system from 1950 to 1965, that is most relevant. In this cohort the absolute differences between the classes were little smaller than they had been for the 1910–19 cohort, educated in the inter-war years, and the relative class chances (as measured by odds ratios) were no more equal either. For example, the higher service:skilled working class odds ratio moved from 9.5 in the oldest cohort to 10.0, 14.3 and finally to 10.7 in the youngest cohort.[6]

As with the 1949 study, we need to conduct a more formal analysis of the data reported in Table 16.2 in order to take account of the full set of odds ratios and in order to allow for sampling variation. As before, we fit a model which allows the distribution of father's class and the number of places at selective schools to vary, but postulates that the association between father's class and entry to selective schooling remained constant over time. (We should also remember that the 1972 study only covered men. We cannot therefore pool men and women as we did with the 1949 study.)

The results when we fit this model to the 1972 data are rather different from those obtained with the 1949 data. In the case of the 1949 data we had to reject the 'no change' model but with the 1972 data the model gives an excellent fit (chi square = 12.32, 18 degrees of freedom, $p = 0.831$). We cannot therefore reject the hypothesis that relative class chances of getting to selective schools had remained constant over the period covered by the four birth cohorts in the 1972 study. There is no sign from this evidence, therefore, that the 1944 Education Act changed the terms on which children from different social class backgrounds competed for places at secondary schools. For whatever reason, then, the 1944 Act did not bring any closer to realisation the ideal 'that the education provided in public secondary schools should be open to children of all classes as nearly as possible upon equal terms' (annual report of the Board of Education for 1909–10, quoted in Floud 1954).

Comprehensive reorganisation

The free secondary education for all of the 1944 Act was followed by comprehensive education for many (stimulated by circular 10/65 issued by the Department of Education in 1965), the raising of the school-leaving age (ROSLA) to 16 years in 1974, and the gradual spread of the Certificate of Secondary Education (CSE), three developments that could not be explored by the 1972 study.

The ROSLA represented a major expansion of educational provision, particularly for the working-class children who had previously left school in large numbers before taking the public examinations of the General Certificate of Education (GCE) or CSE. The wastage of working-class talent from the grammar schools through early leaving and before sitting the public examinations had been seen by many post-war commentators as one of the primary areas where class inequalities reasserted themselves in the tripartite system (Douglas 1968). The ROSLA was a major step in bringing everyone within reach of the major public examinations and might have been expected to enable the working class to catch up. It might have been expected to have considerable impact on the absolute difference between the classes in their educational experience. Comprehensive reorganisation, however, might have been expected to change the terms of the competition between the classes.

Comprehensive reorganisation also necessarily shifts our concerns away from selection at 11 years of age to later stages of the school career, and in particular to the public examinations of GCE and CSE. Indeed, in some respects GCE O levels became the functional equivalent of a place at grammar school before or immediately after the war. Thus for the pre-war cohorts selective education gave access to salaried jobs even for school-leavers who had not taken their school certificate. In the post-war period this became less true and it was the acquisition of O level certificates that became the crucial step on the road to a salaried job (see Heath and Ridge 1983).

We thus change our focus from access to selective schooling to the acquisition of one or more passes at GCE O level. Our central question in this section, therefore, is whether the ROSLA or comprehensive reorganisation has been associated with changes in class inequalities at 16+.

Our data come from the 1983, 1987 and 1992 British Election surveys, which we combine to give us larger frequencies. For the oldest cohorts in these surveys, educated before the war, the public examinations available were the School Certificate and Higher School Certificate. For the post-war cohorts GCE O level and A level were available, and the CSE also became available during this period. Since the School Certificate was not strictly comparable with O level, we

Table 16.3   1983–92 studies: O-level

		% in each birth cohort obtaining an O-level pass			
Father's class		1930–9	1940–9	1950–9	1960–9
Males					
I	Higher service	59	63	87	83
II	Lower service	58	72	78	83
III	Routine non-manual	35	67	65	84
IV	Petty bourgeoisie	25	40	55	61
V	Foremen	24	39	49	70
VI	Skilled working	23	30	44	55
VII	Semi- and unskilled working	16	26	36	46
	All	27	40	53	64
	N	719	856	858	765
Females					
I	Higher service	62	66	82	79
II	Lower service	52	56	71	83
III	Routine non-manual	50	54	64	76
IV	Petty bourgeoisie	27	46	53	77
V	Foremen	38	46	56	75
VI	Skilled working	19	28	41	62
VII	Semi- and unskilled working	14	20	37	52
	All	28	38	52	69
	N	697	886	919	742

shall restrict ourselves to analysis of the cohorts educated post-war, and we shall use as our measure of examination success one or more passes at O level (or grade 1 passes at CSE).

As we can see from Table 16.3, there was a major expansion in the proportion obtaining an examination pass. From 27 per cent in the youngest cohort it rose to well over 60 per cent among the youngest cohort. The growth is continuous and there is no evidence of a kink in the trend corresponding to the relative shortage of selective school places that we observed earlier with the 1940–9 cohort. The explanation for this difference in the two trends is almost certainly that secondary modern schools began to enter pupils for public examinations in the post-war period, whereas, before the war the School Certificate had been the prerogative of the selective schools (see Heath 1984). This policy of entering secondary modern schoolchildren for the CSE thus in a sense compensated for the shortage of grammar school places (a policy incidentally that seems to have been initiated by the schools and parents rather than by the central authorities).

It appears, however, that the growth in O levels was reaching a ceiling in the higher social classes at the end of our period, whereas it was continuing among the other classes. As a result the absolute gap between the classes was tending to decline. Class relativities, in contrast, as measured by odds ratios, showed no consistent trend. In the case of men, for example, the higher service:skilled manual odds ratio moved from 4.8 in the 1930–9 cohort to 4.0, 11.9 and finally to 5.7 in the youngest, 1960–9 cohort. The withering away of class scarcely seems evident from the time series for this particular odds ratio.

Once again we must take account of the full set of odds ratios and of sampling variation. It would be very unwise to attach any especial importance to the sharp increase to 11.9 in the 1950–9 cohort unless it was confirmed by thorough statistical modelling.

In modelling these data we follow the same procedure as with the 1949 study. We first check whether there are any significant differences between the men and the women in their patterns of class inequality. Finding none, we then pool the male and female data, giving us larger numbers to analyse. We next move on to test the 'constant relative chances' model that we had previously applied to the 1949 and 1972 data.

What we find is that, just as with the 1972 data, this 'constant relative chances' model gives an excellent fit to the data. (Chi square 18.8 with 18 degrees of freedom, $p = 0.406$.) We therefore have to reject the hypothesis that class inequalities in the acquisition of O level qualifications declined at the end of our period after comprehensive reorganisation and the raising of the school-leaving age. Of course, this does not necessarily mean that these educational reforms had no effect on class relativities: it could be that in the absence of these reforms class divisions would actually have widened. Nor does it mean that these reforms had no beneficial consequences: the continued rise in the proportions obtaining O level may well owe something to these reforms. But these results do show that there has indeed been persistent class inequality.

Conclusions

These results, therefore, tell us a remarkable story. If we put them together with the results from the 1949 and 1972 surveys, we find that there has been no significant change in class relativities from the 1900–9 birth cohort to the 1960–9 birth cohort. With respect to perhaps the most crucial educational transition facing these different groups of youngsters, then, relative class chances have remained virtually unchanged for much of the century. While the 1907 Free Place Regulations may possibly have had an effect at the beginning of the century, subsequent reforms seem to have had no measurable impact on class relativities, and there appears to have been no general tendency for social class inequalities to wither and die.

These results are all the more remarkable when we remember that the twentieth century has seen a transformation in the educational experience of the population. From being a small minority, it is now the majority of the population, and of almost all classes, who obtain examination certificates such as O levels. But the terms of the competition between the classes has shown little sign of change. It may well be that education policy can have greater effect on the overall levels of education than it can on the class inequalities.

Remarkable though these results may seem, it should be emphasised that many other countries have displayed precisely the same pattern of rising general levels of education but persistent class inequality (Shavit and Blossfeld 1993). The central problem for class theory, therefore, is not why classes have been dying but why they have been so persistent.

Notes

1. The 1983 Oxford-SCPR study was funded jointly by Pergamon Press, the Economic and Social Research Council (ESRC) (grant E00232012) and Jesus College, Oxford; the 1987 Oxford-SCPR study by Pergamon Press, the Sainsbury Trusts and the ESRC (grant A00250005); and the 1992 study by the Sainsbury Trusts and the ESRC (grant Y304253011). We are grateful to David Lee for numerous helpful suggestions which have greatly improved the presentation of this paper, and to the Royal Statistical Society for permission to re-use material published in the *Journal of the Royal Statistical Society*, series A.

2. Father's 'last main' occupation was the basis for these measurements of social status, and this is likely to produce some problems in a cohort analysis. The fathers of the youngest cohort will themselves have been relatively young at the time of the survey, and therefore their last main occupations would tend to be ones at an earlier stage of their careers than the older cohorts'. The data might therefore tend to under-estimate their eventual occupational attainment. Thus 15 per cent of the fathers of the 1920–9 birth cohort were placed in status categories 1–3 compared with 21 per cent of the fathers of the 1890–9 and 20 per cent of the fathers of the pre-1890 birth cohorts.

3. Other scholars have advocated a range of alternative techniques for measuring class inequality. In general, there is no such thing as the one 'correct' measure, and there could reasonably be a number of different conceptualisations of the meaning of class inequality. However, it should be noted that the great advantage of odds ratios is that they are independent of the marginal distributions. Many of the alternatives that have been proposed are not independent of the marginal distributions. Thus if the variance of education changes, these alternative measures necessarily change too. We know that the variance of education has changed markedly over the present century, and the interesting question for us is whether, after taking account of the change in variance, the association between class and education has also changed.

4. Formally, we formulate a logit model in which the dependent variable is the log-odds of attending a selective or non-selective school. In the notation of Fienberg (1980) the model becomes

$$\ln(m_{ij1}/m_{ij2}) = w + wA(i) + wB(j)$$

where A represents father's status and B represents birth cohort. Status categories are numbered from 1 to 4 with category 1 corresponding to higher grade occupations. Cohorts are numbered from 1 to 5 with category 1 corresponding to the pre-1890 cohort. If the term w$AB(ij)$ is added, the model becomes the saturated one, but our main interest is in whether we obtain a good fit without including this term.

5. For some alternative analyses of these data see Halsey, Heath and Ridge 1980, Blackburn and Marsh 1991, Jonsson and Mills 1993, and Kerckhoff and Trott 1993.

6. These odds ratios are rather different from the comparable ones calculated from the 1949 data. The differences will be due, among other things, to the differences in the definition of class and status. We do not know what Hall and Jones included in their higher non-manual category, but it is unlikely to be identical to Goldthorpe's higher service class. And there are certainly differences between the two skilled categories. Hall and Jones, for example, included some routine non-manual workers, and probably included manual foremen as well, whereas Goldthorpe places both these groups in other classes.

CHAPTER 17

Social class and interest formation in post-communist societies

Geoffrey Evans

The debate about class has focused on its demise or otherwise in advanced industrial societies as they have become increasingly *post-*industrial. In contemporary Eastern Europe the question of class takes on a very different form: it concerns not whether the decline of class division is consequent on the decline of industrialism, but whether or not class is likely to become a progressively more important social and political cleavage as the ex-communist countries – with their former ideology of classlessness – attempt the difficult process of transition to liberal democratic forms of conflict resolution. On the one hand, this process portends the emergence of class conflicts associated with the workings of the market place. On the other, commentators from diverse sociological and political perspectives have advanced a variety of explanations for why class divisions in post-communist states should be at best muted, especially when compared with those which emerged in the West.

This issue is of significance not merely for sociological disputes over the efficacy of social class as a source of inequality and interests. The degree and nature of reactions to marketisation have potentially significant consequences for the political character of the new democracies of the region, including, even, whether or not they continue to be democracies. The reasons for this are two-fold.

First, without effective representation of their interests, the 'losers' in the transition process, included among which are people in a range of social categories – the working class, the elderly, the unemployed – are unlikely to see the benefits of playing the liberal democratic game. As a consequence, they are more likely to be susceptible to the populism of anti-democratic demagogues feeding on the privations incurred by marketisation to generate support for their messages of ethnic hatred, nationalist expansion and authoritarian statism. Under these conditions, the popular basis of liberal democracy in the area is likely to be called into question.

Secondly, it has been argued that even if support for democratic processes remains widespread, the patterning of the social cleavages across which post-communist political competition occurs is itself to be consequential for the stability of liberal democracy. Ethnic exclusion and aggressive nationalism are less suited to cross-group political appeals than are the pro-market versus state-interventionist policy orientations which form the key axis of the left–right, class-based political divisions in many Western democracies. As a result, such programmes tend to bring the stability of democratic polities into question, either through secession or international conflicts. Thus even without the rise of anti-democratic movements, the cost of democratic political competition failing to orientate primarily around the running of the economy is that politics is likely to take on a less negotiable and more unstable turn.

Put simply then, the institutionalisation of class conflict via the electoral system is likely to be a significant factor in the process of democratic consolidation. Without it, disadvantaged groups may find anti-democratic demagogues appealing (cf. Zhirinovsky); or politics may orientate around less tractable cleavages, which in turn bring the threat of more severe non-democratic forms of conflict resolution (cf. the former Yugoslavia). Class interest formation and articulation may potentially be consequential for the emergence of 'healthy' democratic processes, but are they present? Or at least, are their underpinnings to be observed even at this fairly early stage in the new Eastern Europe?

The emergence of class divisions in Eastern Europe?

We can divide the discussion of interest formation in Eastern Europe into two general themes. Within each there are a variety of positions, both political and sociological, but these can be aggregated on the basis that they either share doubt concerning the emergence of class divisions in Eastern Europe, or alternatively, they provide grounds for expecting its appearance.

The 'mass society thesis' (Kornhauser 1960) implies that the dissolution of the institutions of civil society under communism produced a pattern of interest articulation at the level of mass collectivism – nation or society – rather than in meso-level organised groups. As a corollary, interests are neither well-formed or articulated and there is predicted to be little evidence of social bases to political preferences. Recent examples of this view can be found in Seymour Martin Lipset's American Sociological Association presidential address (Lipset 1994), in analyses of the role of civil society in Eastern Europe by area specialists (i.e. Lewis 1993; Schopflin 1993), and even in the writings of Marxisant analysts such as David Ost (1993, 1995).

Ost, for example, provides a variety of reasons for the limited nature of class interest formation in post-communist Eastern Europe. Thus in addition to the suppression of social divisions and the lack of interest representation under communist regimes, he argues that since 1989 there has been a pervasive ideology of anti-socialism coinciding with a political focus on the goals of the liberal intelligentsia rather than those of the working class – a focus indicated by evidence of state policies which have tried to eliminate class cleavages and the collapse of socialist aspirations even among Trade Unions. The West's Cold War ideology, with its emphasis on the superiority of capitalism as a provider of economic well-being, has also served to inhibit class-based alternatives to the rectitude of free market practices. Ost even sees the experience of some workers as migrant labourers in the West as a factor reducing their expectations for anything other than complacent appreciation of highly undesirable work and market situations. In consequence of these factors, he suggests that nationalism, religious fundamentalism and 'masculinism' have emerged as non-economic responses to economic discontents among the working class in Eastern Europe (1995:181). For him 'Class sensibility remains weak because of the structure of communism . . . the historical legacy of anti-communism . . . and the policies of post-communist governments' (1995:182).

In contrast to these pessimistic prognoses for the significance of class-based interests in post-communist Eastern Europe, 'modernisation' and rational choice approaches to interest formation in the region imply that the differential possession of resources with which to benefit from capitalist reward structures generates distinct social bases of support for – and opposition to – free market practices. The modernisation thesis emphasises the role played by conflicts of interest remaining from the communist era in shaping current patterns of interest formation (see Hamilton and Hirszowicz 1993:217–37) and Frank Parkin's (1971) disquisition on the patterns of inequality and interest formation in communist societies in the 1950s and 1960s – both of which are clearly at odds with the mass society thesis), whereas rational choice inspired arguments emphasise the role of present resources and future prospects. Herbert Kitschelt, for example, argues that regardless of past events, younger, better-educated, entrepreneurial groups are likely to support marketisation and the rolling back of the state, whereas state-dependent, poorly resourced groups – pensioners, the working class, peasants – will oppose it (Kitschelt 1992:21–7). The difference between these two clusters of groups lies in their differential possession of transferable resources with which to exploit the opportunities for advancement provided by the new system.

Thus different theoretical perspectives on interest formation clearly come to quite different conclusions about the politics of class in Eastern Europe. Fortunately, these conclusions in themselves form hypotheses which can be tested empirically through an analysis of whether social classes appear to be forming a basis of social and political interests in the region. Tests of these hypotheses can indicate the degree to which class divisions are present and their implications for the form that the cleavage structures are likely to take. They can also give us an indication of the robustness of class divisions across differing historical contexts, and thus of the continued relevance of class analysis as a sociological activity.

The data

To examine the issues outlined above I shall use evidence collected in surveys examining social structure and political attitudes and behaviour in nine Eastern European countries: Bulgaria; the Czech Republic; Hungary; Lithuania; Poland; Romania; Russia; Slovakia; and Ukraine, in 1993/4. These surveys are national probability samples with standardised rules for respondent selection procedures, and use sampling frames chosen for their representativeness of each country. Response rates were generally high, averaging 80 per cent across the region, and with non-response resulting mainly from non-contacts. Survey quality was checked using a follow-up study of 10 per cent of the respondents to the initial survey who were randomly selected and re-interviewed a few weeks later.

Each survey includes 300 identical or at least equivalent questions, which were tested on 50–100 respondents in each country prior to their use in the main study. The cross-national comparability of the questionnaries was established through several months of translation and back-translation, as well as cross-translation among the languages employed in the surveys. This process was facilitated by the presence of fluent Slavonic and Hungarian speakers at Nuffield College, academic translators from the School of Slavonic and East European Studies, and the helpful contribution of East European collaborators. Further details of the surveys are available from the author.

The nine countries are at rather different stages of transition, each with different factors which might impinge on the formation of a class basis to interests. Evans and Whitefield (1995) provide an overview of the economic position of most of the countries being considered here, with the exception of the Czech Republic and Slovakia – detailed information on these, and other, Central European countries can be obtained from Winiecki (1994). For a brief sketch, the countries, can be grouped into three blocks: Central Europe; the Balkans; and the former Soviet Union.

The Central European states – the Czech Republic, Poland, Hungary and Slovakia – have been at the forefront of transition. In the Czech Republic, Vaclav Klaus's economic reforms have been arguably the most successful of any former communist state, as evidenced by the fact that his pro-market government is still in power. Poland led the way into the free market for countries in this region when Balcerowicz's 'shock therapy' plan was introduced on 1 January 1990, although Hungary had an established semi-capitalist economy even prior to 1989. Slovakia is probably the least established of the Central European states, with the 'velvet divorce' of 1993 leaving the Slovaks much worse off economically than the affluent Czech lands, and with the vexed issue of the Hungarian minority remaining unresolved. Even for the healthiest of these economies, however, the years after 1988 saw increasing unemployment, a decline in real wages, and a greatly expanded budget and foreign trade deficit. These gloomy statistics were accompanied by others: massive inflation, declining GDP and declining industrial output, although these had bottomed out by 1992. Thus the costs, as well as the benefits, of the market are likely to have had most impact in these countries.

The two Balkan states form a second natural grouping. By 1993 Romania had barely emerged out of the communist era. Liberalisation of either a political or economic kind was little in evidence. There was a poor standard of living, restricted political freedoms, and – with the exception of Transylvania with its substantial proportion of ethnic minorities forming a continued source of internal strife (Shafir 1994), and which was only awarded to Romania after Versailles – little historical connection with democratic procedures or the former German hinterland economies of Central Europe. A similar isolation characterised Bulgaria, though here the democratic system appears to have been stabilised relatively quickly, with former communists quickly proving the dominant party bloc. As with Romania, there is an ethnic dimension to social relations and politics, with the Muslim minority tending to join with the progressive factions in opposition to the former communists, much as the Hungarian minority do in Romania (McIntosh *et al.* 1995, Heath, Evans and Marginean 1994).

Finally, we have three representatives of the former Soviet Union. Russia is the colossus at the heart of this dismembered and still disintegrating empire, in which – although governed by a supposedly pro-West, pro-market leader – marketisation is barely in train and democratic procedures are still open to question (Duch 1994, Whitefield and Evans 1994a). Ukraine was no further down the road to the free market. Even in Lithuania, where prospects were brighter, the situation was such that a government which included many former communists was in power by 1993 (Reisinger *et al.* 1994).

Despite their apparent diversity, in this chapter I will not examine these countries separately. Instead I will draw inferences about the formation of class interests in the region from a pooled analysis in which the samples from all nine countries are combined to give over 16,000 respondents. Inevitably, the marginal distributions of the variables presented in the analyses below vary somewhat cross-nationally. Nevertheless, there is an impressive degree of cross-national similarity in the *patterns of association* within countries between class position and other variables; and it is these patterns of association – between class position and objective and subjective aspects of inequality, and in turn between class position and political attitudes – which are of most relevance for the questions which concern us. For this purpose, therefore, the combined data provides a parsimonious characterisation of the region which avoids the distractions presented by national intricacies, while not unduly misrepresenting the structures of relationships within countries. Moreover, the extremely large number of respondents ensures that robust estimates of class differences are obtained, thus allowing a fine-detailed account of class divisions to be derived. Before looking at the findings of this analysis, however, I will define what is meant by social class, and consequently, how it is to be measured.

Measuring class position

Like John Goldthorpe (see his contributions to this volume) I do not take class to refer to a Marxist dichotomy of capitalists *versus* workers, or to a graduated scale of socio-economic distinctions; rather class is taken to consist of distinctions both in employment status (i.e. between employers, self-employed, employees) and within the broad category of employees. The distinctions within the category of employees arise because 'employees in fact occupy a range of different labour market and work situations, among which meaningful distinctions can and should be made in class terms' concerning variations in 'the labour contract' and 'the conditions of employment' of employees (Erikson and Goldthorpe 1992:41). These primary distinguishing characteristics of employee classes are their conditions of employment, degree of occupational security and 'above all, well-defined career opportunities' (1992:42). An elaboration of Goldthorpe's class concept and its operationalisation via the Goldthorpe class schema is presented in Evans (1992).

The measurement of social class is undertaken using the algorithm developed by Goldthorpe and Heath (1992), with British OPCS occupational unit groups augmented by use of ISCO codes in certain countries and by local information so as to take into account both the range of agricultural occupations in the region and modifications suggested by the remaining intricacies of the former communist occupational structure. From the resulting schema are derived the following categories:

Class I   Professional and higher managerial
Class II   Lower managerial and semi-professionals
Class III   Routine non-manual and service workers
Class IVa   Employers
Class IVb   Self-employed
Class V   Foremen and technicians
Class VI   Skilled manual workers
Class VIIa   Semi- and unskilled manual workers
Class IVc   Farmers
Class VIIb   Agricultural workers

Following convention, in the analysis that follows classes I and II are referred to as the 'salariat', classes VI and VIIa as the 'working class'. Classes IVc and VIIb are in places referred to as 'peasants'. Allocation to a class position is derived from the respondents' occupation and employment status, as recent research suggests that in Eastern Europe allocation on an individual basis is likely to be the most effective strategy (see Marshall *et al.* 1995). For individuals who are not at present working, I take their most recent job.

Inevitably, the application of a class schema developed in the West to a situation in which the characteristics of occupations are likely to reflect, among other things, both former communist reward principles and embryonic capitalist development is fraught with difficulty (although for encouraging signs with regard to the operationalisation of their class schema in Eastern Europe, see Erikson and Goldthorpe 1992). It is likely therefore that the concept of class is going to be less effectively operationalised in Eastern European countries than it is in Britain (for which see Evans 1992). None the less, at this stage in our understanding of class relations in post-communist societies, the insights to be gained from even imperfect measures are likely to make their use worthwhile. After all, the main consequence of any weaknesses in the present system of measurement is that divisions between classes are likely to be underestimated compared with those which would be obtained with improved indicators of class position. Thus refinements in the ways that class is operationalised in Eastern Europe are unlikely to undermine arguments concerning the significance of class in the region, rather they should serve to enhance the importance attributed to class position as a basis of interests.

Analysis

The material bases of class divisions

In this section I shall assess the material inequalities and their subjective counterparts which might provide the basis for the emergence of class-related interests. Thus on the one hand, there is the issue of whether classes in Eastern Europe differ with regard to transferable resources and the presence of institutionally regulated future prospects – a key aspect of the class differences in employment conditions described above – and on the other, there is the question of whether classes are experiencing the dramatic changes of the last five years differently and whether they expect to do so in future years. All of these factors – especially those concerning differences in future prospects (see Evans 1993a) – might be thought consequential for the formation of class-based political preferences.

First, I consider whether class position differentiates individuals in terms of their levels of income, their degree of economic security and chances of economic advancement. Answering this question requires both a consideration of the resources possessed by members of different classes, and a close examination of their employment prospects. For this purpose, Table 17.1 presents the proportion of each class in each of the three countries who have

Table 17.1 Indicators of inequality by social class across nine East European countries (all figures are percentages)

				Goldthorpe class						
	I	II	IIIa + IIIb	IVa	IVb	IVc	V	VI	VIIa	VIIb
Proportion with higher education	67	38	6	22	6	7	8	1	1	1
Proportion unemployed*	4	4	9	3	6	5	6	11	13	16
Proportion on career ladder**	36	33	21	–	–	–	24	16	16	13
Proportion with high income (in top quartile)	41	29	19	45	32	18	33	23	18	12
N =	(1,346)	(2,870)	(2,196)	(122)	(347)	(388)	(662)	(2,489)	(3,252)	(1,200)

*Calculated on the basis of respondents currently in employment or available for work N = 10,087
**Calculated on the basis of respondents currently in employment N = 8,970

higher education, high levels of household income, are on a career ladder, and who are unemployed. As might be expected, there is a remarkably close link between class position and educational attainment. Unemployment, income, and location on a career ladder are also associated in predictable ways, if not to the same degree, with class position.

The link between education and class, although presumably reflecting in large part the influence of prior educational achievement on current class position, tells us that the salariat has a large advantage over other classes in terms of the possession of potentially transferable educational skills with which to benefit from opportunities associated with liberalisation. Income is of interest not only for its use as a resource, but because it serves as a useful indicator of who is doing well out of the transition – and this clearly is *not* the working class: the salariat, entrepreneurs and managers have noticeably higher proportions reporting having high levels of income than do peasants and the working class. For the latter especially, unemployment – which did not officially exist under communism – has been a noticeably more likely outcome of transition than it has for other classes. Finally, future employment prospects display a similar pattern of differences: the salariat contains a considerably higher proportion of employees who report being on a career ladder than do other classes. Although it has to be said that compared with data from Britain (Evans 1992:217), only a fairly low proportion of even the salariat report being on a career ladder.

These objective class differences are also reflected in the experience of the effect of the economic transition on living standards in recent years, and in beliefs about what the future holds. Table 17.2 shows that classes have experienced the economic changes of the last five years differently, and have different expectations about what awaits them over the next five. The salariat and entrepreneurs are not only more likely to report increases in living standards since the end of communism, but expect these to continue. In contrast, peasants and the working class predominantly report a decline in their economic situation; they are more hopeful about the future, but still less confident than members of the other classes. Similar patterns occur for perceptions of promotion prospects, thus adding subjective evidence to the data on career ladders presented in Table 17.1. More generally, the working class are more likely to report having no way at all of improving the standard of living of their family in the future. The subjective evidence on expectations thus confirms the prognoses derived from class inequality in resources.

In sum, from the evidence presented in this section we have seen that members of different classes have different resources with which to benefit from marketisation, have experienced the economic changes associated with transition differently, and have similarly divergent futures. Though it should be remembered that social mobility effects may at least in part explain class differences in reported changes in standard of living over the last five years, the differences in

Table 17.2 Experiences and expectations of different classes (all figures are percentages)

	Goldthorpe class									
	I	II	IIIa + IIIb	IVa	IVb	IVc	V	VI	VIIa	VIIb
Increased household living standard over last 5 years	21	18	16	35	29	19	13	12	9	6
Expected rise of household living standard over next 5 years	31	31	29	44	40	27	27	26	24	16
Proportion reporting no chance of promotion	37	42	50	–	–	–	40	49	61	59
Proportion reporting no way of increasing their present standard of living	24	28	30	18	18	39	30	32	38	56
N =	(1,346)	(2,870)	(2,196)	(122)	(347)	(388)	(662)	(2,489)	(3,252)	(1,200)

future prospects between classes cannot be accounted for in such a way, neither can the evidence on perceptions of widening class inequalities. True, the relations between class position and these perceptions of recent economic changes and expectations for the future are of only moderate strength, but these classes are likely to have started the transition on an already unequal footing: what we have probably been observing therefore is a *polarisation* in the economic circumstances associated with class position, which given the differing prospects reported by respondents in different classes, could be expected to increase over the next five years.

Evidence of class awareness?

Evidence of inequalities between classes is apparent, but on its own it is insufficient grounds for inferring class interest formation. For the latter to occur, class position has to be recognised as consequential for the rewards and costs experienced by people. This requires that people should be aware both of their membership in a class and of inequalities between classes. A starting point for investigating this awareness is therefore to assess whether or not respondents recognise class labels and are willing to ascribe class positions to themselves, and also whether these self-ascribed positions coincide to some degree with their objective class location as determined by the Goldthorpe schema. This latter criterion of class awareness is particularly important if we seek to infer that the expression of class identity through self-placement in a class category is conditioned by experiences based in class relations.

The first column of Table 17.3 shows the distribution of answers to a question enquiring about the respondents' class identification: 'Here are a list of social groups in [country] today. To which of these groups [list in table presented] do you feel you belong?' The list of social categories presented to respondents was selected on the basis of pilot studies and local informants' knowledge. We can see that over 80 per cent placed themselves in one of these social classes without need for further prompting. Moreover, many of those respondents who did *not* choose a class were not actually in the labour market at the time of the survey.

This evidence alone suggests that people in Eastern Europe are aware of their location in a social class. The rest of the table shows, in addition, that the tendency to identify with a particular class is substantially related to respondents' positions in the Goldthorpe class schema. Unsurprisingly, this is most marked for respondents whose Goldthorpe class positions have some overlap with the label used to assess class identification: classes VI and VII (manual workers); class IV (entrepreneurs); and classes I and II (the intelligentsia). With the intermediate classes – routine non-manual workers, foremen and technicians – there is more heterogeneity in self-placement choices, and with agricultural workers there is also a tendency to choose the label of manual worker as well as that of peasant. On the whole,

Table 17.3 Class identification among all respondents and class identification by Goldthorpe class (all figures are percentages)

	Total percentage	Goldthorpe class									
		I	II	IIIa + IIIb	IVa	IVb	IVc	V	VI	VIIa	VIIb
Manual worker	40	6	13	34	27	27	18	46	77	73	31
Entrepreneurs	5	6	5	5	47	42	2	2	3	2	1
Managers	5	15	11	6	4	2	4	9	1	1	1
Intelligentsia	23	61	54	27	13	5	4	18	3	4	2
Peasants	11	2	2	5	4	9	67	5	5	8	53
None of these	17	10	15	24	6	15	6	19	11	12	12
N =	(16,306)	(1,346)	(2,870)	(2,196)	(122)	(347)	(388)	(662)	(2,489)	(3,252)	(1,200)

Table 17.4 Perceptions of the differential effects of economic transition on social classes (all figures are percentages)

	Standard of living has fallen over last 5 years	Standard of living is likely to rise over next 5 years
Group referred to:		
Manual workers	77	29
Entrepreneurs	6	64
Managers and administrators	6	61
Intelligentsia	37	45
Peasants	67	33

N = 16,386

however, these findings indicate that across Eastern Europe the expression of subjective class identity has a substantial link with respondents' experience of being in an 'objective' class position.

Although people in Eastern Europe may recognise their own position in a social class structure, in itself this carries no necessary implications for the development of class interests. For the latter to materialise, an awareness of the advantages and disadvantages associated with class position is necessary. The next step, therefore, is to examine whether respondents are aware of the consequences and correlates of class positions. In particular, are they aware of the impact of transition on different classes, which given their own disposition to place themselves in classes would indicate an awareness of the relative benefits and costs accruing to their class position, and would thus provide a basis for the articulation of differing class interests?

From the evidence in Table 17.4, which shows perceptions of how classes have fared during the previous five years, we can see that the fates experienced by certain classes are agreed on by most people in Eastern Europe. Entrepreneurs and managers are seen more or less universally to be benefiting considerably from the changes; most people think the intelligentsia has also gained from transition. In contrast, manual workers and peasants are seen by most to be bearing the costs. To some degree, the perception of the experiences of the classes varies according to the class of the respondent. Many people in the salariat, for example, do not believe the intelligentsia have benefited from the changes of the last five years, whereas manual workers and peasants take a contrary view. This disagreement does not apply to the perceived fate of peasants and manual workers, however – respondents in all classes are similarly as likely to perceive them to have lost out.

A similar pattern occurs if we examine people's expectations for the next five years. Although the balance of expectations is more positive for peasants and workers than are perceptions of their recent experiences, substantial groups of people believe that class inequalities will continue to polarise. Such polarisation might well be expected to foster the emergence of class differences in responses to the economic upheaval at present under way in Eastern Europe.

The emergence of class interests?

We now assess whether classes have developed different expressed interests. By expressed interests I mean the appearance of class differences in political and economic preferences, particularly those pertaining to support for the unfettered operations of the free market, with its attendant implications for class-related inequality, versus support for a strong interventionist state which limits free market practices and serves to facilitate greater equality of conditions and thus reduce socially structured differences in life chances. Thus if class polarisation in economic conditions has occurred, it should favour the formation of distinct class bases of support for – and opposition to – continued liberalisation, both with regard to the general aim of marketisation and democratisation, and in respect of more specific aspects of economic strategy. By implication, the key political question addressed by an analysis of the class basis of interests in Eastern Europe is whether the economic discontents imposed on the working class and peasants by the transition will result in their rejection of the free market and, in turn, liberal democratic modes of conflict resolution.

These issues are examined in the first instance by enquiring about respondents' support for the aim of building a democratic market society: 'How do you feel about the aim of introducing democracy in [respondent's country], in which parties compete for government? and 'How do you feel about the aim of creating a market economy with private ownership and economic freedom to entrepreneurs?' Table 17.5 presents distributions by class of support for, and opposition to, these goals.

It can be seen from Table 17.5 that classes differ quite noticeably in their expressed support for both the free market and democracy. Working-class respondents tend to be divided on this issue, whereas among the salariat and, predictably, the entrepreneurial classes there is generally a substantial majority in favour. It is useful, however, to go beyond the basics of support for the 'aim' of democracy and the free market and examine respondents' views on some of the issues that emerge from the operation of a market economy. Over time, these attitudes may well be of more consequence than those elicited by references to the emotive but somewhat rhetorical notions of 'democracy' and 'the market'. Also, we know from research in the West that, depending on the context in which particular issues arise, there are likely to be inconsistencies between support for liberalisation in the abstract, and attitudes towards concrete policy proposals (see Mann 1970). Fortunately, in the surveys there are questions which focus on more concrete aspects of economic strategy. These questions juxtapose free market strategies with interventionist ones. Table 17.6

Table 17.5 Support for the free market and democracy by social class (all figures are percentages)

				Goldthorpe class						
	I	II	IIIa + IIIb	IVa	IVb	IVc	V	VI	VIIa	VIIb
Proportion supporting the aim of the free market	79	74	64	79	74	55	66	61	55	42
Proportion supporting the aim of democracy	73	68	56	69	57	52	59	57	50	42
N =	(1,346)	(2,870)	(2,196)	(122)	(347)	(388)	(662)	(2,489)	(3,252)	(1,200)

presents proportions of pro-interventionist and pro-market responses to these items, by class position.

Despite the majority support for the free market observed in Table 17.5, it is clear that when it comes to more concrete policy preferences East Europeans in general are somewhat interventionist. Not surprisingly, however, it is the working class and peasants who provide the strongest electoral base for interventionist policies – policies of the sort endorsed by the various social democratic governments which the last two years have seen elected in Eastern Europe (see Whitefield and Evans 1994b).

The political significance of class cannot be confidently assessed, however, without comparing the effects of class with those of other social bases of economic and political interests. After all, some of these alternative sociological influences on attitudes towards economic policy may be more significant than those concerning class. If this is the case, any argument concerning the importance of class politics would have to be reconsidered.

The candidates for inclusion in a comparative analysis of the social bases of interests are not difficult to ascertain. As noted by Kitschelt above, age is very likely to be a contributory factor to a person's response to marketisation; similarly, the increasing domination of the public sphere by men has been taken to indicate that gender could be an important basis of interests (i.e. Watson 1993); and private versus state sector employment could further be expected to influence attitudes to state intervention, as could dependency on state hand-outs in the form of unemployment benefit or pensions (Dunleavy and Husbands 1985). Income differences are also likely influences on levels of support for marketisation. It should be instructive, therefore, to compare the relative impact of class position on attitudes towards free market versus interventionist strategies with those of income, age, sex, sector, and state dependency (for further comparisons, see Evans, 1996).

For this purpose I present below the results of a regression analysis which takes as the dependent variable (i.e. the thing which is predicted) a scale of 'economic ideology', which juxtaposes free market *vs* interventionist attitudes and is constructed by combining scores on the four items in Table 17.6 (all items are coded so that high scores indicate free market attitudes and low scores indicate pro-interventionist attitudes). To assess the relative size of effects of the different influences on economic ideology, the reader need only observe the magnitude of the coefficients presented in the table.[2]

Table 17.7 shows that even when measured rather crudely (see the technical footnote), social class has a stronger effect on economic ideology than do any other social characteristics. The self-employed and salariat are more pro-free market, whereas peasants and the working class are more pro-intervention, with the intermediate classes – class III (routine nonmanual workers) and class V (foreman and technicians) lying in between. Age has the next strongest impact on economic attitudes, with older respondents being more

Table 17.6 Economic policy attitudes by social class (all figures are percentages)

				Goldthorpe class						
	I	II	IIIa + IIIb	IVa	IVb	IVc	V	VI	VIIa	VIIb
The government should see to it that every person has a job and a good standard of living.	52	59	70	57	55	66	65	70	72	73
OR										
The government should just let each person get ahead on their own.	32	24	15	29	33	13	22	16	15	11
Some people feel that the government should not concern itself with how equal people's income are.	49	42	33	55	42	27	42	34	31	26
OR										
The government should try to make differences between incomes as small as possible.	30	34	44	27	36	46	39	43	48	45
The government should take all major industries into state ownership.	45	46	50	49	46	56	54	55	54	55
OR										
The government should place all major industries in private ownership.	28	26	21	30	30	20	22	20	18	12
The government should just leave it up to individual companies to decide their wages, prices and profits.	49	43	39	54	49	25	39	36	31	24
OR										
The government should control wages, prices and profits.	35	40	42	34	35	45	46	45	49	49
N =	(1,346)	(2,870)	(2,196)	(122)	(347)	(388)	(662)	(2,489)	(3,252)	(1,200)

Table 17.7 Economic ideology regressed on to social class and other predictors

	Standardised beta coefficients
Class	0.19
Age	−0.14
Women	−0.08
Private sector	0.06
Unemployed	−0.04
Pensioners	−0.03*
Income	0.02*
R^2	0.124

All coefficients significant at $p < 0.01$ unless otherwise indicated
*$p < 0.05$
$N = 14{,}378$

interventionist. In addition, consistent with research in the former Soviet Union (Hesli and Miller 1993, Tedin and Yap 1993), women tend to be less liberal on economic issues than are men, while employment in the state sector is associated with pro-market attitudes. Finally there are predictable, although small, effects of unemployment and receiving a state pension, both of which predispose people to support interventionist strategies. Interestingly, income has the weakest effect of all. These findings add further strength to our emphasis on class – which concerns the conditions under which income is obtained – rather than level of that income.

We can conclude that a lack of civil society under communism has not lead to a lack of structured divisions of interests in post-communist Eastern Europe. Predictably, it is the working class, peasants, the elderly, the unemployed, pensioners, state sector workers and women – those who are arguably losing out most in the transition to the free market – who oppose free market practices. Among these social divisions, however, only age comes close to equalling the substantial impact of social class. Moreover, given the effect of class position on the tendency to become unemployed, for example, its impact is probably underestimated by the analyses presented in Table 17.7.

Conclusion

We have seen that in contemporary Eastern Europe class position is a marker for a wide range of inequalities of resources and conditions. These inequalities are in turn reflected in the fates experienced – and expected – by members of different social classes during the process of transition. The concept of social class itself is also clearly meaningful to East Europeans, whose self-location in a classifactory scheme suggests considerable overlap with the academic social class schema developed by John Goldthorpe. In consequence of these factors, class divisions over the goal and method of transition to a market economy have emerged and are likely to shape the nature of political competition in the region. Even when other social differences are taken into account, class positions appears to be central to political and economic interests. Indeed, given the polarisation in the economic situation and corresponding subjective experiences of different classes evident in Eastern Europe, it could be argued that we might even expect to see *stronger* class bases to politics than in the West.

This is not to deny, of course, that within classes there have been diverse experiences during the economic transition. Workers in heavy industry, for example, have fared worse than those in the service sector – although as the decaying sectors of East European economies are the main source of working-class employment, the process of re-structuring hits people in the most vulnerable classes hardest (*Communist and Post-Communist Studies*, special issue 1995). Moreover, if we compare the relative severity and patterning of class divisions in the region with similar evidence from Western countries (see Evans' (1993d) study of class differences in identity and political attitudes in eight Western nations), we find that despite differences in the measurement of class identity and attitudes towards redistribution and inequality, the patterns of class division are very similar. Identity and attitudes appear to be no less class-related in Eastern Europe than they are in the West.

While appreciating the potential such divisions provide for the development of class politics, we should keep in mind that class divisions in expressed interests do not necessarily get translated into any other form of industrial or political action. Moreover, although they are likely to be of consequence for electoral politics, the extent to which divisions of interests between classes are reflected in the programmes adopted by political parties in Eastern Europe will itself be conditioned by a variety of institutional factors which lie beyond an examination of class interest formation *per se*, and which do not therefore come within the purview of this chapter. After all, class analysis cannot be expected to explain the intricacies of elite competition. It can, however, point to the constraints and opportunities provided by divisions of interests derived from the structure of economic relations in Eastern Europe, and their expression through various forms of political action and public opinion. The latter is especially important in that it communicates information to parties and presidential candidates who, if they are concerned to win power, act upon it. In this respect, Whitefield and Evans (1994b) have provided clear evidence of the emerging links between the programmes of political actors and the policy preferences of electorates in Eastern Europe. It should not surprise us, therefore, that in the last two years there has been a rash of socialist electoral successes. In the early post-transition days East European electorates were probably just content to be rid of a disliked system; but such 'negative political legitimacy' quickly gives way to some form of interest based politics.

Such politics need not be about class *per se* – in certain states, for example, Estonia, the ethnic structure is such that ethnic divisions will cross-cut, and quite probably dominate, class-related cleavages over inequality and economic policy (see Evans and Whitefield 1993) – but where there are not powerful alternative sources of political cleavage, then over time we should expect to see class-related issues occupying centre ground.

This process can be represented as one in which the costs of marketisation are sufficiently onerous that many people from disadvantaged social groups are learning that social democracy, rather than free market democracy, is their preferred strategy. From this perspective, the wave of left-wing, in many cases former communist, successes in recent elections in Eastern Europe may be the best indicator of the health of democracy in the region – although as Lipset (1994) and others have suggested, this is likely to depend on the effectiveness of these social democratic governments.

Whether Swedish-style social democratic government can work effectively under such difficult economic conditions remains to be seen. What we can conclude with more confidence from the evidence presented above, is that class position is – as it is elsewhere – a key marker of an individual's location in the cost benefit matrix of transition societies, and thus a pervasive influence on the patterns of interests which are structuring the political conflicts of post-communist democracies.

Notes

1. Paper specially written for this volume [eds].
2. The independent variables in the model in Table 17.7 are measured as follows: age in years; sex (coded male = 0; female = 1); whether or not respondents are on a state pension (no = 0; yes = 1); unemployed (no = 0; yes = 1); and are in, or are in the process of moving into, the private sector (no = 0; yes = 1); self-reported household income. The effects of class are represented through a simple three-category scale of: (i) the 'salariat and self-employed' (composed of classes I, II, Va and Vb); (ii) an 'intermediate' class (classes III and V); and (iii) the 'working class' (semi- and unskilled manual workers). The scale is scored 3,2,1. More complex analyses using dummy variables to represent the effects of class and employment sector (including, for example, co-operatives) confirm these results. Also included in the models are a set of dummy variables representing countries (these coefficients are not reported). The dependent variable measuring economic ideology is a four-item Likert scale evenly balanced in terms of direction of question wording so as to reduce acquiescence response bias. Internal consistency is only moderate (Cronbach's alpha = 0.51), which is to be expected given the small number of items in the scale and the balanced direction of their wording; analyses using a 10-item scale produce the same results (see Evans and Heath (1995), and Evans, Heath and Lalljee (1995) for further elaboration of these scaling issues).

Weak class theories or strong sociology?[1]

David J. Lee

In this editorial conclusion I want to defend the 'strong' conception of class. I accept, like previous authors, that the primary representative of strong class theory throughout this century, Marxist historical materialism, is seriously flawed. This is widely acknowledged by many of its remaining followers even though most would not accept as I would that the damage is fatal. However, the 'death of class' critique is also flawed. It involves a fallacious argument by elimination, according to which, because Marxism went wrong, we must (i) jettison *all* attempt at 'strong' sociological accounts of class and (ii) adopt the 'weaker' individualist class theories and methods associated with Weber. The case has not been made as I see it. Furthermore, as I shall argue, to regard 'weak' and 'strong' class analysis as mutually exclusive is mistaken anyway.

'Strong' class explanation entails the view that class – like many other social phenomena – must at some point be understood as a property of social relationships *per se* and is not simply reducible to the situations and actions of individuals. Indeed class frequently both shapes and constrains, and so to that extent accounts for, the individuality of particular actors, be they persons or groups of persons. I take this type of explanatory strategy to be an important part of what makes sociology itself distinctive; and although that is a view which I obviously do not have space to defend properly here, I see the defence of strong class theory as a key salient in upholding and strengthening the discipline generally.

The following remarks are therefore an attempt to state how a strong account of class might be rehabilitated in sociology, one which addresses some of the crucial issues raised by previous authors in this book and in doing so acknowledges that certain of Marx's insights deserve to be retained. The supporting arguments fall into four groups: methodological, theoretical, substantive and (in a very general sense) political.

The methodology of class explanations

In a celebrated passage in *The Eighteenth Brumaire* Marx argued that people:

> make their own history but they do not make it just as they please; they do not make it under circumstances chosen by themselves but under circumstances chosen directly encountered, given and transmitted from the past. The tradition of all the dead generations weighs like a nightmare on the brain of the living. (Marx 1934:10)

These words constitute one version of the so-called structure-action problem in sociology: at its simplest, how to understand the relation between, on one hand, social behaviour which is constrained by objective circumstances and conditioning; and on the other, social behaviour which is the product of subjective intentions, 'meanings' and reasons. The precise meaning of the quoted words as a guide to Marx's views on the matter has been much debated. Nevertheless, it is possible to take the passage at its face value as merely containing a simple but vital *methodological* insight: namely that to understand social behaviour it must be studied at different levels of analysis. Levels of analysis, such as 'structure' and 'action', are necessary abstractions from a complex reality. They are, however, incommensurate and the one cannot be reduced to the other. The implication, which Marx himself certainly did not always heed, is that any theory which tries overambitiously to incorporate structure and action into the same explanatory framework (or conflate them together as Giddens does with his concept of 'class structuration') will become reductionist and will fail in Holmwood and Stewart's sense (Holmwood and Stewart 1983, 1995 cf. Giddens 1973).

It is the identification of reductionism in existing versions of class analysis which is the rational kernel of 'death of class' polemics. Pahl, for example, finds the 'mantra' of 'structure-consciousness-action' reductionism to be endemic in urban sociology and class analysis. What the Weberian post-modernist critics of class analysis seem to be saying, too, in one guise or another, is that the very concept of class relies on a collectivist methodological reduction.

However, the Weberian method of weak class analysis is reductionist too, albeit in the opposite direction to Marxism. Whereas the Marxist tradition of class analysis has risked reducing all problems of class *praxis* to problems of determining structure, Weberian analysis has tended to see all questions of class analysis as ones of individual class position, formation, action and meaning. There is, in fact, a widely recognised tension in Weber's own work. On one hand, he engaged with substantive matters which sound unquestionably sociological – including, of course, class. On the other, he advocated a methodology which makes the locus of successful sociological explanation 'adequacy at the level of meaning'. Unfortunately for his sociological heirs, Weber in so opting for methodological individualism, aligned himself with a reductionist tradition in social science which is hostile to 'strong' sociology as I have defined it here. Conveyed via Austrian neo-classical economics to Hayek, Popper, Friedman and the rest, methodological individualism tends to be dismissive, not just of Marxism but of methodological 'socialism' (or collectivism) in any form. Individualist methodology, if adhered to rigorously, denies by philosophical *diktat* the principle in Marx's statement, that social phenomena (including class) have to be studied on separate levels of analysis. But as we saw in the introduction, Weberian class analysis has been forced, despite its individualist methodology, to incorporate 'structural' metaphors by default.

In seeking to reject one form of reductionism we emphatically do *not* have to be forced into the arms of the other. By trying to rehabilitate 'strong' class analysis from the detritus of Marxism, I am not claiming that it is somehow 'better' than, or a substitute for, 'weak' class analysis. We cannot study everything at once and each is appropriate for different kinds of problem. 'Strong' problems cannot be explained by 'weak' theories nor 'weak' problems by 'strong' ones. Failure to appreciate this has made it possible, in the wake of the communist debacle, for the critics of class analysis to 'pick off' the separate forms of class research one by one – first the 'strong' and then the 'weak' – and argue that with the different garments gone the Emperor is scantily clad if not actually naked. What is needed, then, to continue the simile, is to ensure that the whole ensemble is in fact still in place and is a fitting one at that. For this we need a more precise account of class than hitherto and a means of determining when and why strong class analysis is appropriate.

Structure, consciousness and action

Marx's brief allusion to tradition 'weighing like a nightmare on the brain of the living' suggests a further methodological argument for strong class analysis. One of the many consequences of explanatory failure and reductionism in existing approaches is their failure to develop a systematic treatment of the middle term of Pahl's 'mantra', i.e. consciousness. A long essay could be written about the status of mental processes in social science and about the tendency of sociologists to ignore or reinvent, albeit in a rather naive and unknowing way, the wheels which turn in psychology around the same issue. A regrettable dualism has developed between the purely mental – i.e. what can safely be left to psychologists – and the truly social. Unfortunately, though, it has in turn become necessary for students of the 'social' to acknowledge that 'mental' phenomena like cognition and 'consciousness' – surfacing in various ways as 'typical meanings', 'rationality' in relation to 'ends', 'identities', 'self-images', 'ideology' and of course, 'class consciousness' – intervene between 'society as structure' and 'society as action', and vice versa. But, with one exception, no serious theory of *collective* consciousness or social thought is available.

The exception of course is found in the work of Durkheim and those influenced by him – of whom the Soviet psychologist Vygotsky is among the most important, if only because the rediscovery of his work has encouraged a sociological turn in psychology itself (Kozulin 1990). In this tradition, however, consciousness/cognition is *constitutive* of both structure and action, not just a black box between them. Alas, because Durkheim had very little directly to say about class, class analysis is one area of sociology which has been virtually uninfluenced by his ideas. This is a pity for it is increasingly recognised that Durkheim (especially as reinterpreted by Vygotsky) pioneered a very subtle basis for a 'strong' theory of collective mental life, and the manner in which social relations are both mentally constituted and 'psychically creative' (Fletcher 1971, 2:271).

First, a careful reading of Durkheim's *Rules of Sociological Method* reveals that he considered it essential, in framing a sociological explanation, to understand how social relations ('society') restrain and limit individual egoism, whether expressed as rational calculation or irrational 'passion'. Since both are potentially limitless in scope such restraint is a precondition of the continuance of social obligation in any meaningful sense at all. Secondly, throughout his entire opus Durkheim pioneered a theory of collective cognition by which psychic boundaries to individual conduct ('classifications') are established and through which both social relations and individual conduct are simultaneously given a 'structure'. The basic element in this collective thought is not mechanistic conditioning but on one hand, active classification of things and activities, of course, and on the other classification of people. This *clas*sification, in the short to medium term at least is 'given' in collective 'representations', that is states of collective consciousness, including language and belief which express 'the way in which the group conceives itself in its relations with the objects which affect it' (Durkheim 1964:xlix). Neither of these principles, it should be emphasised, is a theory as such, so much as the basis of a methodological rule stating what for Durkheim is essential to a strong sociological explanation – and what has to be shown in establishing the validity of this explanation empirically. Note too that while neither violates the rule that explanations should be meaningfully adequate, they do call for an analysis of meaning on separate levels.

What then is involved in utilising these same principles in defence of strong class analysis? The most pressing point of departure is to establish the 'collective representation' of class. However, Durkheim confronted an analogous problem himself. As his interpreters have noted, he felt able to specify the collective representations through which pre-modern societies had constrained the actions of their members: law, morality and most notoriously religion with its powerful categorisations of the cosmic order, its rituals and symbols and its strong sanctions on the growth of egoism as we experience it today. The modern industrial division of labour, however, had undermined the homogeneity and uniformity of collective sentiments and substituted an 'organic' solidarity in which individuality and political doctrines of the 'sacredness' of the individual and of individual self-interest were actually emphasised. How would such an order be able more effectively to establish a spontaneous division of tasks and set boundaries to individual aspiration?

He sought, through his enquiries into totemism, ways to address what he came to call 'the religious nature of modern man'. In fact what he should have been looking at is the religious nature of modern *money*. Is not money a literally awesome collective representation, which in large measure determines the organisational forms and boundaries of individual conduct in an individualistically oriented *Gesellschaft* and furthermore, renders it literally *accountable* to the collectivity? But, as I have argued in greater detail elsewhere, in the role of money as a collective representation also lies the clue to a non-reductionist theoretical account of the persistence of class in modern industrial societies (see Lee 1994).

Money, capital and the 'strong' theory of class

The important point about money is that it is also a form of power. Power, too, however, has to be understood in a strong and a weak sense, i.e. on different analytical levels. Weber characteristically understands power as 'meanings' and 'intentions' in his celebrated definition of power as 'ability to realise one's will against the resistance of others'. But power also can be manifested in a 'strong' i.e. Durkheimian sense as the general power of social relations over individual 'actors', be they persons or collectivities such as organisations and groups (Geiger 1947:242–345). Indeed, power in the 'weak' Weberian sense is arguably precarious unless it can identify itself with 'strong', i.e. social, power. This is, as I see it, exactly how money and class power are linked and why class remains such an entrenched and significant 'phenomenon of the distribution of power' as Weber called it. As anthropologists have noted, money is always both 'heads' as well as 'tails': that is, it is a legal and authoritative collective representation, on one hand, but held by social actors in given denominations on the other (Hart 1986). Or, as Marx points out, through money, and especially through money accumulated as capital the general power of society over human action (in the form of labour) becomes power appropriated by particular persons.

If we are to understand this process properly, however, we again have to jettison Marx and Weber themselves. Just as there were defects in their methodology, so there were defects in their conceptualisations of money and capital. In particular, they remained in various ways under the spell of political economy and economistic thinking (Lee 1994:401–3). In Marx, for example, the accumulation of capital is held only to be possible through the appropriation of surplus value within the context of 'production'. This reification of the 'productive', which derives from Smith and Ricardo, soon began to create problems for his theory of class since it associated class relations proper with the existence of a traditional working class labouring 'productively' in privately owned manufacturing industry. Consequently, it was ill adapted to account for the corporate societies of the twentieth century in which the interpenetration of state and 'industry' grew constantly and a 'non-productive' middle class of administrators and managers became a significant occupational stratum. Marx was also unable to grasp fully the significance of capital accumulation outside the 'productive' sector, through finance, speculation, company take overs and the use of state revenues. As bankers already recognise – and it is time sociology threw off the Marxist reification of production and did the same – capital is *any* accumulated and administered fund of money.

True, Weber, working in a later generation, was able to respond to the actual development of capitalism with a more flexible kind of class analysis. Nevertheless, his work frequently alludes to 'the market' and 'economic action' as if these notions were unproblematic and as if markets could be understood in the idiom of economics, i.e. in terms of general 'economic' laws which supposedly sociology should treat as 'given'. Since this given-ness applied as much to capital accumulation as to other economic processes, the legacy which both he and Marx left to later generations of sociologists is that class inequality can, without being obscure, be associated with 'economic' life chances. Only recently, with the growth of self-doubt in economics itself, has a sociology (and anthropology) of the 'economic' and of markets begun to appear increasingly viable, revealing in the process that 'economic' explanation contains its own failures (Holmwood and Stewart 1995).

Removing the explanatory failures of 'economism', however, in turn shows up in the inadequate treatment of *money* by these writers (Lee 1994; cf. Dodd 1994). For both Marx and Weber and for most sociologists since, money is a 'mere' symbol of something else: namely, 'real' economic relations or the rationality of general economic action. Sociology has thus had very little to say that is not some form of 'economics', about the role of currency in contemporary life and the international flows of money capital which characterise it. Money is in fact of greater significance than a mere symbol of economic relationships: it is the collective representation of *Gesellschaft*, of 'economic' society. We do not have money because we have a market economy. We have an economy and markets because we have money.

If, as the post-modernist myth claims, late twentieth-century life is characterised by the fragmentation and 'globalisation' of social relations and culture, that is nothing new. Even in *The Communist Manifesto* Marx noted that as a result of the capital accumulation process 'all that is solid melts into air' and the traditional moral ties of community are displaced by the cash nexus. It is therefore odd to find so little recognition of the persistence of 'power as money' or of capital accumulation in the works of those who would argue that late twentieth-century capitalism is so fundamentally changed that the concept of class is redundant. The issue is either ignored altogether, or the thesis of the separation of capital ownership from control is treated as if it were established fact. (This particular grand narrative it seems is immune from the scepticism applied to others.) In contrast, as Scott and others are able to show through substantive empirical work, 'strong' class relations in the form of 'impersonal' owner control of accumulated money capital remains of considerable significance in understanding contemporary 'global' society (cf. Chapter 12).

Pecuniary classification and constructing the right classes

Although I cannot do so fully here, I must now illustrate how all of these 'strong' methodological and theoretical arguments might be employed to address the debate which figures significantly in this volume, about surveys of employment or occupation-based research on class position as exemplified in the work of Wright, Goldthorpe and others. The critics argue that at best this work is a 'weak' form of class analysis but that the use of the term 'class' in connection with it is increasingly redundant and one might just as well talk instead about income level or socio-economic grouping. Intuitively, the suggestion that this distinguished work is anything other than *class* analysis seems bizarre to me. As both neo-Weberians and their neo-Marxist colleagues themselves argue, that the grouping of occupations into classes can be justified on the grounds that employment and paid work remain major sources of variation in authority, function, conditions and reward that are of momentous significance for most people. Moreover, the fact that it has been possible to demonstrate this in many different kinds of society over considerable time periods is an argument in itself.

But these grounds for claiming it conceptually as *class* analysis have been weakening, nonetheless. There are for a start the quite distinct classifications, of Wright and Goldthorpe in particular, with their separate rationales. There is the obscurity of the very small group of extremely wealthy and powerful actors, despite the fact that the decisions they take in conjunction with their 'employment' now influence the global 'community'. There is the related conceptual problem of linking research about the distribution and control of capital to 'positional' statistical correlations provided by occupational surveys. There is the problem that those without jobs, not least full-time housewives, the homeless or the unemployed, seem not to have a class position in this sense at all (really?). And there is the plethora of issues raised by the entailment of gender and ethnic differentiation in the elaboration of empirical class structures.

So I come to the same conclusion as Crompton (1993 and above) that as a basis for assigning society into classes, employment is an

251

important part of the story but no means all of it. Employment is one element in what I would call the wider pecuniary classification of people and things. For most people it means belonging to the broad group in highly industrialised societies whose income flow is regular enough to ensure a supply of necessities but whose income and expenditure are broadly in balance. But there are of course others. At the bottom of the heap are to be found unemployed groups, many of them either young adults or the very old, who are so *im*pecunious that they do not have the means to participate in 'normal' social life at all and who, because of the collapse of citizenship systems, experience declassification from mainstream society. Just above them are those who, through irregular income or business failure, or whatever, are building up debt not capital. In turn, *above* the mass of the fairly solvent employed are those members of the true petite bourgeoisie who manage to accumulate money and turn small capital into bigger capital. As Myles and Turegun show above, big capitals do not drive out the small as Marx thought. They have been joined, however, by the new bourgeoisie or service class of both the private and public sector, who are at their most distinctive when they can turn a high income and favourable employment conditions into a source of (mostly) rentier capital. The petit bourgeoisie of both kinds are distinguished, then, by the fact that they also have the opportunity to join the top pecuniary stratum, the owners and controllers of large blocks of personal and public capital. Thus, it would be perfectly possible to develop out of 'strong' pecuniary class analysis a related programme of positional ('weak') empirical research, building on existing employment based frameworks and with the potential to equal them in rigour, especially if one had access to the kind of panel study data now being collected in a number of countries.

The point of these admittedly rather schematic remarks, then, is not to rehearse again the limitations of the conventional frameworks, but rather to stress that to appreciate the exact contribution they have made to class analysis depends on specifying precisely how their methodological and conceptual structure belongs within a wider programme. In this wider programme weak and strong approaches would share a common view of class as pecuniary classification based on relationship to existing means of capital accumulation.

Strong sociology and tendentious politics

I wish to pass finally to some openly non-analytical points about recent criticisms of strong class theory. Too often in critical discussions the suggestion that class analysis (in so far as it is to be tolerated at all) should only think about class in a 'weak' sense, is politically tendentious, whether the authors mean it that way or not. The cramping intellectual influence of the Cold War upon the social sciences lives on in those fresh recitals of the theoretical and predictive failures of Marxist class theory and the accusations of left bias in class analysis and in an implied triumphalism about the benefits of liberal–capitalist *Gesellschaft*. Marshall and Goldthorpe are quite right to complain that the critics of their own brand of class analysis seem totally unable to conceive of 'class' being used analytically, shorn of its revolutionary political associations; and are simultaneously unwilling to recognise that class *analysis* calls for all preconceptions, even neo-liberal ones, to be put on hold. There is even the insinuation that there is something foolish or intellectually disreputable about sociologists who tiresomely still go on with class research despite the manifest collapse of the left political programme; and a specious implication that if the origins of a theoretical idea lay in political utopianism or *gemeinschaflich* nostalgia, its current analytical power must necessarily be questioned. Yet neo-liberalism itself, especially in its free market variants was born of the naive utopian celebration of an idealised *Gesellschaft* that has abolished all fetters on market processes; and relies on a dated anti-nostalgic modernism which equates the good simply with the utilitarian; and individual freedom with *anomie*, or, worse, with mere licence. The fact is that Marxism and liberalism free market have alike failed as political philosophies but they continue to hinder intellectual work.

Conclusion

I have attempted to defend 'strong' class analysis by suggesting that it forms a necessary part of any programme of class research that is equally sensitive to both the strengths and limitations of working at different levels of method and theory in social science. In pursuing such a programme it is necessary to recognise and abandon the reductionism and substantive errors in the traditional class theories which have brought class analysis to its present pass. Much greater use needs to be made of an 'economic' sociology and anthropology in which the role of money in integrating the organic or *Gesellschaftlich* life of the industrial world is acknowledged. And Goldthorpe is no doubt right to suggest that it is the stubborn endurance of class and not its death which will form the focus of such work for many years yet.

Notes

1. I am indebted to constructive disagreements and discussions with various colleagues in the Sociology Department of the University of Essex, notably Ted Benton, David Lockwood and John Scott.

Capitalism, classes and citizenship[1]

Bryan S. Turner

It has often been observed that academics rarely solve problems; they become bored with them and then move on to different issues. Issues do not get satisfactory solutions; they are merely abandoned or recycled. There is a strong sense of boredom with the classical debate regarding the existence and nature of social classes. Furthermore, because sociology is often deeply implicated in the social processes it seeks to describe and to understand, it has been profoundly exposed to and shaped by cultural fashions and changes in the intellectual climate. As we argued in the introduction, the assertion of a clear division between the negative social consequences of a capitalist system and the positive benefits of socialism and organised communism was an important feature of class critiques of capitalism. The relationship between sociology and the May Events of 1968 is well known (Lyotard 1988, Plant 1992). The Thatcher period, the presidency of Reagan and the decline of communism have all had a significant impact on the academic analysis of social class and the welfare state. And with the collapse of communism, a reticence about the explicit value of socialist theory has often been combined with a post-modern critique of grand narratives such as Marxism (Lyotard 1984 and 1988). Given Marx's pronouncements on the death of religion in the nineteenth century, the irony is that with the disappearance of communism many writers now see Islam as the only significant challenge to Western capitalist traditions, and it is not surprising therefore that the contemporary role of Islam is often debated in the context of post-modern culture (Ahmed 1992, Gellner 1992, Turner 1994a). The simple dichotomy between capitalism and communism has been complicated by the robust growth internationally of various forms of fundamentalism, of which Islamic revivalism is a leading example. The rise and fall of class analysis is thus a perfect example of the exposure of sociology and social theory to fashions within the intellectual market place.

In this conclusion I want to argue that these fluctuations in the prevailing mood of sociologists need not and should not distract our attention from the systematic importance scarcity and solidarity as perspectives or paradigms on the enduring social realities of communal membership and social conflict. The dialectic of scarcity of resources and the need for social solidarity has been a constant theme of classical sociological analysis (Lockwood 1992). The idiom of class analysis may be subject to fashion but scarcity of resources and inequalities in their distribution are permanent features of all social organisation and action. The authors in this volume and elsewhere who seek to defend the class idiom, however, have failed to show how it remains a viable means of understanding scarcity and inequality in their contemporary forms.

Pseudo-debate in class analysis

In the strong theory of social classes there remain intractable theoretical and empirical problems most of which centre around the question of class distinctiveness in the face of the complexity of concrete events and contexts. How can the existence of separate independent classes with material interests opposed to other classes be demonstrated in the face of considerable cultural, educational, religious and other overlap between them? These difficulties are not restricted to Marxist versions of strong class theory. For example, much of the debate between functionalist theories of stratification and class theories have been around the question of a continuum of inequality versus the presence of sharp ruptures in the social structure. Or again, it has been particularly difficult to integrate the notion of cultural capital and economic capital into a strong version of class theory as Pierre Bourdieu seeks to do in his work on taste and distinction (1984). Bourdieu's theory of social reproduction is a strong version of Marxist views of class. For example, his analysis of educational systems is highly reductionist (Bourdieu 1973). He combines this class reductionist approach to class with a clear anthropological understanding of the autonomy of the cultural component of habitus (Bourdieu 1977). There is as a result a tension between his anthropological understanding of cultural practices and a structuralist view of class position. In addition, dimensions such as gender, age and ethnicity are problematic for the strong economic theory of social classes. It is not enough to argue, as Westergaard does for example, for the empirical link between these other inequalities and 'class'. The failure to incorporate these theoretically into class analysis remains a problem and, as Crompton's chapter on gender illustrates (Chapter 9 in this volume), the empirical association can actually be used to demonstrate the limitations of prioritising class explanations (see also Crompton 1993, Crompton and Mann 1986). Similar critical arguments about the neglect of ageing and generations as principles of stratification can be raised against conventional class theory (Turner 1989).

As we stated in an earlier reply to Goldthorpe and Marshall (above, Ch. 7), neither Holton nor I necessarily believe that class as an empirical phenomenon or as a form of analysis are on the point of extinction. However, the *idiom* of class analysis does require a systematic overhaul in the light of the apparent collapse of strong class theories. To abandon the strong class idiom is quite clearly to restrict the scope and interest of conventional class theories. Goldthorpe and Marshall evidently share this view in their severe delimitation of the range and scope of class analysis as involving 'no theory of history', 'no theory of class exploitation', 'no theory of class-based collective action' and no 'reductionist theory of political action' (see p. 99–102 above). To this list of limitations, we suggested adding the idea that it is also impossible to generate a satisfactory account of a systematic class-based dominant ideology in capitalist societies (Abercrombie, Hill and Turner 1980, 1990).

We referred to neo-Weberian theory such as Goldthorpe and Marshall's as minimalist or 'weak' in that the claims they make about the analytical value and purchase of class research are both limited and descriptive, unlike the maximalist analytical and empirical claims which have been typical of the classical Marxist legacy. This post-Marxist minimalism appears to be perfectly appropriate, given the current difficulties facing Marxism in a post-communist international system. Indeed there is clearly a substantial measure of agreement between us in terms of identifying the deficiencies and limitations in the strong idiom which require an extensive redefinition of class analysis itself. To deny this common ground by insisting that we have not distinguished different class idioms adequately is, as Crompton (1993:117) points out, to inject a large element of 'pseudo-debate' into the picture.

The key question which remains, however, is what is left of class analysis as such once the strong class idiom has been rejected in favour of minimalism? Our own entry into the debate (Holton and Turner 1989) was not, as implied by our critics, a bland, a-historical, class-less view of industrial society theory but rather a Weberian *gesellschaftlich* version of class theory. This Weberian approach is based upon the analysis of life chances of individuals within the market place over the life course as a method of studying patterns of economic, political and cultural inequality (Turner 1981). The Weberian case against (functionalist) industrial society theories in this respect remains that they neglect the persistence of structurally generated economic inequality, and thus inter-generational class immobility for many categories of individuals. They are open still to the radical criticism that they offer a rather thinly disguised ideological justification for inherited inequality of opportunity. Motivational commitment and personal investment in education are not rewarded on an individual basis of merit, because for example family inheritance always gives an unfair advantage at birth. Recent attempts to resolve these problems with functionalist theories through the development of so-called neo-functionalism have proved both unsatisfactory and unsuccessful (Alexander 1985).

It is also misleading to suggest that this approach lacks any historical dimension. Our approach is not a-historical, but we have been critical of romantic views of the historical significance of class-based communities as agents of social change. Romanticism with respect to the viability and efficacy of working-class communities as carriers of authentic values and as agents of revolutionary change has been highly characteristic of English Marxist historians and radical students of working-class cultures. This communal quality of class has been illustrated typically by isolated communities characterised by a limited number of occupational groupings. Other studies attempted to find the communal basis of class traditions in religious bonds, especially in terms of the impact of the Methodist sects on British culture (Hoggart 1957, Halevy 1962, Thompson 1968). Our critique of romantic nostalgia for intimate community life and cultural authenticity had been developed earlier in our defence of the legacy of Talcott Parsons's version of social liberalism (Holton and Turner 1986:234); Parsons's sociology can be regarded as unambiguously a defence of modernity against both conservative and radical versions of nostalgia.

In order to go beyond pseudo-debate, it is possible to identify two key issues. The first concerns the scope that remains for class analysis in the weaker *gesellschaftlich* mode and the second involves the problems which are inherent in excessively scientistic accounts of class theory. In terms of its remaining scope, the relevance of a restricted or weaker version of class depends on its capacity to explain patterns of inequality, socio-political attitudes and social action over time. An evaluation of the promise of class theory to accomplish these tasks depends in turn on two inter-related factors, namely the empirical persuasiveness of the various class theories (as offered by Goldthorpe, Marshall, Wright and others) and the salience of class theories in relation to other wider theories which seek to explain the same phenomena. A more elaborate discussion of these issues would take us into the importance of politics, life style, citizenship and culture in relation to class theory (Turner 1988).

The theoretical difficulties that arise here stem from the construction of class categories out of aggregations of occupations and other employment-based characteristics. One illustration is their rather odd reference to 'farm classes' (above:p. 152). One assumes that in principle the list of such classes could be extended to embrace 'university classes', 'sports classes' or 'entertainment classes' as descriptions of occupational aggregates. It also follows that the debate around Goldthorpe's work is not a debate about classes but about the employment structure, systematic employment opportunities, and occupational position and attitudes (Crompton 1993). Such categories have the obvious virtue of being measurable, but they are not sensitive to gender, ethnicity and culture as features of such inequality. Social class continues to be associated with occupational position, but the wider and more interesting issues of power, culture and social action are precluded. The effect is to reduce class to a statistical aggregate having an uncertain and tenuous relationship to consciousness, politics and social action. Within this view of occupational groupings, there are no assumptions about inevitable class conflicts over interests. The weak class theory merely says that there are significant inequalities in society and that these inequalities are organised around differences in purchasing power between occupational clusters. Our challenge to conventional weak theories is, given this minimalist conclusion, why would *class* continue to feature so significantly in the sociological repertoire and vocabulary? Why not refer instead to occupation, economic organisation, labour markets and social attitudes? It is unclear what the concept of class adds to the explanatory significance of studies of, say, occupational mobility, or correlations between occupational position and social attitudes or, as Morris argues, the failure of the labour market to provide employment at all.

The second point is to raise questions about the scientistic presentation of conventional class analysis. Of course, there is no objection in principle to measurement and quantification in empirical research, but it is important to reject the idea that class measurement can be done without some resort to cultural evaluation and questions of value-relevance. To put this objection in sharper Weberian terms, one can ask 'Why are the fruits of class analysis worth knowing?' and 'Why have a range of historical actors, including sociologists, deemed them worth knowing?' The basic point is that it is very difficult 'to aggregate the multiplicity of class positions into categories without having recourse to evaluative cultural criteria' (Holton and Turner 1989:388). Class classifications have been deeply implicated in value-relevant concerns about inequality, exploitation, fairness and citizenship. For example, many of the recent attempts to produce a skill-based classification of occupations are themselves heavily implicated in wider social debates, in particular about the relative contributions of men and women to productivity.

To say that class or occupational classifications are value-relevant is not to argue that they are refractory to scientific investigation, but it is to claim that they are not value-free. How, for example, would the idea of a service class have come to be thematised, if not in relation to the normatively loaded legitimation of claims of professionals and others to be recognised? In other words, the choice of such labels as 'service class' is not a deliberation which arises naturally, directly or unambiguously from survey data relating to occupational clusters. Survey methodologies do not provide any privileged means to settle such arguments. These issues were central to Weber's *Wissenschaftslehre* and the role of ideal types was to address some aspects of this value-relevance problem (Turner 1981).

Solidarity and scarcity

In analytical and historical terms, there has always been a close relationship between economics and sociology. This proximity is very obvious in the work of both Marx, who attempted to understand the relationship between civil society and the mode of production in terms of a political economy which rejected bourgeois theories of utility, and Weber whose principal work was, according to Marianne Weber, *Economy and Society*. We can express the underlying issues in economics and sociology as a debate about the relationship between scarcity and solidarity. Economics emerged as a modern science in the eighteenth century alongside the growth of the consumer society. Conspicuous consumption, positional goods, possessive individualism, narcissism, the reputational self and the leisure class – these concepts attempted to express the new competition for distinction which emerged with industrialisation and with the paradox of scarcity as a consequence of abundance. Endless elasticity of demand meant that scarcity was a condition of an economic surplus and rising social expectations. In a world of infinite desire, affluence created a world of scarcity as the product of modernisation (Xenos 1989). Economics was consequently a science of scarcity which attempted to understand the problem of choice in an environment of limited resources. The classical theory of marginal utility attempted to explain the economics of scarcity, or at least how means are related to ends under conditions of universal scarcity. Sociology has, by contrast, been concerned to understand the grounds of social solidarity in terms of shared values and beliefs, common affective ties and the bonding consequences of collective rituals. Sociology has in other words attempted to provide a general answer to the question: how is society possible? Bringing these two debates together, sociology asks how can society be sustained in an environment of conflicts over scarcity. To some extent, this issue was the central focus of David Lockwood's *Solidarity and Schism* (1992) which examined the nature of disorder within Durkheimian and Marxist sociology. In these concluding observations, I attempt to place a slightly different emphasis on this theme by considering the prospects of citizenship in late capitalism.

Sociology as a discipline arose intellectually as a response to the limitations of the underlying assumptions of marginal utility theory; this response is particularly evident in the work of Weber (Breiner 1995). Weber's paradigm of action (traditional, affectual and rational) was an attempt to overcome the limitations of a utilitarian perspective on means-ends rationalism. Out of Weber's analysis grew a familiar set of distinctions between rational, irrational and non-rational actions, which continues to inform sociology. In particular, Weber's sociology of action pointed towards the limitations of the notion of *Zweckrationalisches Handeln* (or purposively rational, end-oriented actions). It is interesting that Weber's sociology, given the impact of Nietzsche on his work, was open to the complexity of the meanings of rationality in context, including the idea that the rational pursuit of a calling in Protestantism was driven by an irrational quest for salvation. It is doubtful whether Weber ever gave a satisfactory answer to the problem of what actually counts as economic rationality (Sica 1988).

Classical sociology attempted to address two issues, namely to understand the non-rational nature of action, that is the limitations of rational choice models to phenomena like love, religion and charity, and to grasp the non-economic foundations of solidarity. The very word 'sociology' is derived from 'logos' (the study of) and 'socius' (friendship or companionship). Now companionship is a solidarity which grows out of the sharing of bread ('pan'), and sociology could be understood as the analysis of the affective foundations of solidarity. In a more elaborate account, sociology studies the set of contradictory relationships which conjoin scarce conditions with the requirements of collective action and solidarity. The study of the inter-relationships between markets and communities would be a typical example. It is difficult to believe that sociology as a discipline could ever stray too far from these intellectual origins, which is in effect a moral inquiry into the nature of reciprocity under conditions of scarcity.

The relationship between sociology and economics was also the main analytical issue behind the systems theory of Talcott Parsons (Holton and Turner 1986). In *The Structure of Social Action* (Parsons 1937), Parsons criticised economic theory for its failure to solve the problem of social order, which had its intellectual origins in the contractarian theory of the state in the work of Thomas Hobbes, through a rational theory of economic action. Because fraud and force are excellent rational responses to scarcity, economic theory could not explain social order without recourse to residual categories such as sentiments. Parsons attempted to resolve the difficulty through the study of the non-rational components of action, namely shared norms and values which guide action towards collective goals. Although many critics of Parsons argue that he abandoned this promising action theory in adopting a functionalist theory of social systems, the concern for economics and sociology re-emerged in the AGIL paradigm of sub-systems where the principal axis is between the problem of the allocation of scarce resources (economics and politics) and the achievement of internal patterns of solidarity (the domain of sociology and psychology) through such processes as internalisation of norms and socialisation into common values. For Parsons, all social life must resolve the political problem of the (fair) allocation of limited economic resources and the sociological problem of integration through the mobilisation of commitments. How can we achieve normative solidarity in a context of uneven scarcity? If the Hobbesian problem is concerned with the relationship between the state and society, we might argue that the Leibnizian problem of social theodicy considers the problem of how to sustain loyalty to society in the face of systemic inequality.

One traditional answer in classical sociology was that the negative impact of scarcity (class) was masked by the presence of an all-embracing dominant ideology which, in Marxist theory, produced a form of solidarity which was well suited to the underlying needs of economic exploitation. Religion has been, in these theories, a powerful form of social glue. With the decline of religion, a more promising theory was found in citizenship. The merit of T. H. Marshall's approach to class and citizenship was that it presented a promising response to the relationship between scarcity and solidarity within the context of a modern industrial society (Marshall 1981). For Marshall, citizenship was a set of institutions which protected individuals and families from the full impact of the market place. For example, social security was precisely a set of measures to protect individuals from the harshness of economic scarcity. Whereas class was a consequence of economic inequality in the market place, citizenship represented a social response to the inequalities of opportunity and condition which are typical of capitalist societies.

Marshall's theory has been the subject of much contemporary criticism and development (Turner and Hamilton 1994). He failed to develop a differentiated notion of citizenship and his concept of rights (legal, political and social) was too narrow. For example, he did not have an adequate notion of economic rights to which would correspond economic citizenship and industrial democracy. Marshall also failed to incorporate a concept of cultural citizenship in his account of expanding democracy to which educational participation would be related. While these difficulties are significant, Marshall's approach is, nevertheless, valuable because it recognised citizenship is a major source of solidarity in modern secular societies. If markets are the divisive feature of industrial capitalism, then citizenship is an essential ingredient of solidarity as a form of civil religion. Citizenship is the principal fountain of loyalty to the nation-state. Two dimensions of contemporary social change, however, are corrosive of citizenship as a solidaristic principle of welfare-capitalism, namely globalisation and post-modernisation.

Thus, inequality or systemic imbalance in the social distribution of scarce resources (Turner 1986) will continue to be a principal feature of human society as such (for reasons which are related to human desire in a context of inadequate resources) regardless of the rise and fall of strong or weak class theories. As a consequence, sociology will also continue to be a major feature of social reflexivity with respect to modernity and postmodernity. The role of social theory is to comprehend the infinitely complex and changing relations between scarcity and solidarity, and in particular how scarcity is produced out of abundance and solidarity from conflict. The conviction remains, however, that class theory and analysis, far from aiding the search for comprehension, has become its fetter.

Note

1. This chapter is a substantially revised version of R. Holton and B. S. Turner, 'Debate and Pseudo-debate in Class Analysis: some unpromising aspects of Goldthorpe and Marshall's Defence', *Sociology* 28, 3 1994:799–804.

References

ABERCROMBIE, N., HILL, S. and TURNER, B. 1980. *The Dominant Ideology Thesis*. London: Allen & Unwin.

ABERCROMBIE, N., HILL, S. and TURNER, B. (eds) 1990. *Dominant Ideologies*. London: Unwin Hyman.

ABRAMS, M., ROSE, R. and HINDEN, R. 1960. *Must Labour Lose?* Harmondsworth: Penguin.

ABRAMSON, P. and INGLEHART, R. 1992. 'Generational Replacement and Value Change in Eight Western European Societies' *British Journal of Political Science* 22(2):183–228.

ACKER, J. 1973. 'Women and Stratification: A Case of Intellectual Sexism' in J. Huber (ed.), *Changing Women in a Changing Society*. Chicago: University of Chicago Press.

AHMED, A. S. 1992. *Postmodernism and Islam. Predicament and Promise*. London and New York: Routledge.

AHRNE, G. and WRIGHT, E. O. 1983. 'Classes in the United States and Sweden: A Comparison'. *Acta Sociologica* 26:211–35.

AHRNE, G. and GLEMENT, W. 1992. 'A New Regime? Class Representation within the Swedish State'. *Economic and Industrial Democracy* 13:455–79.

ALEXANDER, J. (ed.) 1985. *Neofunctionalism*. Beverly Hills: Sage.

ALFORD, R. 1962. 'A Suggested Index of the Association of Social Class and Voting'. *Public Opinion Quarterly*, 26:417–25.

ALFORD, R. 1963. *Party and Society: Anglo-American Democracies*. Chicago: Rand McNally.

ALLARD, P., BEAUD, M., BELLON, B., LÉVY, A.-M. and LIENHART, S. 1978. *Dictionnaire des groupes industriels et financiers en France*. Paris: Editions du Seuil.

ALLEN, G. 1972. *A Short History of Modern Japan*. Third edition, London: Allen & Unwin.

ALLEN, S. 1982. 'Gender, Inequality, and Class Formation' in A. Giddens and G. McKenzie (eds) *Social Class and the Division of Labour*. Cambridge: Cambridge University Press.

ALTHUSSER, L. 1971. 'Ideology and Ideological State Apparatuses' in *Lenin and Philosophy and Other Essays*. London: New Left Books.

ANDERSON, B. 1983. *Imagined Communities*. London: Verso.

ANDERSON, P. 1979. *Lineages of the Absolutist State*. London: Verso.

ANTHIAS, F. 1991. 'Race and Class Revisited: Conceptualising Race and Racisms'. *Sociological Review*, Vol. 38(1):19–42.

BACCHI, C. 1990. *Same Difference*. Sydney: Allen & Unwin.

BAGGULEY, P. and MANN, K. 1992. 'Idle Thieving Bastards: Scholarly Representations of the "Underclass"'. *Work, Employment and Society*, Vol. 6.

BAKER, K., DALTON R. and HILDEBRANDT, K. 1981. *Germany Transformed*. Cambridge, Mass.: Harvard University Press.

BALDERSHEIM, H. *et al.* (eds) 1989. *New Leaders, Parties, and Groups*. Bordeaux, France: Cervel-Iep.

BALTZELL, E. D. 1958. *Philadelphia Gentlemen: The Making of a National Upper Class*. New York: Free Press.

BALTZELL, E. D. 1964. *The Protestant Establishment*. New York: Random House.

BARBER, B. and DUNCAN, O. D. 1959. 'Discussion of Papers by Professor Nisbet and Professor Berherle'. *Pacific Sociological Review*, Spring:25–8.

BARKER, D. and ALLEN, S. (eds) 1976. *Sexual Divisions and Society*. London: Tavistock.

BAUDRILLARD, J. 1988. *Selected Writings*. Stanford: Stanford University Press.

BAUMAN, Z. 1982. *Memories of Class. The Pre-history and After-life of Class*. London: Routledge & Kegan Paul.

BAUMOL, W. 1967. 'Macroeconomics of Unbalanced Growth'. *American Economic Review* 57:415–26.

BECHHOFER, F. and ELLIOTT, B. 1968. 'An Approach to a Study of Small Shopkeepers and the Class Structure'. *European Journal of Sociology* 9:180–202.

BECHHOFER, F. and ELLIOTT, B. 1976. 'Persistence and Change: The Petite Bourgeoisie in the Industrial Society'. *European Journal of Sociology* 17:74–99.

BECHHOFER, F. and ELLIOTT, B. 1978. 'The Voice of Small Business and the Politics of Survival'. *Sociological Review* 26:57–88.

BECHHOFER, F. and ELLIOTT, B. (eds) 1981. *The Petite Bourgeoisie: Comparative Studies of the Uneasy Stratum*. London: Macmillan.

BECHHOFER, F. and ELLIOTT, B. 1985. 'The Petite Bourgeoisie in Late Capitalism'. *Annual Review of Sociology* 11:181–207.

BECK, U. 1987. 'Beyond Status and Class: Will there be an Individualized Class Society?' in V. Meja, D. Misgeld and N. Stehr (eds), *Modern German Sociology*. New York: Columbia University Press, pp. 340–55.

BECK, U. 1992. *Risk Society: Towards a New Modernity*. London: Sage.

BECK, U. 1994. 'The Debate on Individualisation Theory in Today's Sociology in Germany'. *Soziologie* (Journal of the Deutsche Gesellschaft fur Soziologie), 3:119–201.

BECKER, U. 1989. 'Class Theory: Still the Axis of Critical Social Scientific Analysis?' in E. O. Wright (ed.), *The Debate on Classes*. London: Verso.

BELL, D. 1961. *The End of Ideology*. New York: Collier Books.

BELL, D. 1973. *The Coming of Post-Industrial Society*. New York: Basic Books.

BELL, D. 1979. *The Cultural Contradictions of Capitalism*. London: Heinemann.

BELL, D. 1979. 'The New Class: a Muddled Concept' in B. Bruce-Biggs (ed.), *The New Class*. New Brunswick: Transaction Press.

BENOIT-SMULLYAN, E. 1944. 'Status, Status Types and Status Inter-relationships'. *American Sociological Review* 9:151–61.

BERGER, P. 1987. *The Capitalist Revolution*. Hunts: Wildwood House.

BERGER, S. 1980. 'The Traditional Sector in France and Italy' in S. Berger, M. J. Pearce (eds), *Dualism and Discontinuity in Industrial Societies*, Cambridge: Cambridge University Press, pp. 88–131.

BERGER, S. 1981. 'The Uses of the Traditional Sector in Italy: Why Declining Classes Survive'. See Bechhofer and Elliott 1981, pp. 71–89.

BERGER, S. (ed.) 1981. *Organising Interests in Western Europe*. Cambridge: Cambridge University Press.

BERLE, A. and MEANS, G. 1932. *The Modern Corporation and Private Property*. London: Macmillan.

BERMAN, M. 1982. *All That is Solid Melts into Air: The Experience of Modernity*. New York: Simon & Schuster.

BERNSTEIN, E. 1899. *Die Voraussetzungen des Sozialismus und die Aufgaben der Sozialdemokratie*. Stuttgart: Dietz, 1899.

BERTAUX, D. and BERTAUX-WIAME, I. 1981. 'Artisanal Bakery in France: How it Lives and Why it Survives'. See Bechhofer and Elliott 1981, pp. 155–81.

BIANCHI, S. 1981. *Household Composition and Racial Inequality*. New Brunswick, NJ: Rutgers University Press.

BIRCH, D. 1979. *The Job Generation Process*. Cambridge, MA: MIT Program on Neighborhood and Regional Change.

BLACK, D. and MYLES, J. 1986. 'Dependent Industrialization and the Canadian Class Structure: A Comparative Analysis of Canada, the United States, and Sweden'. *Canadian Review of Sociology and Anthropology* 23:157–81.

BLACKBURN, R. M. and MANN, M. 1979. *The Working Class in the Labour Market*. London: Macmillan.

BLACKBURN, R. M. and MARSH, C. 1991. 'Education and Social Class: Revisiting the 1944 Education Act with Fixed Marginals'. *British Journal of Sociology* 42, 507–36.

BLAU, P. M. and DUNCAN, O. D. 1967. *The American Occupational Structure*. New York: Wiley.

BLOCK, F. 1987. *Revising State Theory*. Philadelphia: Temple University Press.

BLOCK, F. 1990. *Postindustrial Possibilities*. Berkeley: University of California Press.

BLOCK, F. 1992. 'Capitalism without Class Power'. *Politics and Society* 20:277–302.

BOARD OF EDUCATION, 1907. *Regulations for Secondary Schools*, London: Board of Education.

BOLTANSKI, L. 1987. *The Making of a Class: Cadres in French Society*. Cambridge: Cambridge University Press.

BONNEY, N. 1988a. 'Gender, Household and Social Class.' *British Journal of Sociology*, March.

BONNEY, N. 1988b. 'Dual Earning Couples'. *Work, Employment and Society*, March.

BOREHAM, P., CLEGG, S., EMMISON, R., MARKS, J. and STEWART, R. 1989. 'Semi-peripheries or Particular Pathways: The Case of Australia, New Zealand and Canada as Class Formations'. *International Sociology* 4:67–90.

BOTTOMORE, T. B. 1964. *Elites and Society*. London: C. A. Watts.

BOTTOMORE, T. and BRYM, R. (eds) 1989. *The Capitalist Class: An International Study*. New York: New York University Press.

BOURDIEU, P. 1973. 'Les stratégies de reconversion: les classes sociales et le système d'enseignement'. *Social Science Information*, 12:5.

BOURDIEU, P. 1977. *Outline of a Theory of Practice*. Cambridge: Cambridge University Press.

BOURDIEU, P. 1984. *Distinction: A Social Critique of the Judgement of Taste*. London: Routledge & Kegan Paul.

BOURDIEU, P. 1990. *The Logic of Practice*. Cambridge: Polity.

BOURDIEU, P. 1993. *Sociology in Question*. London: Sage.

BOURDIEU, P. and PASSERON, J.-C. 1970. *Reproduction in Education, Society and Culture*. London: Sage.

BOWLES, S., GORDON, D. and WEISSKOPF, T. 1983. *Beyond the Wasteland: A Democratic Alternative to Economic Decline*. Garden City: Doubleday.

BOYD, M. 1990. 'Sex Differences in Occupational Skill: Canada, 1961–86'. *Canadian Review of Sociology and Anthropology*. 27: 285–315.

BRAVERMAN, H. 1974. *Labour and Monopoly Capital: The Degradation of Work in the Twentieth Century*. New York: Monthly Review.

BREEN, R. and WHELAN, C. 1994. 'Social Class, Social Origins and Political Partisanship in the Republic of Ireland'. *European Journal of Political Research*, 26:117–34.

BREIGER, R. 1981. 'The Social Class Structure of Occupational Mobility'. *American Journal of Sociology* 87:578–91.

BREINER, P. 1995. 'Rationality, Self-Interest and Politics. The Political Logic of Economics and the Economic Logic of Modernity in Max Weber'. *Political Theory*, 23:1, 25–47.

BRENNER, J. and RAMAS, M. 1984. 'Rethinking Women's Oppression'. *New Left Review* 144:33–71.

BRIGGS, A. 1976. 'The Language of Class' in A. Briggs and J. Saville (eds), *Essays in Labour History*, Vol. 1, London: Macmillan.

BROOM, L. and JONES, F. 1976. *Opportunity and Attainment in Australia*. Canberra: ANU Press.

BROWN, R. 1982. 'Work Histories, Career Strategies and the Class Structure' in A. Giddens (ed.), *Social Class and the Divisions of Labour*. Cambridge: Cambridge University Press, 119–36.

BRUSCO, S. 1982. 'The Emilian Model: Productive Decentralisation and Social Integration'. *Cambridge Journal of Economics* 6:167–84.

BRUSCO, S. and SABEL, C. 1981. 'Artisan Production and Economic Growth' in F. Wilkinson (ed.), *The Dynamics of Labour Market Segmentation*. London: Academic [?], pp. 99–113.

BRYM, R. J. (ed.) 1985. *The Structure of the Canadian Capitalist Class*. Toronto: Garamond.

BRYM, R. J. 1989. 'Canada'. See Bottomore and Brym 1989, pp. 177–206.

BRYNJOLFSSON, E., MALONE, T., GURBABANXI, V. and KAMBIL, A. 1989. 'Does Information Technology Lead to Smaller Firm?'. Massachussets Institute of Technology, Mimeo.

BURAWOY, M. and KROTOV, P. 1992. 'The Soviet Transition from Socialism to Capitalism'. *American Sociological Review*, 57.

BURNHILL, P., GARNER, C. and McPHERSON, A. 1990. 'Parental Education, Social Class and Entry to Higher Education 1976–86'. *Journal of the Royal Statistical Society*, series A, 153, 233–48.

BURRIS, V. 1980. 'Class Formation and Transformation in Advanced Capitalist Societies: A Comparative Analysis.' *Social Praxis* 7:147–79.

BUTLER, D. E. and KAVANAGH, D. 1992. *The British General Election of 1992*. London: Macmillan.

CALVERT, P. 1982. *The Concept of Class*. London: Hutchinson.

CAMPBELL, A. *et al*. 1960. *The American Voter*. Chicago: The University of Chicago Press.

CANNADINE, D. 1992. Review Article. *New York Review of Books*, No. 17.

CARBONI, C. 1984. 'Observaciones comparativas sobre la estrutura de clase de los paises capitalistas avanzados'. *Revista Espagnol Invest. Sociologa*. 26:129–49.

CHANDLER, A. D. 1963. *Strategy and Structure*. Cambridge, Mass: The Belknap Press of Harvard University Press.

CHANDLER, A. D. 1990. *Scale and Scope*. Cambridge, Mass: The Belknap Press of Harvard University Press.

CHANDLER, A. D. and DAEMS, H. (eds) 1980. *Managerial Hierarchies*. Cambridge, Mass: Harvard University Press.

CHERLIN, A. J. 1981. *Marriage, Divorce, Remarriage*. Cambridge: Harvard University Press.

CHIESI, A. 1982. 'L'Elite Finanzieria Italiana'. *Rassegna Italiana di Sociologia* 23.

CHIESI, A. M. 1985. 'Property, Capital and Network Structure in Italy'. See Stokman *et al*. 1985a, pp. 199–214.

CHODOROW, N. 1989. *Feminism and Psychoanalytic Theory*. New Haven and London: Yale University Press.

CIPOLLA, C. (ed.) 1973a and b. *The Fontana Economic History of Europe*. Vols 3 and 4, London: Fontana.

CLARK, T. 1975. 'Community Power' in A. Inkeles, J. Coleman and N. J. Smelser (eds), *Annual Review of Sociology* 1:217–96.

CLARK, T. 1985, 1986, 1987, 1988. *Research in Urban Policy*. Vols 1, 2A, 2B, 3, Greenwich, CT: JAI Press.

CLARK, T. and FERGUSON, L. 1983. *City Money*. New York: Columbia University Press.

CLARK, T. and INGLEHART, R. 1991. 'The New Political Culture: An Introduction'. Prepared for Clark, T. and Hoffmann–Martinot, V. (eds), *The New Political Culture* (Draft Volume).

CLARK, T., LIPSET, S. and REMPEL, M. 1993. 'The Declining Political Significance of Social Class'. *International Sociology* 8:3, 293–316.

CLARKE, S. 1992. 'Privatisation and the Development of Capitalism in Russia'. *New Left Review*, 196.

CLARKE, S. (ed.) 1989. *Urban Innovation and Autonomy*. Newbury Park: Sage.

CLAWSON, D., NEUSTADT, A. and SCOTT, D. 1992. *Money Talks: Corporate PACs and Political Influence*. New York: Basic Books.

CLEMENT, W. 1975. *The Canadian Corporate Elite: An Analysis of Economic Power*. Toronto: McClelland & Stewart.

CLEMENT, W. 1977. *Continental Corporate Power: Economic Elite Linkages between Canada and the United States*. Toronto: McClelland & Stewart.

CLEMENT, W. and MYLES, J. 1994. *Relations of Ruling: Class and Gender in Postindustrial Societies*. Montreal: McGill-Queens University Press.

COATES, D. 1989. *Britain*. See Bottomore and Brym 1989, pp. 19–45.

COHEN, J. 1982. *Class and Civil Society*. Amherst: University of Massachusetts Press.

COHEN, J. 1985. 'Strategy or Identity'. *Social Research* 52:872–95.

COLE, G. 1955. 'Elites in the British Class Structure' in G. D. H. Cole, *Studies in Class Structure*. London: Routledge & Kegan Paul, 1955.

COLEMAN, P. and RAINWATER, L. (with K. A. McClelland) (1979). *Social Standing in America*. London: Routledge & Kegan Paul.

COLLINS, R. 1971. 'Functional and Conflict Theories of Educational Stratification'. *American Sociological Review* Vol. 36:1002–19.

COLLINS, R. 1975. *Conflict Sociology: toward an Explanatory Science*. New York: Academic Press.

Communist and Post-Communist Studies, 1995. Special issue, 'Blue Collar Workers in Post-Communist Societies', 28, (1):3–118.

CONNELL, R. 1987. *Gender and Power*. Stanford: Stanford University Press.

CONVERSE, P. E. 1964. 'The Nature of Belief Systems in Mass Publics' in D. Apter (ed.), *Ideology and Discontent*. New York: The Free Press, pp. 206–61.

COTTRELL, P. L., LINDGREN, H. and TEICHOVA, A. (eds) 1992. *European Industry and Banking Between the Wars*. Leicester: Leicester University Press.

COXON, A. and DAVIES, P. 1986. *Images of Social Stratification. Occupational Structures and Class*. London: Sage.

CREWE, I. and DENVER, D. (eds) 1985. *Electoral Change in Western Democracies: Patterns and Sources of Electoral Volatility*. London: Croom Helm.

CREWE, I. 1984. 'The Electorate: Partisan Dealignment Ten Years On' in H. Berrington (ed.), *Change in British Politics*. London: Frank Cass.

CREWE, I. 1986. 'On the Death and Resurrection of Class Voting: Some Comments on How Britain Votes'. *Political Studies* 34:620–38.

CROMPTON, R. 1989. 'Class Theory and Gender'. *British Journal of Sociology*, 1:No. 4, 565–87.

CROMPTON, R. 1993. *Class and Stratification*. Cambridge: Polity Press.

CROMPTON, R. 1995. 'Women's Employment and the "Middle Class"' in M. Savage and T. Butler (eds), *Social Change and the Middle Classes*. London: UCL Press.

CROMPTON, R. and GUBBAY, J. 1978. *Economy and Class Structure*. London: Macmillan.

CROMPTON, R. and JONES, G. 1984. *White Collar Proletariat*. London: Macmillan.

CROMPTON, R. and MANN, M. (eds) 1986. *Gender and Stratification*. Cambridge: Polity Press.

CROOK, S., PAKULSKI, J. and WATERS, M. 1992. *Postmodernization*. London: Sage.

CROSLAND, A. 1956. *The Future of Socialism*. London: Jonathan Cape.

CRYSTAL, G. 1991. *In Search of Excess: Executive Compensation in the 1980s*. New York: Norton.

CURRAN, J. and BURROWS, R. 1986. 'The Sociology of Petit Capitalism: A Trend Report'. *Sociology* 20:265–79.

CUYVERS, L. and MEEUSEN, W. 1985. 'Financial Groups in the Belgian Network of Interlocking Directorships'. See Stokman *et al.* 1985a, pp. 148–65.

CYBA, E. 1994. 'Gender Inequalities Between Individualization and Social Class'. *Women's Studies International Forum* 17, 2/3, 169–79.

DAEMS, H. and VAN DER WEE, H. (eds) 1974. *The Rise of Managerial Capitalism*. The Hague: Martinus Nijhof.

DAHL, R. A. 1961. *Who Governs?* New Haven: Yale University Press.

DAHRENDORF, R. 1959. *Class and Class Conflict in Industrial Society*. London: Routledge & Kegan Paul.

DAHRENDORF, R. 1969. 'The Service Class' in T. Burns (ed.), *Industrial Man*, Harmondsworth: Penguin.

DAHRENDORF, R. 1988. *The Modern Social Conflict*. London: Weidenfeld & Nicolson.

DALE, A. 1986. 'Social Class and the Self Employed'. *Sociology* 20: 430–4.

DALTON, R. J. 1988. *Citizen Politics in Western Democracies*. Chatham N.J.: Chatham Publishers.

DALTON, R. J., KUECHLER, M. and BECK, P. A. (eds) 1990. *Electoral Change in Advanced Industrial Democracies*. Princeton: Princeton University Press.

DALTON, R., KUECHLER, M. and BURKLIN, W. 1990. 'The Challenge of New Movements' in R. J. Dalton *et al.* (eds) Challenging the Political Order: New Social and Political Movements in Western Democracies. Cambridge: Polity, pp. 3–22.

DANZIGER, S., GOTTSCHALK, P. 1993. *Uneven Tides: Rising Inequality in America*. New York: Sage.

DAVIDOFF, R. 1986. 'The Role of Gender in the First Industrial Nation'. See Crompton and Mann (eds) 1986.

DAVIDOFF, L. and HALL, C. 1987. *Family Fortunes*. London: Hutchinson.

DAVIS, K. and MOORE, W. 1945. 'Some Principles of Stratification'. *American Sociological Review* 50: 242–9.

DAVIS, M. 1991. *City of Quartz*. London: Verso.

DAVIS, S. and HALTWINGER, J. 1989. 'The Distribution of Employees by Establishment Size: Patterns of Change and Movement in the United States'. University of Chicago. Mimeo.

DE VROEY, M. 1973. *Propriété et pouvoir dans les grandes enterprises*. Brussels: CRISP.

DELPHY, C. and LEONARD, A. 1986. 'Class Analysis, Gender Analysis, and the Family'. See Crompton and Mann (eds) 1986.

DENNIS, N., HENRIQUES, F. M. and SLAUGHTER, C. 1962. *Coal is our Life*. London: Eyre & Spottiswoode.

DEPARTMENT OF SOCIAL SECURITY, 1993. *Households Below Average Income*. London, Her Majesty's Stationery Office.

DEX, S. 1985. *The Sexual Division of Work*. Brighton: Harvester.

DJILAS, M. 1966. *The New Class*. London: Allen & Unwin.

DODD, N. 1994. *The Sociology of Money: economics, reason and contemporary society*. Cambridge: Polity Press.

DOMHOFF, G. W. 1970. *The Higher Circles: The Governing Class in America*. New York: Vintage.

DOMHOFF, G. W. 1983. *Who Rules America Now?* New York: Simon & Schuster.

DOMHOFF, G. W. 1990. *The Power Elite and the State*. New York: Aldine de Gruyter.

DORE, R. P. 1976. *The Diploma Disease*. London: Allen & Unwin.

DOUGLAS, 1968 *The Home and the School*. London: Penguin Press.

DUCH, R. 1994. 'Tolerating Economic Reform: Popular Support for Transition to a Free Market in the Former Soviet Union'. *American Political Science Review* 87, 590–608.

DUNLEAVY, P. 1979. 'The Urban Base of Political Alignment'. *British Journal of Political Science*, 9.

DUNLEAVY, P. and HUSBANDS, C. 1985. *British Democracy at the Crossroads*. London: Allen & Unwin.

DUNLEAVY, P. 1980. 'The Political Implications of Sectoral Cleavages and the Growth of State Employment' *Political Studies*, 28:364–83 and 527–49.

DURKHEIM, E. 1964. *The Rules of Sociological Method* (1895). New York: The Free Press: Collier–Macmillan.

EDER, K. 1993. *The New Politics of Class*. London: Sage.

EDGELL, S. and DUKE, V. 1991. *A Measure of Thatcherism*. London: Harper Collins.

EDWARDS, R. 1988. 'Segmented Labor Markets' in F. Hearn (ed.), *The Transformation of Industrial Organization*. Belmont, CA: Wadsworth, pp. 85–98.

EHRENREICH, B. and EHRENREICH, J. 1979. 'The Professional-Managerial Class' in P. Walker (ed.), *Between Labor and Capital*. Boston: South End, pp. 5–45.

ELSTER, J. 1985. *Making Sense of Marx*. Cambridge: Cambridge University Press.

EMMISON, M. and WESTERN, M. 1990. 'Social Class and Social Identity: A Comment on Marshall *et al*'. *Sociology* 24(2):241–53.

ENGBERSEN, G. 1989. 'Cultures of Long-Term Unemployment in the West'. *Netherlands Journal of Social Sciences* 25:75–96.

ENGELS, F. 1968. *The Condition of the Working Class in England*. Oxford: Blackwell.

ERIKSON, R. 1984. 'Social Class of Men, Women and Families'. *Sociology* 18, 4:465–88.

ERIKSON, R. and GOLDTHORPE, J. 1988. 'Women at Class Crossroads: a Critical Note'. *Sociology* 22:545–8.

ERIKSON, R. and GOLDTHORPE, J. 1992. *The Constant Flux: A Study of Class Mobility in Industrial Societies*. Oxford: Clarendon.

ESPING-ANDERSON, G. 1985. *Politics Against Markets*. Princeton: Princeton University Press.

ESPING-ANDERSON, G. 1990. *The Three Worlds of Welfare Capitalism*. Princeton: Princeton University Press.

ESPING-ANDERSON, G. (ed.) 1993. *Changing Classes*. London: Sage.

ESPING-ANDERSON, G. and KORPI, W. 1984. 'Social Policy as Class Politics in Post-War Capitalism: Scandinavia, Austria and Germany' in J. H. Goldthorpe (ed.), *Order and Conflict in Contemporary Capitalism*. Oxford: Clarendon Press.

EVANS, G. 1992. 'Testing the Validity of the Goldthorpe Class Schema'. *European Sociological Review*, 8, pp. 211–32.

EVANS, G. 1993a. 'The Decline of Class Divisions in Britain? Class and Ideological Preferences in Britain in the 1960s and 1980s'. *British Journal of Sociology*, 44:449–71.

EVANS, G. 1993b. 'Is Gender on the New Agenda?' *European Journal of Political Research*, 24, pp. 135–58.

EVANS, G. 1993c. 'Class, Prospects and the Life-Cycle: Explaining the Association between Class Position and Political Preferences'. *Acta Sociologica*, 36:263–76.

EVANS, G. 1993d. 'Class Conflict and Inequality' in R. Jowell, L. Brook and L. Dowds (eds) *International Social Attitudes: the 10th British Social Attitudes Report*. Aldershot: Dartmouth.

EVANS, G. 1994. 'An Assessment of the Validity of the Goldthorpe Class Schema for Men and Women' in R. M. Blackburn (ed.), *Social Inequality in a Changing World*. Cambridge: Cambridge Social Research Group.

EVANS, G. 1996. 'Mass Political Attitudes and the Development of Market Democracy in Eastern Europe', forthcoming in L. Whitehead (ed.) *Political and Economic Liberalisation*. Oxford: Oxford University Press.

EVANS, G. (ed.) 1996. *The End of Class Politics?* Boulder: Westview Press.

EVANS, G. and HEATH, A. 1995. 'The measurement of left–right and libertarian–authoritarian values: comparing balanced and unbalanced scales', *Quality and Quantity*, 29: 191–206.

EVANS, G., HEATH, A. and LALLJEE, M. 1996. 'Measuring Left–Right and Libertarian–Authoritarian Values in the British Electorate'. Forthcoming *British Journal of Sociology* 47.

EVANS, G. and WHITEFIELD, S. 1993. 'Identifying the Bases of Party Competition in Eastern Europe'. *British Journal of Political Science* 23, 521–48.

EVANS, G. and WHITEFIELD, S. 1995. 'The Politics and Economics of Democratic Commitment: Support for Democracy in Transition Societies'. *British Journal of Political Science* 25(4), 485–514.

FEATHERMAN, D. and HAUSER, R. 1978. *Opportunity and Change*. New York: Academic.

FEATHERMAN, D. and SELBEE, L. 1988. 'Class Formation and Class Mobility: A New Approach with Counts from Life History Data' in M. Riley and B. Huber (eds) *Social Structure and Human Lives*. Newbury Park: Sage.

FEATHERMAN, D., SELBEE, L. K. and MAYER, K. U. 1989. 'Social Class and the Structuring of the Life Course in Norway and West Germany' in D. Kertzer, J. Meyer and K. W. Schale (eds) *Social Structure and Aging*. Hillsdale, New Jersey: Erlbaum.

FEATHERMAN, D. and SPENNER, K. 1990. 'Class and the Socialisation of Children: Constancy, Change or Irrelevance?' in E. M. Hetherington, R. M. Lerner and M. Perlmutter (eds) *Child Development in Life-Span Perspective*. Hillsdale, New Jersey: Erlbaum.

FEATHERSTONE, M. 1987. 'Life Style and Consumer Culture' *Theory Culture and Society* 4(1):55–70.

FEATHERSTONE, M. 1988. 'In Pursuit of the Postmodern'. *Theory, Culture and Society* 5:195–215.

FEHER, F. and HELLER, A. 1984. 'From Red to Green'. *Telos*, 59.

FIELD, F. 1989. *Losing Out: The Emergence of Britain's Underclass*. Oxford: Blackwell.

FIELD, J. 1985. *The 1983 British General Election Survey: Methodological Report*. London: Social and Community Planning Research.

FIENBERG, S. E. 1980. *The Analysis of Cross-Classified Categorical Data*. 2nd edn. Cambridge: Massachusetts Institute of Technology Press.

FLANAGAN, S. C. 1980. 'Value Cleavages, Economic Cleavages, and the Japanese Voter'. *American Journal of Political Science* 24.

FLETCHER, R. 1971. *The Making of Sociology*, 2 vols. London: Nelson.

FLOUD, J. 1954. *The Educational experience of the adult population of England and Wales as at July 1949'* in D. V. Glass (ed.) *Social Mobility in Britain*. London: Routledge & Kegan Paul, pp. 98–140.

FLOUD, R., WACHTER, K. and GREGORY, A. 1990. *Height, Health and History. Nutritional Status in the United Kingdom (1750–1980)*. Cambridge: Cambridge University Press.

FOHLEN, C. 1970. 'France, 1700–1914', in Cipolla 1973b.

FOREST, R., MURIE, A. and WILLIAMS, P. 1990. *Home Ownership, Differentiation and Fragmentation*. London: Unwin Hyman.

FORSE, M. 1986. 'La diversification de la société française vue à travers le mariage et l'ideologie'. *Tocqueville Review* 7:223–33.

FOSTER, J. 1974. *Class Struggle and the Industrial Revolution*. London: Weidenfeld & Nicolson.

FRANKLIN, M. 1985. *The Decline of Class Voting in Britain*. Oxford: Clarendon Press.

FRANKLIN, M. *et al.* 1992. *Electoral Change: Responses to Evolving Social and Attitudinal Structures in Western Countries*. New York: Cambridge University Press.

FRANKS, J. and MAYER, C. 1992. *Corporate Control: A Synthesis of the International Evidence*. Unpublished paper, London Business School and University of Warwick.

FRITZELL, J. 1992. 'Income Inequality Trends in the 1980s: A Five Country Comparison'. Working Paper 73, Luxembourg Income Study.

FUKAYAMA, F. 1992. *The End of History and the Last Man*. Harmondsworth: Penguin.

GAGLIANI, G. 1981. 'How Many Working Classes?' *American Journal of Sociology* 87:259–85.

GALLIE, D. 1988. 'Employment, Unemployment and Social Stratification' in D. Gallie (ed.) *Employment in Britain*. Oxford: Basil Blackwell, pp. 465–92.

GALLIE, D. 1990. 'John Goldthorpe's Critique of Liberal Theories of Industrialism' in J. Clark, C. Modgil and S. Modgil (eds), *John H. Goldthorpe: Consensus and Controversy*. London: Falmer Press.

GAMBLE, A. 1979. 'The Free Economy and the Strong State'. R. Miliband and J. Saville (eds), *Socialist Register*. London: Merlin Press.

GANS, H. J. 1990. 'Deconstructing the Underclass'. *Journal of the American Planning Association* 56, 271–7.

GANZEBOOM, H., LUIJKX, R. and TREIMAN, D. 1989. 'Intergenerational Class Mobility in Comparative Perspective'. *Research in Social Stratification and Mobility* 8:3–55.

GEIGER, T. 1947. *Vorstudien zu einer Soziologie des Rechts*. Aarhus and Copenhagen: Hermann.

GELLNER, E. 1992. *Postmodernism, Reason and Religion*. London and New York: Routledge.

GERSCHENKRON, A. 1962. *Economic Backwardness in Historical Perspective*, The Belknap Press of Harvard University Press.

GIDDENS, A. 1973. *The Class Structure of the Advanced Societies*. London: Hutchinson.

GIDDENS, A. 1976. *The New Rules of Sociological Method*. London: Hutchinson.

GIDDENS, A. 1984. *The Constitution of Society*. Oxford: Polity Press.

GIDDENS, A. 1990. *The Consequences of Modernity*. Cambridge: Polity Press.

GIDDENS, A. 1993. *Modernity And Self-Identity*. Cambridge: Polity Press.

GILLE, B. 1970. 'Banking and Industrialisation in Europe, 1730–1914' in Cipolla 1973a.

GLASS, D. V. (ed.) 1954. *Social Mobility in Britain*. London: Routledge & Kegan Paul.

GLAZER, N. 1988. *The Limits of Social Policy*. Cambridge: Massachussets.

GOLDBLATT, P. 1990. 'Mortality and Alternative Classifications' in *Longitudinal Study: Mortality and Social Organization*. London: HMSO: 163–92.

GOLDEN, M. and PONTUSSON, J. (eds) 1992. *Bargaining for Change: Union Politics in North America and Europe*. Ithaca: Cornell University Press.

GOLDTHORPE, J. 1971. 'Theories of Industrial Society: Reflections on the Recrudescence of Historicism and the Future of Futurology'. *Archives Européennes de Sociologie* 12:263–88.

GOLDTHORPE, J. 1979. 'Intellectuals and the Working Class in Modern Britain', Fuller Bequest Lecture, University of Essex. Reprinted in D. Rose (ed.), 1988, *Social Stratification and Economic Change*. London: Hutchinson.

GOLDTHORPE, J. 1982. 'On the Service Class, its Formation and Future' in A. Giddens and G. Mackenzie (eds) *Social Class and the Division of Labour*. Cambridge: Cambridge University Press, 162–85.

GOLDTHORPE, J. 1983. 'Woman and Class Analysis: In Defence of the Conventional View'. *Sociology* 17, 4:465–88.

GOLDTHORPE, J. 1984a. 'Women and Class Analysis: A Reply to the Replies'. *Sociology* 18, 4:491–499.

GOLDTHORPE, J. 1984b. 'The End of Convergence: Corporatist and Dualist Tendencies in Modern Western Societies' in J. Goldthorpe (ed.), *Order and Conflict in Contemporary Capitalism*. Oxford: Clarendon Press.

GOLDTHORPE, J. 1985a. 'Social Mobility and Class Formation', CASMIN Paper No 1.

GOLDTHORPE, J. 1985b. 'Soziale Mobilitat und Klassenbildung. Zur Erneuerung einer Tradition soziologischer Forschung' in H. Strasser and J. H. Goldthorpe (eds) *Die Analyse sozialer Ungleichheit*. Opladen: Westdeutcher Verlag.

GOLDTHORPE, J. 1986. 'Trends in Intergenerational Class Mobility in England and Wales 1972–1983'. *Sociology* 20:1–24.

GOLDTHORPE, J. 1987. *Social Mobility and Class Structure in Modern Britain* with Llewellyn, C. and Payne, C. Oxford: Clarendon Press. Second edn, (First Edition, 1980).

GOLDTHORPE, J. 1990. 'A Response' in Clark, J., Modgil, C. and Modgil, S. (eds) *John H. Goldthorpe: Consensus and Controversy*, London: Falmer.

GOLDTHORPE, J. 1992. 'Employment, Class and Mobility: A Critique of Liberal and Marxist Theories of Long Term Change' in H. Haferkamp and N. Smelser (eds), *Modernity and Social Change*. Berkeley: University of California Press.

GOLDTHORPE, J. 1996. 'Modelling the Pattern of Class Voting in British Elections, 1964 to 1992' in Evans, G. (ed.) *The End of Class Politics?* Boulder: Westview Press.

GOLDTHORPE, J. and HEATH, A. 1992. 'Revised Class Schema 1992'. *JUSST Working Paper no. 13*, Nuffield College and SCPR.

GOLDTHORPE, J. and HOPE, K. 1974. *The Social Grading of Occupations: A New Approach and Scale*. Oxford: Clarendon Press.

GOLDTHORPE, J., LOCKWOOD, D., BECHOFFER, F. and PLATT, J. 1969. *The Affluent Worker in the Class Structure*. Cambridge: Cambridge University Press.

GOLDTHORPE, J., PAYNE, C. and LLEWELLYN, C. 1978. 'Trends in Class Mobility'. *Sociology* 12, 441–68.

GORDON, D., EDWARDS, R. and REICH, M. 1982. *Segmented Work, Divided Workers*. New York: Cambridge University Press.

GORDON, M. 1949. *American Journal of Sociology*.

GORZ, A. 1982. *Farewell to the Working Class*. London: Pluto.

GOTTSCHALK, P. 1993. 'Changes in Equality of Family Income in Seven Industrialized Countries'. *American Economic Review* 83:136–42.

GOTTSCHALK, P. and JOYCE, M. 1991. 'Changes in Earnings Inequality'. Working Paper 66, Luxembourg Income Study.

GOULDNER, A. 1979. *The Future of Intellectuals and the Rise of the New Class*. New York: Seabury Press.

GRAETZ, B. 1992. 'Inequality and Political Activism in Australia'. *Research in Inequality and Social Conflict* 2:157–77.

GRANOVETTER, M. 1973. 'The Strength of Weak Ties'. *American Journal of Sociology* 78, 1360–80.

GRANOVETTER, M. 1984. 'Small is Bountiful: Labour Markets and Establishment Size'. *American Sociological Review* 49:323–34.

GRAY, P. G. and CORLETT, T. 1950. 'Sampling for the Social Survey (with discussion)'. *Journal of the Royal Statistical Society*, series A, 113, 150–206.

GRUSKY, D. B. 1986. 'American Social Mobility in the Nineteenth and Twentieth Century'. Ph.D thesis; Department of Sociology, University of Wisconsin-Madison.

GUTTSMAN, W. G. 1963. *The British Political Elite*, London: MacGibbon & Kee.

HABERMAS, J. 1976. *Legitimation Crisis*. London: Heinemann.

HALEVY, E. 1962. *The History of the English People in the Nineteenth Century*. 2 vols, London: Benn.

HALL, S. and JACQUES, M. (eds) 1989. *New Times: The Changing Face of Politics in the 1990s*. London: Lawrence & Wishart.

HALL, J. R. and GLASS, D. V. 1954. 'Education and Social Mobility' in D. V. Glass (ed.), *Social Mobility in Britain*. London: Routledge & Kegan Paul, pp. 291–307.

HALL, J. and JONES, D. 1950. 'The Social Grading of Occupations'. *British Journal of Sociology* 1, 31–5.

HALLER, M. 1990. 'European Class Structure: Does it Exist?' in Haller (ed.), *Class Structure in Europe: New Findings from East-West Comparisons of Social Structure and Mobility*. London: M. E. Sharpe.

HALSEY, A. 1977. 'Towards Meritocracy? The Case of Britain' in A. Halsey and J. Karabel (eds), *Power and Ideology in Education*. New York: Oxford University Press.

HALSEY, A. 1987. 'Social Trends since World War II'. *Social Trends*, no. 17 (Government Statistical Service).

HALSEY, A. H., HEATH, A. F. and RIDGE, J. M. 1980. *Origins and Destinations: Family, Class, and Education in Modern Britain*. Oxford: Clarendon.

HAMILTON, G. C. (ed.) 1991. *Business Networks and Economic Development in East and South East Asia*. Hong Kong, University of Hong Kong.

HAMILTON, G. C., ORRU, M. and BIGGART, N. 1987. 'Enterprise Groups in East Asia'. *Shoken Keizai* 161.

HAMILTON, G. C. and BIGGART, N. 1988. 'Market, Culture and Authority: A Comparative Analysis of Management and Organisation in the Far East'. *American Journal of Sociology* 94, Supplement.

HAMILTON, M. and HIRSZOWICZ, M. 1993. *Class and Inequality: Comparative Perspectives*. Hemel Hempstead: Harvest Wheatsheaf.

HARRIS, C. C. 1987. *Redundancy and Recession in South Wales*. Oxford: Basil Blackwell.

HARRISON, B. and BLUESTONE, B. 1988. *The Great U-Turn: Corporate Restructuring and the Polarizing of America*. New York: Basic.

HART, K. 1986. 'Heads or Tails? Two Sides of a Coin', The 1986 Malinowski Memorial Lecture, *Man*, 21:637–656.

HARTMANN, H. 1982. 'Capitalism, Patriarchy and Job Segregation by Sex' in A. Giddens and Held, D. (eds), *Classes, Power and Conflict*. London/Basingstoke: Macmillan.

HARVEY, D. 1989. *The Condition of Post-Modernity*. Oxford: Blackwell.

HAUSER, R. 1972. *Socioeconomic Background and Educational Performance*. Washington, D.C.: Rose Monograph Series, American Sociological Association.

HAUSER, R. 1978. 'A Structural Model of the Mobility Table'. *Social Forces* 56:919–53.

HAUSER, R., DICKINGSON, P. J., TRAVIS, H. P. and KOFFEL, J. M. 1975. 'Temporal Change in Occupational Mobility: Evidence for Men in the United States'. *American Sociological Review* 40:279–97.

HAUSER, R. M. and GRUSKY, D. B. 1984. 'Comparative Social Mobility Revisited'. *American Sociological Review* 49:19–38.

HAUSER, R. M. and GRUSKY, D. B. 1987. 'Cross-National Variation in Occupational Distributions, Relative Mobility Chances and Intergenerational Shifts in Occupational Distributions'. Draft Paper.

HEARN, F. 1978 *Domination, Legitimation and Resistance*. Westport, Conn: Greenwood Press.

HEATH, A. and BRITTEN, N. 1984. 'Women's Jobs Do Make a Difference: A Reply to Goldthorpe'. *Sociology* 18, 4:475–90.

HEATH, A., MILLS, C. and ROBERTS, J. 1991. *Towards Meritocracy? Recent Evidence on an Old Problem*. Joint Unit for the Study of Social Trends, SCPR-Nuffield College, Oxford Working Paper 3.

HEATH, A. 1981. *Social Mobility*. London: Fontana.

HEATH, A. 1984. 'In Defence of Comprehensive Schools'. *Oxford Review of Education* 10, 115–23.

HEATH, A., JOWELL, R. and CURTICE, J. (eds) 1994. *Labour's Last Chance? The 1992 Election and Beyond*. Aldershot: Dartmouth.

HEATH, A. and RIDGE, J. 1983. 'Schools, Examinations and Occupational Attainment' in J. Purvis and M. Hales (eds) *Achievement and Inequality in Education*. London: Routledge & Kegan Paul.

HEATH, A., JOWELL, R. and CURTICE, J. 1985. *How Britain Votes*. Oxford: Pergamon.

HEATH, A., JOWELL, R. and CURTICE, J. 1987. 'Trendless Fluctuation: A Reply to Crewe'. *Political Studies* 35, 256–77.

HEATH, A. *et al*. 1991. *Understanding Political Change: The British Voter, 1964–1987*. Oxford: Pergamon.

HEATH, A. and CLIFFORD, P. 1990. 'Class Inequalities in Education in the Twentieth Century.' *Journal of the Royal Statistical Society*, series A, 153, 1–16.

HEATH, A. and McMAHON, D. 1991. 'Consensus and Dissensus' in R. Jowell *et al*. (eds) *British Social Attitudes: the 8th Report*. London: Social and Community Planning Research.

HEATH, A., EVANS, G. and MARGINEAN, I. 1994. 'Clasa sociala si politica in Europa de Est'. *Revista de Cercetari Sociale* 2:59–67.

HEATH, A., EVANS, G. and PAYNE, C. 1995. 'Modelling the Class/Party Relationship in Britain, 1964–92'. *Journal of the Royal Statistical Society*, forthcoming.

HEITLINGER, A. 1979. *Women and State Socialism*. London: Routledge & Kegan Paul.

HENDERSON, W. 1961. *The Industrial Revolution in Europe*. Chicago: Quadrangle.

HERMAN, E. S. 1981. *Corporate Control, Corporate Power: A Twentieth Century Fund Study*. Cambridge: Cambridge University Press.

HESLI, V. and MILLER, A. 1993. 'The Gender Base of Institutional Support in Lithuania, Ukraine and Russia'. *Europe-Asia Studies* 45, 505–32.

HIBBS, D. 1982. 'Economic Outcomes and Political Support for British Governments among the Occupational Classes'. *American Political Science Review* 76:259–79.

HIBBS, D. 1990. *Wage Compression under Solidarity Bargaining in Sweden*. Stockholm: Trade Union Institute of Economic Research.

HIBBS, D. 1991. 'Market Forces, Trade Union Ideology and Trends in Swedish Wage Dispersion'. *Acta Sociologica*. 34:89–102.

HILFERDING, R. 1910. *Finance Capital*. London: Routledge & Kegan Paul, 1981.

HINDESS, B. 1987. *Politics and Class Analysis*. Oxford: Basil Blackwell.

HIRSCHMEIER, J. 1964. *The Origins of Entrepreneurship in Meiji Japan*. Cambridge, Mass.: Harvard University Press.

HIRST, P. Q. 1977. 'Economic Classes and Politics' in A. Hunt (ed.), *Class and Structure*. London: Lawrence & Wishart.

HOBSBAWM, E. J. 1959. *Primitive Rebels*. London: Manchester University Press.

HOBSBAWM, E. J. 1964. *Labouring Men*. London: Weidenfeld and Nicolson.

HOBSBAWM, E. 1981. 'The Forward March of Labour Halted?' and 'Observations on the Debate' in M. Jacques and F. Mulhern (eds), *The Forward March of Labour Halted?* London: New Left Books.

HOCHSCHILD, A. 1989. *The Second Shift: Working Parents and the Revolution at Home.* New York: Viking.

HODSON, R. 1983. *Workers' Earnings and Corporate Economic Structure.* New York: Academic.

HOFF, J. 1982. 'The Resurrection of the Petty Bourgeoisie? The Scandinavian Experience and its Implications for Marxist Research on Class, State, and Ideology.' Prepared for Int. Conf. State, Cosenza, Italy.

HOGGART, R. 1957. *The Uses of Literacy*, London: Chatto & Windus.

HOLMWOOD, J. and STEWART, A. 1983. 'The Role of Contradictions in Modern Theories of Social Stratification'. *Sociology* Vol. 17, No. 2.

HOLMWOOD, J. and STEWART, A. 1995. 'Social Integration, System Integration, Social Contradiction and Sociological Theory'. Paper presented to Retirement Conference for David Lockwood, University of Essex, Department of Sociology, April 1995.

HOLTMANN, D. and STRASSER, H. 1990. 'Comparing Class Structures and Class Consciousness in Western Societies' in M. Haller (ed.), *Class Structure in Europe: New Findings from East–West Comparisons of Social Structure and Social Mobility.* Armonk: Sharpe, pp. 3–23.

HOLTON, R. 1976. *British Syndicalism 1910–14.* London: Pluto Press.

HOLTON, R. 1992. *Economy and Society.* London: Routledge.

HOLTON, R. and TURNER, B. 1986. *Talcott Parsons on Economy and Society.* London: Routledge & Kegan Paul.

HOLTON, R. and TURNER, B. 1989. *Max Weber on Economy and Society.* London: Routledge & Kegan Paul.

HOLTON, R. and TURNER, B. S. 1994. 'Debate and Pseudo-Debate in Class Analysis: Some Unpromising Aspects of Goldthorpe and Marshall's Defence'. *Sociology* Vol. 28(3), pp. 799–804.

HOPE, K. 1981. 'Trends in the Openness of British Society in the Present Century'. *Research in Social Stratification and Mobility* 1: 127–69.

HOUT, M. 1982. 'The Association between Husbands' and Wives' Occupations in Two-Earner Families'. *American Journal of Sociology* 88:397–409.

HOUT, M. 1988. 'More Universalism, Less Structural Mobility'. *American Journal of Sociology* 93:1358–400.

HOUT, M. 1989. *Following in Father's Footsteps: Social Mobility in Ireland.* Cambridge, MA: Harvard University Press.

HOUT, M. and HAUSER, R. 1992. 'Hierarchy and Symmetry in Social Mobility'. *European Sociological Review* 8:239–66.

HOUT, M., WRIGHT, E. and SANCHEZ-JANKOWSKI, M. 1992. '1991–1992 Class Structure and Consciousness Survey' [Machine Readable Data File and Documentation]. Berkeley: UC Berkeley Survey Research Center.

HOUT, M., BROOKS, C. and MANZA, J. 1995a. 'Class Voting in Capitalist Democracies since World War II: Dealignment, Realignment or Trendless Fluctuation'. *Annual Review of Sociology*, forthcoming.

HOUT, M., BROOKS, C. and MANZA, J. 1995b. 'The Democratic Class Struggle in the United States, 1948–1992'. *American Sociological Review*, forthcoming.

HUMPHRIES, J. 1988. 'Protective Legislation, the Capitalist State and Working Class Men: the case of the 1984 Mines Regulation Act' in R. Pahl (ed.) *On Work*. London: Basil Blackwell.

HYMER, S. 1972. 'The Multinational Corporation and the Law of Uneven Development' in J. Bhagwati (ed.), *Economics and the World Order from the 1970s to the 1990s*. London: Collier–Macmillan, pp. 113–40.

INGHAM, G. 1984. *Capitalism Divided*. London: Macmillan.

INGLEHART, R. 1977. *The Silent Revolution: Changing Values and Political Styles among Western Publics*. Princeton: Princeton University Press.

INGLEHART, R. 1984. 'The Changing Structure of Political Cleavages in Western Society' in Dalton, R. J., Flanagan, S. C. and Beck, P. A. (eds), *Electoral Change in Advanced Industrial Democracies*. Princeton: Princeton University Press.

INGLEHART, R. 1990. *Culture Shift in Advanced Industrial Society*. Princeton: Princeton University Press.

INGLEHART, R. and FLANAGAN, S. 1989. 'Value Change in Industrial Societies' *American Political Science Review* 81(4):1289–1319.

INGLEHART, R. and RABIER, J.-R. 1986. 'Political Realignment in Advanced Industrial Society: from Class-Based Politics to Quality-of-Life Politics'. *Government and Opposition* 21:456–79.

IRWIN, S. and MORRIS, L. 1993. 'Social Security or Economic Insecurity? The Concentration of Unemployment (and Research) within Households'. *Journal of Social Policy* 22, 349–72.

ISHIDA, H. 1993. *Social Mobility in Japan*. Chicago: Chicago University Press.

JENCKS, C. and PETERSEN, P. (eds). 1991. *The Urban Underclass*. Washington, DC: Brookings Institute.

JENKINS, S. P. 1991. 'Living Standards and Income Inequality in the 1970s and 1980s'. *Fiscal Studies* Vol. 12.

JOHANISSON, B. 1989. 'Entrepreneurship in a Corporatist State: The Case of Sweden' in R. Goffee, R. Scase (eds). *Entrepreneurship in Europe*. London: Croom Helm, pp. 131–43.

JOHNSON, C. 1982. *MITI and the Japanese Miracle: The Growth of Industrial Policy, 1925–1975*. Stanford: Stanford University Press.

JOHNSON, P. and STARK, G. 1989. *Taxation and Social Security 1979–89*. London: Institute of Fiscal Studies.

JONES, F. 1991. 'Common Social Fluidity: a Comment on Some Recent Criticism'. Research School of Social Sciences, Australian National University.

JONSSON, J. 1991a. *Towards the Merit-Selective Society?* Swedish Institute for Social Research.

JONSSON, J. 1991b. *Class Formation: The Holding Power and Socio-Demographic Composition of Social Classes in Sweden*. Swedish Institute for Social Research.

JONSSON, J. and MILLS, C. 1993. 'Social Class and Educational Attainment in Historical Perspective: A Swedish–English Comparison, Parts I and II'. *British Journal of Sociology* 44(2):213–47.

JOYCE, P. 1995. *Class*. Oxford: Oxford University Press.

KALLENBERG, A. L. and BERG, I. 1987. *Work and Industry: Structures, Markets, and Processes*. New York: Plenum Press.

KARABEL, J. and HALSEY, A. 1977. *Power and Ideology in Education*. Oxford: Oxford University Press.

KATZENSTEIN, P. 1984. *Corporatism and Change: Austria, Switzerland, and the Politics of Industry*. Ithaca: Cornell University Press.

KATZENSTEIN, P. 1985. *Small States in World Markets: Industrial Policy in Europe*. Ithaca: Cornell University Press.

KATZENSTEIN, P. 1987. *Policy and Politics in West Germany: The Growth of a Semisovereign State*. Philadelphia: Temple University Press.

KATZENSTEIN, P. 1989. 'Industry in a Changing West Germany' in P. J. Katzenstein (ed.) *Industry and Politics in West Germany: Toward the Third Republic*. Ithaca: Cornell University Press, pp. 3–29.

KEANE, J. 1988. *Democracy and Civil Society*. London: Verso.

KERCKHOFF, A. and TROTT, J. 1993. 'Educational Attainment in a Changing Educational System: The Case of England and Wales'. See Shavit, Y. and Blossfeld, H.-P. (eds) 1993.

KERN, H. and SCHUMANN, M. 1984. 'Work and Social Character'. *Economic and Industrial Democracy* 5:51–71.

KERN, H. and SCHUMANN, M. 1987. 'Limits of the Division of Labour. New Production Concepts in West German Industry'. *Economic and Industrial Democracy* 8:151–71.

KERR, C. 1983. *The Future of Industrial Society*. Cambridge, Mass.: Harvard University Press.

KERR, C., DUNLOP, J., HARBISON, F. and MYERS, C. 1969. *Industrialism and Industrial Man*. Cambridge, Mass.: Harvard University Press.

KITCHEN, M. 1978. *The Political Economy of Germany, 1815–1914*. London: Croom Helm.

KITSCHELT, H. 1992. 'The Formation of Party Systems in East Central Europe'. *Politics and Society* 20, 7–50.

KITSCHELT, H. 1994. *The Transformation of European Social Democracy*. Cambridge: Cambridge University Press.

KOCKA, J. 1980. *The Rise of the Modern Industrial Enterprise in Germany*. See Chandler, A. D. and Daems, H. (eds), 1980.

KONRAD G. and SZELENYI, I. 1979. *The Intellectuals on the Road to Class Power*, New York: Harcourt Brace.

KORNHAUSER, W. 1960. *The Politics of Mass Society*. London: Routledge & Kegan Paul.

KORPI, W. 1972. 'Some Problems in the Measurement of Class Voting'. *American Journal of Sociology* 78:627–42.

KORPI, W. 1978. *The Working Class in Welfare Capitalism: Work, Unions and Politics in Sweden*. London: Routledge & Kegan Paul.

KORPI, W. 1983. *The Democratic Class Struggle*. London: Routledge & Kegan Paul.

KOSSALECK, R. 1988. *Critique and Crisis*. Oxford: Berg.

KOZULIN, A. 1990. *Vygotsky's Psychology: a Biography of Ideas*. Hemel Hempstead: Harvester Wheatsheaf.

KRYSHTANOVSKAYA, O. 1993. 'The Emerging Business Elite'. See Lane, D. (ed.) 1993.

KUHN, A. and WOLPE, A. (eds) 1978. *Feminism and Materialism*. London: Routledge & Kegan Paul.

KUTTNER, R. 1983. 'The Declining Middle'. *Atlantic Monthly*, July: 60–72.

LACLAU, E. and MOUFFE, C. 1985. *Hegemony and Social Strategy*. London: Verso.

LAKATOS, I. 1970. 'Falsification and the Methodology of Scientific Research Programmes' in I. Lakatos and A. Musgrave (eds), *Criticism and the Growth of Knowledge*. Cambridge: Cambridge University Press.

LANDES, D. S. 1965. 'Japan and Europe: Contrasts in Industrialization' in W. Lockwood (ed.), *The State and Economic Enterprise in Japan: Essays in the Political Economy of Growth*. Princeton: Princeton University Press, pp. 93–182.

LANDES, D. S. 1969. *The Unbound Prometheus*. Cambridge: Cambridge University Press.

LANE, C. 1992. 'Industrial Structure and Performance: Common Challenges – Diverse Responses'. in J. Bailey (ed.) *Social Europe*. London: Longman.

LANE, D. (ed.) 1993. *Russia in Flux*. Cheltenham: Edward Elgar.

LASH, S. 1990. *Sociology of Postmodernism*. London: Routledge.

LASH, S. and URRY, J. 1987. *The End of Organized Capitalism*. Cambridge: Polity Press.

LAVER, M., MARSH, M. and SINNOT, R. 1987. 'Patterns of Party Support' in Laver, M., Mair, P. and Sinnot, R. (eds), *How Ireland Voted: The Irish General Election of 1987*. Dublin: Poolbeg Press.

LEE, D. 1994. 'Class as a Social Fact'. *Sociology* 28(2):397–415.

LEHMBRUCH, G. 1977. 'Liberal Corporatism and Party Government'. *Comparative Political Studies* 10:91–126.

LEHMBRUCH, G. and SCHMITTER, P. (eds) 1982. *Patterns of Corporatist Policy-Making*. London: Sage.

LEIULSFRUD, H. and WOODWARD, A. 1987. 'Women at Class Crossroads'. *Sociology* 21:393–412.

LENIN, V. I. 1916. *Imperialism: The Highest Stage of Capitalism*. Moscow: Progress Publishers.

LEVY, F. 1988. *Dollars and Dreams: The Changing American Income Distribution*. New York: Russell Sage Foundation.

LEWIS, O. 1968. 'The Culture of Poverty' in D. P. Moynihan (ed.), *Understanding Poverty*. New York: Basic Books.

LEWIS, P. 1993. 'Civil Society and the Development of Political Parties in East-Central Europe'. *Journal of Communist Studies* 9, 5–20.

LINDBLOM, C. 1977. *Politics and Markets*. New York: Basic Books.

LINDER, M. and HOUGHTON, J. 1990. 'Self-Employment and the Petty Bourgeoisie: Comment on Steinmetz and Wright'. *American Journal of Sociology* 95:727–35.

LIPSET, S. 1960. *Political Man. The Social Bases of Politics*. New York: Doubleday. Baltimore: Johns Hopkins University Press, Second Edition 1981.

LIPSET, S. 1985. *Consensus and Conflict*. New Brunswick, NJ: Transaction Books.

LIPSET, S. 1990. 'The Death of the Third Way: Everywhere but here, that is'. *National Interest* 20:25–27.

LIPSET, S. 1994. 'The Social Requisites of Democracy Revisited'. *American Sociological Review* 59:1–22.

LIPSET, S. and BENDIX, R. 1991 [1959]. *Social Mobility in Industrial Society*. New Brunswick, NJ: Transaction Books.

LIPSET, S. and ROKKAN, S. (eds) 1967. *Party Systems and Voter Alignments: Cross-National Perspectives*. New York: Free Press.

LIPSET, S. and SCHNEIDER, W. 1983. *The Confidence Gap*. New York: Free Press.

LIVINGSTONE, D. 1983. *Class Ideologies and Educational Futures*. Sussex: Falmer.

LOCKWOOD, D. 1958. *The Black-Coated Worker*. London: George Allen & Unwin.

LOCKWOOD, D. 1966. 'Sources of Variation in Working-Class Images of Society'. *Sociological Review* 14(3) 244–67.

LOCKWOOD, D. 1981. 'The Weakest Link in the Chain: Some Comments on the Marxist Theory of Action'. *Research in the Sociology of Work* 1, 435–81.

LOCKWOOD, D. 1986. 'Class, Status and Gender', in R. Crompton and M. Mann (eds) 1986:pp. 11–21.

LOCKWOOD, D. 1992. *Solidarity and Schism: 'The Problem of Disorder' in Durkheimian and Marxist Sociology*. Oxford: Clarendon Press.

LOCKWOOD, W. 1968. *The Economic Development of Japan*. New Jersey: Princeton University Press.

LUKER, K. 1984. *Abortion and the Politics of Motherhood*. Berkeley: University of California Press.

LUKES, S. 1984. 'The Future of British Socialism?' in B. Pimlott (ed.), *Fabian Essays in Socialist Thought*. London: Heinemann.

LYOTARD, J.-F. 1984. *The Postmodern Condition: A Report on Knowledge*. Manchester: Manchester University Press.

LYOTARD, J.-F. 1988. *Peregrinations. Law, Form, Event*. New York: Columbia University Press.

MCCAHERY, J., PICCIOTTO, S. and SCOTT, C. (eds) 1993. *Corporate Control and Accountability*. Oxford: Oxford University Press.

MCCLOSKY, H. and BRILL, A. 1983. *Dimensions of Tolerance: What Americans Believe about Civil Liberties*. New York: Russell Sage Foundation.

MACDONALD, K. I. 1974. 'The Hall–Jones Scale: A Note on the Intepretation of the Main British Prestige Coding' in J. M. Ridge (ed.), *Mobility in Britain Reconsidered*. Oxford: Clarendon, pp. 97–115.

MACDONALD, K. and RIDGE, J. 1987. 'Social Mobility' in A. H. Halsey (ed.), *Trends in British Society Since 1990*. 2nd edn, London: Macmillan.

McINTOSH, M., MACIVER, M., ABELE, D. and NOLLE, D. 1995. 'Minority Rights and Majority Rule: Ethnic tolerance in Romania and Bulgaria'. *Social Forces* 73:939–67.

McMAHON, J. and TSCHETTER, J. 1986. 'The Declining Middle Class: A Further Analysis'. *Monthly Labor Review*, Sept:22–8.

McPHERSON, A. and WILLMS, D. 1987. Equalisation and Improvement: Some Effects of Comprehensive Reorganisation in Scotland. *Sociology*, 21, 509–39.

McRAE, S. 1986. *Cross-Class Families*. Oxford: Oxford University Press.

MAIR, P. 1979. 'The Autonomy of the Political: the Development of the Irish Party System'. *Comparative Politics* 11:445–65.

MAIR, P. 1992. 'Explaining the Absence of Class Politics in Ireland' in J. Goldthorpe and C. Whelan (eds), *The Development of Industrial Society in Ireland*. London: The British Academy.

MANN, K. 1992. *The Making of an English 'Underclass'?* Buckingham: Open University Press.

MANN, M. 1970. 'The Social Cohesion of Liberal Democracy'. *American Sociological Review* 35, 423–39.

MANN, M. 1973. *Consciousness and Action among the Western Working Class*. London: Macmillan.

MANN, M. 1986a and b. *The Sources of Social Power*. 2 vols, Cambridge: Cambridge University Press.

MANN, M. 1987. 'Ruling Class Strategies and Citizenship'. *Sociology*, 21, 339–54.

MANZA, J. 1992. 'Classes, Status Groups, and Social Closure: A Critique of Neo-Weberian Social Theory'. *Current Perspectives on Social Theory* 12:275–302.

MARCEAU, J. 1977. *Class and Status in France: Economic Change and Social Immobility*. Oxford: Clarendon Press.

MARCEAU, J. 1977. *Class and Status in France*. New York: Oxford University Press.

MARCEAU, J. 1989a. 'France'. See Bottomore and Brym 1989.

MARCEAU, J. 1989b. *A Family Business? The Making of an International Business Elite*. New York: Oxford University Press.

MARE, R. D. 1980. 'Social Background and Educational Continuation Decisions'. *Journal of the American Statistical Association* 75:295–305.

MARE, R. D. 1981. 'Change and Stability in Educational Stratification'. *American Sociological Review* 46:72–87.

MARKLAND, S. 1990. 'Structures of Modern Poverty'. *Acta Sociologica* 33:125–40.

MARSH, A. 1975. 'The Silent Revolution, Value Priorities, and the Quality of Life in Britain'. *American Political Science Review* 69.

MARSH, C. 1986. *Occupationally-Based Measures of Social Class*. London: Social Research Association.

MARSHALL, G. 1983. 'Some Remarks on the Study of Working-Class Consciousness'. *Politics and Society* 12, pp. 263–301 reprinted in D. Rose (ed.), 1988.

MARSHALL, G. 1988. 'Classes in Britain: Official and Marxist'. *European Sociological Review* 4:141–54.

MARSHALL, G. 1990. 'John Goldthorpe and Class Analysis' in J. Clark, C. Modgill and S. Modgill (eds), *John H. Goldthorpe: Consensus and Controversy*. London: Falmer.

MARSHALL, G. *et al.* 1985. 'Class, Citizenship, and Distributional Conflict in Modern Britain'. *British Journal of Sociology*, 36(2).

MARSHALL, G. 1991. 'In Defence of Class Analysis: A Comment on R. E. Pahl'. *International Journal of Urban and Regional Research* 15(1):114–18.

MARSHALL, G., NEWBY, H., ROSE, D. and VOGLER, C. 1988. *Social Class in Modern Britain*. London: Hutchinson.

MARSHALL, G. and ROSE, D. 1990. 'Out-classed by Our Critics?' *Sociology* 24:255–67.

MARSHALL, G. and SWIFT, A. 1992. 'Social Class and Social Justice'. *British Journal of Sociology*, forthcoming.

MARSHALL, G., ROBERTS, S., BURGOYNE, SWIFT, A. and ROUTH, D. 1995. 'Class, Gender, and the Asymmetry Hypothesis'. *European Sociological Review*, 11:1–15.

MARSHALL, T. [1949] 1973. *Class, Citizenship and Social Development*. Westport: Greenwood.

MARSHALL, T. H. 1981. *The Right to Welfare and Other Essays*. London: Heinemann.

MARSLAND, D. 1987. *Bias Against Business*. London: Educational Research Trust.

MARTINELLI, A. and CHIESI, A. M. 1989. 'Italy'. See Bottomore and Brym 1989, pp. 109–39.

MARX, K. 1934. *The Eighteenth Brumaire of Louis Napoleon*. Moscow: Progress Publishers.

MARX, K. 1976. *Capital*. Vol. 1, London: Penguin.

MARX, K. and ENGELS, F. 1968. *Selected Works*. London: Lawrence & Wishart.

MASSEY, D. S. 1990. 'American Apartheid: Segregation and the Making of the Underclass'. *American Journal of Sociology* 96:329–57.

MASSEY, D. and EGGERS, M. 1990. 'The Ecology of Inequality: Minorities and the Concentration of Poverty, 1970–1980'. *American Journal of Sociology* 95:1153–88.

MAYER, K. and CARROLL, G. 1987. 'Jobs and Classes: Structural Constraints on Career Mobility'. *European Sociological Review* 3: 14–38.

MAYER, K. FEATHERMAN, D., SELBEE, L. and COLBJORNSEN, T. 1989. 'Class Mobility During Working Life: A Cross-National Comparison of Germany and Norway' in M. Kohn (ed.), *Cross-National Research in Sociology*. Newbury Park: Sage.

MAYNARD, M. 1994. *The Incredible Disappearing Woman: Gender and Hierarchy in Feminist and Social Thought* (mimeo). Bielefeld: Bielefeld University Press.

MENSHIKOV, S. 1969. *Millionaires and Managers*. Moscow: Progress Publishers.

MICHALET, C.-A. 1974. 'France'. See Vernon 1974, pp. 105–25.

MILIBAND, R. 1989. *Divided Societies*. Oxford: Oxford University Press.

MILLER, A., HESLI, V. and REISINGER, W. 1994. 'Reassessing Mass Support for Political and Economic Change in the Former USSR'. *American Political Science Review* 88, 399–411.

MILLS, C. WRIGHT. 1946. 'The Middle Class of Middle-Sized Cities'. *American Sociological Review* 11:520–9.

MILLS, C. WRIGHT. 1951. *White Collar: The American Middle Classes*. New York: Oxford University Press.

MILLS, C. WRIGHT. 1959a. *The Power Elite*. New York: Galaxy.

MILLS, C. WRIGHT. 1959b. *The Sociological Imagination*. Oxford: Oxford University Press.

MILWARD, A. S. and SAUL, B. S. 1977. *The Development of the Economies of Central Europe, 1850–1914*. London: George Allen & Unwin.

MINGIONE, E. 1991. 'The New Urban Poor and the Crisis of Citizenship/Welfare Systems in Italy'. Paper presented at the Working Conference on 'Pauvreté, immigrations et marginalitiés urbaines dans les sociéties advancées'. Paris, Maison Suger, May.

MINTZ, B. 1989. 'United States'. See Bottomore and Brym (eds) 1989.

MINTZ, B. and SCHWARTZ, M. 1985. *The Power Structure of American Business*. Chicago: University of Chicago Press.

MIZRUCHI, M. 1982. *The American Corporate Network, 1904–1974*. Beverly Hills: Sage.

MIZRUCHI, M. and SCHWARTZ, M. (eds) 1987. *Intercorporate Relations: The Structural Analysis of Business*. New York: Cambridge University Press.

MORIOKA, K. 1989. 'Japan'. See Bottomore and Brym (eds) 1989.

MORISHIMA, M. 1982. *Why Has Japan Succeeded?* Cambridge: Cambridge University Press.

MORRIS, L. D. 1990. *The Workings of the Household*. Oxford: Polity Press.

MORRIS, L. D. 1995. *Social Divisions*. London: University College London Press.

MOSSER, A. 1983. 'Concentration and the Finance of Austrian Industrial Combines, 1880–1914', in Teichova and Cottrell 1983.

MOYNIHAN, D. P. 1973. *The Politics of a Guaranteed Income*. New York: Random House.

MOYNIHAN, D. P. 1989. 'Towards a Post-Industrial Social Policy'. *Public Interest* 96:16–27.

MULLER, W. and KARLE, W. 1990. 'Social Selection in Educational Systems in Europe'. Paper presented to ISA Research Committee on Social Stratification and Mobility, Madrid.

MURRAY, C. 1984. *Losing Ground*. New York: Basic Books.

MURRAY, C. 1990. *The Emerging British Underclass*. London: Institute of Economic Affairs.

MURRAY, F. 1983. 'The Decentralisation of Production – The Decline of the Mass–Collective Worker?' *Capital and Class* 19:74–99.

MURRAY, F. 1987. 'Flexible Specialisation and the "Third Italy"', *Capital and Class* 33:84–95.

MYLES, J. 1988. 'The Expanding Middle: Some Canadian Evidence on the Deskilling Debate'. *Canadian Review of Sociology and Anthropology* 35:335–64.

MYLES, J. 1990. 'States, Labour Markets and Life Cycles', in R. Friedland and S. Robertson (eds), *Beyond the Marketplace: Rethinking Economy and Society*. New York: de Grueyter, pp. 271–98.

MYLES, J., PICOT, P. and WANNELL, T. 1993. 'Does Postindustrialism Matter? The Canadian Experience', in Esping-Anderson (ed.) 1993, pp. 171–94.

MYLES, J. and TUREGUN, A. 1994. 'Comparative Studies in Class Structure'. *Annual Review of Sociology* 20: 103–24.

NAISBITT, J. and ABURDENE, P. 1990. *Megatrends 2000* London: Sidgwick and Jackson.

NAYLOR, R. T. 1975. *The History of Canadian Business 1867–1914*, vols 1, 2. Toronto: Lorimer.

NEWBY, H. 1977. *The Deferential Worker*. London: Allen Lane.

NEWBY, H. 1982. *The State of Research on Social Stratification in Britain*. London: Social Science Research Council.

NIEUWBEERTA, P. and DE GRAAF, N. D. 1996. 'Traditional Class Voting and the Influence of Varying Class Structures in 16 Western Countries: 1956–90' in Evans (ed.) 1996.

NISBET, R. 1959. 'The Decline and Fall of Social Class'. *Pacific Sociological Review* 2(1):11–17.

NUMAZAKI, I. 1986. 'Networks of Taiwanese Business: A Preliminary Analysis'. *China Quarterly*, 12.

NUMAZAKI, I. 1991. 'The Role of Personal Networks in the Making of Taiwan's *Guanxiqiye*', in Hamilton (ed.) 1991.

NUMAZAMI, I. 1992. *Networks and Partnerships: The Social Organization of the Chinese Business Elite in Taiwan*. Dissertation Submitted to Michigan State University for Degree of PhD.

O'CONNOR, J. 1973. *The Fiscal Crisis of the State*. New York: St. Martin's Press.

OECD, 1992. *Labour Force Statistics, 1970–1990*. Paris: Organisation for Economic Cooperation and Development.

OECD, 1985. 'Employment in Small and Large Firms: Where have the Jobs come from?' *Employment Outlook*, Sept.:64–82.

OFFE, C. 1984. *Contradictions of the Welfare State*. London: Hutchinson.

OFFE, C. 1985a. *Disorganized Capitalism*. Cambridge, Mass: MIT Press.

OFFE, C. 1985b. 'Work: the Key Sociological Category?' in Offe 1985.

OHLIN, G. 1974. 'Sweden'. See Vernon 1974, pp. 126–41.

OLSEN, M. 1965. *The Logic of Collective Action*. Cambridge, Mass: Harvard University Press.

ORNSTEIN, M. 1983. 'The Development of Class in Canada' in J. P. Grayson (ed.), *Introduction to Sociology*. Toronto: Gage, pp. 216–59.

ORNSTEIN, M. 1989. 'The Social Organization of the Canadian Capitalist Class in Comparative Perspective'. *Canadian Review of Sociology and Anthropology* 26:151–77.

OSSOWSKI, S. 1963. *Class Structure in the Social Consciousness*. London: Routledge & Kegan Paul.

OST, D. 1993. 'The Politics of Interest in Post-Communist Societies', *Theory and Society* 22:453–85.

OST, D. 1995. 'Labour, Class and Democracy: Shaping Political Antagonisms in Post-Communist Society', in B. Crawford (ed.) *Markets, States, and Democracy: The Political Economy of Post-Communist Transformation*. Boulder: Westview Press.

PAHL, R. 1984. *Divisions of Labour*. Oxford: Basil Blackwell.

PAHL, R. 1988. 'Some Remarks on Informal Work, Social Polarization and the Social Structure'. *International Journal of Urban and Regional Research* 12, 247–67.

PAHL, R. E. 1991. 'R. E. Pahl Replies' *International Journal of Urban and Regional Research*, 15(1):127–129.

PAKULSKI, J. 1986. 'Bureaucracy and the Soviet System'. *Studies in Comparative Communism* 19(1):3–24.

PAKULSKI, J. 1993. 'Mass Social Movements and Social Class'. *International Sociology* 8(2).

PALMADE, G. P. 1961. *French Capitalism in the Nineteenth Century*. Newton Abbot: David & Charles, 1972.

PARKIN, F. 1971. *Class Inequality and Political Order*. New York: Praeger.

PARKIN, F. 1979. *Marxism and Class Theory: A Bourgeois Critique*. London: Tavistock.

PARSONS, T. 1937. *The Structure of Social Action*. New York: McGraw-Hill.

PARSONS, T. 1949. 'Social Classes and Class Conflict in the Light of Recent Sociological Theory', in T. Parsons (ed.), *Essays in Sociological Theory*. New York: Free Press, 1954.

PATEMAN, C. 1988. *The Sexual Contract*, Cambridge: Cambridge University Press.

PAYNE, J. 1987. 'Does Unemployment Run in Families?' *Sociology* 21, 199–214.

PENN, R. 1981. 'The Nuffield Class Categorisation'. *Sociology* 15, 2: 265–71.

PERKIN, H. 1989. *The Rise of Professional Society*. London: Routledge.

PERLO, V. 1957. *The Empire of High Finance*. New York: International Publishers.

PETERS, T. and WATERMAN, R. 1982. *In Search of Excellence*. New York: Warner Books.

PHILLIPS, K. 1991. *The Politics of Rich and Poor: Wealth and the American Electorate in the Reagan Aftermath*. New York: Harper.

PHILLIPS, K. 1993. *Boiling Point: Democrats, Republicans and the Decline of Middle Class Prosperity*. New York: Random House.

PICKVANCE, C. 1977. 'From Social Base to Social Force: Some Analytical Issues in the Study of Urban Protest' in M. Harloe (ed.), *Captive Cities*. Chichester: Wiley, pp. 175–86.

PIORE, M. and SABEL, C. 1984. *The Second Industrial Divide: Possibilities for Prosperity*. New York: Basic.

PIZZORNO, A. 1978. 'Political Exchange and Collective Identity in Industrial Conflict' in Colin Crouch and Alessandro Pizzorno (eds), *The Resurgence of Class Conflicts in Western Europe since 1968*. Vol 2. London: Macmillan.

PLANT, S. 1992. *The Most Radical Gesture: The Situationist International in a Post-Modern Age*. London: Routledge.

POULANTZAS, N. 1975. *Classes in Contemporary Capitalism*. London: NLB.

PRANDY, K. 1990. 'The Revised Cambridge Scale of Occupation'. *Sociology* 24, 629–55.

PRINGLE, R. 1988. *Secretaries Talk*. London: Verso.

PRODI, R. 1974. 'Italy'. See Vernon 1974, pp. 45–63.

PRZEWORSKI, A. and SPRAGUE, J. 1986. *Paper Stones: A History of Electoral Socialism*. Chicago: University of Chicago Press.

RADAEV, V. and SHKARATAN, A. 1992. 'Etacratism: Power and Property – Evidence from the Soviet Experience'. *International Sociology* 7(3): 301–16.

RAFTERY, A. and HOUT, M. 1993. 'Maximally Maintained Inequality: Expansion, Reform, and Opportunity in Irish Education, 1921–1975'. *Sociology of Education* 66:41–62.

RAINNIE, A. 1985. 'Small Firms, Big Problems: The Political Economy of Small Businesses'. *Capital and Class* 25:140–68.

RAWLS, J. 1972. *A Theory of Justice*. Oxford: Clarendon Press.

REDDING, S. G. 1990. *The Spirit of Chinese Capitalism*. Berlin: Walter de Gruyter.

REICH, R. 1991. *The Work of Nations*. New York: Knopf.

REID, I. 1981. *Social Class Differences in Britain*. London: Grant MacIntyre.

REISINGER, W., MILLER, A., HESLI, V. and HILL MAYER, K. 1994. 'Political Values in Russia, Ukraine and Lithuania: Sources and Implications for Democracy'. *British Journal of Political Science* 24, 183–223.

RENNER, K. [1953] 1978. 'The Service Class' in T. Bottomore and P. Goode (eds) *Austro-Marxism*. Oxford: Clarendon, pp. 249–52.

RENNER, K. 1953. *Wandlungen der Modernen Gessellschaft: zwei Abhandlungen uber die Probleme der Nachkriegszeit*. Vienna: Wiener Volksbuchhandlung.

REX, J. and MOORE, R. 1967. *Race, Community and Conflict*. London: Oxford University Press.

RICHTA, R. *et al.* 1969. *Civilization at the Crossroads*. White Plains N.Y.: International Arts and Sciences Press.

RIDGE, J. 1974. Editorial commentary on O. D. Duncan's proposals for 'Reanalysis of the 1949 survey' in J. M. Ridge (ed.), *Mobility in Britain Reconsidered*. Oxford: Clarendon Press, pp. 23–6.

RIGBY, T. H. 1990. *The Changing Soviet System*. Cheltenham: Edward Elgar.

RINGDAL, K. and HINES, K. 1996. 'Patterns in Class Voting in Norway 1957–89: Decline or "Trendless Fluctuation"?' in Evans (ed.) 1996.

ROBERTS, K., COOK, F., CLARK, S. and SEMEONOFF, E. 1977. *The Fragmentary Class Structure*. London: Heinemann.

ROBERTSON, D. 1984. *Class and the British Electorate*. Oxford: Blackwell.

ROBERTSON, R. 1992. *Globalization. Social Theory and Global Culture*. London: Sage.

ROCHE, M. 1992. *Rethinking Citizenship: Welfare, Ideology and Change in Modern Society*. Cambridge: Polity Press.

ROCHESTER, A. 1936. *Rulers of America*. London: Lawrence & Wishart.

ROEMER, J. 1982a. 'New Directions in the Marxist Theory of Exploitation'. *Politics and Society*, 11(3).

ROEMER, J. 1982b. *A General Theory of Exploitation and Class*. Cambridge Mass.: Harvard University Press.

ROSE, D. (ed.) 1988. *Social Stratification and Economic Change*. London: Hutchinson.

ROSE, R. and MCALLISTER, I. 1986. *Voters Begin to Choose: From Closed Class to Open Elections in Britain*. London: Sage.

ROSENTHAL, N. 1985. 'The Shrinking Middle Class: Myth or Reality?' *Monthly Labor Review* March:3–10.

RUNCIMAN, W. G. 1990. 'How many Classes are there in Contemporary British Society?' *Sociology* 24, 377–96.

RUSTERHOLZ, P. 1985. 'The Banks in the Centre: Integration in Decentralised Switzerland' in Stokman *et al.* 1985a.

SABEL, C. 1982. *Work and Politics*. New York: Cambridge University Press.

SARLVIK, B. and CREWE, I. 1983. *A Decade of Dealignment*. Cambridge: Cambridge University Press.

SARTORI, G. 1970. 'Concept Misformation in Comparative Politics'. *American Political Science Review*. LXIV (4):1033–53.

SAUNDERS, P. 1978. 'Domestic Property and Social Class', *International Journal of Urban and Regional Research*, Vol. 8, 202–207.

SAUNDERS, P. 1981. *Social Theory and the Urban Question*, rev. ed., 1987. London: Unwin Hyman.

SAUNDERS, P. 1984. 'Beyond Housing Classes: The Sociological Significance of Private Property Rights in Means of Consumption'. *International Journal of Urban and Regional Research* 8:202–207.

SAUNDERS, P. 1989. 'Left Write in Sociology' Network, 44, May, Nos 3–4.

SAUNDERS, P. 1990a. *A Nation of Home Owners*. London: Unwin.

SAUNDERS, P. 1990b. *Social Class and Stratification*. London: Routledge.

SAUNDERS, P. 1995. 'Might Britain be a Meritocracy', *Sociology* 29(1): 23–41.

SAUNDERS, P. and HARRIS, C. 1990. 'Privatisation and the Consumer'. *Sociology*, February.

SAVAGE, M., DICKENS, A. and FIELDING, T. 1992. *Property, Bureaucracy and Culture: Middle Class Formation in Contemporary Britain*. London: Routledge.

SCASE, R. and GOFFEE, R. 1982. *The Entrepreneurial Middle Class*. London: Croom Helm.

SCHARPF, F. W. 1984. 'Economic and Institutional Constraints on Full Employment Strategies: Sweden, Austria and West Germany, 1973–1982' in Goldthorpe (ed.) 1984b.

SCHMITTER, P. C. and LEHMBRUCH, G. (eds) 1979. *Trends Towards Corporatist Inter-Mediation*. London: Sage.

SCHMITTER, P. 1974. 'Still the Century of Corporatism?' *Review of Politics* 36:85–131.

SCHOPFLIN, G. 1993. 'The Road from Post-Communism' in S. Whitefield (ed.), *The New Institutional Architecture of Eastern Europe*. London: Macmillan.

SCOTT, A. 1986. 'Industrialisation, Gender Segregation and Stratification Theory' in Crompton and Mann (eds) 1986.

SCOTT, J. 1982. *The Upper Classes*. London: Macmillan.

SCOTT, J. 1985. *Corporations, Classes and Capitalism*, 2nd edn. London: Hutchinson.

SCOTT, J. 1986. *Capitalist Property and Financial Power*. Brighton: Wheatsheaf.

SCOTT, J. 1987. 'Intercorporate Structure in Western Europe' in Mizruchi and Schwartz 1987.

SCOTT, J. 1990a. 'Corporate Control and Corporate Rule'. *British Journal of Sociology* 41, 3.

SCOTT, J. (ed.) 1990b. *The Sociology of Elites*, 3 vols. Aldershot: Edward Elgar.

SCOTT, J. 1991. *Who Rules Britain?* Cambridge: Polity Press.

SCOTT, J. 1993a. 'Corporate Groups and Network Structure', in McCahery *et al.* (eds) 1993.

SCOTT, J. 1993b. *Poverty and Wealth: Citizenship, Poverty and Privilege*. Harlow: Longman.

SCOTT, J. 1996. *Stratification and Power: Structures of Class, Status and Command*. Cambridge: Polity Press.

SCOTT, J. and GRIFF, C. 1984. *Directors of Industry*. Cambridge: Polity Press.

SCOTT, J. and GRIFF, C. 1985. 'Bank Spheres of Influence in the British Corporate Network' in Stokman *et al.* 1985a, pp. 215–33.

SEGAL, L. 1987. *Is the Future Female?* London: Virago.

SENNETT, R. and COBB, J. 1972. *The Hidden Injuries of Class*. Cambridge: Cambridge University Press.

SHAFIR, M. 1994. 'Ethnic Tension Runs High in Romania'. *RFE/RL Research Report* 3:32, 24–32.

SHAIKEN, H. 1984. *Work Transformed: Automation and Labor in the Computer Age*. New York: Holt, Rinehart & Winston.

SHAPRE, A. 1983. 'The Evolution of Class Structure and Income Distribution in Canada, 1961–1981'. Presented at the Annual Meeting Can. Polit. Sci. Assoc., University British Columbia, Vancouver.

SHAVIT, Y. and BLOSSFELD, H.-P. (eds) 1992. *Persistent Inequality: Changing Educational Attainment in Thirteen Countries*. Boulder, Colorado: Westview Press.

SHILLING, C. 1993. *The Body and Social Theory*. London: Sage.

SHILS, E. 1982. 'The Political Class in the Age of the Mass Society', in M. M. Czudnowski (ed.), *Does Who Governs Matter?* DeKalb, Illinois: Northern Illinois University Press.

SHORROCKS, A. F. 1987. 'U.K. Wealth Distribution: Current Evidence and Future Prospects', in E. Wolff (ed.), *International Comparisons of the Distribution of Household Wealth*. New York: Oxford University Press, pp. 29–50.

SHRONFIELD, A. 1969. *Modern Capitalism: The Changing Balance of Public and Private Power*. London: Oxford University Press.

SHUTT, J., WHITTINGTON, R. 1987. 'Fragmentation Strategies and the Rise of Small Units: Cases from the North West'. *Regional Studies* 21:13–23.

SICA, A. 1988. *Weber, Irrationality and Social Order*. Berkeley and Los Angeles: University of California Press.

SILVER, H. (ed.) 1973. *Equal Opportunity in Education: A Reader in Social Class and Educational Opportunity*. London: Methuen.

SMEEDING, T. 1991. 'Cross-National Comparisons of Inequality and Poverty Position', in Osberg, L. (ed.), *Economic Inequality and Poverty: International Perspectives*. Armonk, NY: Sharpe, pp. 39–59.

SMITH, C. 1987. *Technical Workers: Class, Labour and Trade Unionism*. London: Macmillan.

SMITH, D. J. (ed.) 1992. *Understanding the Underclass*. London: Policy Studies Institute.

SNIDERMAN, P., BRODY, R. and TETLOCK, P. 1991. *Reasoning and Choice: Explorations in Political Psychology*. New York: Cambridge University Press.

SOLOMOS, J. 1989. *Race and Racism in Contemporary Britain*. London: Macmillan.

SØRENSEN, A. 1991. 'On the Usefulness of Class Analysis in Research on Social Mobility and Socioeconomic Inequality'. *Acta Sociologica* 34:71–87.

SPÅNT, R. 1987. 'Wealth Distribution in Sweden: 1920–1983'. In Wolff, E. (ed.), *International Comparisons of the Distribution of Household Wealth*. New York: Oxford University Press, pp. 55–71.

SPOHN, W. and BODEMANN, Y. M. 1989. 'Federal Republic of Germany', in T. B. Bottomore and R. J. Brym, eds 1989.

STACEY, M. 1981. 'The Division of Labour Revisited' in P. Abrams *et al.* (eds) *Practice and Progress: British Sociology 1950–1980*. London: Allen & Unwin.

STANWORTH, M. 1984. 'Women and Class Analysis: A Reply to John Goldthorpe', *Sociology* 18, 2:159–170.

STANWORTH, P. and GIDDENS, A. (eds) 1974. *Elites and Power in British Society*. Cambridge: Cambridge University Press.

STEDMAN JONES, G. 1974. 'Working Class Culture and Working Class Politics', Journal of Social History, 7.

STEINMETZ, G. and WRIGHT, E. O. 1989. 'The fall and rise of the petty bourgeoisie: Changing patterns of self-employment in the postwar United States'. *American Journal of Sociology* 94:973–1–18.

STEINMETZ, G. and WRIGHT, E. 1990. 'Reply to Linder and Houghton', *American Journal of Sociology*, 96, 727–35.

STEPHENS, J. D. 1979. *The Transition from Capitalism to Socialism*. London: Macmillan.

STEWART, A., PRANDY, K. and BLACKBURN, R. 1980. *Social Stratification and Occupations*. London: Macmillan.

STOKMAN, F., ZIEGLER, R. and SCOTT, J. 1985a. *Networks of Corporate Power: A Comparative Analysis of Ten Countries*. Cambridge: Polity Press.

STOKMAN, F., WASSEUR, F., ELSAS, D. 1985b. 'The Dutch Network: Types of Interlocks and Network Structure'. See Stokman *et al.* 1985a:112–30.

STOLZENBERG, R. 1978. 'Bringing the Boss Back In: Employer Size, Employee Schooling, and Socioeconomic Achievement'. *American Sociological Review* 43:813–28.

SWARTZ, D. 1985. 'French Interlocking Directorships: Financial and Industrial Capital' in Stokman *et al.* 1985a.

TAWNEY, R. 1922. *Secondary Education for All: A Policy for Labour*, edited for the Education Advisory Committee of the Labour Party. London: Allen & Unwin.

TAYLOR-GOOBY, 1991. 'Attachment to the Welfare State' in R. Jowell *et al.* (eds) *British Social Attitudes: the 8th Report*. London: Social and Community Planning Research.

TEDIN, K. and YAP, O. 1993. 'The Gender Factor in Soviet Politics: Survey Evidence from Greater Moscow'. *Political Research Quarterly* 46, 179–211.

TEICHOVA, A. 1992. 'Rivals and Partners: Reflections on Banking and Industry in Europe, 1880–1938' in Cottrell *et al.* 1992.

TEICHOVA, A. and COTTRELL, P. (eds) 1983. *International Banks and Central Europe, 1918–1939*. Leicester: Leicester University Press.

THISTLE, S. 1992. 'Between Two Worlds'. Unpublished Ph.D dissertation, Department of Sociology, University of California, Berkeley.

THOMPSON, E. P. 1968. *The Making of the English Working Class*. London: Penguin (Second Revised Edition).

THOMPSON, E. P. 1964. 'Time, Work Discipline and Industrial Capitalism'. *Past and Present*.

THOMPSON, E. P. 1965. *The Peculiarities of the English* in R. Miliband and J. Saville (eds), *Socialist Register* No. 2. Merlin Press: London: 331–361.

THUROW, L. 1983. *Dangerous Currents: The State of Economics*. Oxford: Oxford University Press.

TILLY, R. 1974. 'The Growth of Large Scale Enterprise in Germany Since the Middle of the Nineteenth Century' in Daems and Van der Wee (eds) 1974.

TILLY, R. H. 1986. 'German Banking, 1850–1914: Development Assistance for the Strong'. *Journal of European Economic History*, 15.

TODD, J. and BUTCHER, B. 1982. *Electoral Registration in 1981*. London: Office of Population Censuses and Surveys.

TOMINOMORI, K. 1979. 'Big Business Groups and Finance Capital in Post-War Japan', *Hokudai Economic Papers* 9.

TOURAINE, A. 1985. 'An Introduction to the Study of Social Movements'. *Social Research* 52(4):749–88.

TOWNSEND, P. 1979. *Poverty in the United Kingdom*. Harmondsworth: Penguin Books.

TOWNSEND, P. 1991. *The Poor are Poorer*. . . . Bristol: Department of Social Policy and Social Planning, Bristol University.

TOWNSEND, P. 1993. 'Underclass and Overclass: The Widening Gulf' in G. Payne and M. Cross (eds) *Sociology in Action*. London: Macmillan.

TOWNSEND, P. and DAVIDSON, N. (eds) 1982. *Inequalities in Health*. Harmondsworth: Penguin Books.

TOWNSEND, P., CORRIGAN, P. and KOWARZICK, U. 1987. *Poverty and Labour in London*. London: Low Pay Unit.

TREIMAN, D. J. 1970. 'Industrialism and Social Stratification' in E. O. Laumann (ed.), *Social Stratification: Research and Theory for the 1970s*. New York: Bobbs-Merrill.

TREIMAN, D. J. and YIP, K.-B. 1989. 'Educational and Occupational Attainment in 21 Countries' in M. Kohn (ed.), *Cross-National Research in Sociology*. Newbury Park: Sage.

TURNER, B. 1981. *For Weber: Essays on the Sociology of Fate*. London: Routledge & Kegan Paul.

TURNER, B. 1986. *Equality*. London: Tavistock.

TURNER, B. 1988. *Status*. Milton Keynes: Open University Press.

TURNER, B. 1989. 'Ageing, Status Politics and Sociological Theory'. *British Journal of Sociology* 40(2):588–606.

TURNER, B. 1990. *Theories of Modernity and Post-Modernity*. London: Sage.

TURNER, B. 1994a. *Orientalism, Postmodernism and Globalism*. London and New York: Routledge.

TURNER, B. 1994b. 'The Postmodernization of the Life Course: Towards a New Social Gerontology'. *Australian Journal of Aging*, Vol. 13(3): 109–111.

TURNER, B. 1996. *Citizenship and Capitalism – The Debate over Reformism*. London: Allen & Unwin.

TURNER, B. and HAMILTON, P. (eds) 1994. *Citizenship, Critical Concepts*. 2 vols, London: Routledge.

TYLECOTE, A. 1992. *The Long Wave in the World Economy*. London: Routledge.

USEEM, M. 1984. *The Inner Circle – Large Corporations and the Rise of Business Political Activity in the US and UK*. Oxford: Oxford University Press.

USEEM, M. and KARABEL, J. 1986. 'Paths to Corporate Management'. *American Sociological Review* 51:184–200.

VALLI, L. 1986. *Becoming Clerical Workers*. London: Routledge & Kegan Paul.

VANNEMAN, R. and CANNON, L. W. 1987. *The American Perception of Class*. Philadelphia: Temple University Press.

VERNON, R. (ed.) 1974. *Big Business and the State: Changing Relations in Western Europe*. Cambridge: Harvard University Press.

VILLAREJO, D. 1961. 'Stock Ownership and the Control of Corporations, Parts I–III. *New University Thought*, Vol. 2. Reprinted in Scott 1990b, Vol. 2.

WACQUANT, L. 1993. 'Red Belt, Black Belt: Articulating Color, Class, and Place in Chicago's Ghetto and the Parisian Periphery'. Unpublished manuscript. Forthcoming in *International Journal of Urban and Regional Research*.

WALBY, S. 1986. *Patriarchy at Work*. Cambridge: Polity.

WALBY, S. 1990. *Theorising Patriarchy*. Cambridge: Polity.

WALKER, A. 1991. 'Poverty and the Underclass' in Haralambos, M. (ed.), *Developments in Sociology*, Vol. 7, Ormskirk, Causeway Press.

WANNELL, T. 1991. 'Trends in the Distribution of Employment by Employer Size'. Research Paper 39. Analytical Studies Branch, Stat., Canada, Ottawa.

WATERS, M. 1989. 'Citizenship and the Constitution of Structured Social Inequality'. *International Journal of Comparative Sociology* 30(3–4):159–80.

WATERS, M. 1991. 'Collapse and Convergence in Class Theory'. *Theory and Society* 20:141–72.

WATSON, P. 1993. 'Eastern Europe's Silent Revolution: Gender'. *Sociology* 27:471–87.

WEAKLIEM, D. 1991. 'The Two Lefts? Occupation and Party Choice in France, Italy, and the Netherlands'. *American Journal of Sociology* 96 (May):1327–61.

WEAKLIEM, D. and HEATH, A. F. 1996. 'Class Voting in Britain and the United States: Definitions, Models and Data' in G. Evans (ed.) 1996.

WEBER, M. 1914. 'The Economy and the Arena of Normative and De Facto Powers', Part Two of *Economy and Society* in Weber 1978.

WEBER, M. 1920. 'Conceptual Exposition', Part One of *Economy and Society* in Weber 1978.

WEBER, M. 1948. *From Max Weber*. London: Routledge & Kegan Paul.

WEBER, M. 1978. *Economy and Society* 2 vols (trans. G. Roth and C. Wittich). Berkeley: University of California Press.

WEISS, L. 1984. 'The Italian State and Small Business'. *European Journal of Sociology* 25:214–41.

WEIZMAN, L. 1985. *The Divorce Revolution*. Stanford, CA: Stanford University Press.

WESTERGAARD, J. H. 1992. 'About and beyond the "underclass"'. BSA Presidential Address, *Sociology*, November.

WESTERGAARD, J. H. 1995. *Who Gets What?* Cambridge: Polity Press.

WESTERGAARD, J. and RESLER, H. 1975. *Class in a Capitalist Society*. Harmondsworth: Penguin.

WESTERGAARD, J., NOBLE, I. and WALKER, A. 1989. *After Redundancy*. Oxford: Polity Press.

WHITEFIELD, S. and EVANS, G. 1994a. 'The Social Background to the December Elections in Russia: Public Attitudes and the Transition Experience'. *Post-Soviet Affairs* 10, 38–60.

WHITEFIELD, S. and EVANS, G. 1994b. 'The Ideological Bases of Political Competition in Eastern Europe'. Presented at the American Political Science Association annual conference, New York, September 1994.

WHITEHEAD, M. 1987. *The Health Divide: Inequalities in Health in the 1980s*. London, Health Education Council.

WHYTE, J. H. 1974. 'Ireland: Politics Without Social Bases' in R. Rose (ed.), *Electoral Behaviour: A Comparative Handbook*. New York: Free Press.

WILLIAMS, R. 1973. *The Country and the City*. London: Chatto & Windus.

WILLIAMS, R. 1976. *Keywords*. London: Fontana.

WILSON, W. 1978. *The Declining Significance of Race*. Chicago: University of Chicago Press.

WILSON, W. 1987. *The Truly Disadvantaged: The Inner City, the Underclass, and Public Policy*. Chicago: University of Chicago Press.

WILSON, W. 1991. 'Studying Inner-City Dislocations'. *American Sociological Review* 56, 1–14.

WINIECKI, J. 1994. 'East-Central Europe: A Regional Survey – the Czech Republic, Hungary, Poland and Slovakia in 1993'. *Europe–Asia Studies* 46, 709–34.

WOLFF, E. 1991. 'The Distribution of Household Wealth: Methodological Issues, Time Trends, and Cross-Sectional Comparisons' in L. Osberg (ed.), *Economic Inequality and Poverty: International Perspectives*. Armonk, NY: Sharpe, pp. 92–133.

WONG, G. 1991. 'Business Groups in a Dynamic Environment: Hong Kong, 1976–86' in Hamilton (ed.) 1991.

WONG, S. 1985. 'The Chinese Family Firm: A Model'. *British Journal of Sociology*, 36.

WONG, S. 1988. *Emigrant Entrepreneurs*. Hong Kong: Oxford University Press.

WONG, S. 1991. 'Chinese Entrepreneurs and Business Trust' in Hamilton (ed.) 1991.

WONG, R. and HAUSER, R. 1992. 'Trends in Occupational Mobility in Hungary under Socialism'. *Social Science Research* 21:419–44.

WOOD, S. (ed.) 1982. *The Degradation of Work?* London: Hutchinson.

WOOD, S. (ed.) 1989. *The Transformation of Work*. London: Hutchinson.

WRIGHT, E. 1978. *Class, Crisis, and State*. London: New Left Books.

WRIGHT, E. 1979. *Class Structure and Income Determination*. New York: Academic Press.

WRIGHT, E. 1985. *Classes*. London: Verso.

WRIGHT, E. 1989a. 'Women in the Class Structure'. *Politics and Society* 17:35–66.

WRIGHT, E. 1989b. 'Rethinking, Once Again, the Concept of Class Structure' in Wright *et al*. *The Debate on Classes*. London: Verso.

WRIGHT, E. 1990. 'Explanation and Utopia in Marxism and Feminism'. Paper presented at the Annual Meeting of the American Sociological Association, Washington, DC, August 11–15.

WRIGHT, E., COSTELLO, C., HACHEN, D. and SPRAGUE, J. 1982. 'The American Class Structure'. *American Sociological Review* 47:709–26.

WRIGHT, E. and MARTIN, B. 1987. 'The Transformation of the American Class Structure, 1960–1980'. *American Journal of Sociology* 87:1–29.

XENOS, N. 1989. *Scarcity and Modernity*. London and New York: Routledge.

YANITSKY, O., forthcoming. *One Hundred Interviews with Informals*. Moscow.

ZEIGLER, R., BENDER, D. and BIEHLER, H. 1985. 'Industry and Banking in the German Corporate Network', in Stokman *et al*. 1985a.

ZEIGLER, R., REISSNER, G. and BENDER, D. 1985. 'Austria Incorporated', in Stokman *et al*. 1985a.

ZEITLIN, M. 1989. *The Large Corporation and Contemporary Classes*. Cambridge: Polity Press.

ZUBOFF, S. 1988. *In the Age of the Smart Machine: The Future of Work and Power*. New York: Basic.

ZYSMAN, J. 1983. *Governments Markets and Growth: Financial Systems and the Politics of Industrial Change*. Ithaca: Cornell University Press.

The Editors

David Lee studied at the London School of Economics and at the Universities of Liverpool and Birmingham. He held lectureships in sociology at the University of Sheffield and Essex and became Senior Lecturer in Sociology at Essex in 1977. He has written numerous articles on education, training, skill and occupational stratification and was the author (with Howard Newby) of *The Problem of Sociology* (1982) and (with Dennis Marsden, Jean Duncombe and Penny Rickman) of *Scheming for Youth* (1990). He contributed over eighty entries to the *Concise Oxford Dictionary of Sociology* (1994). He is now retired and able to treat sociology as an occasional hobby.

Bryan S. Turner completed his undergraduate degree and postgraduate research at the University of Leeds (1963–69) and subsequently held lectureships at the universities of Aberdeen and Lancaster before taking up a Chair of Sociology at Flinders University (1982–88). He was an Alexander von Humbolt Fellow at Bielefeld University in Germany (1987–88). He then held Professorships in General Social Science at the University of Utrecht (1988–90) and University of Essex (1990–93). He returned to Australia in 1993 to take up the foundation Chair of sociology and Foundation Dean of Arts at Deakin University. He is also a Fellow of the Australian Academy of Social Science and currently President of the Australian Sociological Association (1994).

His major publications include *Weber and Islam* (1974), *Marx and the End of Orientalism* (1978), *For Weber* (1981), *Religion and Social Theory* (1983), *The Body and Society* (1984), *Citizenship and Capitalism* (1986), *Medical Power and Social Knowledge* (1987), *Status* (1988), *Max Weber, from history to modernity* (1991), *Regulating Bodies* (1992), and *Orientalism, Postmodernism and Globalism* (1994). He was co-author of the *Penguin Dictionary of Sociology*.

He has been a founding member of the editorial board of *Theory Culture & Society* (1982), founding co-editor of the new journal *Body & Society* (1995) and founding editor of the new *Journal of Citizenship*

Studies. What little leisure time he has is allocated to watching Australian football, especially the Geelong Cats, jogging, exploring the Australian landscape, drinking South Australian wines, collecting books and swimming.

Notes on contributors

Clem Brooks is Assistant Professor of Sociology at Indiana University, Bloomington. He has published papers on political attitudes, voting, and class consciousness. He is currently working on a study of change in the bases of American political behaviour and a study of the evolution of liberalism in the contemporary U.S.

Rosemary Crompton is Professor of Sociology at the University of Leicester, England and was formerly Reader in Sociology at the University of Kent. Her publications include *Class and Stratification* (with J. Gubbay) *Economy and Class Structure* (1977), (with G. Jones) *White Collar Proletariat* (1984) (with K. Sanderson) *Gendered Jobs and Social Change* (1990).

Terry Nicholls Clark is Professor of Sociology and Chair of the College Sociology Programme at the University of Chicago. His books include *Prophets and Patrons: The French University and the Emergence of the Social Sciences; City Money* and *Research in Urban Policy* (Five Vols.)

Peter Clifford is a Fellow of Jesus College, Oxford, and is Reader in Mathematical Statistics in the University of Oxford. He specialises in the statistical aspects of mathematical modelling in the social, medical and physical sciences.

Geoffrey Evans is a Fellow in the Centre for European Studies, Nuffield College, and was formerly a Lecturer at the London School of Economics. He was a member of the British Election Studies team in 1987 and 1992, a co-author of *Understanding Political Change*, (Pergamon, 1991) and has written numerous articles on social structure, ideology and political behaviour. Since 1992 he has also been engaged in survey studies of Eastern Europe.

John H. Goldthorpe is an Official Fellow at Nuffield College, Oxford. His previous publications in the field of social stratification include *The Affluent Worker* series (with David Lockwood and others, 1968–9), *Social Mobility and Class Structure in Modern Britain* (Second Edition 1987), (with Robert Erikson) *The Constant Flux: A study of Social Mobility In Industrial Societies* (1992).

Anthony Heath is a Fellow of Nuffield College, Oxford. He is co-director of the ESRC's Centre for Research into Elections and Social Trends (CREST). He specialises in the statistical analysis of survey data and his books have included *Origins and Destinations* (1980), *Social Mobility* (1981), *How Britain Votes* (1985) and *Understanding Political Change* (1991).

Robert Holton is Associate Professor of Sociology, and Director of the Centre for Multicultural Studies at Flinders University of South Australia. He is author of *Cities, Capitalism and Civilisation* and *Economy and Society*, and co-author (with Bryan Turner) of *Talcott Parsons on Economy and Society*, and *Max Weber on Economy and Society*.

Micheal Hout is Professor of Sociology and Director of the Survey Research Center at the University of California, Berkeley, where he has taught since 1985. He is the author of over three dozen articles on social stratification, political sociology, and demography. Most recently he and five Berkeley colleagues have written *Understanding American Inequality: Beyond the Bell Curve Controversy* which will be published early in 1996.

Seymour Martin Lipset is Hazel Professor of Public Policy, George Mason University. His books include: *Political Man*; *Class, Status and Party*; *Agrarian Socialism*; *The First New Nation*; *Revolution and Counterrevolutions*; and *The Politics of Unreason*. He served as editor of *Public Opinion Magazine* and both founded and served as President of the International Sociological Association's Research Committee on Political Sociology.

Jeff Manza is Professor of Sociology in the University of Pennsylvania.

Gordon Marshall is a Fellow of Nuffield College, Oxford. His publications include *Presbyteries and Profits* (1990, 1993), *In Search of the Spirit of Capitalism* (1982, 1993), *In Praise of Sociology* (1990) and (with others) *Social Class in Modern Britain* (1988). Most recently he edited *The Concise Oxford Dictionary of Sociology* (1994).

Lydia Morris is Professor of Sociology at the University of Essex. She has been researching unemployment, labour market change and gender relations for some years. She is the author of *The Workings of the Household* (Polity Press, 1990) *Dangerous Classes* (Routledge, 1994) *Social Divisions* (London: UCL Press, 1995).

John Myles is Professor of Sociology at Florida State University. He is co-author of *Relations of Ruling* (McGill, 1994).

Jan Pakulski is Associate Professor of Sociology at the University of Tasmania, Australia. He writes on social movements, social stratification and social change in Western and East European societies. He is author of *Social Movements* and co-author (with S. Crook and M. Waters) of *Postmodernisation*.

Ray Pahl is Research Professor in Sociology at the University of Kent at Canterbury, England. His previous publications include *Divisions of Labour* (1984).

John Scott is Professor of Sociology at the University of Essex and was previously Professor at the University of Leicester. His books include *Corporations, Classes and Capitalism* (Second Edition 1985), *A Matter of Record* (1990), *Who Rules Britain?* (1991), *Social Network Analysis* (1991) and *Poverty and Wealth* (Longman, 1994).

Adnan Turegun is Instructor in Sociology at Carleton University, Ottawa, Ontario, Canada.

Malcolm Waters is Professor of Sociology at the University of Tasmania, Australia. He writes on social theory, social stratification and long-term social transformation. He is author of *Class and Stratification*, *Postmodernisation* (with S. Crook and J. Pakulski), *Modern Sociological Theory* and *Globalization*.

John Westergaard is Professor Emeritus at the University of Sheffield and occasional Visiting Professor at Copenhagen University, Denmark. His publications include *Class in a Capitalist Society* (with Harriet Resler) (1975), *After Redundancy* (with Ian Noble and Alan Walker) (1989) and *Who Gets What?* (1995).

Index of principal topics

Age and class, 16, 95, 135, 147–8, 189, 194, 240, 242
Alford Index, 45, 54, 200–1, 207(n. 2)
Anti-scientism, *see* sociology
Australia, significance for class analysis of, 5, 19, 23, 67
Authority relations, 35–6, 41, 43, 46, 156, 157. *See also* Hierarchy managerial, 175, 179

Boundary problem in class analysis, 17–18, 32–3, 62, 64–5, 105, 150, 189–90
Bourgeoisie, 17, 52, 65, 68, 75–6, 94–5, 154–6, 175–6, 200, 230

Capital, 4–5, 38, 45, 52, 65, 82, 94, 96, 133, 143, 155, 159–70, 171, 174, 175–6, 249–51, 254
    money and, 251, 249–51
    small capital, 65, 172–4. *See also* Cultural capital, Ownership and Control; Wealth
Capitalism, Capitalist development, patterns of, 2–3, 5–9, 63, 68, 71–83, 93, 96, 100, 116, 120, 123, 144, 149, 159–70, 175, 226–7, 231, 238
    gender and, 116, 120
    middle class and, 175–9
    under post-communism, 165–6, 226–7, 231
Capitalist class, *see* Bourgeoisie
Car ownership, 110
Citizenship (and welfare state), 8, 11, 19, 41, 69–70, 71, 79–80, 152–3, 185, 176–9, 196, 238, 240
    welfare dependency, 152–3, 185, 240
Class,
    as concept, typologies of, 61–3, 71, 88, 119
    conflicting perceptions of, 1–2, 61–3, 115, 119–120, 125–6, 156–7

'death of class' thesis, 9–19, 42–48, 49, 51, 53–39, 60, 69–70, 71, 98, 108–9, 137, 141, 159, 183, 197, 199–200, 210, 225, 145, 225, 252–3, 254–5
    decomposition of, 65–67, 76–78
    defined by contributors, 42, 50–51, 59n, 115, 141–2, 230
    definition and measurement, problems of, 41, 61, 64–5, 91–2, 96, 103–4, 105, 112–3, 115, 117–9, 121–2, 129–32, 140, 180–2, 184, 186, 187–90, 199–202, 213, 217, 230–31
    demographic formation, 105–6, 111–2, 128–132, 168
    'in-itself' and 'for itself', 5, 95, 142, 156
    in Britain, 142–144
    in Japan, 1
    myths of classlessness, 4–9
    necessity of in sociology, 50–51
    'non-egalitarian classlessness', 60
    see also Class analysis, Class explanations, Gender and class, Social Class formation, Underclass
Class analysis
    absolute and relative measures in, 105, 112, 140, 214–5
    comparative research, significance of, 139–140, 212–8
    defined by contributors, 2, 51, 98–104
    employment-aggregate approaches, 41, 65, 115–6, 117, 119, 121, 140, 251–2, 256–8
    ethnographic studies in, 121
    evidence and method in, 5–9, 88, 102–4, 108–9, 112–3, 120, 121, 133, 129, 171, 181–3, 190–1, 207, 228–9
    historical context of, 2–3, 94–5, 116–7, 254
    in British sociology, 15, 87–8, 147
    labour market change and, 191
    levels of analysis in, 9–10, 29–33, 62, 115, 119–22, 246–7

Index of authors